GNOSTIC
PHILOSOPHY

GNOSTIC
PHILOSOPHY

*From Ancient Persia
to Modern Times*

TOBIAS CHURTON

Inner Traditions
Rochester, Vermont

Inner Traditions
One Park Street
Rochester, Vermont 05767
www.InnerTraditions.com

Library of Congress Cataloging-in-Publication Data

Churton, Tobias, 1960-
  Gnostic philosophy : from ancient Persia to modern times / Tobias Churton.
      p. cm.
  Includes bibliographical references and index.
  ISBN 1-59477-035-2 (pbk.)
  1. Gnosticism. I. Title.
  B638.C48 2005
  299'.932—dc22

                                                                        2004023351

Printed and bound in the United States by Lake Book Manufacturing, Inc.

10 9 8 7 6 5 4 3

Text design and layout by Priscilla Baker
This book was typeset in Sabon, with Berling, Avenir, and Griffin as display typefaces

Spiritual values we know;
religious values we can only guess at.

MICHAEL POWELL TO GAVIN MILLAR,
BBC ARENA, 1980

Contents

Foreword by Christopher McIntosh   xi

Acknowledgments   xv

Introduction   1

PART ONE
Antiquity

ONE   **Before the Gnostics**   10

     Also Sprach Zarathushtra   12

     The Wise Lord   13

     That Old Devil Time   16

     Mithra the Mediator   20

     Enter the Demiurge   22

TWO   **From the Magi to St. Paul**   26

     Jewish Themes   34

     The Anthropos: Man   34

     Sophia   37

     The Unknown God and the Demiurge   40

     Philo of Alexandria   42

     The Essenes   51

     The Book of Enoch   57

     Life at the Dead Sea   63

     Jesus   73

     Stone Theology   75

     Paul   83

THREE   **The First Gnostics**   89

Gnosticism   89

Hans Jonas: The Gnostic Religion   101

The Irresistible Character of Gnosis; or,
"The Spirit Is Willing"   109

Being Is Seeing   110

Clement of Alexandria: The Gnosis Truly
So-called?   115

PART TWO
The Middle Ages

FOUR   **Magic in the Middle Ages**   122

Neoplatonic Theurgy   124

Celestial Hierarchies   129

Light Metaphysics   130

After the Pact   134

Kabbalistic Magic   135

Roger Bacon   139

FIVE   **The Sufis**   144

The Insights of Sufism   146

Sufis and Philosophy   151

Maulana Jalal-ud-din Rumi: Sufi Master   154

Interesting Times   155

SIX   **The Troubadours**   160

Prologue: The Two Worlds   160

What Is a Troubadour?   163

Miraval   166

The Ladies in His Life   169

Loba   169

The Rules of Love: Miraval's Guide to
Successful Courtship   177

Was the Fine Love a Spiritual Love?   184

The Allegory of Love   186

Troubadours and Cathars   189

	The Last Song	194
	The Joy That We Have Lost	196
	Creation Is the Product of Pain	197
	Were the Troubadours Sexual Mystics?	199
SEVEN	**The Knights Templar**	201
	Templars and Cathars	206
	The Templars and the Gral	213
	Baphomet	219
	Templars in Search of the Stones	223
	Kilwinning	226
	Conclusion: Gnostics in the Temple?	229

PART THREE
Enlightenment

EIGHT	**Jacob Böhme's Theosophick Cosmos**	234
	Böhme's Life	236
	Elements of Böhme's Theosophy	239
	The Influence of Jacob Böhme	245
	William Law	246
	Romantic Philosophy	251
	The Neo-Rosicrucians	254
	William Blake	255
NINE	**Germany 1710–1800: The Return of the Rosy Cross**	260
	The Gold und Rosenkreuzers	264
	Masonry in Germany	266
	Radicals Under Attack: Gold und Rosenkreuz vs. the Illuminati	272
	A Real Rosicrucian King (on the Throne of Prussia)	277
	Rosicrucians in Poland	282
	Russia	283
	The Asiatic Brethren	286
	Romanticism	289

TEN	**Freemasonry in France**	291
	The Elect Cohens	293
	Éliphas Lévi Zahed: A Great Socialist	
	Magician and Occult Revivalist	298
	Lévi's Legacy	302
	Magic Revives in France	305

PART FOUR
The Modern Age

ELEVEN	**A New Aeon: Aleister Crowley**	314
	Aiwass: Messenger of the Gods	329
	The Book of the Law	332
	The Crisis	338
	Aleister Crowley: Sex Magician	343
	Sexual Alchemy	358
TWELVE	**Light in the Jar**	366
	Carl Jung	367
THIRTEEN	**Gnosis and the New Physics**	371
	The Copenhagen Interpretation	375
FOURTEEN	**Gnosis Today: A Personal View**	387
	Rudolf Steiner	387
	Gnosis and Ecology	390
	Neo-Gnostics	393
	Cinema	396
	Hipgnostics: Popular Music	398
	The Arts	402
Notes		406
Bibliography		448
Index		455

Foreword

*G*nostic Philosophy is a book that speaks to the condition of our age. If ages correspond to metals, as certain of the ancient Greeks thought, then this is an age of lead, the metal of Saturn. We are ripe for a transmutation. For the alchemist, the gleam of precious metal in the depths of the earth is analogous to the gleam of the divine spirit held captive in the physical realm, as the gnostic puts it.

At the core of Gnosticism lies a powerful metaphor: There is not one creator but two, one true, the other false. The false one, the Demiurge, keeps our spirits captive in the world of matter, away from the divine light above. Yet through the ages, a tradition of knowledge has been handed down, veiled in imagery and symbol, telling us where we came from and how we can find our way back. This knowledge, or gnosis, can set our spirits free if we are receptive to it.

In speaking of this worldview, I use the word *metaphor* deliberately because, like the author of this book, I believe that much mischief has been caused by taking it in a literal and physical sense, as many present-day gnostics and scholars of Gnosticism continue to do. One of Tobias Churton's most interesting arguments is that this literal interpretation is a distortion or parody of the true gnosis, stemming arguably from a misunderstanding of early Gnostic writers such as Valentinus—yet it was the parody that came to be generally signified by the word *Gnosticism*. Hence, writers such as Plotinus attacked the Gnostics because, as Churton puts it, some of them "had got hold of an excellent stick and caught the wrong end of it."

If, however, the dualistic worldview of the Gnostics is taken as a spiritual metaphor, it becomes a powerfully transforming message: All of us are spiritually less than we could be, but we have somewhere within us the knowledge of how to raise ourselves up toward the stars. Seen in this perspective, the Demiurge becomes, in Churton's words, the "world-making perceptual faculty of human beings," which tries to be God and thus hinders the spirit from communion with the true God.

The metaphor of Gnosticism opens up another possibility, which is to view the world as a jest or a kind of conjuring trick, with the Demiurge as the conjuror whose skill we admire, knowing that sooner or later the show will end and we shall leave the theater. With this viewpoint, Gnosticism ceases to be a negative, melancholy worldview and becomes instead a playful, celebratory one. If the world is a trick or a jest, why not play along with it as with a party game? Perhaps this is ultimately the way to transcend it.

The Dutch historian Huizinga, in his classic book *Homo ludens,* deals with playfulness and its importance in human culture throughout history. This spirit of playfulness is, I believe, an important vein running through the gnostic tradition. It is the same phenomenon we find among certain Buddhist sages, who cultivate humor as one path to enlightenment. Thus, there has always been, in both East and West, the tradition of the "laughing master." Churton mentions an early example in the figure of the Samaritan Simon Magus.

When I wrote my own book on Rosicrucianism, which is one aspect of the gnostic tradition, I did not take into account the importance of this quality of playfulness. Hence, I failed to appreciate the real significance of the word *ludibrium,* or "jest," which Johann Valentin Andreae used to describe his work *The Chemical Wedding of Christian Rosenkreuz,* one of the key early Rosicrucian documents. Only later did it strike me that Andreae intended the word *ludibrium* in the spirit of *Homo ludens,* and that the same spirit runs through much of Rosicrucianism. This thought struck me again when I read Churton's illuminating chapters on the Rosicrucians in this book's companion, *The Golden Builders.* In that book, Churton skillfully places the Rosicrucians in the context of the emerging gulf between science and religion, a gulf they wished to bridge by creating a universal system of knowledge linking religion, science, philosophy, and art. The Rosicrucians embodied this vision in a brilliantly created mythology with a strong element of playfulness. This playful spirit informs *The Gnostic Philosophy* as well.

One of the more recent "laughing masters" featured in this book is Aleister Crowley, whose path was through sex and humor, neither of which find favor in the West when combined with religion—hence the vilification that has been heaped on Crowley's head. When we rediscover the spirit of *Homo ludens,* perhaps we shall look more kindly on the "Great Beast." Meanwhile, Churton's affectionate and perceptive treatment of Crowley is a valuable corrective to much misunderstanding about him.

One of the notable achievements of Churton's book is to demonstrate how thinkers as far apart in time as Crowley and Valentinus can be placed in the tradition of gnostic thought. Churton shows how the same tradition links the Sufis, Neoplatonists, medieval magicians, troubadours, kabbalists, Jacob Böhme, William Law, Freemasonry, the psychology of Carl Jung, the Rudolf Steiner movement, the songs of John Lennon, and much else.

If "laughing masters" such as the much maligned Aleister Crowley are the heroes of this book—as the much neglected Johann Valentin Andreae was a hero of Churton's last book—the villains are the people of lead who perpetuate the age of lead. These are the promoters of stifling religious dogma or crass materialism, in every age. Yet Saturn, the planet of lead, is also the planet of time and therefore of transformation. A millennial mood is struggling for air in a polluted world, as it was when the Rosicrucian manifestos first began to circulate. And the gnostic tradition is still available to us as a source of inspiration for change. This book brings that tradition alive in all its richness and gives us hope that we may succeed in transmuting the lead into gold.

CHRISTOPHER MCINTOSH, AUTHOR OF
*THE ROSICRUCIANS: THE HISTORY, MYTHOLOGY, AND
RITUALS OF AN ESOTERIC ORDER*

Acknowledgments

This book could not have been written without the superb facilities of the Bibliotheca Philosophica Hermetica (J. R. Ritman Library, Amsterdam). I am also indebted to help received from my mother and father, Victor and Patricia Churton, and from Ms. Sarah Miller.

For permission to study the Yorke Collection at the Warburg Institute, I am deeply grateful to the former library curator, Dr. William Ryan. For a series of sparkling interviews, I am likewise indebted to Professors Hans Jonas, Gilles Quispel, Elaine Pagels, and R. McLachlan Wilson, and to the late Dr. Kathleen Raine. Special thanks are also due to Art Schiemann, director of the Warmonderhof Anthroposophical Farm in Holland, for showing me how spirit and nature work together.

The chapter on the Knights Templar benefited greatly from the detailed knowledge of the Masonic historian Matthew Scanlan.

The friendship, encouragement, good humor, original scholarship, and fraternal guidance of Christopher McIntosh have been central to the long gestation and fruitful birth of this work. In particular, part 3 ("Enlightenment") owes everything to Dr. McIntosh's pioneering work in what was the dusty attic of eighteenth- and nineteenth-century Freemasonry and occultism.

Special thanks are due to my special agent, Tuvia Fogel, for his patient faith.

This book *has* been a long time in coming. There has been turmoil and heart searching. There have also been luminous helpers on the way. I thank God for the friendship of the late bishop of Växjö (Sweden),

Professor Jan Arvid Hellström (who died in a car accident just as we had begun to formulate Stone Theology).

Enormous gratitude is due again to my parents, Victor and Patricia Churton, and to Julian Jones, Philip Wilkinson, Caroline Wise, Columba Powell, Sally de Beaumont, Patrick and Karla Hickman-Robertson, Thelma Schoonmaker-Powell, Vanilla Beer, Steve George, Andrew Brown, Jean Gimpel, David and Belinda Parsons-Scott, Jim, Gay, and Pattie Parsons, Brian Averill, the late Robert J. "Bob" Vincent, Peter Maxwell-Jones, and Doug and Hilary Pickford; all have encouraged, helped, and indulged my own particular madness.

Behind every great book is a great woman; without Joanna Churton, this work would not have been completed.

Introduction

Unless you have devoted years of study to the subject, you will have your work cut out if you propose writing about the Gnostics. It is an enormous field and intricate beyond imagination.

MONTAGUE SUMMERS TO JOHN SYMONDS, MARCH 13, 1948

t the tender age of twenty-five, I wrote a book called *The Gnostics* to accompany a series on British television's Channel 4. I hoped at the time that this would be my last word on a subject that had fascinated me in many different ways since my midteens. *The Gnostics* contained concise chapters on the Nag Hammadi library, the early Gnostics, those medieval "heretics" known as the Cathars, the Hermetic philosophy of the Renaissance, William Blake, and a review of some contemporary gnostic phenomena, all packed neatly into 150 libel-free pages. Having done that, I thought I could get back to filmmaking—and leave the printed word alone.

I was wrong.

Seven years later, in 1993, an enthusiast of *The Gnostics* finally persuaded me that the time was ripe for a follow-up. And now here we are; more than a decade has passed. What took me so long? Perhaps the time was not then quite ripe after all. Perhaps *I* was not ripe.

There is a certain ritual in the Ancient and Accepted Rite of Freemasonry wherein the candidate is conducted around seven concentric circles seven times, gathering fundamental spiritual insights on the way, this being a symbolic preamble to the conferring of the degree. The circuits represent a lifetime's journey. One goes round in circles, all right! But at the center of this little cosmos, a pelican feeds its young on its own blood.

This book represents a journey to the center of the circle.

Each of *The Gnostic Philosophy*'s fourteen chapters, though arranged chronologically for convenience, is a kind of mirror of the others. It does not matter where one begins reading; the center of the circle will always be there. Whether one is looking at the so-called Age of Reason, the Middle Ages, the modern age, or the pre-Christian era, gnostic philosophy remains the same dynamic, liberating power. Existing in time, it points beyond time. It calls us to wake up from materialist vision to a more profound, higher, and more centered perception. Whether the expression of the gnosis is apparently Christian, classical, Jewish, magical, Islamic, Buddhist, Hindu, Eastern, or Western, the wisdom of the ages speaks to us as it did to our ancestors—if we choose to listen. Many religious traditions assume that if we go back far enough, we are all related. "All art is one, man, one."[1] This book is testimony to that insight.

Yes, the field of the gnostics *is* enormous, if not quite "intricate beyond imagination," as Montague Summers wrote over half a century ago. When Hans Jonas's masterpiece *The Gnostic Religion* appeared in the 1950s, the philosopher insisted that the teachings of Mani and the Hermetic corpus be included in his survey. By extending the field of study, Jonas wanted gnosticism to be liberated from its restricted significance as an early Christian heresy. He saw its appearance as a world-historical event; the Gnostics were apparently the first existentialists.

Kurt Rudolph's *Gnosis* (1985) not only updated Jonas's work on the Mandaeans of Iraq but added the Bogomil-Cathar heresy to its itinerary as well. James M. Robinson, supervising editor of the *Nag Hammadi Library in English* (1977), went so far as to draw parallels between the second-century Gnostic movement and the counterculture movements of the 1960s. Meanwhile, Joost Ritman, a Dutch businessman, collector, and latter-day Rosicrucian, was assembling a Hermetic-Gnostic library of original books and manuscripts. The library's contents included early Gnostic texts, the medieval Grail romances, medieval mystics, all aspects of alchemy, Neoplatonism, the Renaissance Hermetists, the early Rosicrucian movement, Jacob Böhme, John

Pordage, Jane Lead, some Freemasonry, Rudolf Steiner, and every scrap of world scholarship on these and kindred subjects. Ritman's achievement goes by the name of the Bibliotheca Philosophica Hermetica, and it stands tall in old Amsterdam.

Joost Ritman's perception of the vast scope and significance of the subject happily coincided with my own youthful enthusiasm, and there was mutual delight when we met to collaborate on the award-winning British TV series *Gnostics* in 1986. That delight informed my first popular book on the subject, a book that established the breadth of vision needed to see *Gnosis* in its full historical contours, albeit an aerial view.

Most scholars of Gnosticism (a word that generally refers to the Gnostic movements of the early Christian period) have accepted that such a pan-historical perspective lies outside their specialist remit. The subject as a whole has lain scattered among the copious works of Christian theologians, historians of philosophy, specialists in the history of occultism, discreet societies, and literary historians. My design in this book has been to bring these far-flung estates under single management—not so much for reasons of efficiency as to demonstrate coherence where coherence exists.

There is another factor that has informed the making of this book. During the last twenty years, a number of pseudo (or alternative) histories have muddied the waters and stirred up a welter of conspiracy tales told (sometimes) with journalistic flourish, but these are for the most part misleading—as this book shows. Truth is stranger than fiction, and a good deal more bracing.

The chief problem with "alternative history" is that for those unacquainted with the best scholarship on the subject, with no yardstick to measure the truthfulness or accuracy of the new historical perspective, the chance of entering an imaginative space dominated by the unreal is all too likely. A journey through the unreal is an unreal journey; the blind begin to lead the blind. In the case of conspiracy theories, the results of exploitation of history may be quite deadly. For many malcontents, history is a powerful spur to destruction; a fair account, on the other hand, helps us understand a little more. If you want absolute certainties, you'll be prepared to believe anything.

An ancient authority wrote that he believed in order that he might understand. Well, I follow neither this line nor its corollary: to know in order that I might believe. My line is simply: "*This* is fascinating. I want to know why." I want to know *what* is fascinating about it, and I want to know *why* I am fascinated by it. In short, I want to understand it. And it is to this urge to understand—in this case, the Gnostic philosophy—that this book is directed. That is to say, while I trust the work to be scholarly and of interest to academic study, it is intended for everyone who wants to understand better the essence of the gnostic story. This may be a small market, but I hope it is neither a provincial nor an unhappy one.

GNOSTIC PHILOSOPHY

This book might have been called *The Hermetic Philosophy* but for the fact that it has been preceded by a herald. That herald is my book *The Golden Builders: Alchemists, Rosicrucians and the First Free Masons*, published in the United States in 2005. *The Golden Builders* concentrated chiefly on the Hermetic, alchemical, proto-Masonic, and, above all, Rosicrucian aspects of the gnostic story. That book and this one, *Gnostic Philosophy,* complement each other. The subject matter of *The Golden Builders* fills the chronological gap between parts 2 and 3 of this book (late Middle Ages to the late seventeenth century).

The gnostic story is not, thankfully, an account of the historical progress of an idea (I leave that to nineteenth-century German idealists); it is the story of an idea that has repeatedly promoted such historical progress as our species has enjoyed over the last twenty-five centuries. That idea I am calling the gnostic philosophy. What do I mean by the phrase?

Hans Jonas's most widely read book, referred to earlier, was called *The Gnostic Religion,* yet the chief interest of Gnosis (to him) lay in the Gnostics' relationship to contemporary philosophy. It would be Elaine Pagels *(The Gnostic Gospels)* who focused on the Gnostics' relationship to religion—particularly orthodox Christianity. When we add to these considerations the phenomenon of the Hermetic Gnostic tract—spiritual philosophy that can be understood without recourse to religious organization—we may be led to think of gnosis as a philosophy of religion, or simply as a religious (or mystical) philosophy—or, indeed, as gnostic philosophy! Hermetic philosophy itself has been called a *religio mentis,* a religion of the mind. This suggests that a hybrid status may be required for the phrase *gnostic philosophy,* because it blurs the customary boundaries between religion (an organized system of belief) and philosophy (an inquiry into truth values). Gnosis may be thought of as taking the latter road, only to burst explosively into the realm of the former.

The German church historian Adolf von Harnack (1851–1930) clearly felt the discomfiting tingle of a disharmonious phenomenon when he (wrongly) described Gnosticism as "the acute Hellenization of Christianity."[2] There was Hellenization, but it occurred in the context of a long-term cross-pollination. Experienced by Greeks, Egyptians, and Jews based in Egypt after Alexander the Great's invasion in 331 B.C., the ensuing *mélange à trois* in part promoted the peculiar thought-world of the second-century Gnostic heretic. Harnack, like the church fathers who wrote against Gnostics, saw an uncomfortable conflation of religious and dialectical philosophical categories in the phenomena later collectivized by scholars in the word *Gnosticism.*

When we look, for example, at the famous Valentinian Gnostic speculation (strongly identified with Alexandria), we may think we are looking at philosophy become myth: the personification—even deification—of *ideas.* Valentinus' aeons are the pleromic "thoughts" or archetypal ideas of the divine mind extended (and ultimately warped) all the way into the created world, in which they can be discerned by the awakened mind and heart. In the pleromic microcosm of the individual *pneuma* (spirit), like discerns like, and pneuma comes home. The theme of *gnosis* as a parable or myth of the reflexive consciousness is explored in chapter 3. This parable or myth denotes a philosophical hypothesis *and* a religious— or, better, mystical—experience: the recovery of spiritual perception and identity.

This book places religious and philosophical questions side by side with scientific and historical questions. Religion practices what philosophy (especially Platonist and Neoplatonist philosophy) thinks about, and philosophy thinks about what religion practices. This was seen as the proper order of things in antiquity; theology was the queen of the sciences. Modern science, in contrast, at least as most people understand it, represents an apotheosis of measurement that has made the stars more distant from us and us from our selves. (The status of modern science in relation to *Gnosis* is explored in chapter 13.)

I hear an objection rising from my dialectical alter ego: Is not *Gnosis* a mere coterie of philosophies—some would say a half-baked coterie at that—not a single philosophy of life? These anarchic games with the cosmos and its creator or creators—can they possibly be properly described as a philosophy?

Obviously, I think so. However, the gnostic approach to life is not that of the literary monolith that we have become accustomed to think of when we use the term *philosophy*. One thinks of the big guns with their mighty tomes: Descartes, Wittgenstein, Nietzsche, Confucius, Locke, Aristotle, Kant, to name but a few.

The gnostic philosophy certainly represents a thoroughgoing inquiry into truth values. The patristic authority Tertullian (second century A.D.) complained that it was *questions* that made people heretics, questions such as, Where does humanity come from, and why? Where does evil come from, and why? Classic Gnostics claim to have found their literal philosophy in *knowing* whence they come, why they are here, and whither they are going. Gnostic works are chock-full of questions, many abstract and dizzyingly metaphysical. But as I try to explain in chapter 3, we should beware of materialistic interpretations of the characters that appear in the myths associated with Gnosticism. Some Gnostics called the creator of the universe Saklas, "Fool"; one wonders if they would have said so to his face!

Much of the scandal of Gnosis was in daring to answer *too many* of these questions. "Did they think deeply *enough?*" opponents have asked. The great Egyptian Neoplatonist Plotinus regarded the writings of the *gnostikoi* he opposed as the decadence of philosophy.

Gnosis is philosophy as spiritual liberation. It is also a religion built of speculation and invention—almost an antireligion—and the explosion of philosophy into its mythic and mystical origins. It is a philosophy that could feast on a religion, a magical religion that could become a philosophy, and a magical philosophy that could become a religion. It was trouble from the start! *Gnosis* is the most suppressed religion and philosophy in history. Discuss.

The Gnostic philosophy was also an attitude that expressed a philosophy; it is so today. But it is not just an attitude, rebellious or otherwise. The philosophy is characterized by key premises flexibly repeated.

The link over time and space lies in the receptivity of the subject to the gnostic experience par excellence: initial spiritual alienation in the world, leading to a certainty that the realization of this state is itself the key first step to transcending the grief of separation from the world. The tragedy remains, but the triumph is won already. The Gnostic Jesus, for example, "crucifies the world"; the cross becomes a flowering tree. The pain leads to rebirth. It transpires, for the gnostic, that the pain resides not so much in alienation from the world, but in estrangement from the source of spirit. The spirit is a stranger, alien, or exile in the world; the "uncomely stone" is the pearl of great price. We must make a choice, and in doing so, we may find that this world is not at all what we thought it was. In *this* world: paradox, compassion, and confusion. In the gnostic's real world—the world of spirit: laughter, life, love, liberty, and Light.

The world sundered eventually resolves itself into the realization of the One: the infinite variety of the cosmos or reflection of the Self (as above, so below). Salvation is awakening; seeing is being. We did not know our home until we had left it. Then we found that infinity was our home and eternity our destiny. This expression of *gnosis,* of course, belongs to its more optimistic presentation, and especially to its alchemical and Hermetic expression in the vision of the *unus mundus,* or "one life."[3]

In *gnosis,* consciousness of being *is* being. The Gnostic would laugh at the modern behaviorist biologist who considers him- or herself to be on the last lap of science in seeking to locate "consciousness itself." As if awareness could be subject to itself! the Gnostic would scoff. The search for consciousness as object indicates that the seeker is *not* truly alive to the profundity and mystery of being. ("The dead are not alive, and the living will not die" is one of the author's favorite gnostic *logia.*) Our materialist world would come under the Gnostic's strictest censure, be it scientific materialism, consumer materialism, or, perhaps most dangerous of all, religious materialism—thinking of God as an angry man and us his trigger fingers. The fruit of *gnosis* in this world is peace and a certain certainty.

The Gnostic figure of the Demiurge, the false or blind creator, helps us see the constraints of biology, as the image of its specter, abstract reason *(agnosis)*, helps us see mental constraint. But consciousness is *in potentia* infinite (this is what I believe it means to be made in "the image of God"); we can, in this world, only move upward on an ever-increasing scale—or sink to the bottom of the great chain of being. As the latter-day theurgist Aleister Crowley wryly asserted: "The more necessary anything appears to my mind, the more certain it is that I only assert a limitation."[4]

Only the philosophy of gnosis guarantees infinity in the created and eternity in the uncreated worlds. Gnosis—knowledge, spiritual knowledge—certainly represents (for the gnostic) philosophy itself—the love of *sophia* (wisdom)—in its purest state. It is no surprise that it has outlived the Wittgensteinian fantasy that words cannot express anything but themselves. *Gnosis* is also a magical philosophy: Words express powers. The right use of words (poetry or the making thereof) invokes or evokes psychic energies—from the healing balm of the bedside manner to the destructive rants of the hateful priest, mullah, or power-hungry politician.

Gnosis is good for women. Only the Gnostics saw Mary Magdalene and her powers of spiritual wisdom as the equal and probably superior figure to the argumentative, bullying, and misperceiving male disciples. It could have been a Gnostic—and not blues singer Willie Dixon in his "Backdoor Man"—who wrote so succinctly: "The men don't know, but the little girls understand." The troubadours are also a part of this story.

I was educated in a world where the sciences reigned supreme. The mystery of immeasurable being awaited and still awaits understanding. The gnostic philosophy has helped me in my dim cave to understand something of the truth. I hope readers may likewise enjoy this intellectual and spiritual adventure.

> *I bowed down my ear a little, and received her [Sophia, or Wisdom], and got much learning. I profited therein, therefore will I ascribe the glory unto him that giveth me wisdom.*
> ECCLESIASTICUS 11:16–17

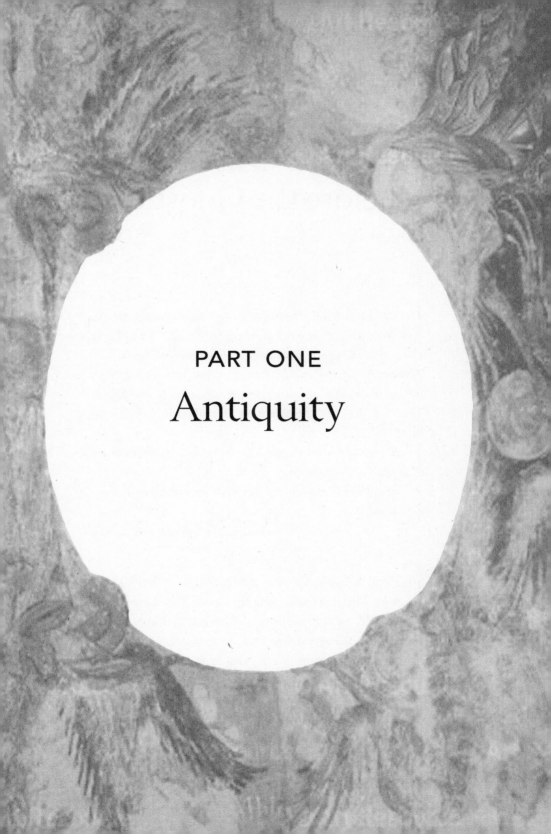

PART ONE

Antiquity

ONE

Before the Gnostics

The Goddess said: "Spirit, through Spirit you attained your greatness. Praise the greatness of Spirit." Then Light knew that the mysterious Person was none but Spirit. . . . The power of the mind when it remembers and desires, when it thinks again and again, belongs to Spirit. Therefore let Mind meditate on Spirit. Spirit is the Good in all.

It should be worshipped as the Good. He that knows it as the Good is esteemed by all.

You asked me about spiritual knowledge, I have explained it.

FROM KENA UPANISHAD 4.1, 5, 9

Spiritual knowledge was prized at least half a millennium before Christ. Hindu metaphysicians speculated on the life of the spirit in a collection of Sanskrit writings known as the Upanishads. The word *upanishad* means "at the feet of . . ." and clearly refers to initiatic instruction. Something was being imparted from on high. What was it?

The Upanishads explore the relationship of the individual self *(atman)* to the cosmic soul (Atman, the Self) or Brahman. To realize the unity of individual atman with Brahman involves the spiritual experience of *jnana*, knowledge.

10

The Sanskrit noun for knowledge, *jnana,* is of the same root as both the English verb *to know* and the Greek word *gnosis* (knowledge). In the quotation above, *jnana* is used to denote spiritual knowledge, a higher knowledge acquired not through the activity of the natural human being, but through experience of the spirit.

This knowledge is explored in the Chandogya Upanishad:

This is my self [*atmantar*] within the heart, smaller than a grain of rice, than a barley corn, than a mustard seed, than a grain of millet or than a kernel of a grain of millet. This is myself within the heart, greater than the earth, greater than the atmosphere, greater than the sky, greater than these worlds. Containing all works, containing all desires, containing all odors, containing all tastes, encompassing this whole world, without speed, without concern, this is the self of mine within the heart; this is *Brahman*. Into him, I shall enter, on departing hence.[1]

Christians will immediately recognize the reference to the mustard seed, an image Jesus used as a likeness for the kingdom of heaven, which, though appearing insignificant to the eyes of the world, yet contains a hidden glory that will in time manifest itself in the world.

From the point of view of *Gnosis,* it is significant that the essence of the individual self is of the same nature as Brahman. That spiritual being is divine is the prized discovery of the gnostic. According to Renaissance sages such as Pico della Mirandola, writing some two millennia after the Upanishads, this discovery constitutes the absolute basis of human dignity.

According to this conception, to kill a person is not to kill, but to offend the divinity in the human being, whose will it is to express itself in this form. This very deduction is present in some of the Gnostic writings discovered near Nag Hammadi in Upper Egypt in 1945. Indeed, the author was delighted to discover within that collection what appears to be a paraphrase of the Katha Upanishad in the work entitled The Dialogue of the Saviour. The Egyptian Gnostic text reads: "The Lord [said] to them, 'Be prepared before the All. Blessed is the man who has found the interpretation [about his thought (?)], the struggle with his eyes. *He did not kill nor was [he] killed,* but he came forth victorious' " [my emphasis].[2] Compare this to a passage on the indestructibility of the divine Self in the Katha Upanishad: "The Self knows all, is not born, does not die, is not the effect of any cause; is eternal, self-existent, imperishable, ancient. How can the killing of the body kill Him? He who thinks that He kills, he who thinks that He is killed, is ignorant. *He does not kill nor is He killed"* [my emphasis].[3]

Suddenly it becomes crystal clear why some Christian Gnostics (from the second century A.D. onward) regarded the orthodox crucifixion-atonement doctrine with disdain. For these Christian Gnostics, the "living Jesus" (as they called him) was nothing less than a manifestation of the Self. He did not kill nor was he killed. He was *Life,* as well as being the Way and the Truth.

The Upanishads' identification of the individual self (atman) with the Self (Brahman) is a quintessential teaching of *Gnosis.* And it occurs in India at least five hundred years before Christ.

ALSO SPRACH ZARATHUSHTRA

The prophet Zarathushtra (Zoroaster) is thought to have lived in eastern Persia between circa 628 and 551 B.C. He is generally regarded as the father of cosmic dualism, and the religious tradition that bears his name has also been seen as a major influence on the development of *Gnosis.*

Dualism is a proverbial characteristic of gnostic philosophy. In the gnostic context, dualism means that the universe embodies a contest of opposing principles. Terrestrial life exhibits a struggle between good and evil, life and death, beauty and ugliness, love and hate, right and wrong, even spirit and flesh, while the whole drama finds its sublime image in the contrast of Light and Darkness, or enlightenment and ignorance: gnosis and *agnosis.*

There is little doubt that the dualist element within *Gnosis*—as also within Judaism, Christianity, and Islam—owes something to Persian speculation between the sixth century B.C. and the first century A.D. What that something could be we now explore.

THE WISE LORD

At about the same time as Gotama (the Buddha, or "enlightened one")
was born in India, Zarathushtra was preaching a religion in Persia that
he claimed had been revealed to him by a supernatural being called
Ahura Mazdah, which means Wise Lord.

According to Zarathushtra's seventeen surviving hymns (the
Gathas), Ahura Mazdah created a company of good gods, the Amesha
Spentas (Bounteous Immortals) and a host of bad gods called *daeva*s
(demons). These forces were governed, respectively, by a good or holy
spirit (the Spenta Mainyu) and by an evil or destructive spirit (the
Angra Mainyu). In the Yasna, the sacred liturgical texts of the Avesta
(the Zoroastrian Scriptures), followers of Zarathushtra were enjoined
to follow the good spirit exclusively in thought, word, and deed and to
avoid the snares of the bad spirit, often called simply the Lie, and his
followers, the Liars: "By his [Ahura Mazdah's] wisdom let him teach
me what is best, even he whose two awards, whereof he ordains, men
shall attain, whoso are living or have been or shall be. In immortality
shall the soul of the righteous be joyful, in perpetuity shall be the torments of the Liars. All this doth Ahura Mazdah appoint by his
Dominion" (Yasna 45.6–7).

Thinking people might observe an inconsistency in this exhortation
to moral goodness. If the Wise Lord reigns supreme and demands right
action, why would he also be responsible for an evil spirit? Clearly,
Zarathushtra saw religious virtue in making a free choice for the
good—and how could such a choice be made without the temptation of
evil? But this does not really answer the question of how evil might flow
from good.

Part of the solution to this question may lie in the possibility that
Zarathushtra's Wise Lord owed his origins to a yet more ancient Indo-
Persian god more ambivalent in character than Ahura Mazdah.[4] This
more ancient god contained in his nature the ambivalence of life experience. He represented the perception of an eternal balance of light and
darkness necessary for the progress of the seasons and their promise of
renewed life. This god was called Zurvan, a daunting figure who
appears to be a deification of the principle of time.

By the end of the fourth century B.C., a change in the Zarathushtrian scheme, noted by Eudemus of Rhodes (a pupil of Aristotle), seems to have occurred. Ahura Mazdah had become Ohrmazd. As such he was now one of a pair of opposing powers, with Ahriman, the principle of evil, his opponent: "Both the Magi and the whole Aryan race . . . call by the name *Space* (τοπον, *topon*) or *Time* (χρονον, *chronon*) that which forms an intelligible and integrated whole, and from which good god and evil demon were separated out, as some say, light and darkness before these."[5]

Behind the duo Ohrmazd and Ahriman stands Zurvan. But speculation on the nature of time—especially regarding the requirement that a transcendent deity must himself in some way transcend time (being its creator)—led the Persians to distinguish two forms or aspects of time: *Zurvan akarana*, infinite (more properly, *eternal*) time; and *Zurvan daregho-chvadhata*, the Zurvan who "for a long time follows his own law," or "Time of long Dominion," finite (or relative) time. This highly significant distinction can be compared to Plato's description of time as "the moving image of eternity."[6] What does this mean? It means that time, as human beings experience it, may be regarded as a kind of copy or image of the extension characteristic of the heavenly life, or, in Plato's terms, the life of the aeons.

The aeons may be described as supracosmic "time units," eras or epochs that determine the extending time that we experience on earth. Indeed, the biblical expression translated as "eternal life" means literally "aeonic life"—that life enjoyed by spiritual beings. Another way of putting it is to say that if our time is a crafted copy, then the aeon represents its original mold, or archetype. We must understand this distinction if we are ever to grasp the significance of gnostic thinking. Things in our world are *like* things above, being derived from them. If God is reality, our universe is the movie, with all the vividness of neo-realism.

Let us look at a more intimate way of expressing the distinction. When people have intense feelings of perception—either of beauty, say, or of falling in love and its corollary—people are wont to speak of the "timeless moment," or the moment when "time stopped still." This is the staple experience of romance. Very profound prayer may also share this characteristic. At such a moment, one gets a glimpse of an almost angelic existence. We fear the moment being "snapped." This state is analogous to what is meant by aeonic life.

We can also see that the familiar distinction between finite life and infinite life is inadequate. For example, some people say they could never bear an unending existence in heaven. To them, it sounds like torture. The reason is because both finite and infinite are descriptions of time: one curtailed, one extended.

The problem for the followers of Zarathushtra was that they appear to have had no wholly adequate way of expressing that time is relative and not absolute—which, by the way, is one reason why Einstein is so significant for spiritual theology! Time is a category, like space, of the existence of the cosmos. By speaking of Zurvan akarana, speculators on the doctrines of Zarathushtra were, I think, trying to indicate a state of being outside the time category altogether. The nearest they could come to this concept in the intelligible language that was available to them was to speak of *infinite* time. And the best way to think of this, and certainly the most natural for the ancients, was to think of infinite time as a circle without beginning or end. This was the way the planets appeared to wander, hence the idea of time moving in cycles or revolutions. In alchemy we have the image of the serpent or dragon bent in a circle swallowing its own tail—and the serpent was an image both of immortality (it sheds its skin) and of the spirit hidden within the visible world.[7]

The idea of infinite time is useful because when one thinks about it, cyclic time infinitely extended is hardly time at all, as we know it. We know time chiefly through observing change and death—either of people or, in the winter months, when nature goes underground. We see time in a linear way. Infinite time is so inconceivable to the mind—if not to mathematics—that it would seem to indicate something else. This something else we tend to call *eternity*. This is what Plato meant by "Time is the moving image of eternity"—a mechanical copy of a more profound reality.

It might be objected that the sages could surely have conceived of a dimension absolutely unconditioned by space and time. They did. They called it Zurvan akarana. But they could not simply drop the temporal dimension, first because Zurvan was the god of time, and second because of the philosophical difficulty of defining *being*.

When we say that something *is,* we cannot escape from the immediate sense that it must in some way *extend.* And when we think of extension, our minds automatically generate the categories of space (presence) and time (duration). It might appear that there is no escape! And it is this very experience of being stuck with space and time that leads us on to the next area where speculation on the work of Zarathushtra influenced the development of gnosis.

THAT OLD DEVIL TIME

Zarathushtrian sages gave finite time the duration of 12,000 years. Humans live and die under the dominion of this massive burden of time. The predicament was the source of much soul searching, a Jewish version of which appears in the Wisdom text called Ecclesiastes (c. fourth century B.C., by Qoheleth, the Preacher), where, under time's dominion, we are informed: "Vanity of vanities, saith the Preacher, all is vanity" (Eccl. 12:8). The book is full of anguish, representing a resigned and sometimes quite skeptical protest against Wisdom traditions advocating the simple idea that a wise life leads to an avoidance of disaster:

> For what hath man of all his labour, and of the vexation of his heart, wherein he hath laboured under the sun? For all his days are sorrows, and his travail grief; yea, his heart taketh not rest in the night. This is also vanity.
>
> All go unto one place; all are of the dust, and all turn to dust again. Who knoweth the spirit of man that goeth upward, and the spirit of the beast that goeth downward to the earth? Wherefore I perceive that there is nothing better, than that a man should rejoice in his own works; for that is his portion: for who shall bring him to see what shall be after him? (Eccles. 2:22–23; 3:20–22)

A Persian text of roughly the same period as Ecclesiastes is as eloquent, if not as succinct, on the subject of the pain of time: "As to him whose eyes Time has sewn up, his back is seized upon and will never rise again; pain comes upon his heart so that it beats no more; his hand is broken so that it grows no more, and his foot is broken so that it walks no more. The stars come upon him [astral fate, escape from which was the primary task of the primitive *gnosis*], and he goes not out another time: fate came upon him, and he cannot drive it off."[8]

As time wore on, the problem of innocent suffering, the capriciousness of much experience, and the failure of simple wisdom to account for the visible wastage of life became acute. For those who adhered to the view that their God was good and just, it became necessary to point out that since God was a God of time, he knew the times for all recompense. Jews were encouraged by Persian-influenced sages to look to the end of the wicked, held within the providential economy of God's temporal scheme: "He spoke to me, 'At the beginning of the world, before heaven's gates were set up, I determined it, and thus it was created by me and no other; so, too, the end is created by me and no other' " (2 Esd. 6:1–6).

Persian sages were not so fortunate, having to contend not only with the light of Zurvan akarana, who, as one might expect, came to be identified with the light of Ohrmazd, but also with the terrifying determinism of Zurvan daregho-chvadhata, later identified with the dark power of Ahriman. According to the German scholar Gerhard von Rad, Israel was saved from the grim fatalism of Persia by the power of its monotheism, its belief in the unity of creation: "And was the position of man in the world as a creature among creatures not established in such a way that he could never take up either an entirely objective position in relation to the world or the position of a mere observer? It was the way in which he was tied to the experiential basis of his knowledge which prevented him from moving towards any type of *gnosis*."[9]

While this may have been true for Jews in the fourth century B.C., when they were subject to relatively benign rule as a semi-independent satrapy of the Persian Empire, the same cannot be said to obtain after the conquests of Alexander the Great. The subsequent period left the Promised Land first in the hands of the Ptolemys and then, after the invasion of Palestine by Antiochus III (the Great) in 200 B.C., in the hands of the Seleucid dynasty.

In December 167 B.C., Antiochus IV (Epiphanes) profaned the

Jewish Temple by erecting "the abomination of desolation"—a statue of Zeus Olympius—in the Holy of Holies. This epoch-marking event signaled not only the beginning of armed Jewish resistance under the very able Judas Maccabaeus (Judas the Hammer), but also a crisis among Jewish sages, who were forced to consider again just what kind of temporal scheme their God had in mind for them.

From out of this crisis there emerged among Jews a new class of prophetic literature: *apocalyptic*. The word means literally "to bring out of hiding." And this is primarily what the authors of apocalyptic tracts believed they were doing. They were interested in secrets. Most particularly, they were interested in the secret time plan of God. Where earlier sages had maintained that justice would be satisfied in respect to those wicked who appeared to get off scot-free by contemplating their end, apocalyptic writers reassured doubters with a phantasmagorical vision of that end. And in the Greek, the word takes on a wholly new flavor. The word for "end" is *eschaton*. Hence, *eschatology* deals with the Last Things.

Apocalyptic prophets perceived that a great darkness had fallen over their people. Ancient texts and prophecies were scoured for clues to when the light would return. They did not seek in vain. Had not the prophet Isaiah spoken of a child of a virgin who would bring the light of God back to the people and redeem Israel from sin and oppression? Did not the prophet Amos speak of a Day of the Lord when the world of corruption would cease? Did not Jeremiah speak of a time when the Law of God would be written in the heart of all believers and foreign oppression would end? Did not the prophet Ezekiel write of "the likeness as the appearance of a man" upon a heavenly throne? Surely, they surmised, all that was befalling Israel had been foretold. If therefore the Book of Time was already written, then might not servants of the Lord be given access to it, as interpreters? "O my Lord, what shall be the end of these things? And he said, Go thy way, Daniel: for the words are closed up and sealed till the time of the end" (Dan. 12:8–9).

And so we have Apocalyptic: pseudonymous works describing visions and dreams of the past, the present, and the future. We have ascents to heavenly places; we have revelations of divine mysteries; we have numerological interpretations; we have manifestations of angels;

we have terrifying beasts; we have the revelation of an elect people; we have judgment of the wicked; we have portents, predictions, promises. We hear of saints "tried in the fire as gold"; we hear of a coming light in the darkness. In short, we have a kind of *gnosis:* a total explanation of the destiny of the Jewish people—their past, present, and future—and of the world they lived in: "And after seven days the world, that yet awaketh not, shall be raised up, and that shall die that is corrupt. And the earth shall restore those that are asleep in her, and so shall the dust those who dwell there in silence, and the secret places shall deliver those souls that were committed unto them. And the most High shall appear upon the seat of judgement, and misery shall pass away, and the long-suffering shall have an end" (2 Esd. 7:31–33).

And what of the Persian sages who venerated Zarathushtra? Had not their kingdom also been broken by foreigners? Did they not also have apocalypses? *They did not need them.* Why? Because while the Jews had to explain bad tidings in the context of one righteous God who must be shown to do right in the end, the Zarathushtrians could ascribe the worse to the reign of Zurvan-Ahriman, awful as that might be. Meanwhile, they had to look to Ohrmazd for guidance and seek him in the image of that holy fire which had become a feature of Zarathushtrian temples.

Nevertheless, the Zarathushtrian influence was deeply pervasive, and nowhere more so than in the conception of Satan. Whereas before the time of Alexander "the Adversary" in Jewish literature merely occupied the position of prosecuting counsel in the court of God (see the Book of Job), by the time the Romans gained a strong foothold in Palestine (between 63 B.C. and the time of Jesus), "the Satan" had become the living symbol of the darkness over Israel—and indeed the world: the very shadow of the Spirit.

The Jesus of the Gospels calls him "the prince of this world." He is very much like Ahriman, but for the fact that his power is subordinate to that of the Holy Spirit. And yet he has power over the principalities of the world and, furthermore, over earthly time. His kingdom has duration, but it is relative—not unlike Zurvan daregho-chvadhata: finite time. According to Jesus, Satan's kingdom is of *this* world and will end, while that of Jesus is of the aeons: eternal life. "It is not for you," says the resurrected Christ to his disciples in Acts 2:7, "to know the times or the seasons which the Father hath put in his own power." What had the true disciple, the holy one, to do with time?

By A.D. 50, Paul could tell the Corinthians, without fear of contradiction, that the flesh of humankind goes to Satan, along with all that dies and perishes for good. This idea of linking Satan to created flesh was to have far-reaching consequences for the development of Gnosticism.

Perhaps the most powerful punch that the development of Zarathushtrian thought and experience brings to the first and second centuries A.D. is the sundering of worlds—a view that Jesus seems to have accepted, but with his own subtle twist.

The world-denying, otherworldly spirit is inevitable once one posits a dualist system operating in a single world. Something in human beings rebels against the idea of beng sandwiched between two vast forces that tear through every fiber of their being. If human joy is not to be wrecked by sorrow, humankind must somehow hold apart the dominions of light and darkness. And what more sane solution could be found than to posit two worlds of influence—stressing, of course, that one is, as far as humans are concerned, higher than the other? And what more obvious a way could be found of doing this than by maintaining that that which is visible is less than that which is invisible?

So the flesh becomes the shadow of the spirit. The flesh is subjected to the world of change and corruption, but the spirit finds its home in eternity. Only the spiritual alchemist can solve the problem: *The kingdom of heaven is nigh and within you.* The spiritual world is not broken off from the world of sense—although the reverse might appear to be so—the spiritual kingdom is found *within* this world. As the Gnostic Gospel of Thomas puts it, "The kingdom of the Father is spread over the earth, but men do not see it."[10]

MITHRA THE MEDIATOR

As Jewish apocalyptists sought an intermediary between the world of heaven and of earth in the form of "the son of man" coming as an anointed king *(messiah),* it should not be thought that certain Persian believers could do without some link between the mighty forces of Ohrmazd and Ahriman. For the task, some breakaway Zarathushtrians pondered the ancient god Mithra, linked before the time of Zarathushtra with Varuna, the Vedic god of the heavens, whom Zarathushtra had for some reason abandoned in favor of Ahura Mazdah.

Plutarch, born in Chaeronea, Greece, about four years before Paul's sojourn in Corinth, and a priest of the Delphic Oracle, wrote in his *De Iside et Osiride* (On Isis and Osiris, 46) that Mithra was the mediator between Ohrmazd and Ahriman. Mithra was the redeemer of humankind from the dark power of Ahriman. Votive offerings were presented to Ohrmazd and disaster-averting or mourning offerings were presented to Ahriman. Ahriman, principle of (necessary) darkness, was venerated or propitiated in rites where Mithra was the mediator—thus marrying, as it were, heaven and hell, and reconciling (or rather attempting to reconcile) the cosmos to itself.

According to the poet Statius, writing in A.D. 96, Mithra's followers had established an independent cult that operated throughout the Roman Empire, a cult whose followers met in caves and underground chambers. Mithraic sanctuaries have been discovered from Hadrian's Wall to Persia. An image frequently gracing the sanctuaries is that of the young man Mithra, sporting a Phrygian cap, killing a great bull with a dagger thrust to the neck. A dog and a snake leap to catch the spurting blood as a scorpion catches his sperm; men gather three ears of corn from his anus. Blood, corn, and sperm are, of course, all phases of the principle of life.

On one side of the image is a figure with a torch facing upward, while on the other, the torch faces downward: a classic image of dualism. The dog, scorpion, and serpent almost certainly refer to the stellar constellations of those names; the ears of corn are self-explanatory. This was a syncretistic cult, combining elements from Zarathushtra, Osirian worship, possibly Ophism, and the popular fertility cults of Attis and Cybele. In that the cult permitted only men, we may infer that it was complementary to the cult of Isis, which members' wives may have frequented.

No wholly Mithraic manuscripts have survived, so forming an idea of the beliefs and practices of Mithraism is not straightforward. We know there were seven grades of initiation (an important parallel to gnostic systems), corresponding to some extent to the ascent through the seven planetary spheres, and the names of these grades are suggestive: Raven, Bride, Soldier, Lion, Persian, Runner of the Sun, and Father.

Initiation involved dramatic sequences, including the visceral struggle of the aspirant with men dressed as beasts (related to the constellations?), following which the aspirant was dressed in a zodiacal garment. A cultic meal of bread and water, or wine, was served to celebrate the victory of Mithras (Mithra in his Roman form) over the slain bull.

The bull, called Apis, was a form of the sun god Osiris, and we may wonder whether Mithras is not here slaying Osiris and playing the role of Set, god of the sun in the south: the sun darkened (night = death). This interpretation would form a happy complement to the feminine worship of Isis, who puts Osiris back together again. Roles of man as warrior and woman as preserver would thus be neatly kept. On the other hand, the slaying of the cosmic monster Ti-amat (a dragon) by the Babylonian god Marduk may lie behind the myth.[11]

One inscription refers to Mithras saving his followers by the shedding of eternal blood: a great image to inculcate a sense of value in soldiers, among whom Mithras was so popular, while the fruit of this struggle, in the form of bread and wine, was shared among cult members. Mithras's birthday coincided with the birthday (winter solstice) of the sun: December 25, our Christmas.

ENTER THE DEMIURGE

In many Mithraic sanctuaries stood the statue of a monstrous being. He has a lion's head on a man's body. The body is wrapped in huge serpentine coils. The figure is winged (Time?), and he holds a long staff with keys (to the kingdom?). He has zodiacal signs over his body and sometimes a thunderbolt on his chest. This terrifying figure is surely Zurvan-Ahriman: the all-devouring lion as a symbol of finite time. The serpent coiled: the sun's ceaseless ecliptic; the zodiac: fate—the powers of the *heimarmene* (Greek, meaning the "cloak of the months").

Zurvan-Ahriman is the power behind irrevocable destiny, the

power of the stars. The study of astrology is the study of his operation. Thus, we can see clearly why astrology has played such a significant role in gnostic doctrines. Astrology is to give Zurvan-Ahriman his due—how to avoid the worst his power portends. While humankind at large languished under the weight of the stars, the Mithraist had a mediator, Mithra, who, it seems, could clear a way through the seven planetary spheres and put the advanced believer in touch with Ohrmazd, god of light, as Zurvan akarana: eternity.

This breaking-through of the power of the earthly governors (the zodiac) is a central motif in the development of *Gnosis*. It represents the promise of a timeless miracle. We can see its influence in orthodox Christian doctrine as well: "Sun and moon bow down before Him," as the hymn puts it. When Christian Gnostics came to speak of Christ's outwitting the power of the archons (literally, "rulers") who try to kill him because he knows the secret of how to transcend them, the Mithraic scheme gives us an idea of what they meant.

The explosion of archontic power by Christ represented for many Christians in the first and second centuries A.D. the very substance of the Gospel: good news indeed for those fearful of fate, as ancient people undoubtedly were—and, in many cases, as we are still. (Needless to add, perhaps, that sharing in the triumph over the archons also put believers one up on the merely worldly power of imperial Rome. Believers were not afraid of Roman authority. They could resist without either arms or armies and in the end would triumph.)

We now come to a key Gnostic conception, one that caused consternation to the enemies of Christian *gnosis* in the second century A.D. Insofar as the Demiurge claimed to be the highest God, then the Demiurge, the awful creator of the material universe, was for Gnostics a false god. The Gnostic had *seen through* his deceptive handiwork, and, free of it by virtue of knowledge, could "look down" on it. Enemies of the Gnostics regarded this posture as one of insufferable arrogance. The radical Gnostic could reply that such a position was as nothing compared to the supreme destructiveness and arrogating offense of the Demiurge—himself the blind god who knows no higher than himself.

In their Secret Book (Apocryphon) of John, written sometime in the second century A.D., we hear of how the Demiurge, here called Ialdabaoth, took counsel with the archons and created the seven planets—hence the false god's claim to "have none before him." (The zodiac provided the image for the grim fetters that held humans in ignorance, or agnosis: that is, "without gnosis").

Reckoning the Father in heaven preached by Jesus to be superior in character to the God of much of the Hebrew Bible, it was natural for Gnostics to identify any lesser conception of the highest God with the Demiurge, who had, they believed, blinded Jewish people to the central *gnosis*.

The link between the Gnostic Demiurge and the Mithraic Zurvan-Ahriman conception of a cosmic creator of the finite and transcendable is revealed in an attack on the doctrines of the Christian Gnostic Marcus. His followers, the Marcosians, are pilloried in Bishop Irenaeus of Lyons' monumental books *Against the Heretics* (Adversus haereses), written in about A.D. 180:

> [The Marcosians] declare that the Demiurge, desiring to imitate the infinitude, and eternity, and immensity, and freedom from all measurement by time of the Ogdoad[12] above, but, as he was the fruit of defect, being unable to express its permanence and eternity, had recourse to the expedient of spreading out its eternity into times, and seasons, and vast numbers of years, imagining, that by the multitude of such times he might imitate its immensity. They declare further, that the truth having escaped him, he followed that which was false, and that, for this reason, when the times are fulfilled, his work shall perish.[13]

Thus, we can now see how the apocalyptic hope of a "time" when time's dominion would cease is joined at last to the figure of the Gnostic Demiurge. This was the figure whom Gnostics saw in Christ's image of "the prince of this world": a prince whose reign is finite and relative, and who will, in short, run out of time.

Little did the Roman armies who moved eastward in the first century B.C. know that the East was in the throes of a vast spiritual revolution. As the Roman bureaucracy superseded ancient self-governing cities and regions, individuals had perforce to seek in religion what they had lost in civic self-realization. The very roads constructed for armies and for trade would provide the means for a slow spiritual takeover from the East. Ancient religious currents began to seep into the veins of the empire. Not surprisingly, a world redeemer was widely expected. The hope sprang like a spark out of a creeping darkness that was enveloping the East. Men and women desired release from Zurvan-Ahriman,[14] the Lord of the zodiac, the power of Satan.

The East awaited a sign.

TWO

From the Magi to St. Paul

Now when Jesus was born in Bethlehem of Judea in the days of Herod the king, behold there came magoi *[Greek] from the east to Jerusalem, saying, Where is he that is born King of the Jews? For we have seen his star in the east, and are come to worship him.*

(MATT. 2:1–2)

Who were these *magoi* who came "from the east"?

The word we translate as "magi" would not have been at all strange to readers of Matthew's Gospel in the last quarter of the first century. Magi, it seems, were to be found everywhere. Gaius Plinius (who died in the famous Vesuvius volcanic deluge of A.D. 79) wrote in his *Natural History* (30.6) of how the science of the magi had been brought to Greece by the Persian Asthanes. Asthanes had accompanied Xerxes to that country (c. 480 B.C.). From there, Pliny tells us, magian arts had spread to Italy, Gaul, and even Britain.

Perhaps the art became thoroughly debased by shallow and unscrupulous practitioners, for by the first century Pliny describes the art of the magus as "a thing detestable in itself. Frivolous and lying as it is, it still bears however, some shadow of truth upon it; though reflected in reality by the practice of those who study the arts of secret poisoning, and not by the pursuits of magic." Magic, even then, carried an ambiguous status and a questionable past.

Philo of Alexandria, a generation before Pliny, distinguished between scientific magi and a class of charlatans and sorcerers who also took the name. This distinction became a perennial one. In the fifteenth century, for example, the neo-Neoplatonist Pico della Mirandola, in making a great case for the dignity of the magian art, sharply distinguished between sacred *magia* ("the perfection of all philosophy") and *goetia* (referring to the evocation of demons). The latter was "a thing to be abhorred so help me the God of truth, and a monstrous thing."[1] In declaring this, Pico was merely echoing an age-old perception that there was a respectable magus and a demonic imitation.

The tone of Matthew's description of the Magi's arrival at Jerusalem "from the east," an account with no negative connotations at all, can refer only to the respectable magi.[2] Where had they come from?

In about 587 B.C., the Jewish prophet Jeremiah (39:3, 13) described the head of the Magian caste in Babylon as being accorded equal status with the princes of that city. This man was Nergal Sharezar, whom Jeremiah called Rab Mag—that is, Chief Magus.

The Greek historian Herodotus, writing some thirty years after the defeat of Xerxes' Persian navy by Themistocles at Salamis (480 B.C.), fascinated Greek readers with an account of a priestly caste of Magi. The Magi had lived as one of the six tribes of the Medes[3] (northern Persia) until the transfer of power to the Persians in 550 B.C.:

> The Magi are a very peculiar race, differing entirely from the Egyptian priests, and indeed from all other men whatsoever. The Egyptian priests make it a point of religion not to kill any live animals except those which they offer in sacrifice. The Magi, on the contrary, kill animals of all kinds with their own hands, excepting dogs and men. They even seem to take a delight in the employment, and kill, as readily as they do other animals, ants and snakes, and such like flying or creeping things. However, since this has always been their custom, let them keep to it.[4]

Herodotus also describes how the Median king Astyages went to the Magi to find out if a dream he had had, wherein his grandson Cyrus was made king, had any truth in it. (This is the same Cyrus, by the way, whose edict of 538 B.C. would give the Jews permission to rebuild their temple in Jerusalem after the return from exile in Babylon.)

> Proceeding to consider what he [Astyages] should do with Cyrus, his grandchild, he sent for the Magi, who formerly interpreted his dream in the way which alarmed him so much, and asked them how they had expounded it. They answered, without varying from what they had said before, that "the boy must needs be a king if he grew up, and did not die too soon." Then Astyages addressed them thus: "The boy has escaped, and lives; he has been brought up in the country, and the lads of the village where he lives have made him their king. All that kings commonly do he has done. He has had his guards, and his doorkeepers, and his messengers, and all the other usual officers. Tell me then, what think you does all this tend?" The Magi answered, "If the boy survives, and has ruled as a king without any craft or contrivance, in that case we bid thee cheer up, and feel no more alarm on his account. He will not reign a second time. For we have found even oracles sometimes fulfilled in an unimportant way; and dreams, still oftener, have wondrously mean accomplishments." "It is what I myself most incline to think," Astyages rejoined; "the boy having been already king, the dream is out, and I have nothing more to fear from him. Nevertheless, take good heed and counsel me the best you can for the safety of my house and my own interests." "Truly," said the Magi in reply, "it very much concerns our interests that thy kingdom be firmly established; for if it went to this boy it would pass into foreign hands for he is a Persian: and then we Medes should lose our freedom, and be quite despised by the Persians, as being foreigners. But so long as thou, our fellow-countryman, art on the throne, all manner of honours are ours, and we are even not without share in the government. Much reason therefore have we to forecast well for thee and thy sovereignty. . . . As for the boy, our advice is, that thou send him away to Persia, to his father and mother."[5]

Needless to say, Cyrus's Persian army conquered Media. The Magians revolted, whereupon Cyrus's successor, Cambyses, severely repressed them.

A century or so later, the Magi were still known as enchanters, astronomers, dream interpreters, and prophets, flourishing in some kind of uneasy relationship with the official Zarathushtrian priesthood. By the first century their name had become associated with anyone adept in secret lore and magic. There were even Jewish magi, such as Elymas, or Bar-Jesus, described as "a sorcerer, false prophet" (Acts 13:6), based at the court at Paphos in Cyprus, who contested there with Paul and Barnabas.

Meanwhile, the religious influence of the Magians was still strong among the Parthians (Arsacid dynasty, 250 B.C.–A.D. 225), who, by grace of Rome, controlled what had once been the Persian Empire. According to Strabo, the Magians formed one of two councils of the Parthian Empire—so they represented no mean influence in the East.

As far as the first-century A.D. general public was concerned, magic operated in a world ruled by destiny, whose visible agents were the unreachable stars above them. Naturally, anyone with knowledge of the stars, anyone who could predict their movements and relate them to ordinary life, was both powerful and useful. For people of goodwill, the aim of magic was to wrest control of destiny from the apparently evil, hostile powers and to give it to those who claimed powers of healing and positive influence. Thus, to have a demon at one's disposal did not necessarily mean the demon's master was evil. The demon could become a slave in the cause of good. (The debate involved in this power is implicit throughout the New Testament: If he (Jesus) casts out a demon, ask his opponents, is his power from Satan?) Magi used spells, charms, elaborate ceremonies, astrology, and possibly some kind of alchemy to shield their followers from evil, or Ahriman.

According to Professor Howard Clark Kee,[6] Magi assessed Jesus as magically significant on account of the miracles attested to him. Indeed, Jesus' name appears as a suitable "name of power" to be invoked in acts of healing magic in the first-century Magical Papyri, discovered in Egypt.

It was not difficult to compare Jesus' alleged magical powers with those of the Greek sage Pythagoras (c. 582–500 B.C.), whose followers were so much admired by Philo of Alexandria. Pythagoras's skills in healing, prediction, and commanding the weather were claimed by enthusiasts of a first-century B.C. revival of Pythagoras's reputation, to be derived from the Chaldeans (southern Babylonia) and the Magi. According to the Gospels, Jesus maintained that his powers came directly from God, because, as far as he was concerned, the demons worked only for the Enemy (hence, in part, the conflict between the early Church and what one might call the magical establishment).

While it may be that the *magoi* of Matthew 2 came to Jerusalem, and thence to Bethlehem, to greet the birth of one of their own—as in contemporary Tibet, where Buddhist monks use magic and dream interpretation to locate their reincarnated Lama—the references in Matthew 2 to Magi seeking the one "born king of the Jews" suggests, from the Magian point of view, that their visit was quite routine.

Magi moved around the East to visit kings and emperors on numerous recorded occasions. King Herod the Great was subject to at least two visitations in a single decade. The *Antiquities* of the first-century Jewish historian Josephus records a visit by Magian envoys bearing gifts after the completion of Caesaria Maritima in 10–9 B.C. (Caesaria was to be the chief base for the Roman administration of Judaea). Dio Cassius, Suetonius, and Pliny all describe an amazing procession of Magi who came to pay homage to the emperor Nero in A.D. 66. They were led by Tiridates, the king of Armenia.

Armenia lay northeast of Commagene. Commagene lay fifty miles northwest of Edessa (northeast Syria), home to the great Jewish-Christian community where Matthew's Gospel is thought to have been composed. Astrology flourished in Commagene.[7] Perhaps the Matthaean Magi came from Commagene.

In any case, Tiridates and the Magi were accompanied by the sons of three of the neighboring Parthian rulers, and the triumphal procession from the north Euphrates region certainly passed through Edessa (perhaps shortly before the composition of Matthew)[8] and Aleppo. Aleppo was another Jewish-Christian region where magic and "primitive" Christianity existed in close proximity. The *Gnosis* of Syria was strongly influenced by Magian practices. The Western churches had reason to be suspicious of the Eastern church's relations to magic.

Magi seem to have had a curious propensity for turning up at the right place at the right time. (They were clearly concerned with the

whole question of time and doubtless played an active part in speculations on the Zarathushtrian tradition.) Cicero, for example, reports
that on the night Alexander the Great was born, the temple to Diana at
Ephesus burned down. Apparently, Magi were there and cried out at
daybreak that the plague and bane of Asia had been born that night.
They were right.

The scope and perhaps universality of Magian interests is further
attested to by Seneca, who left us an account of how Magi in Athens visited Plato's tomb, offering incense in recognition of the philosopher's
divinity. What is particularly striking in all this is the apparent independence of spirit and of activity ascribed to the Magian caste.[9] Their
movements might sometimes appear to have been initiated by higher
motives than the usual terrestrial considerations of state or religious
organizations. Magi took their cue from natural signs in both the earthly
and the celestial orders. We might say that they rubber-stamped destiny.
As for the particular Magi—Matthew does not tell us how many there
were—who appeared in Jerusalem seeking "his star," they could have
made their journey from a number of places.[10]

Apart from Commagene and Harran (about fifty miles southeast of
Edessa and a center for astrology and, later, Hermetic philosophy),
Babylon had established itself as the world leader in astroscience, and
there were many Jews resident there. These Jews could have fleshed out
astronomical observations and astrological interpretations connected
with the birth of a king in Israel with knowledge of messianic prophecies. A world redeemer from the East was widely expected throughout
the empire at the turn of the Christian era. Naturally, the Jews hoped
and believed such a figure would be their promised messiah, or king.
However, the confusion over where the king of the Jews was to be born,
evident on the arrival of the Magi at the court of King Herod the Great,
does to some extent militate against their journey having been spurred
by prophecies such as that in Isaiah 60.

The Magi were, moreover, dependent on the king's scribes for further information, while Isaiah's prophecy belongs properly to hopes surrounding the return of Jews from Babylonia in the fifth century B.C.:
"Arise, shine; for thy light is come, and the glory of the LORD is risen
upon thee. . . . And the Gentiles shall come to thy light, and kings to the

brightness of thy rising. . . . The multitude of camels shall cover thee, the dromedaries of Midian and Ephah; all they from Sheba shall come: they shall bring gold and incense; and they shall shew forth the praises of the LORD" (Isa. 60:1, 3, 6).

While this kind of predictive coincidence was very much in the province of Magian interests, the passage carries too great a weight of self-justifying Jewish triumphalism to have been of determinative interest to the apparently more objective Magi. (Worshipping a king was good form; the capitulation of all Gentiles to the God of Israel was not on the Magian agenda.)

The Matthaean Magi could also have come from Arabia. An Arabic Gospel of the Infancy (dated between the second and fifth centuries A.D.) refers in its seventh chapter to "some magi" who "came to Jerusalem according to the prediction of Zoroaster [Zarathushtra]."[11] The famous gifts of gold and frankincense were associated with the desert camel trains from Midian in northwest Arabia and with Sheba in the southwest. According to Herodotus, frankincense (an aromatic constituent of incense) was found only in Arabia. (Myrrh, incidentally, was used in oils for embalming and anointing, while magical charms were sometimes written in myrrh ink.)

In the Hebrew Bible, "people of the East" was a name frequently applied to the Qedemites, or desert Arabs. The Qedemites had a reputation for wisdom in astroscience (four Arabian tribes took their names from the stars), and it would be surprising if there were no Magi among them.

About 120 B.C., Dhu Nowas, the Arabian king of Yemen (Sheba), had converted to a form of Judaism. There were Jewish colonies around Medina in the first century. Justin Martyr's *Dialogue with Trypho* (78, c. A.D. 160) is emphatic that "the magi came to him [Herod] from Arabia." However, he goes on to say that in coming to worship Christ, they showed that they had revolted against the "bondage" of the demon (magic) "which held them captive." He then locates this demonic "dominion" in Damascus and Samaria (associating Samaria and Syria with demonic [pagan] magic). Furthermore, he reckons that "none of you [non-Christian Jews] can deny that Damascus was, and is, in the region of Arabia, although it now belongs to what is called Syrophoenicia."[12]

The polemical thrust of Justin prevents us from taking his account strictly historically. It is noteworthy, however, that Justin associates the Magi with exactly that place where twenty years later the orthodox Christian bishop of Lyons, Irenaeus, will say that the heresy of the "*gnosis* falsely so-called" had its birth in the person of the Samaritan Magus, Simon. Again, this could be a general and possibly ill-informed polemic against the competitive power of magic as a rival mode of salvation. This refutation, it must be said, is wholly absent from the account of the Magi in Matthew.

What had the Magi seen that made them travel to Jerusalem in search of one born to be king of the Jews? Dr. David Hughes, lecturer in astronomy and physics at Sheffield University in the United Kingdom, has made a thorough scientific study of all the extant evidence surrounding the so-called Star of Bethlehem and has come to the following informed conclusion:

> The physical occurrence that made up the star of Bethlehem was the series of conjunctions, the apparent coming together in the sky and accompanying risings and settings of the major planets Jupiter [associated astrologically with kingship] and Saturn [associated astrologically with Israel] in Pisces. The Piscean conjunction is rare enough to have been considered unusual. It was possible to predict the conjunction, and Babylonian magi had done just that, as the cuneiform tablets testify. The phenomenon had an inherent astrological message which equated it directly with "his star." Historically it occurred at the right time, in 7 B.C. And finally, even though it was an extremely significant event to a trained astrologer, in reality it consisted of two perfectly normal planets moving as usual along their ordained celestial paths. This is why Herod and the people of Jerusalem could easily miss its significance.
>
> The choice of a specific day is really stretching the evidence too much, but if one day has to be selected I think we would be safest with the day that the Magi probably chose, the day of the acronychal rising. (An outer planet rises acronychally when it is at opposition, on the opposite side of the Earth to the Sun. It rises in the east as the Sun sets in the west and remains in the sky all night, being due south about midnight.) This means that Jesus was born on the evening of Tuesday, September 15, 7 B.C.[13]

JEWISH THEMES

Persian speculation by no means had a monopoly on those ideas that in their development would constitute the Gnosticism of the second century A.D. Jewish speculation had a considerable influence.

The prophets of ancient Israel, as is well known, were constantly attempting to get their hearers to recognize the uselessness of material gods, images (idols), or anything false that interrupted the communion of God and God's people. One of the problems with which prophets such as Jeremiah, Deutero-Isaiah, and Ezekiel had to contend was the materialistic fear felt by Jews in exile in Babylon that being separated from Jerusalem (the Temple) meant being separated from God. It became important throughout this terrible crisis of faith to emphasize the idea of God dwelling in the heart, and, furthermore, to explain the physical exile in Babylon as being the direct result of, or judgment on, a former spiritual exile.

The hope for a restored Temple was predicated on the belief that it could happen only when the hearts of believers had been purged and God could be worshipped spiritually. Jeremiah (c. 625–587 B.C.) longed for a day when the Law would be written in the heart. A restored Temple would require a spiritually renewed faith and a new purity of worship: "They shall ask the way to Zion with their faces thitherward, saying, Come, and let us join ourselves to the LORD in a perpetual covenant that shall not be forgotten" (Jer. 50:5). What is meant by this "perpetual covenant that shall not be forgotten"? Could it not be understood as union with God in terms of spiritual knowledge?

The Babylonian Exile (597–538 B.C.) made the heaviest possible demands on the prophets of Israel, and they sought divine inspiration from visionary experiences, in which the terrible physical events could be seen spiritually and meaningfully. In the extremity of the crisis, the prophetic word seems to have gained access to numinous archetypes formerly sleeping in the bosom of the Hebrew faith.

THE ANTHROPOS: MAN

In 593 B.C., the prophet Ezekiel experienced a vision of the personified glory of the Lord. This occurred in Babylon, four years after the first deportation of the Jews of Judah to Babylonia and roughly contemporaneous with the period of the writing of the Hindu Upanishads. The glory of the Lord appeared to Ezekiel in the form of Man:

> And above the firmament that was over their heads was the likeness of a throne, as the appearance of a sapphire stone: and upon the likeness of the throne was the likeness as the appearance of a man above upon it.
>
> This was the appearance of the likeness of the glory of the LORD. And when I saw it, I fell upon my face, and I heard a voice of one that spake. And he said unto me, Son of man, stand upon thy feet, and I will speak unto thee. And the spirit entered into me when he spake unto me, and set me upon my feet, that I heard him that spake unto me. And he said unto me, Son of man, I send thee to the children of Israel, to a rebellious nation that hath rebelled against me. (Ezek. 1:26, 28; 2:1–3)

This vision of Ezekiel became, in the words of Professor Gilles Quispel, "the stock theme of Jewish mysticism,"[14] and it may be the origin of the Anthropos, the divine archetype of Man that is so important to Gnosticism: the human being as spiritual being.

In the second century B.C., for example, the Jewish (and notably) Alexandrian playwright Ezekiel Tragicus refers to this figure, the divine Man, in his Greek drama *Exodus*.[15] Moses has a dream of Man (Greek: Phōs, [Au 5] "heroic man"; also "light"—a great pun) sitting on a throne on the top of Mount Sinai with a crown on his head bearing a scepter. Man then gives a crown to Moses and invites him to sit on a throne next to God. (The account is somewhat reminiscent of the account of the Transfiguration in the Synoptic Gospels.)

The prophet Ezekiel's vision[16] is also the origin of the kabbalists' Adam Kadmon, the macrocosm in the form of Man. Soon after 160 B.C., the figure appeared as the "Son of man" in the Book of Daniel, becoming a staple of apocalyptic tracts thereafter. The figure is the origin of the "Son of man" theme, which the Christ of the Gospels takes as his own. He becomes the last, or "second," Adam, in Paul's letters: the glory of God, the light of heaven in whose "body" the Christian is invited to participate through the baptismal sacrament.

Possibly under the influence of Alexandrian Jews, the figure of the Anthropos becomes the star of the Graeco-Egyptian Hermetic *Poimandres,* where the heavenly Poimandres (described as the authentic *nous,* or Mind), reveals to the mystagogue Hermes Trismegistus the way to gnosis.[17]

The philosophical *Hermetica* reveal that God generated a Son, who is yet androgynous: both Phōs (Adam, Man, Light) and Zoë (Life, Eve). Desiring to imitate the creative powers of the divine spheres, the heavenly Man descends to the outer rim of the spiritual world, sees his image reflected in the "waters" of the material world, falls in love with said image, and descends further into nature. From his beautiful image, the rulers of nature fashion the first human being, both mortal in his natural part and immortal, because he is made in the divine image:

> But Mind [nous], Father of all, he who is Life and Light, gave birth to Man, a being like to Himself. And he took delight in Man, as being his own offspring; for Man was very goodly to look on, bearing the likeness of his Father. With good reason then did God take delight in Man; for it was God's own form that God took delight in. And God delivered over to Man all things that had been made.
>
> And having learnt all the substance of the energies and received a share of their nature, he willed to break through the bounding circle of their orbits; and he looked down through the structure of the cosmos, having broken through the sphere, and showed to downward-tending Nature the beautiful form of God. And Nature, seeing beautiful Man who bore the form of God, smiled with insatiate love of Man, showing the reflection of that most beautiful form in the water, and its shadow on the earth. And he, seeing the form, a form like his own, in earth and water, loved it, and willed to dwell there. And the deed followed close on the design; and he took up his abode in *matter-without-Logos* [my emphasis]. And Nature, when she had got him with whom she was in love, wrapped him in her clasp, and they were mingled in one whole; for they were in love with one another.
>
> And that is why Man, unlike all other living creatures upon earth, is twofold. He is mortal by reason of his body, he is immortal by reason of the Man of eternal substance. He is immortal, and has all things

in his power; yet he suffers the lot of a mortal, being subject to *heimarmene* [Destiny or Fate; the Stars]. He is exalted above the structure of the heavens; yet he is born a slave of Fate. He is bisexual, as his Father is bisexual, and sleepless, as his Father is sleepless; yet he is mastered by carnal desire and by oblivion.[18]

For those Hermetists, or followers of Hermes, who may have met in small coteries for instruction in Egypt during the second century and perhaps beyond, gnosis consisted in the act of recalling to consciousness their divine origin. This recollection, as it were, reversed the adventure of the Anthropos, enabling aspirants to "rise again" to rejoin the spiritual realm whence their spirit had come, eschewing their natural part. This process constituted the Hermetic-Gnostic *palingenesia*, or rebirth, attained through noetic (that is, of the divine mind, *nous*) or prayerful meditation.

The Anthropic image is almost certainly a conceptual descendent of Ezekiel's visionary experience in Babylon in 593 B.C.

SOPHIA

In that she [Wisdom] is conversant with God, she magnifieth her nobility;[19] yea, the Lord of all things himself loved her. For she is privy to the mysteries of the Knowledge [gnosis] of God, and a lover of his works. (Wisdom of Sol. 8:3–4)

In the Wisdom of Solomon, written no later than the first century A.D., Wisdom (Greek, Sophia) is revealed as the companion of the Lord. This beautiful work of Jewish speculative thought (to be found in the Apocrypha of the Hebrew Bible) puts forward a positive, personalized vision of the Sophia of God, who will later come alive as a key, if initially tragic, figure of the precosmic divine drama in second-century Valentinian Gnosticism.

The origin of the Sophia speculation is almost certainly Alexandrian Jewish—and it is in Alexandria (the meeting place of East and West) that the most intense period of Gnostic development took place, from the first century A.D. onward.

The voice of Sophia can be heard crying out from the Nag Hammadi library in such works as *The Thunder, Perfect Mind,* as the wisdom of the Greeks and the gnosis of the barbarian, saint and whore, bridegroom and bride:

> *I was sent forth from [the] power,*
> *and I have come to those who reflect upon me,*
> *and I have been found among those who seek after me.*
> . . . .
> *For I am the first and the last.*
> *I am the honoured one and the scorned one.*
> *I am the whore and the holy one.*
> *I am the wife and the virgin.*
> *I am the mother and the daughter.*
> *I am the barren one*
> *and many are her sons.*[20]

In the once lost book *Eugnostos the Blessed,* composed no later than the second century, Sophia appears explicitly as the consort of the Immortal Man:

> All the immortals, which I have just described, have authority—all of them—by the power of the Immortal Man and Sophia, his consort, who was called "Silence," because in reflecting without a word she perfected her greatness.[21]

According to inscriptions of the eighth century B.C. found in the Negev and near Hebron, the God of Israel had the Canaanite goddess Ashera as a spouse. In the fifth century B.C., Jewish soldiers at the (Egyptian) Elephantine garrison (near Assuan) venerated another pagan fertility goddess, called Anat Jahu, wife of the Lord. However, it is most likely that the origin of the femininity of Jewish Wisdom lies not here but in the person of the Egyptian goddess Maat.

Maat expressed the principle of truth, right, justice, basic order, and world order, with correspondences in the later Greek Stoic concept of Logos and the Chinese Tao. Lady Wisdom, as she appears in the Jewish

Proverbs (where it is recommended that one follow her as a whore through the back streets), survived as the Hokma (Wisdom) principle, especially at Alexandria, where she became the great Gnostic heroine.

The love between the Lord and the Sophia expressed in the Wisdom of Solomon is paralleled in Gnostic writings such as the Gospel of Mary (Berlin Codex) in the love of Jesus for Mary Magdalene. A great deal is made of the despising of Mary's testimony by the all-male disciples: She is treated much as Sophia is treated by those "of the world." But Gnostics were taught to venerate her message. Indeed, in the Nag Hammadi Gospel of Philip, the identification of Mary Magdalene with Wisdom is explicit: "As for the Wisdom who is called 'the barren,' she is the mother [of the] angels. And the companion of the [Saviour] is Mary Magdalene. [But Christ loved] her more than [all] the disciples [and used to] kiss her [often] on her [mouth]."[22]

While these references have naturally encouraged observers to wonder about some kind of historical sexual relationship between Jesus and Mary, it is clear to this author, given the background of Sophia speculation, that a Gnostic Immortal Man-type Jesus would *have* to have a Sophia-type consort or companion. Mary Magdalene fit the bill perfectly, especially as there was speculation that Mary of Magdala and the woman taken in adultery were one and the same person. What better companion for Jesus than *She* the Whore, she who offers herself to all: Wisdom, the divine slut of heaven and earth?

Irenaeus, along with other orthodox heresiologists, attributed the existence of the Gnostics' threat to orthodoxy to the activity of the Samaritan Magus, Simon. Simon appears in a walk-on part in the Acts of the Apostles, chapter 8, giving us the word *simony* for the sin of purchasing spiritual preferment. The Magus is reported to have attempted to buy the secret of the power of the Holy Spirit that the apostles had at their occasional disposal.

Professor Quispel finds it significant that the Magus Simon came from Samaria. The Samaritans were the last survivors of the Ten Tribes of northern Israel, who, though despised by orthodox Jews in general, kept the basic Mosaic Law but rejected much of the remainder of the Bible. They also retained a tradition of Wisdom being the personal creator of the world, an idea central to Valentinian Gnosticism.

Views attributed to Simon the magician suggest he regarded Wisdom as God's wife, also called Holy Spirit or God's First Idea, and the Mother of all. She descended to nature and gave birth to angels who created the world. But these angels kidnapped her, whence, according to Simonian tradition, she reincarnated in a series of bodies, including that of the Helena "whose face launched a thousand ships" against Troy.

Simon, "the great power of God," claimed to have finally picked her up in a Tyrian brothel in Phoenicia, and "redeemed her" as his consort. It would be interesting to know how much he paid for her freedom. If the tradition is based on fact, it would seem that Simon was as humorous a figure as the magus Aleister Crowley two millennia later, with a magician's taste for ironic symbology.

The Sophia archetype is clearly of pre-Christian origin and was a figure of gnosis before Gnosticism.

THE UNKNOWN GOD AND THE DEMIURGE

The Jewish philosopher Philo of Alexandria, a contemporary of Jesus, wrote polemics against those who taught of two gods; at the same time, Philo himself called the Logos (the divine instrument of creation) "a second god," "archangel," "Lord," and "Name."

After Philo's time, Jewish rabbis complained of heretics (minim) who believed that God had a representative who bore his name, Jao (an abbreviation of Y H W H, the proper name of God) or Jaoel. These Jewish heretics also said that this figure sat on a throne next to God's and was called Metatron. Metatron became a significant figure in what Gershom Scholem called "Jewish Gnosticism," which contains much of what is now generally referred to as the Kabbalah.

Some dissident Jews, called Magharians, said that all anthropomorphic names in the Hebrew Bible referred not to God, but to the angel Metatron, who created the world. In the Gnostic Apocryphon of John, which is dated before A.D. 185, something like this angel appears as the Demiurge, or "the archon who is weak," with three names: Ialdabaoth, Saklas, and Samael.

Saklas means "fool," so called because he does not know that there is One higher than he. He is thus the "jealous god," jealous of his superior from whom the original "perfect Man" derives. Saklas is directly hostile to the first human being, whom he and his fellow powers create after marveling at the divine Anthropos: "the Man, and the son of Man" whose reflection they see "in the waters."[23]

"Come," says Ialdabaoth, in a terrifying parody of the Genesis account of the creation of Adam, "let us create a man according to the image of God and according to our likeness, that his image may become a light for us."[24] Having made a "luminous" man, the archons recoil in jealousy, for their combined efforts have made a being greater than themselves individually: "And when they recognised that he was luminous, and that he could think better than they, and that he was free from wickedness, they took him and threw him into the lowest region of all matter."[25]

This is hard-core Gnosticism, where the false god has become a perfectly sinister deity. The philosopher Hans Jonas, for one, has doubted it could possibly be the work of Jews—especially since its knowledge of Hebrew scripture seems limited to the book of Genesis, which certainly did fascinate Gentile readers. In a short and typically clear paper on gnosis, Professor Quispel observes, "Only people who had been brought up to believe every word of the Bible, and to cling to the faith that God is one, and yet found reason to rebel against Law and Order may have been inclined toward the Gnostic solution: God is one and the Bible is right, but anthropomorphisms like the handicraft of a creative workman and personal lawgiving are to be attributed to a subordinate angel."[26]

Perhaps Quispel is right, but there is all the difference in the world between a subordinate angel and the vicious, scheming, sinister bunch of archons who make Man only to kick him into the dark dungeon of matter, there to all but tread the life out of him. This was the disturbing revelation of cosmoclastic Gnostic texts such as the Apocryphon of John.

If anything, the case suggests what might have occurred when a tradition of gnosis—in this case, with a Jewish speculative lineage—got into the hands of a determined representative of Gnosticism. The case indicates clearly the need to define the essential difference between gnosis as a spiritual commitment to and awareness of divine union and the use made of gnostic (small *g*) material to create the kind of thorough-going, grand-plan, "Here's-Your-Answer" Gnosticism.[27]

PHILO OF ALEXANDRIA

The Greco-Egyptian city of Alexandria occupies a key position in the intellectual development of *Gnosis,* so it is not surprising to find that the first-century figure whose thought comes closest to the developed or even classical Gnosticism of the second century resided there. The Jewish philosopher Philo was an elder contemporary of both Jesus and Paul, dying at about the time the latter established a church in Corinth, some five hundred miles northeast of Alexandria, across the Mediterranean.

Alexandria had become the great mixing bowl of Greek and Eastern philosophy, and Philo's work attests to just how far Jewish speculation in Egypt had advanced during the Ptolemaic period as a result of this interaction.

Philo's audience spoke Greek, and in translating the personalist language of the Hebrew Wisdom, legal, and prophetic books into the abstract terminology of Plato and Pythagoras, he not only created a new theological language but also contributed to that peculiar blend of abstraction and mythology so characteristic of the temper of the later Gnostic writings.

According to Professor Henry Chadwick, although "some of the raw material of Gnosticism can be found in Philo, he is not, except in the vaguest sense, himself a Gnostic."[28] This must be taken to mean that Philo did not consider a formulaic *gnosis* to be the sole mode of redemption from the powers of the world—but the roots of such a view are evident in his works, of which, happily, for once we have a signifi-cant quantity.

Philo attempted to explain the nature and relationship of God to human beings in philosophical and intellectually respectable terms to an audience curious about the religion of the Jews. His biggest philo-sophical problem was how to explain the difference in quality between the postulated perfection of God and the imperfection and catastrophic quality evident in humankind and the visible creation. Since this issue was of prime importance to the Gnostics, who were much preoccupied with the question of the origin of evil, Philo's influential framework is well worth examining.

One of the most characteristic Gnostic ideas is that of an utterly transcendent Father whose essential nature is completely beyond intellection. Insofar as God is beyond (being the author of) the Ideas of which the universe is an expression, God is remote from this world. There is nonetheless a link to this world. In a sense, this idea involves the old Persian problem of the relation of finite to infinite time, but in Alexandria the problem was expressed in different terms, though still leading to similar conceptual conclusions.

Philo describes God as One, or, in Greek terms, as the Monad. He does not mean that God is the first in a series of numbers (as in Pythagorean abstraction), for according to Philo, God is "beyond the Monad," being self-sufficient, immutable, and independent of—in the sense of not needing—the world. Philo was perhaps the first to see the Platonic Ideas as God's thoughts. This would have fascinated Platonists, for whom the eternal (note!) Ideas represented the basis for human thought. Thus Philo's transcendent God dignified the pursuit of philosophy—most pleasing to the Greeks!

How is the link made between the utterly transcendent and the world we live in? Philo developed the notion of a Great Chain of Being, filled out to a "perfect fullness,"[29] or as a magnetic chain.[30] The governing principle of this relation between transcendent God and lower world Philo calls the *Logos,* a term borrowed from Stoic philosophy and usually translated as the Word. It can mean the "world-reason," or the principle of order, or the divine mind extended. Essentially the Logos is the divine power that holds together the All. In humans, the Logos is the principle of intelligibility, or the plumb line, level, and square of the universe, if you like.

Philo calls the Logos the "Idea of ideas," content to combine abstract terminology with personal and poetic language, since for him divinity is manifest in both the personal and the impersonal orders—in fact, for Philo they are really the same. Thus the Logos is called (in language highly resonant to readers of the first chapter of John's Gospel) the "first-begotten Son of the uncreated Father," "second God," and even "the man of God."[31]

Like the later Gnostics, Philo speculated on the meaning of Genesis 1:26: "And God said, Let us make man in our image, after our likeness: and let them have dominion . . . over every creeping thing that creepeth upon the earth."

He saw the passage as describing the creation of the heavenly Adam, distinct from the earthly man, whose creation he saw in Genesis 2:7: "And the Lord GOD formed man of the dust of the ground, and breathed into his nostrils the breath of life; and man became a living soul."

Philo was thus able to get the two accounts to correspond to the Platonic distinction of the sensible and the intelligible worlds. We have already seen to what use Paul put this distinction when enjoining the Corinthians to put the spiritual man before the man of flesh. The later Gnostics used the distinction to classify human beings as hylics (or materials—with no chance of redemption) and pneumatics (or spirituals who were saved by possession of gnosis).

Again, in terms so reminiscent of the first chapter of John's Gospel ("In the beginning was the Word . . ."), Philo speculated that as archetype of the heavenly Mind, the Logos was the heavenly Adam (Paul called Christ the "second Adam," redeemer of the sin of the first or earthly Adam).

As manna, or "bread" (cf. Paul's "spiritual meat" and the Gospel of John's "bread of life" that comes from heaven), the Logos is, according to Philo, God's heavenly food to humankind. The Logos is God immanent in the creation: the vital power holding together the hierarchy of being. The Logos is God's viceroy;[32] it is midway between creator and creature.[33] The Logos is the high priest who intercedes or mediates with God on behalf of frail mortals (cf. the Persian Mithra)—the supreme God being too remote to have direct intercourse with the world.

Philo, possibly thinking of the Stoic doctrine of the World-Soul that sustains and interpenetrates all creation, and who is worshipped in parts (those parts pertaining to the elements as separate gods), maintains that although the less enlightened take the Logos for God, he is in fact God's image. Again we might think of the possible Persian influence on Plato, where Platonism holds time to be the "moving image of eternity." According to Philo, the "divine man"—he refers to Moses at the burning bush—is, in fact, indwelled by the Logos.

Philo calls the Logos an archangel, a governor of angels, rather like the Gnostic Sophia who is credited with their creation. Indeed, according to Professor Chadwick, the language of the personified Hokma (Greek: Sophia) is never far away when Philo speaks of the Logos. It would seem that for Philo, Wisdom and the Logos are indeed the same. For a richer picture of Philo's Logos, then, we need only refer to such passages of Jewish Wisdom as Proverbs chapter 8:

> Receive my instruction, and not silver; and knowledge rather than choice gold. For wisdom is better than rubies; and all the things that may be desired are not to be compared to it. I wisdom dwell with prudence, and find out knowledge of witty inventions. . . . By me kings reign, and princes decree justice. By me princes rule, and nobles, even all the judges of the earth. I love them that love me; and those that seek me early shall find me. . . . The LORD possessed me in the beginning of his way, before his works of old. I was set up from everlasting, from the beginning, or ever the earth was. . . . When he prepared the heavens, I was there: when he set a compass upon the face of the depth: . . . Then I was by him, as one brought up with him: and I was daily his delight, rejoicing always before him; rejoicing in the habitable part of his earth; and my delights were with the sons of men. (Prov. 8:10–12, 15–17, 22–23, 27, 30–31)

Philo's work bears eloquent testimony to the idea that contemplation of and speculation about the works of the Logos will reveal secrets. In some passages, he regards God's "power" mediating between God and the world as mysteries, and in some degree esoteric.[34]

Philo believed that Moses had experienced a second birth when called to be a prophet, his mind replaced by the divine spirit. (This is a doctrine very close to the "bowl of nous" story in *Corpus Hermeticum* 4.) This gift of the divine spirit was made to those who had attained the heights of holiness by training *(ascesis)* and discipline. Philo clearly feels he has at times shared in this gift. He speaks of how the veil of the letters of the Hebrew Pentateuch (the Five Books of Moses) must be penetrated to uncover their spiritual meaning. Philo believed Moses had intended his work to be taken allegorically.

This enthusiasm for allegory was to have profound effects on the development of Gnosticism and on its practical wing, alchemy, which inhabits a veritable landscape of poetic allegory.

In "De cherubim" 27, Philo refers to higher meanings being made available to him by an inner voice within his soul, which he says is often possessed and able to divine matters beyond its knowledge. Philo believed the gift did not necessarily require retirement into solitude—revelation could occur in the midst of a crowd—but he held it to be nonetheless true that the senses were a constant distraction to spiritual perception. In this regard, Philo took great comfort from the words of God to Jacob in Genesis 11:3: "I will be with thee."

Sometimes, when sitting down to write, Philo would see only a blank, even though his mind was ready. Suddenly, ideas fell upon him like rain, causing him to enter a state of "corybantic frenzy, losing consciousness of everything, of the place, of anyone else present, of myself, of words spoken, of lines written."[35]

For Philo, the experience of redemption meant losing self in something higher. That experience of losing self justified for Philo the superiority of prophetic revelation over philosophical thought. To add weight to his point of view, he referred readers to Plato's ecstatic side when, in the *Phaedrus,* the soul remembers its primal dance among the Ideas. Philo described mystical ecstasy as like being "on fire."[36] The soul is "stirred and goaded to ecstasy, dancing and possessed so that it seems drunk to the onlooker."[37]

This experience led to spiritual gnosis and enabled Philo to formulate ideas on not only the destiny of the soul, but how it came to be that the soul should require experience of release from the bonds of this world.

Like the Gnostics, Philo held that during this life the soul was something of a pilgrim and a sojourner, with no firm root in the world of nature. He wrote of how, when the mind soars up to initiation in the Lord's mysteries, it judges the body to be bad and hostile.[38] The soul has descended into the bondage of flesh, like Israel in Egypt, and must seek its Exodus.

This dualism is very close to the classical Gnostic position. The aspirant must advance to a complete absence of passion (απαθεια, *apatheia*). The Gnostics of the second century developed this idea into a full pictorial itinerary. Within it human beings are progressively stripped of passions (those powers that hold them to the earth), which are handed over to their respective governors (frequently linked to the zodiacal powers) as the humans rise toward the Pleroma, or Fullness, of the purely spiritual realm, beyond the stars.

The goal for Philo is the vision of God, of "seeing and being seen."[39] According to Philo, God is knowable by the mind, but in himself he is unknowable. We can know *that* God is, but not *what* God is. The crown in this cognitive process ultimately belongs not to inferential reasoning, but rather to intuition.

Philo, like the Gnostics, continually stresses the gulf between the transcendent God and the creature. Unlike some Gnostics, Philo's divine spark of *pneuma* (spirit) is not regarded as being undifferentiated in identity with the One; rather, Philo speaks of an "unbroken union with God in love," with the soul as God's bride.[40] Nevertheless, there is a stress on deification: To see God, human nature must first *become* God (θεον γενεσθαι).

For Philo, the soul certainly belongs in a higher realm than that of earth, regardless of whether that higher realm is itself derived from or co-substantial with God. The question is: How did the soul get wrapped up in a lower world to begin with? In attempting an answer, Philo came very close indeed to the understanding shared by many Gnostic groups in the second century.

For Philo, being fallen is inherent in being created, so that even in respect to the best human beings, sin is "congenital." The flesh, as Plato would say, is still a tomb. Sin, according to Philo, has its root in pride (a view from which Paul would not have dissented); the lust to become equal to God is for Philo the root of sin.[41] This might seem paradoxical, since Philo also sees the goal of spiritual life as being the vision of God. Enjoying the vision of God entails becoming divine.

From the philosophical point of view, there is something of a conundrum here, and Philo, like the Gnostics, takes a certain amount of refuge in a mythology of the Fall. Philo wrote of a fall of souls brought about by their satiety with the divine goodness—like bees heavy from an excess of honey.

Some souls descend to bodies; others become ministering angels, known as *daimones* by the pagans. (Philo identifies the Greek heroes with angels.) This does not get around the problem of evil in the world, but Philo nonetheless makes an important contribution to the question with ideas that will receive more systematic treatment from the cosmoclastic Gnostics.

Because God can cause only good, God is not responsible for evil. Responsibility lies elsewhere. Looking at Genesis 1:26, Philo notes that the God who created humans spoke in the first person plural: "Let *us* make man . . ." The Lord was obviously, he deduced, assisted by subordinate powers. They were doubtless responsible for the *mortal* part of humans—a neat trick (cf. Plato's *Timaeus* 41, where we hear of a subordinate "maker" or "demiurge"). For Philo, that inferior angels shared in the creation explains the existence of evil. He thus foreshadows the radical Gnostics' darkest secret: A bad creator, impersonator, and confidence trickster had a part in the making of the cosmos.

The question involved here is intractable and results in part from the problem of source and derivation. If, like the Greeks, the philosopher holds that the source or archetype is always better than the "copy" (as water is purest nearest the spring), then how can he explain that the Good was responsible for the not-good? Why *can't* the Source make a perfect copy? Philo answers that the ultimate source was not responsible for the copy; it was the work of an assistant. The assistant must be in some way *less than* the Source because otherwise it could not possibly be described as being subordinate!

On the basis that you find this tautology intelligible, it is difficult to avoid concluding that you have only two options for explaining the situation. Either you take the later third-century Neoplatonic view—based on naturalness as a quality of divine creation (that sound, for example, loses its resonance over distance), and that's just the way things are, no evil intended—or you take the mythological view that some kind of dramatic rupture has occurred beyond the sphere of the perfect Good, prior to the creation of the cosmos and its powers. Or—a big *or*—God has reasons to be inconsistent with what we think, for the best of reasons: God is. If we were meant to know, we would be told. Suffering is a mystery; God knows best.

Perhaps the problem here lies in how far the spiritual world is to be inhibited by natural categories. Platonists have held that the natural derives its character from the spiritual, but as a kind of copy or image. While this has a certain logic, it does not explain how it came to be that man *qua* natural man has a spiritual part that is not entirely at ease with nature. This was the question to which the second-century Gnostics thought they'd found the solution—and their solution was not very far from Philo's.

The logic of the situation demands that the soul should return to its source. This is fine if the angels above are, as it were, on your side. Persian speculation, however, and a good deal of popular astrological belief suggested otherwise. The powers above were quite terrific and not well disposed to doing favors for human beings—especially if the favor involved them in helping the aspirant reach what they themselves could not—the godhead. This could only happen if a way *through* the lower angels, or archons, or zodiacal *heimarmene,* was found.

Christian Gnostics found their Way in Jesus' defeat of Satan, exhibited by the latter's inability to secure Jesus' permanent demise by crucifixion, and by Jesus' subsequent gift of pneumatic knowledge (the Holy Spirit) to his followers. Non-Christian Gnostics simply looked to the gnosis itself as providing the key to the prison gates.

As for the creation of the material cosmos, Sophia speculation led Alexandrian and Alexandrian-influenced Gnostics (such as Valentinus around A.D. 150) to ascribe the fault to *her.* They had perhaps read of how Sophia had played with the Lord (Prov. 8:30). Had she perhaps played a bit too much? According to many Gnostics, she most certainly had. Her yearning to know the unknowable, her desire, her intense passion to grasp the ungraspable (Wisdom + Pride = Fall) led her to autoconceive a version, a copy, a kind of unauthorized phantom pregnancy—note the Platonism plus myth—of the creative powers of the transcendent Father.

Through this illegitimacy, she falls from the perfect harmony of the Pleroma. She gives birth to subordinate and, being the product of disharmony, warped powers. Like her, they are seized with the desire to know her fully and create in their turn the manifest cosmos in which Sophia wanders destitute and whorelike among the sons of men, crying for release, begging for pity from the merciful Father. The bright planets who stud her cosmic garment likewise "wander," suggesting an order beyond themselves.

Meanwhile, in the conflagration—or the Pleroma's Big Bang—sparks of spirit have fallen like a burst placenta, or, more particularly, like an abortion caught in a half-life of space and time. The sparks of *pneuma,* or spirit, then lie dormant beneath the weight of space, time, and *matter.* The only hope for human beings, according to this view, was that the spark be brought into consciousness, with all its attendant memory of the divine home, and the human soul be released from bondage by the "living Jesus"—the "perfect fruit of the Pleroma," as the Valentinians called him. Once all the sparks were returned home, the wounded Pleroma would be healed and the wicked cosmos destroyed. The stars would fall: the promise of the apocalypse.

No doubt Philo would have been horrified by all this. The cosmos, far from being a manifestation of the Logos—however imperfect—had become a bloody mess, and ordinary human life absolutely intolerable. But surely we can now begin to see how it happened that the long-term conflation of Persian speculation with apocalyptic failure,[42] and the heady development of Greco-Egyptian and Jewish philosophical speculation in Alexandria, came to generate the phenomenon known to scholars as Gnosticism. In fact, there is something almost inevitable about the phenomenon, given the nature of the human mind under such a mighty array of conditions.

Before going any further, however, it must be stated that it is possible that those ideas which have traditionally been seen as the province of Gnosticism, and especially the subsequent interpretation of those ideas, represent something of a perversion of a purer gnosis. It may be said that the radical Gnostics' stunning spiritual and literally anarchic rebellion used the language of gnosis without control or restraint. So, while the appearance of people calling themselves Gnostics belongs securely to the second century A.D. and beyond, it may be more accurate to see their Gnosticism as an incident in the unfolding passage of gnosis through time.

When all is said and done, *Gnostic* is only a word, like *Christian*, which may denote whatever the bearer may wish it to denote. On the other hand, two major characteristics of gnostic (note small *g*) thought have been, first, its lack of dogmatism; and second, its playfulness in formulating ideas, on the simple basis that it is the *spirit* that counts. In telling a story, it may be possible to destroy the essence of what is being told. In the past, historians and theologians have taken the far easier route of describing gnosis in the ready-made terms provided by its enemies.

Since the epoch-marking studies of Reitzenstein, Nock, and Festugière;[43] Bultmann;[44] and Jonas[45]—and now even more particularly, since the receipt of texts from the Nag Hammadi library—scholars across the world widely disagree as to what a Gnostic really is and what constitutes the gnosis. This, of course, could all be part of the Gnostics' extraordinary joke on the values of the world. They have a tendency to turn the world upside down—perhaps because the world *is* upside down, and there is a lack of truth in it.

The first major theologian to write in copious and quite exhausting—if not exhaustive—detail about the Gnostics (Irenaeus in c. A.D. 180) described their beliefs as the "gnosis falsely so-called," thereby implying, to anyone who noticed, that there just might be a gnosis *truly* so-called. While many have gone on to investigate what was described as false, how many have sought what was true?

THE ESSENES

Philo of Alexandria admired two religious groups above all others. These were the Pythagoreans (whose master Pythagoras, they believed, had learned his secrets from the Magi and the Chaldeans) and the Essenes.

There has been much speculation on the nature of the Essenes. For a long time, scholars have associated them with the supposed sectaries of Khirbet Qumran, once the alleged holders of the world-famous Dead Sea Scrolls. This was an easy mistake to make. Flavius Josephus (born in Judaea in A.D. 37 or 38) wrote that there were four sects of the Jewish religion. He described the beliefs of three of them: the Sadducees, the

Pharisees, and the Essenes. The fourth group, the Qanna'im (Hebrew), known generally as the Zealots (from the Greek *zelotai*), he did not describe. The reason is almost certainly that Josephus held them responsible for bringing ruin to his country during the Jewish revolt against the Romans of A.D. 66–70. Josephus usually describes the Zealots as "bandits." It was natural to suppose, with such a biased conception in mind, that the "sectaries of Qumran," with their extensive literary interests (thought unlikely if the Zealots were primarily warriors) and some other characteristics similar to those in Josephus's description of the Essenes, must have been Essenes.

Since a number of Qumrani documents have features in common with early Christianity, some writers have gone on to suggest that the Essenes were the fount of a tradition that, following the disappearance of the Jerusalem Mother Church after A.D. 70, went underground in some way. For example, the War Scroll refers to a war between the Sons of Light and the Sons of Darkness. This suggestion of a Gnostic-type dualism has led some writers to think of links to the Bogomil and Cathar gnostic heresies of the Middle Ages.[46] This picture is certainly an interesting and to some extent attractive one. Unfortunately, evidence advanced to promote it is highly ambiguous and frequently tendentious. A primary problem is that it is most unlikely that the principles sustaining the renegade community of Qumran were in fact those of the Essenes.

It is surely significant that the two Jewish writers of the first century who have anything good to say about the Essenes both wrote with a Gentile audience in mind. The extant writings of the Dead Sea sect generated out of the sect itself cared not a jot for the opinions of non-Jews and looked for the destruction of those they called the Kittim, a designation used for the Romans and their non-Jewish allies: "No peaceful Essenes these."[47] Of course, that does not mean that the Essenes shared all the apologetic interests of Philo of Alexandria and Flavius Josephus, but it is hardly likely that the latter should recommend respect to a group that desired the annihilation of foreigners.

Philo of Alexandria sought principles of universality in the ancient writings of the Jews and doubtless saw such principles alive among his admired Essenes. As for Josephus, he tells us that for three years before the age of nineteen, he chose to be a disciple of one Banus who lived in the desert in great austerity: "I was informed that one, whose name was Banus, lived in the desert, and used no other clothing than grew upon trees, and had no other food than what grew of its own accord, and bathed himself in cold water frequently, both night and day, in order to preserve his chastity. I imitated him in these things and continued with him three years."[48]

Since this passage occurs in a paragraph wherein he speaks of investigating the beliefs of the Sadducees, Essenes, and Pharisees (finally choosing the discipline of Pharisaic life), it is reasonable to suppose that Banus may himself have been one of the Essenes. Josephus never associates the Essenes with the practices of the Zealots. Nevertheless, it is now clear that the Zealot movement was not only an armed resistance movement, but also a distinctly religious movement. The Zealots' deepest motives and most profound and often moving convictions can be found in the Qumrani War Scroll, along with a range of associated commentaries, prayers, legal texts, hymns, and community guidelines.[49]

Similar ideological distinctions and associated bitterness and acrimony may be found in the contemporary Israeli political and religious scene. We have only to compare the activities of the first-century Jewish Sicarii (the "dagger-men" who killed Jews in the city streets for cooperating with Romans) with recent politico-religious assassinations in the modern state of Israel. The extreme right-wing political movement in Israel lives side by side with moderate right-wing, liberal, pacifist, and mystical groups and individuals—pretty much, it seems, as did analogous parties in first-century Judaea. So if the Essenes were not the same as the sectaries associated with Qumran, who were they?

It is interesting that Philo regarded both the Essenes and the Pythagoreans as the best exemplars of the spiritual life, for Josephus begins his account of the Essenes by saying that the latter "live the same kind of life as do those whom the Greeks call Pythagoreans."[50]

Pythagoras, apart from making famous contributions to geometry and mathematics (both of which were taken by him or by his followers as symbolic disciplines with relevance to the soul), founded a religious order for men and women. The order believed in preparing for successive lives, a staple expectation of the Indian subcontinent both at that time and today. This secret order became not only a religious sect but also a political force in southern Italy, where Pythagoras (c. 582–500 B.C.), a native of Samos in the eastern Aegean, had finally settled down.

The view most associated with Pythagoras, and which has become a perennial one—and certainly perennial among many gnostics—is that there is an absolute duality between soul and body. The soul is imprisoned in the body, a condition from which Pythagorean prescriptions— magical prescriptions—hoped to liberate it. Empedocles, a pre-Socratic philosopher familiar with the Pythagorean doctrine, wrote of the human as a divine being fallen from a heavenly state into a corrupt body. His lament for his condition would not have looked out of place among the texts of the Nag Hammadi library: "One of these I now am, an exile and a wanderer from the gods, for that I put my trust in insensate strife. . . . I wept and wailed when I saw the unfamiliar land. . . . For I have been ere now a boy and a girl, a bush and a bird and a dumb fish in the sea."[51]

The Pythagorean view also left an indelible mark on Plato and most of the later Platonists. Whatever the beliefs of the first Pythagoreans, those following Pythagorean tradition in the time of Josephus and Philo are more properly called Neo-Pythagoreans and had a more developed, syncretistic teaching.

One significant Neo-Pythagorean doctrine concerns the psychic autonomy of the pneuma, or spirit, which held that while the soul *(psyche)* had been swallowed by matter, the mind (*nous*—a word frequently interchangable with *pneuma*) was, as it were, left outside and constituted the *daemon*[52] of the human being. The Neo-Pythagorean nous seems to be identical with the Gnostic figure of the Anthropos, who comes from beyond the realm of the archons as the adversary of the planetary spheres (the heimarmene). Just how much of these doctrines was familiar to the Jewish Essenes it is impossible to ascertain.[53] We are almost completely dependent on the brief disclosure of Josephus concerning the Essenes, to which we must now turn.

In his *Antiquities*, Josephus tells us of one Manahem, an Essene who attempted to advise Herod the Great (d. 4 B.C.). Manahem not only "conducted his life after an excellent manner, but had the foreknowledge of events given him by God also." Josephus considers the Essenes' gift of prophecy as being due to the strict and irenic probity of their personal lives: "Essenes have, by their excellent virtue, been thought worthy of this knowledge of divine revelations." Manahem's prophecy having been found to be true, Josephus tells us that Herod the Great afterward "continued to honor all the Essenes."[54] What being honored by Herod meant we do not know, except to say that he did not regard the Essenes as a threat to his power. This was a rare privilege from a man regarded by many Jews as a puppet king and Roman collaborator who had had his wife, his wife's mother, and two of his sons executed.

If Manahem had tried to assist Herod, he would have earned the undying hatred of the "Qumran sectaries" and Jewish patriots elsewhere. However, there is no hint of political bias on the part of the Essenes. In *War of the Jews,* Josephus refers to another Essene prophet, Judas, who "never missed the truth," who predicted the rise of Alexander Jannaeus (c. 104–76 B.C.), the Maccabaean priest-king who was a hero of the "Qumrani" messianic sect.

Josephus tells us that the Essenes were to be found throughout his country, moving around from town to town and city to city, a peripatetic lifestyle familiar to us from the Gospel accounts of Jesus. Asceticism played a part in their practices: "Essenes reject pleasures as an evil, but esteem continence, and the conquest over our passions to be virtue." They shared property, were suspicious of women, and were poor, dressing in simple white garments until the clothing was worn out. On journeys they took nothing with them save a weapon against thieves. They were known for their extraordinary piety, sobriety, and moderation, praying before sunrise and bathing in cold water together as an act of purification. Josephus describes them as "ministers of peace" and "eminent for fidelity." Essenes, he says, "restrain their power." Furthermore, "swearing is avoided by them"; "they take great pains in studying the works of the ancients"; and they "inquire after such roots and medicinal stones as may cure their distempers." Essenes were also said to be stricter in their observance of the Sabbath than other Jews.

In spite of a general proscription on oath taking, initiates did take oaths of piety, justice toward humankind, hatred for the wicked, and assistance for the righteous. The initiate was to be "perpetually a lover of truth." It is significant that their virtues are contained in the words *hesed* (piety) and *zedek* (righteousness); it seems that Josephus regarded their practice of these virtues as definitive and probably expected his readers to compare them with the terroristic practices of the armed resistance movement.[55]

In his *Antiquities,* Josephus applies these virtues to the teachings of John "that was called the Baptist . . . who was a good man [possibly a euphemism for 'Essene,' but unproven], and commanded the Jews to exercise virtue, both as to righteousness towards one another, and piety towards God, and so to come to baptism; for that the washing would be acceptable to him [God], if they made use of it, not in order to the putting away, of some sins, but for the purification of the body: supposing still that the soul was thoroughly purified beforehand by righteousness."[56] We must try to avoid thinking of baptism as practiced by the Essenes as being the same in meaning as that practiced by Josephus's older contemporary St. Paul, for whom baptism was a definitive rite of entry into "Christ's body."

We cannot say whether or not John was an Essene, but it is true that his behavior conforms to that idea of the righteous and pious Essene held by Josephus.[57] The cardinal virtues of hesed and zedek are also evident in Jesus' confirmation that people should love their neighbors as themselves (righteousness) and that they should love God above all (piety). In the general Gnostic theory, right acts proceed from right knowledge: If we have gnosis of God, we are necessarily saved from the blindness that normally prevents us from loving other human beings and which inhibits the love of God. This concept of gnosis is, of course, morally removed from the brand that self-consciously sets up a spiritual elite. On the other hand, hatred of the wicked is also counted for righteousness among the Essenes, so it would not be impossible to hold to both a spiritual and a moral concept of elite behavior.

According to Josephus's account of Essene doctrines, there are definite signs of Gnostic illuminist ideas: "These are the divine doctrines of the Essenes about the soul, which lay an unavoidable bait for such as have once had a taste of their philosophy."

The idea of the ascent, or rather re-ascent, of the soul is primary. Bodies are corruptible; souls are immortal and continue forever. Souls are "united to their bodies as in prisons, into which they are drawn by a certain natural enticement; but that when they are set free from the bonds of the flesh, they then, as released from a long bondage, rejoice and mount upward."

The initiate "swears to communicate their doctrines to no one any otherwise than as he received them himself; that he will abstain from robbery, and will equally preserve the books belonging to their sect, and the names of the angels."[58] This reference to their special books and to the names of the angels may help us further grasp Essene doctrines. While we do not have any books extant that can definitely be said to be Essene books, we do have one book from the period that in certain important respects would not have been considered to be beyond Essene interests, or even, possibly, provenance. That book is the apocryphal and apocalyptic *Book of Enoch,* a work known primarily in an Ethiopic copy of an Aramaic original. It was certainly available in our period, since fragments of it have been discovered among the documents comprising the Dead Sea Scrolls.

THE *BOOK OF ENOCH*

The *Book of Enoch* is in fact a collection of books.[58] The books deal with the end of the world, the cause of human depravity, astronomical corrections to the calendar, the coming messiah (called the "Son of Man," the "Lord of the sheep" [90.20–27], and the "Lamb"), the names and destiny of the angels, the revealing of the "holy sons of God," and the nature of the heavenly kingdom.

We also learn of the history of the Jews from the creation to the first century B.C., the nature of Sheol (Hell), the blessed destiny of the righteous, and the downfall of the wicked. The *Book of Enoch* is a positive compendium of all the chief features of apocalyptic literature, and from its language and dramatic myths we can learn much about the formative imagination of first-century Jewish and Christian literature. It also provides us with crucial information that appears to have been developed by the Gnostics.[59]

We can see from the following quotation how well the book would fit into the thought-world of the Essenes:

The book written by Enoch for all my children who shall dwell on the earth; and for the future generations who shall observe uprightness and peace. Let not your spirit be troubled on account of the times; for the Holy and Great One has appointed days for all things. And the righteous one shall arise from sleep, and walk in the paths of righteousness, and all his path and conversation shall be in eternal goodness and grace. He will be gracious to the righteous and give him eternal uprightness, and he will give him power so that he shall be with goodness and righteousness, and he shall walk in eternal light. (90.1–4)

That the *Book of Enoch* contains lists of angels there is no doubt. The leaders of the fallen angels are listed in 6.7 as Semiazaz, Arakiba, Rameel, Kokabiel, Tamiel, Ramiel, Danel, Ezeqeel, Baraqijal, Asael, Armaros, Batarel, Ananel, Zaqiel, Samsapeel, Satarel, Turel, Jomjael, and Sariel (all sounding of Babylonian or Median origin). The names may well be synonymous with those of observed stars, since in 43.1 ff. we read of the weighing of the stars in scales of divine judgment "according to their proportion of light: the width of their spaces and the day of their appearing, and how their evolution produces lightning [like sparks off a grindstone]: and their revolution according to the number of the angels, and they keep faith with each other."

In 20.1 ff. we are given "the names of the holy angels who watch": Uriel, Raphael, Raguel, Michael, Soraqael, Remuel, and Gabriel—and their particular tasks. The four archangels are listed in 40.9 ff.: Michael, Raphael, Gabriel, and Phanuel. Another list of the chiefs of the hundreds of fallen angels, or "Satans" (adversaries of humankind), occurs in 69.2 ff., wherein we find the name of the mighty angel Azazel, the angel that Irenaeus asserted to be the master of the Gnostic Marcus.[60]

In addition to the lists of angels and the general ideological thrust of the *Book of Enoch,* which ties in with Josephus' reference to Essene works, one further passage might be cited as suggesting either an Essene provenance for the book or at least a spiritual tradition shared among Essenes and the book's authors. We know from Josephus that the Essenes wore white garments, bound by a girdle at the waist (as did the Mandaeans and Sufis centuries later). Enoch, patriarch of the Jewish people, one who traditionally did not die but who was transported directly to heaven (Genesis 5:24), explains that after his "spirit was translated and it ascended into the heavens" he "saw the holy sons of God. They were stepping on flames of fire: *Their garments were white and their faces shone like snow.* . . . And the angel Michael . . . showed me all the secrets of righteousness. And he showed me all the secrets of the ends of the heaven, and all the chambers of all the stars, and all the luminaries, whence they proceed before the face of the holy ones. . . . And he translated my spirit into the heaven of heavens, and I saw there as it were a structure built of crystals, and between those crystals tongues of living fire. And my spirit saw *the girdle which girt the house of fire,*[61] and on its four sides were streams full of living fire, and they girt that house" (71, 1–14; emphasis mine).

It may be that this "house of fire" is a vision of a spiritual being, a visionary and ideal human who contains the Head of Days and the archangels within him. At the climax of the vision, an angel tells Enoch: "This is the Son of Man who is born unto righteousness" (71.14). In this context, the visionary Son of Man could represent the transfigured Essene in his translated spiritual aspect: Enoch himself *in himself*—after he has (to borrow Josephus's expression) "mounted upwards" to, in Neo-Pythagorean terms, his daemon, his nous, the autonomous Anthropos (archetype of man) beyond the stars, beyond the body, beyond the soul—the House of Fire. It is an intoxicating vision: "This is the Son of Man who hath righteousness, with whom dwelleth righteousness, and who revealeth all the treasures of that which is hidden, because the Lord of Spirits hath chosen him. . . . And this Son of Man whom thou hast seen shall raise up the kings and mighty from their seats, and shall loosen the reins of the strong, and break the teeth of the sinners" (46.3–4).

And thou, child, shalt be called the prophet of the Highest: for thou shalt go before the face of the Lord to prepare his ways; to give knowledge [*gnosis*] of salvation[62] unto his people by the remission of their sins, through the tender mercy of our God; whereby the dayspring from on high hath visited us, to give light to them that sit in darkness and in the shadow of death, to guide our feet into the way of peace.

And the child [Jesus] grew, and waxed strong in spirit, and was in
the deserts till the day of his shewing unto Israel. (Luke 1:76–80)

In addition to enlightening us as to the imaginative world behind
parts of the New Testament, as in the above parallel (there are many
examples), other features of the *Book of Enoch* appear to have influenced aspects of second-century Gnosticism.

First of all, the depravities of the human condition are not ascribed
to Adam's sin (as St. Paul taught) but to the machinations of a host of
fallen angels called the Watchers. The Watchers "saw and lusted after"
the "beautiful and comely daughters" of men, and resolved "to choose
us wives from among the children of men and beget us children"
(Genesis 6.1–3). These children were giants, and they soon corrupted
and perverted humankind through every kind of bestial wickedness (cf.
Genesis 6:4, where the "sons of God" impregnate the "daughters of
men" to produce the "mighty men which were of old, men of
renown"—with no negative effects implied).

According to Enoch, the Watchers disobeyed the Lord of Spirits and
taught humans secrets and mysteries without restraint or moral guidance, the ensuing scene resembling an orgy of libidinous excess. The
angel Azazel taught people to make instruments of war; he taught them
about the metals of the earth, the use of antimony, cosmetics, and jew-
elry. In short, he was responsible for fornication and godlessness.

Semjaza taught enchantments and root cutting (herbal lore and
drugs). Baraqijal taught astrology; Kokabiel the constellations;
Ezeqeel knowledge of clouds; Sariel the course of the moon. Enoch is
sent by the Lord of Spirits to condemn Azazel, an angel, and his host,
telling Enoch that the Watchers should intercede for human beings,
not he for them. Enoch is to tell the Watchers that "though ye were
holy, spiritual, living the eternal life, you have defiled your selves
with the blood of women, and have begotten with the blood of flesh,
and as the children of men, have lusted after flesh and blood as those
who do die and perish" (15.4). Here, surely, we have a root for the
Gnostic conception that the rulers of the stars, the archons, are evil,
and that from their dominion the Lord of Spirits desires humankind's
liberation.

Furthermore, there is the idea that some humans have received the effulgence of the spiritual, eternal life and should return to the heavenly realm where spirit belongs. Thus we can see that in the end-of-the-world itinerary of such works as the *Revelation of St. John the Divine* (the Apocalypse of the New Testament), the arrival of the Lamb is preceded by, among other things, the fall of the stars and zodiacal disruption. We can see the veritable birth of a Jewish Gnosticism from out of the fires of apocalyptic literature.

The *Book of Enoch* furthermore provides a basis for the kind of rebellious inversions of myth that some Gnostics reveled in. If Gnostic Ophites (serpent-worshippers) could venerate the serpent who offered Eve the forbidden fruit of the tree of knowledge of good and evil, then it is not unlikely that Azazel could have appeared to radical Gnostics (such as Marcus in c. A.D. 180) as a revealer of gnosis.

In 9.6 the "sons of men" complain to the "Lord of the ages": "Thou seest what Azazel has done, who hath taught all unrighteousness of earth and revealed the eternal secrets which were in heaven, which men were striving to learn." A radical like Marcus may have considered Azazel a friend of humankind, and his opponents dedicated to keeping humankind in ignorance.

The *Book of Enoch* even contains what appears to be a proto-Gnostic Sophia myth. In 42.1–3 we read of the discomfiture of Wisdom (Hokma; Greek: Sophia):

Wisdom found no place where she might dwell; then a dwelling-place was assigned her in the heavens. Wisdom went forth to make her dwelling among the children of men, and found no dwelling-place. Wisdom returned to her place and took her seat among the angels. And unrighteousness went forth from her chambers: [some Valentinian Gnostics attributed the creation of the cosmos and its creatures to an abortion of Sophia called Archamoth] whom she sought not she found, and dwelt with them, as rain in a desert, and dew on a thirsty land.[63]

Josephus was not ignorant of the idea of the angelic fall. In *Antiquities* he tells us how the posterity of Seth esteemed God as the

Lord of the universe for seven generations. Then came the black day when "many angels of God accompanied with women, and begat sons who proved unjust, and despisers of all that was good, on account of the confidence they had in their own strength, for the tradition is that these men did what resembled the acts of those whom the Grecians called giants."[64]

Josephus writes that it was Noah, not Enoch, who called humankind's plight to God's attention, resulting in the Deluge. It is noteworthy to hear of Seth in this context. The Sethians were a group or groups of (possibly Jewish) Egyptian Gnostics in the second century and beyond whose works appear in the Nag Hammadi library.[65] According to Josephus, the children of Seth were "the inventors of that peculiar sort of wisdom which is concerned with the heavenly bodies, and their order. And that their inventions might not be lost before they were sufficiently known, upon Adam's prediction that the world was to be destroyed at one time by the force of fire, and at another time by the violence and quantity of water, they made two pillars; the one of brick, the other of stone: they inscribed their discoveries on them both."[66]

The Gnostic Sethians called themselves the "immovable race," the original children of Adam who had resisted the enticements of the dark angels and remained true throughout time, or so they claimed.

One final word on the Gnostic implications of the *Book of Enoch*. Gnostics were condemned by orthodox bishops for believing the resurrection to be a spiritual experience. This claim of the Gnostics must be taken seriously when we consider passages such as the following, when an author of *Enoch* describes the salvation of the "righteous and elect":

And the righteous shall be in the light of the sun,
And the elect in the light of eternal life:
The days of their life shall be unending,
And the days of the holy without number.

And they shall seek the light and find righteousness
with the Lord of Spirits:
There shall be peace to the righteous in the name of the
Eternal Lord.

And after this it shall be said to the holy in heaven
That they should seek out the secrets of righteousness,
the heritage of faith:
For it has become bright as the sun upon earth,
And the darkness is past. (58.3–5)

The experience of gnosis had, as can be seen from many writings in the Nag Hammadi library, fulfilled these conditions. For the Gnostic the darkness was indeed past. The collapse of Zealot power between A.D. 70 (the fall of Jerusalem) and A.D. 132–35 (the Bar Kokhba rebellion), along with the expulsion of Jews from Jerusalem, led to a failure of terrestrial apocalyptic hope. However, it is now clear that the apocalyptic vision, in the face of the continued depravity of the world in general, became for many completely internalized. The vision returned whence it came. The result: Gnosticism. As for the Essenes, the name disappeared, but the tradition lived on.

LIFE AT THE DEAD SEA

The terrestrial apocalyptic vision had certainly not been abandoned by those whose sectarian writings were found near Khirbet Qumran. In their writings (commonly known as the Dead Sea Scrolls), we see this vision emblazoned in text after text of ecstatic expectation: that a final battle would soon take place in which they would take arms and take part—a truly cataclysmic maelstrom of righteous vindication. The Messianic War would result in a holy Israel, a cleansed Temple, and the defeat and destruction of those who failed to worship Y H W H.

However, two years after the explosion of Zealot revolt against the Romans (A.D. 66), it was not God's army of invincible Sons of Light who emerged from the ashes of Qumran, but the Roman Tenth Legion. Its commander, Vespasian, became Josephus's guardian, and the historian would eventually persuade himself that it was the Roman general who was the Coming One of contemporary prophecy, earning Josephus ample leisure to pen those histories from which we have been quoting.

Josephus does not give us any information about Jews who may have lived out in the wilderness at Qumran. This is not altogether surprising. He was by mature training a Pharisee with an intense dislike of the excesses of what can broadly be termed the "messianic movement." For information about the sect, we must look to the texts themselves.

This task is now an easier one since Professor Robert Eisenman and others broke the stranglehold on publication of the scrolls in 1990, releasing to the public for the first time a number of fragmented texts. There can be no doubt that the movement now associated with Qumran saw itself as being in that tradition of righteous (or Zadokite) resistance to foreign domination established by Judas Maccabaeus in the middle of the second century B.C.

Judas had retaken Jerusalem from the troops of the Seleucid king Antiochus IV, destroyed the image of Zeus that had been erected there, and rededicated the Temple to Y H W H in December 165 B.C. Thus began the Hasmonaean dynasty, one of Jewish priest-kings (named after Hasmon, an ancestor of Judas). The dynasty fell in 38 B.C. when the Idumaean Arab Herod, chief minister to the high priest Hyrcanus II, and derived from a family of forced Jewish converts, captured Jerusalem from the Hasmonaean Antigonus with a detachment of troops from the army of the Roman general Mark Antony. Antigonus, the last Hasmonaean king, was sent to Mark Antony in Antioch and beheaded. Herod, trusted friend of the Roman Empire, married Mariamme, daughter of the Hasmonaean Alexandra, and imposed an iron grip on Israel.

This is the political background to the stance of the "Qumrani" religious rebels. They abhorred the Herodian rule with its pro-Hellenization and pro-Roman policies. They also abhorred those surviving members of the Hasmonaean dynasty (who were Pharisaic in outlook) who collaborated with the Herodians (such as Alexandra and Mariamme's younger brother Aristobulus, who was made high priest by Herod and subsequently murdered at the latter's order in 31 B.C.).

The strange thing is how Herod could have allowed the "Qumranis" to survive, being such a ruthless tactician with a nose into all Judaean business. It is impossible to date the scrolls any more accurately than sometime between 100 B.C. and A.D. 100. They do contain a "Hymn to King Jonathan"—apparently Alexander Jannaeus, who reigned between 103 and 76 B.C. So either the more political texts were held in secret during the reign of Herod (who died in 4 B.C.) or they were composed during the crisis of Herodian rule when Roman governors took over the running of Judaea in A.D. 6.

There is, however, another possibility as to why Herod may not have persecuted the "Qumrani" sect—namely, that no such group dwelt at Qumran at all, the link between scrolls and site being fortuitous.

Norman Golb's *Who Wrote the Dead Sea Scrolls? The Search for the Secret of Qumran* has not been popular with scholars convinced of the existence of a Qumrani messianic sect.[67] However, reading the book with an unbiased mind makes reference to its principal findings a scholarly imperative.

While dismissing, as I do, the identification of the strictly sectarian writings with the Essenes, Golb makes the highly significant point that the archaeological evidence at Qumran has been made to fit the preconception of some kind of sectarian monastery; a scriptorium, for example, has been designated on pure conjecture. Golb sees Qumran as a militarily defended site or trading post; the secretion of the scrolls to the north is to be seen in the context of a removal of texts from imminent Roman destruction in Jerusalem circa A.D.70, the caves being convenient for this purpose.

The patristic writers Origen and Timotheus bear literary witness to scrolls being found "near Jericho." The likelihood is that library material may lie undiscovered throughout the Judaean wilderness (as the Dead Sea "Copper Scroll" also intrinsically asserts). The scrolls represent, then, a diverse archive collection, not necessarily the documents of one group, even though a significant number of documents (such as the "Manual of Discipline") betoken a consistent and exclusive religious attitude.

As Baigent and Leigh's popular text *The Dead Sea Scrolls Deception* shows, there is too much scholarly, political, and religious heat about the subject to ascertain a consensually objective view.[68] On the currently available evidence, this author doubts the existence of a "Qumran sect" and will continue to put this and like phrases in quotation marks, denoting a point of view within Zealot activity in the first centuries B.C. and A.D.

Having established this much, what is the significance of the point of view associated with Qumran to our story—especially since its authors were so strictly attached to the Jewish Law, the Torah, an interest that might seem inimical to gnosis?

First, great claims have been made for the origin of the Christian church among the "sectaries of Qumran."[69] Because the present work maintains that there is an identifiable gnosis in the teaching of Jesus as recorded in the New Testament, we might also seek it in the Qumran material. Second, while there were no Gnostics represented in the scrolls, recent releases of scroll material strongly indicate a gnosis—understood as elite spiritual knowledge—active in Judaea at the turn of the Christian era.

Regarding the first question, then, the following elements of early Christian belief and language have been located in the scrolls:

1. A host of texts describing the Messiah, for example, *NASI* (Leader) 4Q 285 (plate 2), which refers to "a staff" that "shall rise from the root of Jesse" (fragment 7, line 2), "the Branch of David" (fragment 7, line 3), as well as the possible killing of the "Leader" (fragment 7, line 4) by the high priest—though the latter assertion depends upon complexities involved in the translation of separate fragments.

2. Documents concerning "Works Reckoned as Righteousness" (4Q 394–98; 4Q 397–99, plates 13 and 14), wherein language and attitudes very closely parallel the biblical Epistle of James, the latter possibly being the same James recorded in Acts as Jesus' brother, the head of the Jerusalem church until Herod Antipas beheaded him.

3. Belief in the coming "New Jerusalem" (4Q 554, plate 3), familiar to readers of the Apocalypse of St. John, and a description of the dimensions of same, attributed in a pseudepigraphical text to the prophet Ezekiel.

4. An apocalyptic vision of the near future, using and elaborating on texts central to the apocalyptic and messianic themes evident in the Gospels, especially the Book of Daniel, pseudo-Danielic texts, and, notably, the *Book of Enoch,* already discussed.

5. General hostility to the establishment running the Temple in Jerusalem, together with the "Qumran sect's" plans for a new and purified Temple order.

What are we to make of all this? There can be no doubt whatsoever that the Dead Sea Scrolls add a wholly fresh and authentic dimension to our knowledge of the New Testament (and vice versa). In some ways, the experience of reading the scrolls is one of rediscovering the first-century Judaean scene after the accreted barnacles of two thousand years of orthodox interpretation and sacred iconography have been stripped clean away. The *Titanic* of pre-A.D. 70 Judaea has undoubtedly been raised. But is Jesus on board?

The last time this author studied the scrolls—before the release of the fifty withheld documents—the unavoidable deduction was that had the canonical Jesus entered the "community of Qumran," the sectaries would not have recognized him as the messiah. They would probably have stoned him to death for being too casual and disruptive in his attitude both to the Mosaic Law and to foreigners in Israel.

Because we have no documents (save possibly the Epistle of James) from the Mother Church of Jerusalem, we can never be certain that the Gospels were not composed with a movement in mind of the Christian Church away from its Jewish roots. This might have followed the revolt against the Romans of A.D. 66. Professor S. G. F. Brandon has argued not only that Jesus' entourage included at least one Zealot (this is so) and that Jesus himself was crucified as one, but also that Jesus was himself sympathetic to certain causes of the Zealots.[70] Jesus understood his mission in terms comprehensible solely within the context of contemporary Judaism. After all, had not his "friend" (?) John the Baptist been beheaded at the behest of Herod's sister Salome, an enemy of the Hasmonaeans within Herod's immediate family?

The critical text with respect to this whole question is the one wherein Jesus' Jewish opponents try to trap him on the issue of paying tribute to Rome (see Mark 12:13–17; Luke 23:2). This was a burning question. Imposition of tribute was perhaps the single biggest issue leading to the revolt against the Romans of A.D., at the very time when it is thought Mark was compiling his Gospel in Rome. To those zealous for Y H W H's Law, tribute to Rome meant apostasy to Y H W H, for it meant taking wealth from God's Holy Land and giving it to a heathen who was himself worshipped as a god. "Thou shalt have no other gods before me" rang the ancient commandment—and it rang throughout Judaea. Y H W H was sole Lord—and Jesus would have been the first to affirm this.

Jesus' answer, that his interlocutors should "render unto Caesar the things that are Caesar's, and unto God the things that are God's," is presented in Mark as foiling his opponents. The implication may have been that since Caesar's image was on the coin used by Jesus to demonstrate his point, paying tribute with Caesar's money was all right with him. Had he thought otherwise or had he been of the Zealot frame of mind, the retort might have been, "Pay tribute to Rome? Never!"

However, accepting that this is an authentic logion of Jesus (what else can we do?), Jesus' answer is exceedingly profound. He leaves it in the first instance for individuals to think about and to decide on what is God's and what is Caesar's. (We might assume that Jesus is somehow indifferent to the word *Caesar* in a way a Zealot never could have been.) But the entire thrust of his teaching is that *all* things belong to God—the rule of Satan himself will end when God wishes it. All things will ultimately pay tribute to God—Caesar included. In other words, it is impossible to give Caesar anything that is not God's, and since Caesar is God's also . . . Give God His due! Do not confuse Caesar and God: that is the Gentiles' problem!

Jesus was not interested in money. We can envision how Jesus might have looked at and held the coin, as if to say, "Do you think we should give our lives for *this?*" He knew that as far as his materialist opponents were concerned, behind the Caesar–God problem lurked the mammon–God problem. Who owns what? So, they were jealous for God's Holy Land on God's behalf—so what! Can God not take care of God's own? I hope readers will pardon my presumption.

Had Jesus visited the supposed "Qumran sect," he would, I think, have looked at the community, with their hopes for changing the nature of the world from without, with pity. They had confused two worlds, and, what was worse, they were prepared to subject the spiritual powers to the requirements of the material world, thereby grossly undervaluing a vastly superior treasure. With a viewpoint like that, no wonder there were few mourners at his crucifixion!

The depth of Jesus' spiritual teaching is utterly lost on those who expect Jesus to have taken sides. This statement surely includes many organized Christian bodies that are content to gag their prophets when occasion demands. Religion has always stood in need of being rescued from its priests! Sincere priests of spiritual religion will understand what I am saying here.

I write this as I hear on the news that Israeli settlers on the West Bank regard it as their duty to God to defend the borders of the Holy Land against "foreign" interference. Does God need guns? Or do we need God? The events of the first century, and the first-century mentality, are replayed because many of us have been brought up to think in the terms and images of the first century. Perhaps we need to "move on" to the second century, when sensitive people realized that the apocalyptic hope *(materially expressed)* had led to a political catastrophe. The Gnostics rebelled against the prevailing thought of their time. They looked beyond borders and nations and religions to the heart of the human experience: the silent center that is seldom heard. They knew that "the world ended in fire" when the world of materialist perception gave way to the spiritual consciousness, awareness, and knowledge hidden within it. "Those who have the ears to hear, let them hear." Our world is being destroyed by blind people speaking in God's name. Rampant egos make their words appear big. This is how a Gnostic would perceive our current, so-called insoluble crises. The spiritual perspective is deep and difficult to grasp.

Jesus' perspective is entirely removed from that of "Qumran." Much has been made of common language. Doubtless, many Englishmen shared the argot of Harrow in the late nineteenth century—that doesn't mean they all went on to share the political or moral outlook of Winston Churchill. Indeed, Jesus shares concepts and language familiar to "Qumran," as well as to the Pharisees, to the Essenes, to the Sadducees, to Josephus, to the Samaritans, to the peasants, prostitutes, and publicans—even to the Romans—but he does something exceptional with this language. He transvalues it to such an extent that it is unlikely that his first disciples—some of whom may well have been to some degree in sympathy with the "Qumran" point of view—properly understood him. Do *we* understand him?

Indeed, it may be that it took the annihilation of the terrestrial apocalyptic hope for some bright sparks (a.k.a. some Gnostics) to see the point. Neither Pilate, nor the Sanhedrin that condemned him, nor probably his own disciples, could see—really *see*—what he was talking about. And if we wish to know in what terms his Judaean opponents *did* see him—and those opponents certainly included at least one disciple (named perhaps after the great Maccabaean liberator)—then we need only look at the politico-religious picture presented by the Dead Sea Scrolls.[71]

Regarding the second question—gnosis at Qumran—we can see from the evidence that the "community" lived in two different worlds, apparently simultaneously. There was a politico-religious conflict with (it was believed) an eventual historical denouement with the coming of the Era of Light, and an inner spiritual world whence they extracted their precious visions. This latter side of "Qumrani" life has proved to hold a more enduring value. When we think, for example, of Paul's claim to spiritual knowledge (gnosis),[72] we can be reasonably sure that he was familiar with the kinds of spiritual treasury once preserved near Qumran.

While it seems that Pharisaic rabbis in this period forbade psychological introspection into the nature of one's being, some "Qumranis" pondered deeply on what they called "the Mystery of Existence," seeking "the Knowledge of the Secret of the Truth":

> Also, do not take Riches from a man you do not know, lest it only add to your poverty. If (God) has ordained that you should die in [you]r poverty, so He has appointed it; but do not corrupt your spirit because of it. Then you shall lie down with the Truth, and your sinlessness will He clearly proclai[m to th]em (the recording angels). As your destiny, you will inherit [Eternal] bliss. [For] though you are Poor, do not long for anything except your own portion; and do not be swallowed up by desire, lest you backslide because of it. And if He restores you, conduct yourself honorably. And inquire among His children about the Mystery of Existence; then you will gain knowledge of the inheritance and walk in Righteousness. (4Q416, 418, plate 22, fragment 10, column 2, lines 6–11)

Though you are poor, do not say "I am penniless, so I cannot seek out knowledge." (Rather) bend your back to all discipline and through al[l Wisdo]m, purify your heart, and in the abundance of your intellectual potential, investigate the Mystery of Existence. And ponder all the Ways of Truth, and consider all the roots of Evil. (fragment 10, column 2, lines 13–15)

If you take a wife in your poverty, take her from among the daughter[s of . . .] . . . (fragment 10, column 2, line 21)

from the Mystery of Existence. In your companionship, go forward together. With the helpmate of your flesh . . . (fragment 10, column 2, line 22)

Do not exchange your Holy Spirit for any Riches, because no price is worth [your Soul]. Willingly seek the face of him who has authority over your storehouse, and in his own tongue, and in his own tongue [speaks with him] . . . (4Q 416, 418, plate 22, fragment 9, column 2, line 6)

Do not forsake your Laws, and keep (secret) your Mysteries. (fragment 9, column 2, line 8)

If He assigns His service to you . . . (don't allow) sleep (to enter) your eyes until you have done it . . . (fragment 9, column 2, line 9)

Do not sell your Glory for money, and do not transfer it as your inheritance, lest your bodily heirs be impoverished. (fragment 9, column 2, line 18)

There is a striking and tantalizing fragment that Eisenman calls the "Demons of Death" from a series of what he calls "Beatitudes" (4Q 525, plate 12), a text that contains a Wisdom discourse from a teacher to his "sons" (pupils):

[Now, hear me, all my sons, and I will speak] about that Wisdom which God gave me . . . (column 1, line 1)

[For He gave the Kn]owledge of Wisdom and instruc[tion] to teach
[all the sons of Truth . . . (column 1, line 2)

Bring forth the knowledge of your inner self and in . . . meditate.
(fragment 2, column 4, line 19)

Darkness . . . poison . . . [all] those born [on the earth] . . . Heaven
. . . (column 5, line 1)

. . . serpents in [it, and you will] go to him, you will enter . . . there
will be joy [on the day] the Mysteries of God [are revealed] for[ever]
. . . (column 5, line 2)

The problem for us in all this is that we cannot be certain about the
substance of what is meant by the "Mystery of Existence" and the
"inner self" of the pupil. Nevertheless, it is clear from the ecstatic and
highly imaginative character of some of the new fragments that the
authors of the works clearly found authentic spiritual wisdom in their
meditations on God and God's Law. They recognize that there are hidden mysteries in their "holy spirits" that can be accessed and that offer
ecstatic visions of the life of God within them.

The sense of certainty gained from these experiences, however, is
always used to justify the strict Torah-consciousness of the community.
This undoubtedly puts their gnosis more in the category of apocalyptic
revelation than of Gnostic liberation. The "knowledge" invariably concerns the secrets of God's heavenly places, while the Messiah invariably
appears as a separate being. There is a kind of half-light about the
works, in retrospect—a dawning consciousness. While the reliance on
external legal formulas for understanding spiritual experiences may
have proved a weakness for the community as eschatological comman-
dos, the vein of spiritual discovery nonetheless proved to be a comfort-
ing treasure afterward.

As stated earlier in this chapter, the apocalyptic hope eventually
became almost entirely internalized. Perhaps it is at this point that we
can discern the beginnings of that tree called Jewish Gnosticism, or
rather the Kabbalah (especially Merkabah—that is, "chariot" or

"throne" mysticism), a tradition of piety and redemption from the material world sought through inner exploration.

Themes and language such as those found in the following fragment were to be developed by Jewish communities in the Middle East (particularly in Baghdad), to emerge in medieval Europe among certain pious Jews of Spain and the Languedoc:[73]

> Secret Wisdom and image of Knowledge and Fountain of Understanding, Fountain of Discovery and counsel of Holiness and Secret Truth, treasurehouse of Understanding from the sons of Righteousness. (From "The Chariots of Glory," 4Q 286–87, plate 21, manuscript A, fragment 1, line 6)
>
> . . . of Your Holiness and the chariots of Your Glory with their (mu)ltitudes and wheel-angels, and all [Your] Secrets, Foundations of fire, flames of Your lamp, Splendors of honor, fi[re]s of lights and miraculous brilliances, [hon]or and virtue and highness of Glory, holy Secret and pla[ce of Spl]endor and the highness of the beauty of the Fou[ntain]. (Manuscript A, fragment 1, lines 3–4)

It may be that we see the roots of the kabbalistic tradition in the Qumran fragments published by Eisenman and Wise. However, it is as likely that the movement of Jewish gnosis—and its frequently accompanying magic—was more profitably developed in the relative safety of Babylonia, Alexandria, and Syria and in initiated circles in the Diaspora generally. Nevertheless, merely to know that some kind of Kabbalah existed historically at least as early as the first century A.D. not only is a boon to scholarship, but also gives us new tools for understanding the Jesus both of the New Testament and of the so-called Gnostic Gospels.

JESUS

Then Judas appointed certain men to fight against those that were in the fortress, until he had cleansed the sanctuary. So he chose priests of blameless conversation, such as had pleasure in the law: Who cleansed the sanctuary, and bore out the defiled stones into an unclean place.

And when as they consulted what to do with the altar of burnt offerings, which was profaned; they thought it best to pull it down, and
laid up the stones in the mountain of the temple in a convenient place,
*until there should come a prophet to shew what should be done with
them.* (The Temple in December, 165 B.C.: 1 Macc. 4:41–46)

About 180 years after the event described above, Jesus was active
in Israel, engaged in the construction of a new spiritual Temple. "And
he brought him [Simon] to Jesus. And when Jesus beheld him, he said,
Thou art Simon the son of Jona: thou shalt be called Cephas, which is
by interpretation, a stone" (John 1:42).

It is a strange fact that the Aramaic word *cephas,* when written in
Greek (as it was in the Gospel of John), adds up, according to the Greek
"cabala," to 729. $\kappa = 20$, $\eta = 8$, $\phi = 500$, $\alpha = 1$, $\varsigma = 200$. Just a coincidence? Seven hundred twenty-nine happens to be 9 cubed. Where
(according to the cosmological conceptions of late antiquity) 9 represents eternity (the realm of the aeons) beyond the seven spheres of the
cosmos, $9 \times 9 \times 9$ could represent (to the initiate of the symbolic art
of building)[74] the corner of an infinite cube. It happens that the Holy of
Holies of Solomon's Temple was a cube (1 Kings 6:20). In the Book of
Revelation, the symbolic New Jerusalem is a cube also: "And the city
lieth foursquare, and the length is as large as the breadth: and he [an
angel] measured the city with the reed, twelve thousand furlongs. The
length and the breadth and the height of it are equal. And he measured
the wall thereof, an hundred and forty-four [12×12] cubits, *according to the measure of a man,* that is, of the angel" (Rev. 21:16–17). But
what of the Temple? "And I saw no temple therein: for the Lord God
Almighty and the Lamb are the temple of it" (Rev. 21:22).

The Temple of the New Jerusalem is a spiritual temple. Why a
cube? According to Nigel Pennick, author of *Sacred Geometry,*
Pythagoras expressed a tradition in which building ratios were related
directly to musical ratios: "The symbolic cube . . . like the city of
Revelation or the Jewish Holy of Holies, contains the consonances of
the universe."[75] Gordon Strachan, author of *Christ and the Cosmos,*
explains: "Why should the cube be thought to contain the consonances
of the universe? Because the ratios of its sides and edges are all equal

and can therefore be said to be one to one, 1:1. But the ratio 1:1 in music, represents the note of unison or full string-length and the full string-length contains within itself the vibrations of all the other musical intervals."[76]

Very interesting, no doubt, but what has this got to do with Jesus? In the second chapter of John, Jesus goes into the Temple in Jerusalem—a mighty new structure built by Herod the Great—and causes a major fracas. He makes himself a whip resembling a cat-o'-nine-tails and drives out the sheep and oxen waiting to be sacrificed on the altar. Not content with that, he then overturns the tables of the money-changers (whose job it was to change non-Jewish money for special Temple coins to pay for the sacrificial beasts) and tells all those within earshot that they had turned "my Father's house" into "an house of merchandise."

While doubtless rendering unto God what was God's, this was nonetheless disorderly conduct on a grand scale. To top it all, he then suggests the Temple itself might be destroyed: "Destroy this temple, and in three days [9 × 9 × 9] I shall raise it up." To which the author of John adds: "But he spake of the temple of his body" (John 2:19 21). Quite possibly, but *which* body?

STONE THEOLOGY

And he beheld them, and said, What is this then that is written, The stone which the builders rejected, the same is become the head of the corner? *Whosoever shall fall upon that stone shall be crushed; but on whomsoever it shall fall, he shall be winnowed.* (Luke 20:17–18)

This fascinating text has gone largely unnoticed by orthodox theologians—a pity, since it not only contains what could be described as the quintessence of Jesus' spiritual teaching, but it also reveals his peculiar—not to say alchemical—conception of the new Temple. Jesus quotes from Psalm 118, verses 22 to 24: "The stone which the builders refused is become the head stone of the corner. This is the LORD's doing; it is marvellous in our eyes. This is the day which the LORD hath made; we will rejoice and be glad in it."[77]

Jesus, apparently reinterpreting a long-standing prophetic tradition regarding the Temple, refers to what is clearly a supernatural stone: the stone rejected by the "builders." The implication is clear enough. Taking the words of the psalm allegorically (as Jesus did), the "builders" represent those who controlled the practice of the Jewish religion, and they have rejected the vital principle of the house of God—without which the true Temple will certainly fall, as all earthly structures must. (The Temple of Jesus' day was destroyed by the Romans as a result of Jewish resistance in A.D. 70, and has never been rebuilt.)

Following the psalmist and a prophecy of Isaiah (28:16), Jesus looks to "the day which the LORD hath made" and clearly believes that that day has now come. The Day of the Lord (Yom Yahweh) has been realized in his own appearance. The missing stone *anoints* (*christos* means "the anointed"); it is God's (rejected) gift, knowledge of the Holy Spirit—the formative principle of a new and spiritual Temple.

Furthermore, the stone to which Jesus refers has supernatural powers. If ignored, that is to say if one "falls upon it," ignorance of the stone will crush the spiritually blind. Jesus' hearers may have enjoyed—but were more likely mystified by—the joke within the saying: that it is not the stone which falls from the sky that crushes the ignorant (as one might naturally suppose), but the stone they choose to ignore. Contrary to expectation, then, it is the stone that falls from the heavens that produces the positive effect—that is, it *winnows* the one on whom it falls. Why "winnows"? To winnow is to separate the grain from the chaff (Greek: λικμαω, *likmao*: an agricultural image for an alchemical process—the recovery of the grain—often identified in alchemy with gold).

This separating process is what Jesus on numerous occasions claimed to be his essential purpose. Jesus says he brings not peace but a sword: A sword separates; he divides the "sheep from the goats." In Mark 15:37 the veil of the Temple that separated the people from the Holy of Holies—the Divine Presence—is rent from top to bottom immediately after Jesus exhales pneuma (Greek for spirit) at the climax of the crucifixion (the Greek verb is *exepneusen*).

There is, I think, the strong suggestion of an alchemical process here—an analogy not lost on later alchemists who would write of the *crucifixion* of the *mercurius* principle. The use of the winnowing metaphor is as precise as other poetic images Jesus uses (such as the cleansing fire that, in basic alchemy, separates gold from its accreted impurities). When wheat is winnowed, the farmer thrusts it up into the air with a fork and lets the *wind* blow away the useless chaff. Etymologically, the word for "spirit" in Hebrew (*ruach*—feminine) means breath, or wind—air.[78] While everyone knows that at the coming of the Holy Spirit upon the apostles at Pentecost the room was filled with the sound of wind (Acts 2:2–3), the Greek language preserves the root link between "air" and "gold," a most suggestive parallel in the alchemical context.

In Greek, "air" is *he aura* (feminine), while "gold" is *to auron* (neuter).[79] Thus, the coming of the Stone initiates a spiritual apocalypse, that is, a revelation of what has been formerly hidden—namely, the Spirit; or, in the winnowing metaphor, the grain. Everyone knows the parable of the sower; it is the *grain* that is sown in the world. The grain is, of course, to make *bread:* "for the bread of God is he which cometh down from heaven, and giveth life to the cosmos" (John 6:33).

If Simon was a stone, and he (Jesus) was the stone that came from above to winnow the grain from the chaff, what kind of "body," what kind of "temple" was Jesus proposing? Could it be something to do with the "house of fire" described earlier in the *Book of Enoch,* in which Enoch divined the figure of the Son of Man? The author of John seems to think so; he litters his Gospel with suggestive inferences:

> Verily, verily, I say unto you, Hereafter ye shall see heaven open [spiritual vision], and the angels of God ascending and descending upon the *Son of man.* (John 1:31)
>
> But as many as received him, to them gave he power to become the sons of God, even to them that believe on his name: Which were born, not of blood, nor of the will of the flesh, nor of the will of man, but of God. (John 1:12–13)
>
> And this is life eternal, that they might *know* thee the only true God. (John 27:3)

The Jesus of John comes like the alchemical Stone to divide the image from the reality and give birth to a child of God. Had it not all been prophesied before? There were, as we have seen, Jews who knew something of what was coming. They need only have read their prophet Malachi (meaning "my messenger"), who declared sometime, it is supposed, between 475 and 450 B.C. that the Lord would send a "messenger, and he shall prepare the way before me: and the Lord, whom ye seek, shall suddenly come to his temple, even the messenger of the covenant, whom ye delight in: behold, he shall come, saith the LORD of hosts. But who may abide the day of his coming? And who shall stand when he appeareth? for he is like a refiner's fire, and like fuller's soap. And he shall purify the sons of Levi [the priesthood], and purge them as gold and silver, that they may offer unto the Lord an offering in righteousness" (Mal. 3:1–3).

Impressive though this is—and we could speculate on whether the Gospels' account of Christ does not have within it the presence of a myth descending into history with all the key events prewritten in prophecies[80]—the defining stroke is still missing: that is, that *he,* the anointed, is the cornerstone of the Temple that the builders threw away, the eternal stone and measure. The missing measure is the Son of Man: MAN. Not the earthly man, the average clod or stone in need of shaping, but the "house of fire," the Hermetic man of nous: the spiritual man, he whom the Gnostics called the Anthropos, the archetype beyond the image.

So when Jesus beholds Simon, he sees beyond the image presented to him (Simon the fisherman) and penetrates to what Simon has never before seen in himself. Jesus sees in him a spiritual block of the new Temple—and in that Temple, the righteous sacrifice is neither bird nor beast, neither man nor money, but self (ego)-sacrifice. Surrender the image; return to the real. Thus to *know* Jesus, the archetypal Son of Man, is to know the true God: It is to know thy*self*. This is gnosis, and the New Testament is full of it, for those with the eyes to see.

It is a curious fact that those people who have undergone a conventional Christian religious education will tend to remember Jesus' teaching in terms of his imaginative parables. And yet it would appear that Jesus himself regarded his parabolic teaching as being chiefly for the benefit of those outside his inner circle. According to Mark 4:31, Jesus told his disciples: "Unto you it is given to know the mystery of the kingdom of God: but unto them that are without, all these things are done in parables."

And yet the Synoptic Gospels (Matthew, Mark, and Luke—widely considered the earliest and therefore the more authentic Gospels) seldom seem to give us "these things" and continue to relate parable after parable. Surely, then, we cannot rely on the Synoptic Gospels for "knowledge of the mystery of the kingdom of God." But, except the considerably later Gnostic Gospels and of course the maverick Gospel of John, what have we to go on? Can we try to find the mysteries within the parables? Well, this was pretty much the point of view of the authors of the Gnostic Gospels. They saw the parables as allegories and their constituent features as symbols with spiritual meaning. They wanted to be on the *inside*. Perhaps at times they read in principles that were not originally there, but sometimes I think they hit gold by reading *through* a parable.

Mark 4:31–32:

> The kingdom of God "is like a grain of mustard seed, which, when it
> is sown in the earth, is less than all the seeds that be in the earth. But
> when it is sown, it groweth up, and becomes greater than all the herbs,
> and shooteth out great branches; so that the fowls of the air may lodge
> under the shadow of it."

Jesus' parable appears to be based on a dream of the Babylonian king Nebuchadnezzar as related in Daniel 4:12 ff. (based on a passage in Ezekiel 17:22 ff.). In Daniel, Nebuchadnezzar calls for Daniel to explain a dream that the Magi and the Chaldeans have failed to interpret. It's a case of Y H W H versus the Magi—and we can guess who is going to win. The Babylonian king tells of how he dreamed he saw a tree that filled the heavens: "The leaves thereof were fair, and the fruit thereof much, and in it was food for all: the beasts of the field had shadow under it, and the fowls of the heaven dwelt in the boughs thereof, and all flesh was fed on it."

Daniel tells the king that the tree represents his earthly kingdom.

But there's an unpleasant catch to the dream. The king goes on to relate how the tree was suddenly cut down, leaving only a stump. Daniel tells the king that the stump is to serve as a reminder that "thou know that the most High ruleth in the kingdom of men, and giveth it to whomsoever he will. And whereas they [a "holy one" and a "watcher"—cf. the *Book of Enoch*] commanded to leave the stump of the tree roots; thy kingdom shall be sure unto thee, after that thou shalt have known that *the heavens do rule*" (my emphasis).

Jesus reinterprets the dream (it is interesting, this relation of dreams to parables) from the realm of the earthly kingdom (the seen) to the spiritual kingdom (the unseen). Thus the kingdom of God is like the seed that was sown in earth (the world of material vision) at the beginning of history when God "breathed his Spirit into Adam." The significance of this was lost in the earth—the spirit, like an atom, was "too small" to see, and yet this long period of gestation has at last borne fruit in a spiritual kingdom: In the kingdom of God the heavens do indeed rule. The spirit is the sustaining principle of all things. In alchemical terms, the fruit of the tree is the Stone.[81] The new spiritual kingdom breathes pneuma, spirit, giving life to all things that are truly alive. The alchemist calls this spirit the mercurius that can penetrate all things and exists as the formative principle of all things.

According to Carl Jung, "The possessor of this penetrating Mercurius can 'project' it into other substances and transform them from the imperfect to the perfect state."[82] "And when he [Jesus] had said this, he breathed on them; and said unto them, Receive ye the Holy Spirit [pneuma]" (John 20:22).

"The imperfect state," says Jung, "is like the sleeping state; substances lie in it like the 'sleepers chained in Hades' and are awakened as from death to a new and more beautiful life by the divine tincture extracted from the inspired stone." Christ the Stone calls for an awakening, that the "seed" (one thinks of Philo's *logos spermatikos*) may penetrate through the earth to the fresh air (pneuma) and grow: "But when the fruit is brought forth, immediately he putteth in the sickle, because the harvest [gold] is come" (Mark 4:29).

When the spirit emerges from the human being, the Father brings it back to Himself: This is the rebirth. The human is reborn in God. To be reborn in the spirit, it is necessary to die to the earth.

At this point, we may recall the Neo-Pythagorean doctrine discussed in our treatment of the Essenes: that when the soul was swallowed by matter, only nous (mind or spirit) was left. The task of the psychically autonomous nous is to retrieve the psyche (soul) buried in matter. Thus the pneuma (spirit), as the Son of God, descends into matter and then frees itself from it, brings healing and salvation (the branches of the tree) to all souls.

Jung analyzed the actual psychic process whereby Jesus—and you and I—could look on events in the outside world, especially in nature, and find "parables" for the spiritual process. The Idea of the descending Son of God pertains to the nous that lives "a life of its own in the psychic non-ego."[83] This Idea instantly projects itself "whenever it is *constellated* in any way—that is, whenever attracted by something analogous to it in the outside world." This "sacramental" perception will always appear as "knowledge from beyond," or, as the Gnostics called it, "knowledge of the heart":

For this reason error grew angry at him, persecuted him, was distressed at him, [and] was brought to naught. He was nailed to a tree; he became a fruit of the knowledge of the Father, which did not, however, become destructive because it [was] eaten, but to those who ate it it gave [cause] to become glad in the discovery. For he discovered them in himself, and they discovered him in themselves, the incomprehensible, inconceivable one, the Father, the perfect one, the one who made the all, while the all is within him and the all has need of him, since he retained its perfection within himself which he did not give to the all.[84]

In Gnostic terms, the Son of God comes from beyond the seven spheres (the heimarmene); in contemporary psychological jargon, from the psychic nonego. The Pythagorean nous, free of matter, seems to be identical to the Anthropos (Son of Man), adversary to the planetary spheres and whom the Demiurge (the "Fool" or lord of the spheres—and of the elements) tries to imitate.

In the Hermetic *Poimandres,* the Anthropos rends the circle of the spheres (as the veil of the Temple is rent when Jesus exhales pneuma at the climax of the crucifixion in John, the reverse movement of the redemptive opus; John 19:30) and looks down to the earth and water (of which "natural man" is composed), sees his reflection, and proceeds to project himself into the elements, whereupon physis (nature) locks him in passionate embrace (or in Valentinian imagery: nails him to her tree).

According to Jung, these Gnostic visions "stand for an unconscious component of the personality ["He was in the world, but the world knew him not"] which might well be endowed with a higher form of consciousness transcending that of the ordinary human being. As a matter of fact, we are dealing here with a content that up to the present has only very rarely been attributed to any human personality. The one great exception is Christ. As *huios tou anthropou* (son of man) and *theos huios* (son of God), Christ embodies the God-man, and as an incarnation of the Logos by 'pneumatic' impregnation, he is an avatar of the divine *Nous.*"[85]

According to Jung, "Christianity was assimilated through Gnosticism."[86] This was possible because there was already a significant (if largely unseen) gnostic component in Jesus' spiritual teaching.

It is I who am in you [pl.], and you are in me, just as the Father is in you in innocence.[87]

Now since it has been said that you are my twin and true companion, examine yourself that you may understand who you are, in what way you exist and how you will come to be.[88]

These are the secret sayings which the living Jesus spoke and which Didymos Judas Thomas wrote down. And he said, "Whoever finds the interpretation of these sayings will not experience death."[89]

Thomas said to them, "If I tell you one of the things which he told me, you will pick up stones and throw them at me; a fire will come out of the stones and burn you up."[90]

Jesus said, "I shall give you what no eye has seen and what no ear has heard and what no hand has touched and what has never occurred to the human mind."[91]

I am the light which exists in the light, I am the remembrance of the Pronoia [Providence]—that I might enter into the middle of darkness and the inside of Hades.[92]

You walked in mud,
and your garments were not soiled,
and you have not been buried in their filth,
and you have not been caught.[93]

And he that was dead came forth, bound hand and foot with grave-clothes: and his face was bound about with a napkin. Jesus saith unto them, Loose him, and let him go. (John 11:44)

"Let him go." Lazarus was free.

PAUL

Sometime between A.D. 50 and 60, probably during the reign of the Roman emperor Claudius, an extraordinary Jew called Paul wrote a letter to a community of Christians in Corinth. In it, he reminded his hearers that it was he who had first brought salvation to them, but although first, he was still but an agent of the Stone: "According to the grace of God which is given unto me, as a wise master mason [αρχιτεκτων, master builder/mason or architect], I have laid the foundation, and another buildeth thereon. But let every man take heed how he buildeth thereupon. For other *foundation stone* can no man lay than that is laid, which is Jesus Christ" (1 Cor. 3:10).

Paul, who had been most thoroughly hit by the Stone, here attempts to explain what this implies for such sins as pride. Some of the Corinthian Christians were claiming to be the exclusive followers of the wisdom of one Apollos, others of Cephas (Simon Peter), others of Paul himself. Paul exhorts them to understand that there is only *one* Spirit of

God and the "body" of that Spirit is the Temple comprising all its Christian members. How, therefore, he asks them, can they find conflict among themselves? They stand or fall on one foundation stone. And they shall be "tried" as such.

Paul cleverly employs the image of the chemist or metallurgist who, in purifying gold-bearing matter, would heat the material to a thousand degrees in a bone-ash vessel to "try" or separate the gold from its accreted impurities. In the imaginative inner context in which Paul places the image, the fire that tries or judges can be understood as *alchemical fire,* and Paul shows no hesitation in bringing its power to bear upon the Corinthians: "Every man's work shall be made manifest: for the day shall declare it, because it shall be revealed by fire; and the fire shall try every man's work of what sort it is. If any man's work abide which he hath built thereupon, he shall receive a reward. If any man's work shall be burned, he shall suffer loss: but he himself shall be saved; yet so as by fire. Know ye not that ye are the temple of God, and that the Spirit of God dwelleth in you?" (1 Cor. 3:13–16).

Was Paul familiar with the following quotation from the apocalyptic second book of Esdras, composed sometime between the first century B.C. and his own day? "Then shall they be known, who are my chosen; and they shall be tried as the gold in the fire" (2 Esd. 16:73).

This passage refers to the trials of the Jewish Maccabaean "saints" (literally: holy; pious; pure ones) of the second century B.C. who underwent martyrdom for their faith at the hands of the Seleucid dynasty. The descendants of the Maccabaean religious and military revolt were still active in Paul's day, and their struggle was fresh in Paul's mind. Everywhere he went he was harassed by Gentile-dismissing Jewish opponents who demanded that non-Jews who professed faith in the messianic Jesus adhere strictly to the Jewish Law. Paul, who had formerly held much in common with these so-called Judaizers, was doubtless regularly reminded of his apostasy from their cause—the extraordinary nature of which can be gleaned from recently published sections of the Dead Sea Scrolls.[94]

For Paul, unlike his detractors, the true arena of struggle lay not in Judaea but in the universal war between the natural man and the spiritual man: "But the natural man receiveth not the things of the Spirit of

God: for they are foolishness unto him: neither can he know them, because they are spiritually discerned" (1 Cor. 2:14).

The alchemical fire emanating from the Stone would judge who had built most truly upon the foundations of the spirit. Of this Paul was supremely confident—and subsequent events would seem to have justified his faith in love over and above the Zealot sword—a thought worthy of reflection as once again we see a recrudescence of the Zealot spirit in contemporary Israel.

In redefining the nature of the saint from Maccabaean Zealot to Christian spirituality, he was striking an ax into the root of the beliefs of many of his compatriots. It is little wonder, then, that he stressed the idea that "in Christ" there is neither Jew nor Greek, neither slave nor free. For Paul, the master mason of a new Temple, there could be no going back. Unfortunately, his new saints in Corinth did not seem to understand what kind of spiritual revolution he was promulgating.

The ongoing theme of Paul's heartfelt letter concerns the spiritual gifts that come from the Spirit of God and that have now come into the possession of the saints. It appears from his letter that not only had members of the Corinthian assembly fallen from spiritual awareness into fornication and general sexual libertinism (sainthood for Paul was expressed in moral holiness) but that possessors of spiritual gifts felt themselves to be vying with one another for primacy as well. Paul tries to make it plain that from the perspective of the Holy One, all gifts serve the common good, and that while a one-legged person may make an excellent and respected teacher, he or she would still be less useful to someone drowning than would a person with two legs. The Christian body needs *all* its parts: "For to one is given by the Spirit the word of wisdom; to another the word of knowledge [*gnosis*] by the same Spirit; to another faith by the same Spirit; to another the gifts of healing by the same Spirit; to another the working of miracles; to another prophecy; to another discerning of spirits; to another divers kinds of tongues; to another the interpretation of tongues. But all these worketh that one and the selfsame Spirit, dividing to every man severally as he will" (1 Cor. 12:8–11).

In the following chapter (13), Paul really drives home the message in words that have astonished men and women for nearly two millennia: "Though I speak with the tongues of men and of angels, and have not love, I am become as sounding brass, or a tinkling cymbal. And though I have the gift of prophecy, and understand all mysteries, and all knowledge [*gnosis*]; and though I have all faith, so that I could remove mountains, and have not love, I am nothing."

All spiritual gifts—including gnosis—exist to serve the cause of love. But at the end, a knowledge never envisioned shall embrace all: "For now we see through a glass, darkly; but then face to face: now I know in part; but *then shall I know even as also I am known*" (1 Cor. 13:12; my emphasis). The ultimate gnosis awaits those who have transcended the limitations of the natural man, whose pride has been conquered by love.

Whatever else might be grasped from Paul's words, it is clear that he regards gnosis—spiritual knowledge—as a bona fide gift of the Spirit. As we might expect, scholars continue to join battle over the nature of the gnosis present in Corinth. It has been asked whether Corinth saw the first outbreak of this "heresy." The problem with this line of thinking is that, first, Paul does not have any truck with the idea of heresy, and second, he does not see gnosis as being a problem for the Christian assembly. He regards it as a gift among other gifts. It is clear from the tone and context of the letter that Paul takes gnosis in its plain meaning, the gift of spiritual knowledge. He also sees absolute spiritual knowledge (intimate cognitive awareness of God) as the goal of the spiritual life. He also makes it plain that what we can know in our earthly state—however exalted this might be—is nothing when compared to the ultimate state of spiritual people following their resurrection: "So also is the resurrection of the dead. It is sown in corruption; it is raised in incorruption: It is sown in dishonor; it is raised in glory: it is sown in weakness; it is raised in power: It is sown a natural body; it is raised a spiritual body. There is a natural body, and there is a spiritual body" (1 Cor. 15:42–44).

Gnosis of God is central to Paul's understanding of salvation. He is also aware that this gift is not available to all—and that in its fullness it is not available to himself, even though he says he knows many mysteries that the Corinthians are not ready to hear. This caveat explains to some extent why Paul was such a hero to Christian Gnostics. It can hardly be denied that Paul sanctioned the gift while doubting that religious speculation could alone lead to the ultimate knowledge. Of course, by setting so much store by the gnosis of God, he undoubtedly whetted the appetites of those naturally—or supernaturally—born with the gift of religious speculation and spiritual knowledge. Indeed, his surviving works are full of intimations of a flexible spiritual system conducive to the full flowering of what scholars call Gnosticism in the century after his death.

Nevertheless, it must be stressed that from the works of Paul alone, we cannot deduce a full-fledged Gnostic doctrine at work among the Corinthians. Indeed, much of the development—at least of Christian Gnosticism—owes its genesis to speculation on the letters of Paul, combined with the Gospel of John, which came into circulation toward the end of the first century.

There was already in Paul's day a long line of tradition that attempted to generate coherent philosophies out of the sayings of inspired sages. It is perhaps because Paul was so acutely aware of this—he had, after all, been venerated as the incarnation of Hermes during his travels around Asia Minor—that he stresses that his wisdom is foolishness to the world, scandalous and absurd both to Jerusalem and to Athens. And that while he may call himself a wise (σοφος) master mason, he is so only because he works on the foundation stone of the true messiah, the Logos of God.

The decisive difference between Paul's understanding of gnosis and that of those who called themselves Gnostics in the second century lies in this. The Gnostics saw the possession of a salvific knowledge as not only the primary but also the *sole* mode of release from the grip of the spiritual darkness that they believed was inherent in the fabric of the natural cosmos. For them, Jesus was responsible for bringing an exclusive gnosis into the world of men and women, and this gnosis had a quite specific content, such that it could itself be presented as *the* gospel, or "good news," for those who could appropriate it.

The attraction of this view is obvious. Christianity becomes more than a story of a suffering and resurrected messiah, through which the Christian enters by the mystery of baptism and sacrament; it becomes a complete and absolute system of knowledge—and this knowledge becomes itself the key to spiritual liberty. The idea of a spiritual elite follows naturally—and it was perhaps some prescience of this that drove Paul to stress that gnosis is *one* of a range of spiritual gifts with no exclusive rights to primacy in the Body of Christ. Nevertheless, Paul gave the Gnostic movement a certain amount of ideological ammunition, which can be summarized as follows:

1. Belief in the distinction between the natural human and the spiritual human.
2. Belief that Christ had shattered the powers of nature's spiritual governors (Colossians 2:15, 20).
3. Belief that the flesh belongs to Satan and cannot inherit the kingdom of God (1 Cor. 5:5).
4. Belief that the redeemed spiritual person or "saint" is superior not only to the natural order but even to the angels (1 Cor. 6:3).
5. Belief that the power of the Jewish Law held no control over Gentile converts.
6. Belief that prophecy was a continual gift of God.
7. Belief that gifted Christians had access to the mind ($\nu o \nu \varsigma$) of Christ (1 Cor. 2:16).
8. Belief that gnosis was a genuine gift of the Spirit.
9. Belief that the climax of the spiritual journey could be expressed in terms of knowledge.

Paul did not invent these ideas. Indeed, much of what seems to have constituted the kinds of gnosis with which he was familiar, as well as the accompanying mysteries of that gnosis, had been the subjects of speculation by religious sages and their initiated followers for some five centuries. It may be that only the paucity of written material from before that time prevents us from regarding spiritual speculation as being of even more ancient provenance. However, on the basis of the extant evidence, the momentum of speculation does seem to increase steadily after the sixth century B.C.

The time has now come to examine those who explicitly called themselves Gnostics—among whom many regarded Paul as their ideological progenitor—who in the second century A.D. held fast to a range of beliefs known to scholarship as Gnosticism.

THREE

The First Gnostics

At first I spoke to you in parables and you did not understand; now I speak to you openly, and you (still) do not perceive.

THE APOCRYPHON OF JAMES, NH CODEX 1, PAGE 7, LINES 1–6

GNOSTICISM

*I*t must stand as one of the greater ironies of the history of Christianity that the name of the man who, from the doctrinal point of view at least, most thoroughly divided the Church meant "peace." Irenaeus (c. A.D. 120–202) wielded a doctrinal sword through the air of Christian thought whose reverberations may still be felt today. Of all the works written against the Gnostics, his have been by far the most influential. When we seek the meaning of the word Gnosticism, it is chiefly to his work that scholars have, until very recently, gone for definition.

In the year A.D. 180, Irenaeus was the bishop of Lyons. The see of Lyons on the borders of Gallia Narbonensis had been founded by a Greek-speaking mission from Smyrna in Asia Minor led by Pothinos, a pupil, like Irenaeus, of the martyr Polycarp. Church tradition, and Irenaeus himself, tells us that Polycarp had sat at the aged feet of the apostle John. This must be significant when we consider that Irenaeus opposed what he considered to be a gnosis "falsely so-called." It is likely that any gnosis *truly* so-called would, in the understanding of Irenaeus, be consistent with a Johannine tradition.

Irenaeus's opposition to the "false" gnosis would seem to have stemmed from painful experiences undergone during the persecution of Christians by the emperor Aurelius in A.D. 177. The hideous treatment of the martyrs of Lyons and Vienne would become notorious in the annals of the Church; Irenaeus experienced them at first hand. The word *martyr* means "witness," and the nature of that witness was very important to bishops such as Irenaeus in promoting the message to non-Christians.

The significance of martyrdom would, from Irenaeus's point of view, be lost should observers be confused over what precisely it was that Christians were dying *for*. Thus it was that during the Aurelian persecution, Irenaeus visited Rome to remonstrate with the bishop there for holding what Irenaeus regarded as false doctrines.

While in Rome, Irenaeus also encountered an old friend from his days as a pupil of Polycarp. To Irenaeus's horror, his old friend had embraced the teaching of the Egyptian poet and Gnostic theologian Valentinus. (Valentinus had been in Rome about two decades earlier.) What Irenaeus found both in Rome and in southern Gaul among those calling themselves Gnostics was not consistent with what he had been taught by Polycarp, and for which teachings Polycarp had himself perished at the stake. Unsettled by his discovery, Irenaeus set about exposing the doctrines of "those who called themselves Gnostics" with great thoroughness, posing as one interested in their "secret" ideas. What he discovered from these Gnostics, and the manner in which he presented what he had discovered, has shaped our ideas of gnosticism from that time to the present—tarring Gnostic ideas forever with the brush of heresy, on which charge Gnostics could be condemned and excluded from the Church.

Irenaeus's aim in producing his five-book *Against Heresies* was to ensure that henceforth no one to whom his work was accessible could possibly confuse the "false gnosis" with the tradition of the apostles as he understood it.

On the other hand, Gnostic Christians themselves claimed to be the *true* Christians, holders and guardians of a privileged tradition of insight into what they considered to be the real meaning of Christ's teaching.

Now, if a person claims to be a Christian and claims to have attained higher knowledge and deeper wisdom, it is logical to suppose that the content of this knowledge may represent the authentic nature of the message itself. Thus the claims of *gnosis* represented a challenge to Irenaeus's authority as a bishop or "shepherd" of the Christian Church. Not surprisingly, therefore, the arguments Irenaeus piles up against his chosen Gnostics revolve around the question of authority. On whose authority, Irenaeus asks, do Gnostics hold their peculiar beliefs?

The argument between Irenaeus and the heretics would have tremendous ramifications for the development of the Christian Church into a doctrinal-control system. The results of this development—theocratic imperialism—account partly for the perennial interest in the Gnostics. In retrospect, Gnostics can be presented to appear as rebels with a cause. Indeed, each successive age has tended to see them in terms of that age's particular conflict with received authority.[1]

For those unfamiliar with Irenaeus's "blasphemous and mad" Gnostics, as he called them, it is necessary to delineate what he found objectionable in their views. However, we must bear in mind that he was talking about very specific groups (in southern Gaul and in Rome), of whom only a portion took the name *gnostikoi*, gnostics, as their ideological *nom d'ésprit*, or nickname.

1. Objectionable was their view that salvation is attained through receipt of a secret knowledge: knowledge of how to extricate the transmundane spirit in humans from material envelopment, both corporeal and cosmic. Both body and cosmos are regarded with suspicion.
2. Also troublesome was their belief that humanity is divided into three types. First, there are the *pneumatikoi,* or "spirituals" (who have awakened to their real nature through gnosis). Second, the *psychikoi:* psychics, whose soul-nature may be guided by faith, but who yet still stand in need of exceptional moral effort and spiritual enlightenment. Third, the *hylikoi,* hylics—that is, the "materials": those who are aware only of matter and who, in belonging to matter alone, have no chance of salvation. They are, from the spiritual point of view, already "dead."

3. Also on Irenaeus's list was these groups' belief that the cosmos is a calamity and birth a catastrophe. The absolute God had no intention of producing a material universe. It came about due to a Fall within the original divine being. The original divine being (called the Pleroma, or Fullness) consisted of a coterie of conceptual emanations: the archetypes, or aeons, who derived their origin from an unknowable depth or profundity (Greek: *bythos*), also called the Father. The emanated archetypes were presented both as Platonic ideas and as spiritual beings, among whom the most significant were Anthropos (humanity) and Sophia (Wisdom).

As we have seen in the previous chapter, some Gnostics traced the origin of the material universe (perhaps allegorically) to a tragedy, the result of Sophia's endeavoring foolishly to understand the unknowable. All that she could achieve was a material copy, a *false conception,* resulting in a *miscarriage* in which she loses herself in baleful wanderings, exiled from the Pleroma (a mythic type for the status of the aspirant before receiving gnosis).

The tragic cosmos, far from the Pleroma, is made subject to the government of beings, archons ("rulers"), who, while fascinated by the light of the Pleroma above them, are essentially hostile to, or jealous of, the purely spiritual. (All this speculation was intended to satisfy or perhaps to stimulate existential questions regarding how evil came to be in the world, and how human beings came to suffer in a world of ubiquitous evil.)

According to the consensus of Irenaeus's Gnostics, human beings are the handiwork of the chief archon, the Demiurge. He has various names but is sometimes identified with the creator-God and legal judge of the Hebrew Bible. In Gnostic mythology, he is pitted against the Anthropos, the primal human, who had appeared before the archons to their envy and astonishment (cf. the manifestation of the "Son of man" in Ezekiel 1:26).

In the process of exile from the Pleroma, sparks of pneuma (spirit) were trapped in the cosmos by the jealous archons and unhappily lodged within some human beings, who thus faced the appalling prospect of seeing the light while being cruelly separated from it by the apparently impenetrable bars of matter. This situation typifies for the Gnostic the distress of the spiritual human's predicament: spirit trapped in matter. That is to say, humans are not simply born into the world; they are brutally "thrown" into this prison of the soul.

For Irenaeus, the idea that the Gnostics were superior to their creator was both absurd and blasphemous. Indeed, it is precisely at this point that we can detect what would for the bishop of Lyons differentiate between the false and the true gnosis. The Johannine tradition, as evinced in the Gospel of John, revealed to Irenaeus that eternal life consisted in knowledge of "the only true God": "This is eternal life, that they know [the Greek verb is *gignoskosin*] thee the only true God, and he whom thou hast sent Jesus Christ" (John 17:3).

For Irenaeus, "the only true God" was the one of whom Jesus had spoken: the creator of heaven and earth and all things therein, patently superior to all created existence. Of course, some Gnostics would doubtless have interpreted the passage as referring to the absolute Father beyond creation. To announce the absolute Father's existence, Jesus had to do battle with Satan, the "prince of this world." While Satan kept men and women in ignorance, or agnosis, "the only *true* God" was for Gnostics the "alien God" whom Gnostics had discovered within themselves.

On consideration, the problem posed by the Gnostics goes back to the Persian difficulty with time. What was the divine pneuma doing wrapped up in a world of transience? The philosophical crux of the argument lies in the fact that whereas the Gnostics desired that the pneuma be redeemed from creation, Irenaeus expected the redemption of *all* creation.

Irenaeus looked to an eventual resurrection and fulfillment of God's purposes at the end of time; the Gnostics claimed that the resurrection had for them already been experienced upon their joyful receipt of gnosis, so awakening to their spiritual nature. In defense of this assertion, they could quote Jesus: "The kingdom of heaven is nigh and within you."

4. The great secret of radical Gnostics consists in knowing and understanding the precosmic Fall myth (in one of many variant forms) and in being given the keys to liberate the exiled pneuma from the grip of the archons. (The characteristic chord of gnosis is the yearning for the absolute in pain, the major seventh of the entire philosophy and the psychological basis of its attractiveness.[2])

5. Not infrequently, these groups refer to the holder of the keys to liberation as Jesus: an emanated energy of the Father, sent out of the Father's love to benighted earth in order to awaken the dormant Gnostics to their true identity. Jesus is thus the Gnostic par excellence; he is not a man in the ordinary sense of the word.

    The crucifixion itself is a fraud, a trick effected to outwit the Demiurge. The archons got a death from the body (its essential nature)—but the spiritual being could not be destroyed. Rather, as the unknown author of the Gnostic Gospel of Philip put it: He "came crucifying the world." Some Gnostics denied Jesus' participation in the crucifixion altogether, claiming that another (sometimes Simon of Cyrene) was crucified in his place. Indeed, the wholly spiritual Jesus finds the spectacle of the earnest, blind crucifiers to be a source of intense, even ironic amusement, thus coining the image of the "laughing Savior." Gnostics are expected both to see and to share the joke: "For my death which they think happened, happened to them in their error and blindness, since they nailed their man unto their death. It was another upon whom they placed the crown of thorns. But I was rejoicing in the height over all the wealth of the archons and the offspring of their error, of their empty glory. And I was laughing at their ignorance" (from *The Second Treatise of the Great Seth*).[3] Before returning to the Pleroma, the Savior instructed a number of disciples as to the true gnosis. These instructions were written, it was claimed, in secret books known exclusively to Gnostics.

6. The Gnostic groups believed the emanatory powers (aeons) of the Father were projected within the Pleroma in co-dependent pairs (male and female natures), with names such as Mind and Truth and Logos and Life. Consistent with this was that one valid way for the spirituals to express the gnosis—or to return to

the One—was through a pneumatic sex sacrament. This "divine union" was available only to pneumatics—for sexual gnosis had nothing to do either with material procreation or with animal lust.

Sex might be used either allegorically or in fact as part of Gnostic ceremonies. Semen could be regarded as a sacramental substance, as an image for the *Logos spermatikos* (the spermatic Word cast into the world) or pneumatic spark—the fugitive fragments of spirit, diffused in nature. Fertility was seen as a metaphor for spiritual growth. (This was how some Christian Gnostics interpreted Christ's parable of the sower who sowed seed in barren earth.)

7. The Gnostics, who claimed to owe their being to a higher power, felt free to disregard the Ten Commandments and to live by their own light because the Demiurge was responsible for these negatively expressed injunctions. Essentially free of any external authority whatsoever, the Gnostic could "walk tall" in the world—and, should we share the Gnostics' symbol of water as denoting matter, the Gnostic could "walk on water" as well.

8. Irenaeus found objectionable the Gnostic notion that humankind's essential predicament is the product not of sin, but of unconsciousness. When humans become conscious, when they experience gnosis, they are free to disentangle themselves from the passions (nature's grip on the spirit, working through the soul).

This could be achieved either by asceticism or by becoming indifferent to the passions, permitting their manifestation with detached indifference on the principle that what the body does or does not do is either irrelevant or a necessary education on the path to pure spirituality. (This was particularly the case among the followers of the proto-communist Gnostic teacher Carpocrates, an intellectual anarchist who coined the dictum "Property is theft.")

9. Gnostics gave women an equal spiritual role in their services. By emphasizing the androgynous character of the spiritual, Gnostics enabled particular devotion to either the male or the female

aspect of divine emanations. Thus Sophia, for example, conceived of as feminine, could effectively be adored as a kind of goddess within, and as a road to, God.

10. Some Gnostics used demonic magic as a means of ascending through the archontic spheres to obtain assistance from celestial and supercelestial beings. Indeed the cosmogony of the Gnostics is in all essentials a magical one, populated by beings who could be influenced by the right magical codes, symbols, and passwords.

This ambiguity with regard to cosmic control was deeply threatening to people such as Irenaeus, who saw God as being in sole charge of human history. Irenaeus's hatred of magic strongly reflects the fact that the Christian Church had grown up in direct competition with magic, and in Irenaeus's time the main ideological battle had by no means been won. (Irenaeus was convinced that the author of the Gnostic heresy was Simon Magus, a Samaritan magician whose followers called him the "Great Power of God" and who appears in a walk-on part in the eighth chapter of the Acts of the Apostles and in sundry apocryphal works.)

The Gnostics discussed by Irenaeus held ideas utterly suffused with the speculations of the Eastern Magi. This is clear from his statements on *The Deceitful Arts and Nefarious Practices of Marcus,* whose ideas of the Demiurge were shown in the last chapter to have been influenced by Persian (and probably Magian) speculations on the nature of time.

"It appears," wrote Irenaeus, that Marcus "really [was] the precursor of Antichrist. For joining the buffooneries of Anaxilaus[4] to the craftiness of the magi, as they are called, he is regarded by his senseless and crack-brained followers as working miracles by these means."[5]

The means constituted the stock-in-trade of the Eastern magicians, who were such an ambiguous feature of late antique culture. Irenaeus complains of Marcus's addiction to philters, love potions (drugs), "familiar demons," prophecies, the defiling of women, numerology, the secret meaning of letters, astrology, and Satanism. In addition to claiming intimacy with a female spiritual creature called Charis ("Grace"), Marcus was also, according to the bishop of Lyons, a follower of Azazel, a "fallen and mighty angel." Irenaeus is particularly astonished at the Marcosian logic whereby the creator of the cosmos could have been the end result of a series of defects, a position that Hans Jonas has identified as hard-core Gnostic. It is interesting to find this position right in the heart of the philosophy of a Magus. Marcus is described as "a perfect adept in magical impostures, and by this means drawing away a great number of men, and not a few women, he has induced them to join themselves to him, as to one who is possessed of the greatest knowledge and perfection, and who has received the highest power from the invisible and ineffable regions above."[6]

It is perhaps strange that Irenaeus continued to see the gnosis "falsely so-called" as a heresy or deviation from apostolic Christianity. After all, he had discovered many of its doctrines to be derived from, as far as he was concerned, non-Christian or alien sources, sources that for him had no authority in the Christian Church proper. Perhaps this was because he could not see Christianity as anything other than the supreme knowledge and foundation of truth everywhere. Irenaeus never envisioned Christianity as a sect or as a religion among other religions.

For him, Christ the Logos was the revelation of the *fons,* or source philosophy. While this point of view may seem foreign to the contemporary world, it is certain that Irenaeus, as a progenitor of the catholic and orthodox ("straight-teaching") idea, did see things this way. He was not prepared to tolerate the idea of a rival religion that claimed Christ for its prophet. Thus, the "false gnosis" must be vanquished by and within the Church. For him, it was a poison within the body of the Church, and he was simply doing God's work. Indeed, the Catholic Church has been battling with the gnostic "poison" ever since, regarding it as far more dangerous to its well-being than merely other religions, which, from its own theory, must ultimately recognize the absolute historic primacy of the Church Catholic, however that recognition is made.

Irenaeus's conception of the church was not, however, primarily institutional—and obviously not Rome-based. For him the Church was a spiritual inevitability of history. It embodied a revelation of God Himself, whose dynamism and growth would eventually see the triumph of Christ over all in all. As far as he was concerned, the Gnostics were retarding that process by unauthorized, divisive, and dangerous speculation. The Gnostics, their opponents believed, were joyfully indulging in a satirical game at their expense.

We, however, are not compelled to see things that way. Indeed, it is now widely held that from the historical point of view, Gnosticism may be regarded as a semiautonomous religion in and of itself ("semi" since it took in so many conceptions from various religious sources, including the New Testament). In his introduction to *The Nag Hammadi Library in English,* Professor James M. Robinson writes, "Gnosticism seems not to have been in its essence just an alternate form of Christianity. Rather it was a radical trend of release from the dominion of evil or of inner transcendence that swept through late antiquity and emerged within Christianity, Judaism, Neoplatonism, the mystery religions, and the like. As a new religion it was syncretistic, drawing upon various religious heritages. But it was held together by a very decided stance, which is where the unity amid the wide diversity is to be sought."[7]

This statement is borne out to some extent by the contents of the Nag Hammadi library. There we find Valentinian Christian works rubbing shoulders with pagan works of religious philosophy and speculation stemming from the followers of the works of Hermes, Plato, and Zarathushtra, as well as hard-core Gnostic works such as the Apocryphon of John. We also find Jewish Gnostic or Jewish-influenced Sethian work and, in addition, magical texts and works that would not be entirely out of place in the library of an orthodox Christian or Jewish mystic.

Two things should here be noted, however. First, the Nag Hammadi library represents the eclectic interests of a community that prized the gnosis in Upper Egypt; it does not necessarily reflect the full range of Gnostic experience throughout the eastern and western empire of late antiquity. Second, this community undoubtedly saw itself as Christian. That is to say, as far as this community was concerned, its members felt themselves to be in touch with the authentic revelation of Jesus and their opponents to be out of touch with this revelation. One text, the Apocalypse of Peter,[8] refers to the orthodox bishops of the third century as "dry canals" who cannot provide spiritual instruction, only aggressive orders. Another text *(Eugnostos the Blessed)* even comes in two versions: an original, wherein one Eugnostos is the provider of spiritual instruction, and a copy *(The Sophia of Jesus Christ),* in which the instruction is put in the mouth of Jesus.

These Egyptian Gnostics listened to the voice of him whom they called the "living Jesus," whose voice they found in a number of spiritual traditions—and, especially, in themselves. For them, this voice of the awakening spirit constituted authority enough for the composition of their books. Jesus himself, it should be noted, never forbade the making of books in his name. He never wrote one himself and made it clear that it was the Holy Spirit that would inspire his followers and not necessarily his recorded logia. Paul himself had told the Corinthians that "we" have the mind (nous) of Christ—and Paul taught without recourse to the books of the New Testament!

The Egyptian Gnostics whose sacred works comprise the Nag Hammadi library undoubtedly believed that gnosis was integral to, and indeed the prime component of, the revelation of Jesus. Irenaeus, who was aware of the existence of secret Gnostic books—particularly the Apocryphon of John—was convinced that their message was not consistent with that of the four nonsecret Gospels of Matthew, Mark, Luke, and John. However, the Egyptian Gnostics both used and approved of the so-called canonical Gospels. Much of their teaching was based on commentary on the Gospels, and they considered it to be based on valid interpretations of the conventional sayings of Jesus.

The Egyptian Gnostics seem to have suspected that the Church had not gone deeply enough into the meaning of Jesus' teaching, being too preoccupied with apocalyptic expectations of the return of Christ in time and preparation for the end of the world. Christian Gnostics took the "second coming" and the "end of the world" as allegories and symbols of inner, spiritual processes. (Indeed it must be added that the temporal apocalyptic interpretation of Jesus' message has been a perpetual cause of embarrassment to the Church to this day.)

Gnostics were very keen on allegory and the power of parabolic and symbolic images. Take, for example, this quotation from the Gospel of Philip: "Truth did not come into the world naked, but it came in types and images. One will not receive truth in any other way. There is a rebirth and an image of rebirth. It is certainly necessary that they should be born again through the image. What is the resurrection? The image must rise again through the image."[9] This statement appears to be the product of a meditation on John 3:5–7: "Verily, verily, I say unto thee, except a man be born of water and of the Spirit, he cannot enter into the kingdom of God. That which is born of the flesh is flesh: and that which is born of the Spirit is spirit. Marvel not that I said unto thee, Ye must be born again."

The Gospel of Philip interprets this theme in language with the most powerful kinship to that of spiritual alchemy. Note particularly the explanation of the transformative fire: "It is from water and fire that the soul and the spirit came into being. It is from water and fire and light that the son of the bridal chamber [the "resurrected" spirit of the Gnostic] (came into being). The fire is the chrism, the light is the fire. *I am not referring to that fire which has no form,* but to the other fire whose form is white, which is bright and beautiful, and which gives beauty." Following a paraphrase of the alchemical *Smaragdine Table of Hermes Trismegistus* (put into the mouth of Jesus), the Gospel of Philip goes on to comment on the crucifixion (quoting Mark 15:34) and then on the denouement to the "division" of Christ on the cross, the resurrection: "The [Lord rose] from the dead. [He became as he used] to be, but now [his body was] perfect. [He did not possess] flesh, but this [flesh] is true flesh. [Our flesh] is not true, but [we possess] only an image of the true."[10]

This Gnostic author is telling us that in the rebirth referred to in the Gospel of John, the reborn person acquires spiritual flesh: a body that, the author goes on to say, is invisible to the world. The one reborn becomes like the Christ of John's Gospel, who was in the world but the world knew him not: "When we were begotten [through Christ] we were united. None shall be able to see himself either in water or in a mirror without light. Nor again will you be able to see in light without water or mirror. For this reason it is fitting to baptize in the two, in the light and the water. Now the light is the chrism."[11]

This fascinating meditation, a state of mind that so masterfully destroys the material vision by allegorizing into alchemical symbol the images of light and fire, bringing forth a being with the gift of spiritual vision, seems as far away as could be imagined from Irenaeus's "blasphemous and mad" Gnostics. Well, blasphemous, perhaps; Irenaeus may himself have appeared mad to somebody.

We might even begin to wonder whether a clear understanding of what is encompassed by the term *Gnosticism* is even possible. Of course, it might be that between the time of Irenaeus and the time of the composition of the Gospel of Philip (held generally to be a Valentinian work)—perhaps up to a century later—the ideas of Valentinus had undergone development. Perhaps certain (hard-core?) aspects of original Valentinianism had been ditched or reinterpreted by some Gnostics. But this only further emphasizes the question of when *gnosis* ceases to be defined as Gnosticism.

In spite of our ability, in retrospect, to *construct* a Gnostic religion, was there, in late antiquity, really such a thing as *the* Gnostic religion?

HANS JONAS: THE GNOSTIC RELIGION

The brilliant twentieth-century philosopher Hans Jonas certainly believed that we can speak of such a phenomenon.[12] He pinpointed the appearance of organized Gnostic culture as a major eruption into the human story, the first time human beings came systematically to the awareness of a great and terrifying gulf between humankind and the natural world—a tremendously shocking and subversive consciousness.

Insofar as Gnosticism expressed the experience of a sinister imprisonment in the world, an essential hostility to the cosmos, and an at once both pessimistic and optimistic proclamation of humankind's essential *otherness*, Jonas saw Gnostics as being, to an extent, precursors of the existentialist philosophy of his teacher, Martin Heidegger. The very currency of these ideas in late antiquity—before their time, so to speak—marked for Jonas not only a world-historical event, but also the essential point of definition of the Gnostic religion.

For Hans Jonas, a Gnosticism without hostility between the demiurgical world and the spiritual Pleroma, and thus between the Gnostic and the creator God of the Jews, would be unworthy of being classed as essential Gnosticism. Gnosticism demanded a "transcendent history" of the divine being itself: a truly epic conflict, involving the whole scheme of grim constraint of the spirit by the zodiacal and demonic-archontic powers. Gnosticism required the whole to be seen as a grand all-encompassing repair operation, whereby the transcendent Being returned being to Being. Any definition of Gnosticism deprived of the majority of these features would be inadequate. Jonas advanced these features as being definitive at the International Colloquium on the Origins of Gnosticism held at Messina in April 1966.

The dark and literally world-shattering vision of the Gnostics provided Jonas with the Gnostics' central interest for himself, for modern philosophy, and for the contemporary world situation, or crisis. This contemporary crisis may be characterized by the following pressing phenomena:

1. Personal and social alienation.
2. The transfer and insecurity of traditional cultures.
3. The fear of imminent catastrophe; endemic violence.
4. Loss of trust; the collapse of many traditional forms of authority, and unease with regard to new types.
5. The sense of a civilization out of joint and even worn out.
6. The widespread grasping for sources of immediate gratification; the despair of failed satisfaction; and the rush toward either personal oblivion or fundamentalist redemptive figures.

Many of these features were present to the experience of people in the world of late antiquity (the second to sixth centuries A.D.). The Gnostic message seems both to have been stimulated by them and to have provided welcome solace to those who found in the gnosis a transcendent experience beyond the vicissitudes of time. For, despite the darkness of a good part of the Gnostic vision of the world, unlike nihilism—to which, according to Jonas, it is a distant cousin—it bore a definite meaning. Gnosis was still, in spite of its catastrophic and terrific nature, a value system, albeit a very strange one:

Where there is a conflict of values, we have to take sides. So strangeness then, our alienation, does not mean simply that there is nothing to hold on to, but it means that there is a great battle going on in which our souls are engaged. And *that* has meaning. Now the Gnostic answer to the human predicament was a curious mixture of utter pessimism and utter optimism.

As regards the chances to make sense of this world, it was very pessimistic, but in terms of our chances to elevate our being beyond, above the world, it was tremendously optimistic. We may even say it exhibited an overbearing arrogance: that with the right knowledge, if you really look through this whole fraud of the world, this deception that struts around as the great irreality and only produces intoxication in us, dullness of sense, drunkenness or sleep—if we break through that, we can not only espy something, we can make ourselves part of it through the act of *knowing* itself. Provided, of course, it is not the wrong knowledge of the *archons,* of the Demiurge, or of the "lord of this world," but the true.

Now the significance for us is, first of all, the sense of déjà vu regarding what these people experienced and what they sought an answer to; and secondly, that while all these answers may have been fantastic, imaginative mythology, their type of experience is somehow parallel to ours and therefore their answer is at least worth listening to.[13]

If we seek our definition out of our own historical or personal crisis, then undoubtedly it is difficult to avoid Jonas's existential emphasis as the principal criterion for the definition of Gnosticism. However, there have been a number of significant dissenters from this emphasis.

Possibly the chief, and certainly the best-known, dissenter from the Jonas definition has been Professor Elaine Pagels, author of the very popular study *The Gnostic Gospels.*[14] Pagels to some extent follows the broadly Christian-Jungian approach of Professor Gilles Quispel of Utrecht. Quispel was responsible for bringing the Jung Codex (of the Nag Hammadi library) to the attention of scholars, after he had bought the Codex on May 10, 1952, from an agent in Brussels.[15]

Professor Pagels's first book on the Gnostics demonstrated, through a selective reading of the Nag Hammadi texts, that a chief background influence on the making of the texts was a political battle for the mind of, and authority over, the Christian churches. The conflict was chiefly between free-range Gnostics and a growing monarchical episcopacy.

Orthodox bishops were trying with gathering success throughout the second, third, and (most successfully) fourth centuries to impose a single tradition and doctrinal and canonical formula upon a once pluriform (and to some extent, multidoctrinal) Christian Church.

Professor Pagels has specialized in the study of the Valentinian Gnostics, Christian Gnostics who followed a tradition of teaching established by the Egyptian Gnostic genius, Valentinus. He was active in Rome and Alexandria after about A.D. 150. Indeed, the heresiarch nearly became bishop of Rome before he was excommunicated. Valentinus's thought is apparently well represented among the fifty-two texts of the Nag Hammadi library, in such works as the Gospel of Truth, the Gospel of Philip, the Epistle to Rheginos, and the Tripartite Tractate.

Pagels told me that the Valentinians "were trying to be the esoteric branch of the Christians the way that Jewish mystics were the esoteric branch of Judaism. I don't think they did think the world was evil and that ordinary Christians were in a state of hopelessness." I asked her if Professor Jonas was right to refer to the Gnostic religion as the "message of the Alien God."

Pagels: Orthodoxy says God is the wholly other, and the Gnostics speak about the world as alien because it interrupts their communion with God, which is the essential kinship. So whenever you speak of "alien," you're presupposing kinship somewhere else. Professor Jonas chooses to presuppose a kinship between cosmos and humankind—and God is the wholly other. He's orthodox Jewish/Christian in the way he thinks.

Churton: Do you think any Gnostics held a positive view of Nature?

Pagels: Yes. If you look at Irenaeus's *Against the Heretics* regarding his discussion of Valentinian Christians, then you would see an image of the world—as you said, a Neoplatonic image—straight out of Plato's *Timaeus* (which Valentinus and his followers used): "Time is the moving image of eternity." These are Christians who are in the Church. That's why Irenaeus thought they were so deceptive—because they pretend to be "like us," he says. Most people can't tell them apart!

Churton: Except, that is, as regards their view of the Demiurge. The two big attacks that Irenaeus made were with respect to, first, the Demiurge, and second, their negative view of the God of the New Testament and much of the Hebrew Bible themselves.

Pagels: My claim is, of course, that the Valentinians thought of the Demiurge not as an evil being—guilty, as it were, of making the world for malicious reasons, as Jonas maintains—but as a deficient being who doesn't fully comprehend the whole creation with which he is engaged.

Churton: Do you think the Demiurge is, in a sense, a part of the mind of God?

Pagels: I think so. And I also think that these people were fascinated by the question of how symbols function. The Valentinians say that the Demiurge is an *ikon tou theou* [Greek], "an image of God." And I think they're talking of our images of God. When we say "God," we're using images, and they're trying to point out—some with irony, others with parody—that our images of God are in a way a travesty, or at least they're very limited. When they are not wrong, they are at least very deficient. So they say that our images for God—that he's the Father, or that he's the creator—are images. They're not wrong; they're deficient. Other, more radical Gnostics would say that they're totally erroneous.[16]

Soon afterward, I put these points to Professor Jonas.

Churton: Would you say that the Valentinian idea, in crude, literal terms, is that we are in the mind of God, and that the mind of God is not a wholly pure thing—the heart of it is, to use our expression, "pure," but that there are aspects of it, when it expresses itself, that are at least a diminution—

Jonas: Sure, oh, yes.

Churton: —and that the Demiurge is a projection of the mind of God? So we're not separate from the mind of God; that is to say that God is not truly "unknown"—I mean, God is unknown in his essential being, but that we're not cut off wholly from God. This is the gist of what Professor Pagels was saying yesterday.

Jonas: Oh, yes, that's true. But it becomes actualized only through the acquisition and the exercise of gnosis. We're not automatically part of the mind of God. This is a potential, because these estranging, intervening forces [the archons], these have put us at a great distance from our source. And it is this great distance between the darkness of this world and the transmundane luminosity of the divine mind that has to be bridged. It's bridged first by knowledge, but it is also bridged by a certain way of life. But as regards this, there were many different conceptions, including libertinism—the permission to do anything because you are not bound to the laws of this world.

Churton: Yes, but Elaine Pagels was disagreeing with something in your book. For instance, the cover refers to the "message of the Alien God," and she felt that not all the Gnostics thought that God was alien, nor that the Father and the Demiurge were necessarily separate.

Jonas: One has to beware of oversimplification in formulating Gnostic doctrines. There were so many lines of Gnosticism that it's always dangerous to bring them down to one formula. I think Plotinus [Neoplatonic philosopher, c. A.D. 200], who wrote a treatise in his Enneads called "Against Those Who Consider the World Evil, and the Creator of the World Evil," had it essentially right in his title. Some of the doctrines he quotes there were Valentinian or certainly close to Valentinian.

With regard to the creation, something happened [i.e., went wrong in the Pleroma, resulting in creation]—the emanations of being from the One were not a natural progression, an expending of the divine light, as Plotinus saw it, but necessarily involved a diminution or tragedy—a devolution. In Plotinus, the grades of being emanating from the One leading to the visible world always retain a bond, drawing their origin from the reality of the One—that bond is never lost or broken in Plotinus—even down to the existence of matter. While it represents the minimum, it is still derived, not wholly alien.

The Gnostic view is really different from that. Something happened that led to a breach. One can speak of a tragedy. One can speak of a suffering. One can speak of an erring Sophia who had lost her way, who tries to turn back but cannot find her way back to the Father, to her origins. This, Plotinus rightly felt, was the decisive difference between his philosophy and that of the Gnostics.

Now, there may have been among the many Gnostics those who saw things more harmoniously, less tragically, less disharmoniously than others. Clearly if you start, as Mani did [Gnostic-type prophet of the world religion Manichaeanism; born A.D. 216 in Babylonia], with the assumption of an original principle of evil, hostile to the good, then you have a polarization right from the outset. The Valentinians were much more subtle and sophisticated. The polarity now experienced, which the existing world presents to us, is the outcome of a mystery of divine Self-estrangement. Parts of divinity have become estranged from their origin and have to be reunited.

In Plotinus, it [the cosmos] would never be any different from what it is now. The whole ladder of being, the hierarchy, would always be there, because if the Fullness [the Pleroma] were really full, that means that the utter, most distant rims of being will always be there. The Gnostics thought that this is a passing, tragical history of divine reality, that this will ultimately be wound up, as it were, when all the alienated Spirit is returned to the Pleroma.

Churton: Do you think the Gnostics would have been sympathetic to the Big Bang theory?

Jonas: Yes! "That is the way the Demiurge operates! Brutal force. *Right!* Very nice. That is his style!—Pity we didn't think of it ourselves!"

Okay, I won't deny that Elaine Pagels may have a point that not all Gnostics were such dualists. It's a matter of emphasis. Which Gnostics do interest us? Those whose thinking was somehow in a general Platonic line—I don't think they are particularly interesting, because the real Platonists could do that better.

But those who really scandalized Plotinus, who told these really sinister stories—to whom the Demiurge was an arrogant, tyrannical being—they are the ones who make the flesh creep. Therefore I choose my emphasis. Who doesn't?

When I read these long lamentations in Mandaean literature[17] about our exile in the world, and wandering in the aeons, seeking for the way back; and how the knowledge of life breaks into the world from outside and shows the way . . . There is this constant theme of the Alien Man: This is the messenger from the godhead. Either, seen from here, the godhead is alien, or seen from "there": we have become alienated.[18] It's a matter of perspective. But a great alienation has taken place, and that has to be overcome again.

Gnostics claim recognition of two things in our situation, as it is. First, that it is the consequence of a divine Fall. Second, that they recognize the true source of being to which Gnostics must return: the knowledge of our being here and now in its true light. And seeing this in its true light means that you also gain knowledge of the lost, true existence of the soul or spirit.

So that it is a recognition of the world for what it is, and that can only be gained if it is joined to a knowledge of the history of how it has come to be, what it has become, and then the *gnosis theou*: gnosis of God. You may remember that I put great emphasis on a brief saying of the *Excerpta ex Theodoto* [a negative comment on a Gnostic author by the second-century Latin-speaking theologian Tertullian]. Tertullian's enquiry into gnosis yields the definition that it is the "knowledge of who we were, what we have become, where we have come from, whereunto we have been thrown. Where we go, from what we have been freed, where we are bound to return." This is the polarity. There's always two things: "where we were," "what we have become"; "where we are now," "where we are bound to go"; "where we came from," "into what we have been thrown."

These are the existential facts. This tension between these two poles keeps Gnosticism alive, and therefore any attempt to harmonize this would take the sting out of Gnosticism. A pervading feeling of distress is there. Our being, the creation as such, has created a *distressing* condition. Where that distress isn't there, and where you don't have if not an evil Demiurge, then at least a stupid or blind Demiurge—he may not be evil; if he's not evil, then he's blind—if you don't have that, then I wouldn't say you had genuine Gnosticism. I would regard it almost as a criterion where you could draw the line.

THE IRRESISTIBLE CHARACTER OF GNOSIS; OR, "THE SPIRIT IS WILLING"

It certainly seems to this author that Hans Jonas wins his case for a definition of Gnosticism. However, this is the gnosticism of what Jonas has called "the core Gnostic writers," and the strong implication is that Gnosticism here refers to a number of specifically Gnostic groups whose teaching is essentially a systematized—even concretized—grand-plan philosophy of religion. The teaching answers specific questions, questions that the more orthodox second-century Latin legalist and theologian Tertullian declared to be those which "make people Gnostics": that is, Where does humanity come from, and why? And where does evil come from, and why?

The whole mythological structure examined by Jonas, as well as being an intense *cri de coeur,* is basically a construct envisioned to answer these questions; somebody or something, other than the supposed spiritually pure, good God, must be responsible for the suffering fate of the spirit in the world. Who's to blame? Answer: the creator—and he is not the absolute God.

This intuition is expressed in the otherwise banal popular joke about the Almighty: God is alive and well but is now working on a less ambitious project. The metaphysical problem that these Gnostics attempted to address is still with us: How can a good God create a world that contains evil?

At this point, the author must confess to some dissatisfaction with the idea that the mythic system thought to comprise the gnosis within Gnosticism does in fact exhaust it. Must it be that the cosmic speculation on the origins of evil and of people ascribed to the Gnostics does in fact constitute the heart of their message—or more precisely, the heart of their teachers' message?

Perhaps the ease with which we can grasp Gnostic doctrines (the progressive Fall from the Pleroma; the creation of the Demiurge; passwords and so on to assist reascent) might be thought to militate against the notion that this itinerary does in fact represent the whole mystery.

Jonas himself speaks of the Valentinians' subtlety, of their "mystery of divine Self-estrangement." Paul, much studied by the Valentinians, was emphatic that spiritual things are spiritually discerned. The second-century Gnostic myths described by Irenaeus seem materialistic. From an aesthetic point of view, the conflation of spiritual, philosophical, and crude mythological language renders them somewhat monstrous. Even pneuma, the divine spirit, appears as a movable quantity—hardly a conception belonging to a realm beyond time and space!

Gnosis is not mere knowledge of facts, is never as opaque as mere information. Perhaps the Gnostic myths of creation were originally intended as the outer shells of a mystery, hints of a depth not available to the mind in the first instance—even humor-drenched parodies, jokes to shake the mind from its normal distracted, flesh-loving, automatic, egoistic, and passionate course. Has all the attention on the "heresy" of Gnosticism obscured a more profound gnosis within it?

One of the fascinating things about the Valentinian itinerary—or rather the myth attributed to Valentinus by Irenaeus—is that, should we deprive it of a fundamentally materialistic interpretation, the myth can also be taken as a valid and profoundly suggestive theory of perception. Indeed, I should venture to say that this is in fact its psychological basis. From this point of view, the starting question is not, Where did evil come from, and why? but, How does the spirit become enmeshed in matter?

This question may well have been put to Valentinus when he was a teacher in Egypt. (It is certainly related to the practice of Egyptian alchemy and the recovery of the Stone.[19]) How do we explain material existence, once we have said that the absolute is spiritual? Why is not everything spiritual? How was it that it became necessary for a Christ to teach a way to eternal, or spiritual, life? Valentinus may have realized that the *gnosis* of what Jesus called the kingdom of heaven lay in a consideration of the problem of *perception*.

BEING IS SEEING

A basic premise of Valentinian thought is that the so-called material world is relative; it is not absolute. It has a beginning and an end. It is relative, but it is not illusory. But to become enamored of it, to believe in it as the only reality, is indeed to become deluded, to be lost in the illusion: the illusion of a counterfeit eternity. Perhaps we may compare the dilemma with falling totally in love with the first attractive person you meet. Oblivious to the fact that the one you are going to marry is quite different,[20] it might take many painful experiences to reach that person. In becoming deluded, the person becomes lost. The author of the Nag Hammadi Gospel of Truth (almost certainly Valentinus himself) expresses a kindred dilemma most poignantly:

> They were ignorant of the Father, he being the one whom they did not see. Since it was terror and disturbance and instability and doubt and division, there were many illusions at work by means of these, and (they were) empty fictions, as if they were sunk in sleep and found themselves in disturbing dreams. Either (there is) a place to which they are fleeing, or powerless they come (from) having pursued others, or they are involved in striking blows, or they are receiving blows themselves, or they have fallen from high places, or they take off into the air although they do not even have wings. Again, sometimes (it is as) if people were murdering them, though there is no one even pursuing them, or they themselves are killing their neighbors, for they have been stained with their blood. When those who are going through all these things wake up, they see nothing, they who were in the midst of all these disturbances, for they are nothing. Such is the way of those who have cast ignorance aside from them like sleep, not esteeming it as anything, nor do they esteem its works as solid things either, but they leave them behind like a dream in the night. The knowledge of the Father they value as the dawn. This is the way each one has acted, as though asleep at the time he was ignorant. And this is the way he has come to gnosis, as if he had awakened.[21]

According to the Gnostic, only spirit is ultimately real. Time and space (the world of the Demiurge) are not absolutes; they are conditions of perception.

Another premise of Valentinus is that Christ is a spiritual archetype, the "fruit of the Pleroma." He is the Logos, the creative Word or intelligible energy of God, envisioned by Valentinus in a formative spiritual experience in the form of a Child. Jesus the spiritual archetype shows us *what we really are*. He *is* what we really are—that is to say, what we are to *become*, in Paul's language the "second Adam": new Man.

The actual experience of realizing this formerly hidden divine Self is gnosis. This realization belongs to those who have arisen from hylic, to psychic, and, at last, to pneumatic consciousness. (It may well have been a corruption of Valentinus's thought to have regarded these three classes of people as ineluctably separate.)

It is important to see that the tragedy within the Pleroma (the spiritual wholeness) is triggered by thought. Thought generates a consciousness of loss of wholeness, making the dualist or dialectical universe a universe of pain. The "suffering thought" attempts to relocate its home in the primal repose of the One. Valentinus expresses this in the myth of Wisdom (Sophia) seeking to know her mysterious source. We then have the paradox whereby the restitution of the Pleroma is effected by the granting of knowledge that knowledge of the primal depth is impossible. The dialectic set up by the yearning thought, or desire to know the depth/Father, is transcended on a higher plane in the gnosis experience itself.

The Sophia myth is thus revealed as a parable of the reflexive consciousness. It is, in a sense, like the Paradise (Eden) story transposed to the being of God, with Sophia playing the part of Eve, wherein the fatal apple is replaced by a more satisfying fruit: knowledge of why the fruit of dialectical thought (or material consciousness) is poisonous. (Except that the starting point of the Valentinian myth is the very arrival of consciousness—i.e., "they knew that they were naked," and are to be flung out of the paradisiacal Garden.)

This ultimately beautiful myth contains a great perceptual key. Insofar as a human being seeks to *know*, the material world of three or more dimensions discerned by the five senses is created. The more a person seeks to know, the more world is created (cf. Lao-tzu's dictum "The farther one travels, the less one knows"). Thus the human being "falls" into the world.

Materially speaking, the entire myth takes place "in the head," that is to say, in the mind—which is not *in* the head at all. (Plotinus believed that the body is that part of the soul perceived by the five senses.) Hence, the person who is "tired of the world" invariably seeks either innocence (the world unknown) or oblivion (loss of consciousness). It is the transmundane mind of the human being that creates the universe. We search the universe into being, so that, in a sense, spiritual Man created the universe (of his knowing), but has forgotten both how and why he did it. Gnosis aims to restore the lost supracosmic memory; its perennial cry is: *Wake up!*

As the Gospel of Philip puts it: "Men make gods and worship their creation. It would be better for the gods to worship human beings."[22] Bearing this in mind (!), we can understand the nature of the Buddhist trance of *nirodha sammapatti,* in which the meditator experiences the total destruction, the annihilation of the universe, along with, significantly, all semblance of duality. And we find that this condition, the alogical positive-nothing, *no-thing,* is the very characteristic of the Valentinian absolute, *Bythos*—the depth, the unknowable God. And again, we must recall the Valentinian Gospel of Philip's contention that Christ "came crucifying the world." There were Buddhists in Alexandria in the second century.

The Demiurge, the false God who knows no higher than himself, may never have originally been considered by Valentinus to be some kind of external, materialistically conceived being. But as Elaine Pagels has suggested, Valentinus may have thought of him as an image of God in our minds. We can go further than this. Might we not say that the Demiurge is the world-making perceptual faculty of human beings?

That is to say, what we would now call the ego, or false self, which obscures what the Upanishads call the Self, and the Christian Gnostics the "living Jesus" (exactly parallel to the gnostic Blake's "Jesus, the Imagination"), is identical with the Demiurge: the false god. The ignorant monster-god lurks within our own bosom. The derangement that produces the "imperfect" universe is not, then, in God the depth, but in our selves.

My contention here is that the Valentinian myth is absurd, if taken materialistically and according to materialistic rational categories. Irenaeus quite correctly, on this basis, saw its ridiculousness, coming to the conclusion that the myth represented an insanely false gnosis, dangerous and damning. Now, while it may be that many *gnostikoi* were duped, it is this author's contention that the picture presented either to or by Irenaeus, or both, was manifestly a materialistic portrayal of a spiritual system. Plotinus, who also produced a spiritual system, was likewise disturbed by its quasi–spiritual characteristics, lamenting its dire results: world-hatred, creator-hatred, and ego-exaltation. This was why he was so against the Gnostics. Some groups, it seems, had got hold of an excellent stick and caught the wrong end of it.

I would go further. The reason, I think, that Professor Jonas could recognize this materialized, existential gnosis as bearing kinship to the modern existentialism of his teacher Martin Heidegger was because that existentialism was itself one of the grim fruits of the materialism that had overtaken European thought since the so-called Enlightenment. And we are still struggling with that materialism.

The Gnostic secret par excellence is that Man is *(in potentia)* God. (The Christian story of the incarnation of Christ is almost an allegory, or type, of this knowledge—it may even have been Jesus' essential Self-realization that got him crucified.) The reason we do not see "Man is God" as an immediate fact is, according to this interpretation of Valentinus, that our imagination is perpetually creating the world, projecting "God" into it, and falling after "Him" and so into the world.

This explains the Gnostic stress on Self-realization as the key approach to gnosis: a view desperately misunderstood in our egoistic age, which likes to paste "self" before as many nouns as possible, with results so plain to see: lost souls full of themselves, cut off, adrift, deluded, tragic.

The alleged distance that Valentinus sets up between the exiled spirit and the Pleroma may be more of a poetic metaphor than has hitherto been seen. That is to say, the alleged distance between ourselves and the "kingdom of heaven" (aeonic or eternal life) is not so much spatial as it is, if you like, a mere blip of perception, which can be overcome. But it is a tremendously difficult blip to overcome—and it might seem that victory is indeed a billion miles away.

I should like to advance the theory that were we to overcome it, the most distant rim of the cosmos would become as close to us as we are to ourselves. The infinity of the universe is only as infinite as the space between two thoughts. The aim of bona fide Gnostic teaching is to take fallen—or falling—Man back to himSelf.

It is, in the view of this author, this fundamental understanding of Man's sleeping God that is the defining stroke of the gnosis. To awake fully would be to become free of matter: It would be, as it were, to walk on water.

CLEMENT OF ALEXANDRIA: THE GNOSIS TRULY SO-CALLED?

O wondrous mystery!
One is the Father of the universe,
and one also the Word of the universe;
the Holy Spirit, again, is one and
everywhere the same.

CLEMENT, *PAEDAGOGUS* 1.42, 1

And it is manifest that the maker is one;
for soul is one, and life is one,
and matter is one.
And who is that maker?
Who else can he be but God alone?

CORPUS HERMETICUM, LIBELLUS 11(2).11

Clement of Alexandria, who flourished around the year A.D. 200, was a Christian who called himself a Gnostic. He was not declared to be a heretic, and his works have therefore survived in orthodox circles. Of all the extant writings of the first centuries of the Christian era, it may be that those of Clement conform most closely to what Bishop Irenaeus of Lyons might have called the gnosis "truly so-called."

An Athenian convert to Christianity, and head of the famous Catechetical School in Alexandria toward the end of the second century, Clement lived in a society that, rather like our own, had lost its nerve. The death of the dignified emperor Marcus Aurelius in 180 led to a period of grave insecurity. His successors were both extravagant and cruel. Many citizens sought solace in philosophy. The problem was that there was so much competition and hostility among rival philosophical schools that genuine seekers were frequently confused.

Christianity had made much headway, but its common evangelical form failed to satisfy many of the more intellectual and thoughtful questors, Christian leaders often being contemptuous of philosophy. Philosophy was on the whole seen by Church leaders (especially in the West) as an arid, self-destructive, and self-contradictory arena: a place of wrangling, intellectual pride, and fruitless speculation. Christianity was considered by such people to have superseded the need for philosophy.

When the Latin Christian legalist Tertullian, a contemporary of Clement, uttered the famous line "I believe because it is absurd," he revealed not only a contempt for a religion cut-and-dried to suit reason, but also the price to be paid for abandoning a philosophical outlook on religious practice.

To those people who refused to accommodate the idea that their beliefs were absurd, the Athenian Clement spoke. He held out an olive branch to those people who found that the "simple faith" was too simple, and who required a deeper, more encompassing view that could accommodate both rigorous thought and spiritual experience. The Gnostic Hermetists of Alexandria addressed a similar audience, but theirs was a pagan audience, and Clement was convinced that the figure of Christ, understood gnostically, was a central platform for uniting thought, spirituality, and the cream of the empire itself.

Clement had the intuition that truth was not to be discovered from simple formulas, blank statements, or dogmas but, rather like our perception of the world itself, was to be found unfolded and enfolded within a kaleidoscopic pattern of shifting perspectives. Paradox, irony, myth, poetry, contrast, mutual opposites were all, taken as a whole, pathways to the truth.

Arriving at a conclusion resembling the Valentinian idea that "truth did not come into the world naked but came clothed in types and images," Clement realized that the absolute truth that lightened the spirit and, consequently, the body can never be stated and accommodated directly in purely linguistic terms in this world. The world was as much theater as fact, and, as in theater, a statement could be "unreal" but nonetheless true. (As Bertolt Brecht said of his theatrical experiments: "Realism does not consist in reproducing reality, but in showing how things really are.")

Clement realized that imagination and the experience of vision transcended matter-of-fact formulas. The important thing was to gain understanding. As an aid to understanding, Clement composed the beautiful collection of insights called the *Stromateis*. In fact, it is more than a collection; it is a patchwork, a quilt, and the whole effect is built up by the coincidence of many elements. No piece can sum up the whole, and yet the whole is contained in each piece. Clement's theory might now be called holographic, stressing the interrelatedness of all things whatsoever. (Clement's whole is holy.)

Clement was a self-confessed Gnostic. His aim was to bring his students to a state of spiritual vision, not as a single experience so much as a dynamic, growing movement, of which this life on earth formed only a part. As the Egyptian poet Valentinus had regarded Jesus as the "fruit of the Pleroma," Clement saw Christ the Logos as the implicate, unifying factor of all the projected archetypes. This also meant that Clement saw all religions as being the sacred expressions of the divine archetypes, while the divine Logos-Christ, present (if unseen) in all, united the All. He would surely have approved of the following statements from the Gospel of Thomas from the Nag Hammadi library: "Jesus said, 'It is I who am the light which is above them all. It is I who am the All. From Me did the All come forth, and unto Me did the All extend. Split a piece of wood, and I am there. Lift up the stone, and you will find Me there. . . . The Kingdom of the Father is spread out upon the earth, and men do not see it.'"[23]

Clement refused the temptation of some Gnostics to sunder the whole within a dynamic of precosmic conflict, and in this guardedness he shows his profound indebtedness to Middle Platonism. His Gnostic Christianity encouraged him to develop this position, and in fact his system, if it is right to call it so, represents one of the earliest formulations of a type of Christian *Neo*platonism.

The aim of the Neoplatonist is to rise through a dynamic relation of unbroken spiritual levels—an essentially hierarchical chain—so as to return the soul to the One from which the soul is derived. Only the One can see the whole as it is. This One, or God absolute, is in its essential nature unknown, yet the animating principles of his projected being are available to those creatures with the *gnosis* to see them. In fact, the universe receives the good principles, but not in like measure. For Clement, the Gnostic Christian is one who not only receives, but one who also *perceives*: one who has become fully—that is to say, spiritually—conscious.[24]

To a certain extent, Clement shared the view of more radical Gnostic thinkers in seeing faith as only a first step toward gnosis. However, he does not in any way disparage faith as being a condition of negative inadequacy, nor would he say that faith was insufficient to participate in God's scheme of salvation. But it is not an end in itself. There is more exciting territory awaiting exploration.

Clement's Christ-the-Man leads to Christ-the-Logos: the dynamic mind of the universe. Clement's Logos, the central principle of all archetypes, is practically indistinguishable from the Hermetic nous (spiritual mind), in which the Hermetist was symbolically baptized in the experience of Gnostic rebirth: the granting of new eyes and the participation in eternal life. The Hermetic revealer figure Poimandres corresponds very closely to Clement's Gnostic Logos. In Book 7 of his *Stromateis,* Clement writes of the relation of faith to gnosis:

> Faith then is a compendious knowledge of the essentials, but *gnosis* is a sure and firm demonstration of the things received through faith, being itself built up by the Lord's teaching on the foundation of the faith, and carrying us on to unshaken conviction and scientific certainty. As I mentioned before, there seems to me to be a first kind of saving change from heathenism to faith, a second from faith to *gnosis;* and this latter, as it passes on into love, begins at once to establish a mutual friendship between that which knows and that which is known. And perhaps he who has arrived at this stage has already attained equality with the angels. [See Luke 20:36.]
>
> At any rate, after he has reached the final ascent in the flesh, he still continues to advance, as is fit, and presses on through the holy Hebdomad [the seven planetary spheres] into the Father's house, to that which is indeed the Lord's abode ["In my Father's house are many mansions: if it were not so, I would have told you. I go to prepare a place for you," John 14:2], *being destined there to be, as it were, a*

light standing and abiding forever, absolutely secure from all vicissitude.[25] [my emphasis]

Clement's carrot for the questing donkey lay in maintaining the conviction that the one who had attained gnosis had not only become free of the vicissitudes of worldly constraint—that is to say, the Gnostic was "above all that"—but he had also become, in a profound sense, Self-determined. For Clement there really was a clear goal to be reached, and the essence of that goal could be realized in the flesh. Christ had demonstrated the possibility, and his teaching, properly understood, enabled its practicality: "Our Savior, in desiring that the gnostic should be perfect as the Father in heaven, that is, as himself— our Savior who says 'Come ye children and I will teach you the fear of the Lord'—desires that the gnostic should no longer need the help given through the angels, but being made worthy should receive it from himself and have his protection from himself by means of his obedience."[26]

The work of Clement helps us see that gnosis, as it grew in the once charmed city of Alexandria, could take many, and often happily conflicting, forms—Christian, Jewish, and pagan. Whatever the myths employed, the central experience remained constant: the realization that each human being contains a bright spark derived from a higher realm than that available to ordinary perception. Furthermore, this spark can, under discipline and through inspiration, be ignited with startling results in the life of the individual, with astonishingly creative results for all human endeavors.

Gnosis can be seen as a great light pulsing through time: a great underground stream or sacred river that flows ever onward, never resting. Its movement is nearly always unexpected; it helps its exponents see that the human story has not ended, that there is always farther and higher to go, that there is a great deal more in wait for humankind than we might hope for, and that our daily terrestrial vision is clouded by the mists of material obscurity.

"Let him who seeks continue seeking until he finds. When he finds he will become troubled. When he becomes troubled, he will be astonished, and he will rule over the All.[27]

"And being made like to those with whom he [the Anthropos] dwells, he hears the Powers, who are above the substance of the eighth sphere, singing praise to God with a voice that is theirs alone. And thereafter, each in his turn, they mount upward to the Father; they give themselves up to the Powers, and becoming Powers themselves, they enter into God. This is the Good; this is the consummation, for those who have got *gnosis*.

"And now, why do you delay? Seeing that you have received all, why do you not make yourself a guide to those who are worthy of the boon, that so mankind may through you be saved by God?" And when Poimandres had thus spoken to me, he mingled with the Powers.[28]

What characterizes the positive side of the gnostic experience is the insight that we have wings we will not use, a freedom we only dream about, a home we ignore, a fraternity we abuse, a love we will not share, and perhaps, above all, a giant within who is bound to the ground by our own spiritual blindness.

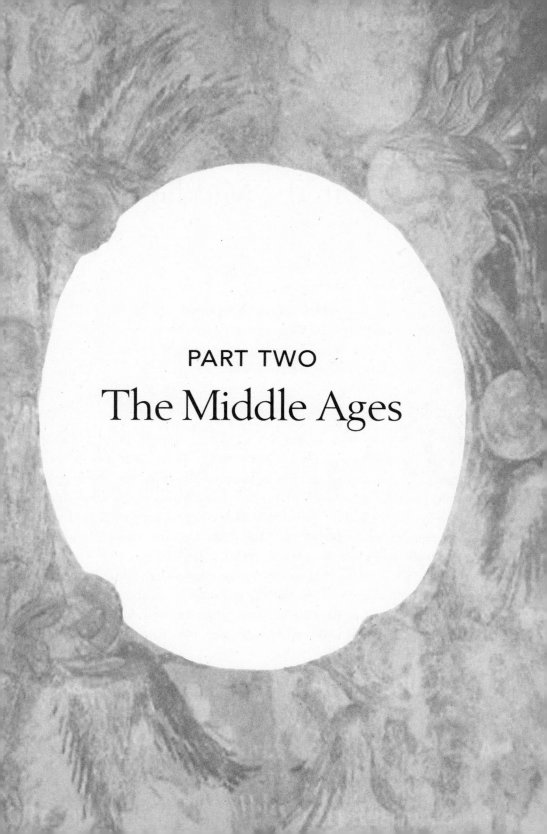

PART TWO

The Middle Ages

FOUR

Magic in the Middle Ages

Man is so infinitely small,
in all these stars: determinate;
Maker and moulder of them all,
Man is so infinitely great!

ALEISTER CROWLEY, "THE POET"

*D*espite the medieval church's appropriation of virtually every magical trick in the book—from the pagan festivals solemnized as Christmas and Easter to the dressing of wells, from the use of formerly pagan sacred places to the substitution of saints for the gods, together with the whole panoply of sacramental magic embodied in the liturgy—the quest for direct magical contact between humans and the unseen powers persisted.

The few who desired to experience the mysteries for themselves became both the inheritors and the transmitters of gnostic traditions. Medieval magic[1] in its highest phase became (along with Catharism, mysticism, alchemy, and Jewish Kabbalah) one of the five great channels of gnosis in the West.

The medieval period is often seen as a golden age of magic. Wizards and warlocks inhabit the popular imagination of the era. Who could forget the venerable Merlin of Malory's late romance, *Morte d'Arthur?* But how many know of Clinschor, the castrated sorcerer? This fantastic individual pops out not from a computer game, but from the pages of Wolfram von Eschenbach's *Parzifal* (early thirteenth century).

Described there as the duke of Terre de Labur, maternal nephew of Vergil of Naples, Clinschor's pursuit of his lover Iblis leads to castration. Not surprisingly, he develops a nasty side, compensating for his deficiency with supernatural potency—a good joke.

Magic in *Parzifal* is firmly linked to the execution of spectacular effects. The knight Gawan enters a mysterious palace upon a shining pavement as smooth and as clear as glass: "With his [Clinschor's] subtle lore he had brought the artifice applied to it from many lands." The palace also boasts an enormous pillar. Like a looking glass, the pillar can see everything within a six-mile radius, day or night. Clinschor's security system is "strong and burnished and so tall that Lady Camilla's sarcophagus might fittingly have rested upon it. Clinschor had brought this masterpiece from Feirefiz's lands." Feirefiz is Parzifal's Muslim half brother who is later baptized. Clinschor's magic certainly derives from the East, but whence in the East is ambiguous:

> I refer not to the land of Persia—it was in a place called Persida that magic was first contrived. Clinschor repaired there and procured the means of bringing to pass by enchantment whatever he fancies. Clinschor has the art of necromancy [conjuration] at his beck unfailingly, so that he can bind men and women with his spells. Of all the worthy people on whom his eye falls not one does he leave without trouble. Clinschor has power over all those beings that haunt the aether between earth's boundary and the firmament, the malign and the benign, except those under God's protection.[2]

While obviously an exotic, imaginary creation, Clinschor's abilities do not belong wholly to fiction; his skills derive from the Arabic world. This ties in with our knowledge of the transmission of Hermetic and Neoplatonist manuscripts from the Sabian translators of Harran and Baghdad to the West from the ninth to the eleventh centuries (the Sabians took the Gnostic *Hermetica* as their scripture).[3]

Clinschor's magic includes ray projection, an activity considered in the twelfth and thirteenth centuries to fall under the creditable discipline of "natural magic" by scholar-scientists such as Friar Roger Bacon, Arnold of Villanova, and Peter Abano. Natural magicians studied ray generation and light amplification, using mathematics and geometry. Clinschor would have recognized a modern physicist as a natural magician.

Wolfram also shows Clinschor's familiarity with the elementary, sublunary, and celestial worlds and their controlling demons. His powers do not, however, extend into the supercelestial realm, the world of archangelic powers, or to those whom these higher powers especially protect. This restriction is well in line with Neoplatonic theurgic lore, highly influenced by Gnostic cosmography.

Central to the mythology of early Gnosticism was the view of humankind imprisoned in a world populated by fallen psychic powers and dominated by hierarchies of archons. The archons personified the demonic powers of the stars; lords of fate, they were the grim guardians whose relative power held spiritual humans in thrall of matter, the realm of their secret dominion.

These powers were not necessarily evil in the modern sense of the word *satanic,* but they were certainly ambiguous from the point of view of the spirit, since they inhibited or even prohibited access of the spirit to its home in the One. Nevertheless, the normal pagan view was that such powers had legitimate control over every aspect of life on earth, and pagan Neoplatonists, as we shall see, recognized that paying these powers their due was necessary for the good health of their lower physical and psychic (soul) nature.

The medieval magus received the bulk of his knowledge of demonology from the late antique period and its philosophical justification from Neoplatonism.

NEOPLATONIC THEURGY

Familiarity with those old demons—and putting them in their place— was the stock-in-trade of the ancient theurgist. The theurgist was a practitioner of a spiritual philosophy (Neoplatonism) and ceremonial magic. The most important theurgic texts were created between the third and sixth centuries A.D.; their most significant authors were Porphyry, Iamblichus, and Proclus.

Porphyry, a follower of and apologist for the greatest Neoplatonic philosopher, Plotinus (b. A.D. 204), recognized that most devout pagans needed ceremonial, cultic affirmation of their position in the cosmos. He tried to reconcile the austere practice of pure philosophy (detachment from the body and absorption in the nous) with contemporary pagan cults. These cults were threatened by the rise of a Christianity that regarded them as idolatry.

Porphyry's reconciliation lay in theurgy or sacred magic, together with the so-called *Oracula Chaldaica* (Chaldean Oracles), fragments of which were available in the Middle Ages. The Oracles contained an eclectic mixture of Pythagorean and Stoic (Middle Platonist) doctrines, along with Persian, Babylonian, and Syrian material. Mithraic elements have also been observed. The word Chaldean was associated with the astronomer-priests of Babylonia discovered by the Greeks after Alexander's conquests. Together with the Egyptians, the Chaldean teachings were thought to represent the ancient wisdom of the East.

The fragments of *Chaldean Oracles* now available tell us something of the structure of the divine hierarchy, but little about the most characteristic gnostic doctrine of third- and fourth-century theurgy. This was the purification of the soul from the barnacles of matter and its raising to its source through magical ceremonies and sacred formulas.

Porphyry's attempt to reconcile philosophy and cult was beset by problems that stemmed partly from his devotion to Plotinus. According to Plotinus, the philosopher is one "who has penetrated the inner sanctuary, leaving behind him the images in the temple"[4]—a belief akin to Christ's dictum that God is a spirit and they that worship God must worship him in spirit and in truth.

Porphyry distinguished between the unclean magician with his worldly concerns (γοης = *goes*; hence *goetia*, black magic) and the divine human (θεός ανηρ, *theos aner*). In his *Epistola ad Anebonem*, Porphyry went so far as to say that theurgy was incompatible with Greek intellectualism, while the Christian Augustine quoted Porphyry that "those who have been purified in their spiritual soul by theurgic art cannot return to the Father."[5]

Porphyry tried to get around his difficulties by dividing the soul into different categories. This seems a typical Egyptian ruse, for in Porphyry's home territory gods could have as many aspects as explication deemed necessary. In *De regressu animae,* Porphyry granted that theurgy was a possible means of purifying the spiritual soul *(spiritalis anima)* and preparing it "to receive spirits and angels and to see gods,"[6] but denied that theurgy had any effect on the higher or intellectual (noetic) soul *(intellectualis anima)*.

The acute problem for Porphyry was that he wanted to keep his philosophical credibility intact while having to admit an inward efficacy derived from theurgy. He could not really get over the sticking point that a true follower of Plotinus's philosophy had already encompassed the magical. Porphyry's compromise was to assert that while the intellectual soul (Plotinus's nous, or "spirit") was capable of attaining the vision of the One, or the unity at the source of all phenomena, without theurgy, the practice nonetheless represented a possible first step in the soul's return to its source. This is rather akin to saying that if a nasty experience with a Ouija board gave a youth some idea that there was more to it than met the eye, then that experience might yet provide a first step to considering genuinely spiritual religion.

While Porphyry believed that a universal way to the One might be possible through a philosophical theurgy, he did not believe that the Chaldean or Egyptian sources he had consulted represented such a path. Iamblichus of Apamea, on the other hand, had no such qualms. For the Syrian Iamblichus, the synthesis of Egyptian, Chaldean, and "philosophical" (Greek) sources offered in his work *De mysteriis* did, in fact, offer the universal way vainly sought by Porphyry.

The work of Iamblichus and later Proclus (410–85) had an enormous impact on the magical tradition. It was absorbed into magical and natural philosophical texts emanating from Harran and Baghdad, often pseudonymously attributed to Aristotle, and passed over to the West in the Middle Ages from Arabic translations from Syriac and Greek and then translated into Latin for the delectation of nervous Western scholars. The gnostic thread in this transmission process is evident from the very first line of *De mysteriis,* where the primacy of Hermetic wisdom is asserted directly: "Hermes, the god who presides over learning, has for long been rightly regarded as common to all priests: he who presides over true knowledge [gnosis] about the gods is one and the same, whatever the circumstances. It was to him too that our ancestors dedicated the fruits of their wisdom, by placing all their own writings under his name."[7]

The theurgy transmitted to the Middle Ages included abundant material of Hermetic origin. Iamblichus claimed to have found his doctrine of pacifying the demons of the soul (to neutralize the passions of the body) in the Hermetic books, where the liberation of the soul from the bonds of Fate (that is, the star-demons, or archons) was many times described. It was due to the abundant but often fragmentary Hermetic material already transmitted in the Middle Ages that the arrival of the apparently complete *Corpus Hermeticum* in Florence in 1460 had such tremendous impact.[8] The ground had been prepared.

Iamblichus was convinced that the Hermetic writings, while having been translated into Greek by those familiar with Greek philosophy, had their origins in the ancient Thoth (Hermes) literature, the pristine wisdom of Egypt. Since the third-century Christian theologian Lactantius *(De divinis institutionibus)* had declared Hermes to be a prophet of Christianity (because the Hermetic writings refer to the "son of God" and describe God as "Father"), Hermetic sources gained respectable currency among Christian thinkers. Hermes' reputation, free of heresy, also helped in the assimilation of Neoplatonic texts.

That Neoplatonic texts showed respect for the figure of Hermes encouraged enthusiasts of such material in the Middle Ages to group magical material under the general authorship (origin) of either Hermes or Solomon, the latter dignified in both the Hebrew Bible and the New Testament. Nevertheless, even the Neoplatonists had some problems dealing with the demonology of Hermetic writings and its connection with a purely (or impurely) vulgar magic. This abiding problem seems to be due to the inescapable conclusion that magic in its intellectual phase bore within it essentially gnostic characteristics, and while it was the inherent gnosis of the *Hermetica* that appealed to the Neoplatonists, the two were really inseparable. It is difficult to escape the conclusion that gnostic theory in its primitive state derived from the ancient magical theories of Egypt and Mesopotamia; indeed, a gnosis without magical quality would be a pretty anemic affair.

Iamblichus himself was struck by a number of strands within the Hermetic writings that seemed to contradict the pagan and Plotinian view of the spiritual cosmos as wholly natural. The "alien" strain in *gnosis*—that humankind's essential nature is not really at home in the world but is suffering a bondage here—was discerned by Iamblichus in the following passage, and one feels that he found this strain unsettling: "The Egyptians do not say that all things are natural. They distinguish both the life of the soul (ψυχη, *psyche*) and that of the intellect (νους, *nous*) from the life of nature, and not just in the cosmic sphere, but as regards us (men) as well."[9]

Gnosis always bore within it these twin moods, first of pessimism regarding humankind's life in bondage to fate and to time and space (a late-Zarathushtrian but pre-Christian view) and second of optimism with regard to humankind's special place and potential in the full scheme of things. Even the orthodox Christian would have to agree that the coming of Christ would have been unnecessary were all well with the world as normally conceived.

Of course, the first explicit Gnostics were attempting to explain how it came to pass that humankind had become involved in such an ambivalent situation in the first place. How had humans gotten into the situation that the only solution to their predicament was to return to where they came from? Their answer, which the Neoplatonists found so difficult to swallow, was that the Pleroma[10] had been wounded by the dynamism of its inner tension and that humankind's existential woe was simply a by-product of the divine drama. However, humans could, through gnosis, participate in its healing.

In the Hermetic writings, gnosis is fundamentally the highest category of perception and the special necessity of the magus. The Hermetic texts gave dignity to the divine task of the magus: Follow the Thrice Greatest and make the link between heaven above and earth below. Know who you are; there is more to the human being than meets the eye. This is the positive message of the Hermetic magus, in the Middle Ages or at any other time.

The beliefs of the theurgists, handed over to the Western Middle Ages by the Sabians of Harran and Baghdad, preserved the realization that humans could be free agents within a divine cosmos. They could engage directly with cosmic powers; they shared in the being of the primal human, called Phōs, "Light." Humans were *in potentia* beings of light closed in a shell, and, like the gods who lived within them, were endowed with immortality and the spark of gnosis. If used properly, this divine knowledge could bring them out of a world of constraint and darkness into a world of freedom, love, light, and truth. This optimistic picture was necessarily held largely discreetly, not least because it stood in head-on collision with the Catholic Church's concept of original sin and purgatorial redemption.

Nevertheless, the Catholic Church held these works in her bosom, in the monasteries and in the libraries of the rich and the wise. In fact, Neoplatonism shaped the dogma and science of the medieval Church, and its study was encouraged, so long as the ultimate authority of the Church to decide on such matters and to control such study was respected.

CELESTIAL HIERARCHIES

The medieval world did not receive an orderly package of late antique philosophical and magical works. All too frequently the inheritance arrived in fragments and as part of copious and often confused compendia. The censor was never far away, and transmission was frequently filtered through anachronistic understanding and plain miscomprehension.

It was in an Irish monastery, as early as the ninth century, that the philosopher John Scotus Erigena translated the *Celestial Hierarchies* from Greek into Latin.[11] A work of fifth-century, possibly Christian, Neoplatonism, falsely ascribed to Dionysius the Areopagite (St. Paul's Athenian convert), the text adumbrates a vision of a tripartite system of heavenly hierarchies. Although deeply influenced by the cosmology of Gnosticism, it was accepted by St. Thomas Aquinas as authentic Christian theology, and thus had great impact, mapping out the supercelestial realms for hundreds of productive years.

While the author held a vigorous and highly influential theology of the *via negativa*—God can only be defined by what God is not, because God's being is unfathomable and indescribable—the hierarchy nonetheless outlined a system of positive knowledge of God-in-extension. God expresses Himself through a series of emanatory principles deriving from the "negative" One (cf. the kabbalists' Ain Soph and the unknowable *Bythos,* "Depth," of the Valentinian Gnostics).

According to the *Celestial Hierarchies,* the divine order consists in the unbroken descent of the divine being through three triads, each corresponding to a person of the Trinity. The supreme hierarchy of the Father consists of the Seraphs, the Cherubim, and the Thrones (cf. the *Hekhaloth* texts). The second triad of the Son consists of the Dominions, the Powers (or Virtues), and the Forces; the third triad consists of the Rulers (cf. the Gnostic archons), the Archangels, and the Angels.

This description of the divine expression was taken to be objective in the Middle Ages, and the system pervades works such as the *Summa theologiae* of St. Thomas Aquinas and the *Paradiso* of Dante. It became a blueprint for the magical ascent of the spirit to gnosis.

LIGHT METAPHYSICS

The works of Proclus and of Dionysius the Areopagite also contributed greatly to what Father F. C. Copleston has called the "light metaphysics" of the Middle Ages.[12] The central significance of the word *light* ought immediately to alert us to a gnostic presence. Light, illumination, the inner sun are perennial gnostic themes. The Nag Hammadi Gospel of Thomas, to take one of many examples, is full of the special understanding of the Gnostic as one who both sees and is in the light: "It is I who am the light which is above them all. If they say to you 'Where do you come from?' say to them, 'we came from the light.'. . . The images are manifest to man, but the light in them remains concealed in the image of the light of the Father. He will become manifest, but his image will remain concealed by his light."[13]

The Gnostic Christ is described as "the light which is in the light": a spiritual reality sustaining the visible aspect of God in the world. The true Gnostic is a person of the light and a light to the world; in the canonical Gospels, we are enjoined not to hide our light under a bushel.

The medieval world did not state this light theme so directly or so explicitly as did the authors of the Nag Hammadi library. However, the vestiges were there for those with the eyes to see them. In the Pseudo-

Dionysian corpus, God—the Neoplatonic One—is light itself: the spiritual and intelligible light, source of material light.

Light flows down to the world by gradation and diminution. Thus, the reverse ascent to the One was experienced as greater degrees of illumination. This theme was to have a great influence on natural philosophers such as the Franciscan Roger Bacon, and we can discern in his studies of physical light a groping for inner awareness of the "light which is in the light."

The philosophy of light goes back even further than the first explicit Gnostics—to Plato, in fact. In the *Republic* (517–18), the absolute good is said to be the source of light in the intelligible world (or sphere of being), and to be the parent or producer of the source of light—namely, the sun—in the visible world. (An extract from the *Republic* was also discovered, with some surprise, in the Nag Hammadi Gnostic library.) Interestingly, it was in a comment on this Platonic light idea that Proclus revealed what Garth Fowden sees as an essential kinship with the Hermetic and pious pagan practice generally of devoting a thrice-daily act of worship to the sun.[14] For Proclus, this act of devotion was a simile for the philosopher's encounter with the One.

In his *Theologia Platonica,* available in the Middle Ages, Proclus spoke of an encounter with "the sun of the light of the intelligible gods" as being like a prostration before the rising sun, when one shut one's corporeal eyes because of the sun's unbearable power and glory. Like the Hermetists, Proclus greeted this spectacle with a hymn of praise and thanksgiving for the paradoxical opening of the (inner) eyes. Such a hymn is preserved in the Nag Hammadi library and is of undoubted Hermetic provenance.[15]

From Baghdad via Spain came Thabit ibn Qurra's *De imaginibus* (Concerning the Imagination) on talismanic, Neoplatonist celestial magic and al-Kindi's important *De radiis* or *Theorica artium magicarum* (Concerning Rays; Theory of Magic Art): talismanic and liturgical magic in the context of a philosophy of causation based on the emanation of rays. Medieval light metaphysics was necessarily bound up with ray theory.

Abu Yusuf Ya'qub ibn Ishaq al-Kindi, the first Arab Muslim philosopher (born in 850 in the southern Arabian peninsula and educated in

Baghdad), also translated the *Uthulujiyya* (Theology) of Aristotle. This work was not by Aristotle but was in fact a commentary by Porphyry on books 4 to 6 of the *Enneads* of Plotinus, and was known in the West as the *Liber de causis,* or *Book of Causes.*

The book represents a kind of gnosticizing of Plotinus, describing the descent of the soul from the pure incorporeal realm of "intelligence" into the world of sense and corporeality. Showing conceptual kinship to the Valentinian myth of the yearning Sophia, the book reveals how the soul produces the world of perception out of its pain and desire to give form to the ideal or intellectual forms that are present to it.

The forms derive from the soul's origin in the active intellect of God the One. In short, the soul or spirit (*intellectus,* to the Latins in this context) creates reality. This gnostic theory of perception was to have great impact in the West for centuries and is currently being revived in the world of quantum physics as well as in the Continental philosophy of perception and optics.

Al-Kindi's *De radiis* was highly influential on two thirteenth-century geniuses: Friar Roger Bacon and Robert Grosseteste. It was particularly influential because it tried to explain through a natural philosophy that astral and other magical effects could be understood without demonology, through the propagation of astral and other "natural" rays.

The theory of this "natural magic" runs as follows: The nature of a star is emitted as a ray. All terrestrial events are the product of a total harmony of rays in the heavens, a view frequently blended with both geometry and the more mystical light metaphysics. Events could be shown as having "natural," not demonic, causes, the basis for the natural magicians' defense against the imputation of vulgar magic leveled against them.

Robert Grosseteste interpreted al-Kindi's work as grounds for believing that the essence of light is the formative and structural principle of the universe. According to Grosseteste, in a striking conceptual premonition of Einstein's famous formula ($E = mc^2$), the universe is the result of the union of formless prime matter and "light," of which visible light is only an aspect. Our word *radiation,* of course, is derived from the idea of astral rays.

Grosseteste believed that a point of "light" can produce a sphere of any size—again a striking premonition of the hidden potential within the atom—and that light formed the basis of spatial dimension and physical extension. Thus, humans' essential being was *light,* a somewhat gnostic view. For Grosseteste, light was the principle and model for all natural operations, including the emanation of species and the virtues of things; as with light, all causes of natural effects operate by lines, angles, and figures. The differences among phenomena depend on the laws of optics, geometry, and perspective.

Geometric optics thus became the basis for a mathematical philosophy of nature, affecting and effecting everything, including astrology. For example, a stellar virtue was understood to act more strongly when concentrated rather than when diffused through refraction or reflection, or when striking perpendicularly rather than obliquely, due to the numerically lower angles of incidence of those rays when reaching the earth.

Astral influences were regarded not as occult forces or demonic powers but as rays that behaved as light. Thus, mathematics had become a divine science, or science of the divine. The full implications of this shift in perspective would have to wait until the seventeenth century for its fulfillment in the scientific revolution.[16] Nevertheless, Grosseteste's universe was still magical, but the magic was determined by an understanding of mathematical and physical laws. The deterministic power of the stars had been theoretically overcome by the illumination gained by knowledge of their mathematical nature. Knowledge was empowering. Gnostic-influenced manuscripts oversaw the birth of natural magic, the critical stage before the birth of modern science, the latter rejecting its mother in infancy.[17]

However cogent the scientific defense against imputations of sorcery might appear to us, the magical and Neoplatonic context of the emerging science ensured opposition. Neoplatonic protocols for dealing with spiritual powers were retained in the Middle Ages because medieval magic owed virtually everything to the development of magic in the late antique period. Paradoxically, just as the higher magic of the Middle Ages was transported practically intact from the late antique Greco-Roman and Greco-Egyptian worlds, so the formula for its condemnation was also transported from that world. The old conflict between church and magic was simply taken out of mothballs and replayed.

AFTER THE PACT

It was on the basis of the demonology of the late antique age, and in its developed form among the Neoplatonists, that Augustine (d. 430) developed the very doctrine that would condemn the practitioners of that doctrine's source.

Augustine believed that the efficacy of magical effects in the pagan world was due to the intervention of demons. Following from this premise, all magical practices, words, and gestures formed a series of signs, comparable to human language but particularly audible to demons.

In the Christian itinerary, demons were understood as devils, servitors of the Antichrist—with the added irony that that is pretty much how the radical Christian Gnostics saw the issue as well! According to Augustine (*De doctrina Christiana* II), the condition for communication between human and demon was the making of a contract effected by the signification of magic signs.

Thomas Aquinas (d. 1274) was inspired by Augustine's pact doctrine and transformed it into a systematic base for a theory of superstition. By amplifying the Augustinian doctrine through a distinction between intentional contracts and tacit contracts with demons, Thomas established for each superstitious manifestation the "fact" of a demonic pact.

In the thirteenth-century commentaries on the *Sentences* (of Peter Lombard), elaboration of this doctrine of contracts took place, stressing the apostasy involved in demonic pacts. We now begin to see the emergence of the Western image of the secretive, sinister sorcerer, bound by baleful pacts:

> They set themselves up as prophets by practicing the pronunciation of holy names, or sometimes they only direct their attention upon them without actually pronouncing the words. Then a man is seized by ter-

ror and his body sinks to the ground. The barrier in front of his soul falls, he himself steps into the center and gazes into the faraway, and only after a while, when the power of the name recedes, does he awaken and return with a confused mind to his former state.

This is exactly what the magicians do who practice the exorcism of the demons. They conjure one from their midst with unclean exorcisms, in order that he may tell them what has perhaps been happening in a faraway country. The conjurer falls down on the ground where he was standing and his veins become cramped and stiff, and he is as one dead. But after a while he rises without consciousness and runs out of the house, and if one does not hold him at the door he would break his head and his limbs. Then when he again becomes a little conscious of himself, he tells them what he has seen.[18]

This extraordinary description comes from the pen of Moses Taku, possibly from Tachau in Germany, writing in the early thirteenth century. He is describing the activities of kabbalistic magicians. A pious disciple of Jehudah the Hasid, Moses Taku did not approve.

KABBALISTIC MAGIC

In the middle of the last century, Gershom Scholem demonstrated beyond all reasonable doubt not only that Kabbalah ("received tradition") could be rightly described as Jewish Gnosticism, but also that its practice was inherently bound up with magical ideas and, sometimes, practices.[19]

The link with magic is evidently through the stress on the power of names, of words—to wit, the seventy-two names of God (God's projected "virtues": that is, in magical understanding, God's nature). To have the *name* is to share the power of the essence of the thing itself. Chanting, meditation, and certain kinds of prayer all share the magical belief in the efficacy of words. While today words float about from the tongue like airy cotton candy, words and the knowledge of grammar and language held magical powers for the medieval magician and gnostic contemplative.

Their framework was that of the mystical ascent, directly parallel to Neoplatonic and Gnostic spiritual ascent formulas, and was to be found in what is called Merkabah ("chariot" or "throne") mysticism, described in the Hekhaloth texts deriving from Mesopotamian and Palestinian Jews.

The mystical journey also used magical seals to ward off the opposition of the gatekeepers. These figures are analogous to the Gnostic archons, the guardians of the celestial spheres who bound not only the earth without, but also the spirit of God within. This ascent was always preceded by ascetic practices of purification to avoid archontic or demonic influences and attraction. The purification process could last twelve days, or forty.

Here is an account of these practices given by Hai ben Sherira, head of the Babylonian academy, in about A.D. 1000:

> Many scholars were of the belief that one who is distinguished by many qualities described in the books and who is desirous of beholding the Merkabah [corresponding to the Gnostic Pleroma], and the palaces of the angels on high, must follow a certain procedure. He must fast a number of days and lay his head between his knees and whisper many hymns and songs whose texts are known from tradition. Then he perceives the interior and the chambers, as if he saw the seven palaces with his own eyes, and it is as though he entered one palace after the other and saw what is there.[20]

Accounts of the aeons encountered on such journeys made their way from Baghdad and Syria to Provence. There, systematic attempts were made to edit them in the twelfth century, in works such as *Bahir,* the oldest kabbalist text, based partly on the highly esteemed work *Raza Rabba,* or Great Mystery, known to be extant in the East in the tenth century and permeated by Hebrew Gnostic quotations.

Other important works that formed the basis for mystical and magical practice were grouped in a work called *Maaseh Bereshith,* which included the highly significant and brief (no more than 1,600 words) *Sefer Yetsirah* (Book of Creation).

Thought to have been written between the third and sixth centuries, and clearly demonstrating Gnostic influence on speculative Jewish circles, the work outlined a theory of everything, based on the ten primordial numbers—the Sefiroth—and the twenty-two letters of the Hebrew alphabet. From these "thirty-two paths of wisdom" kabbalists believed God made all: a total system without beginning or end.

The Sefiroth were understood not merely as numbers of scale but also as living, creative beings whose manifold combinations in harmony with the twenty-two paths explained all possible manifestations in the cosmos, providing contemplative routes for the soul to actively philosophize or contemplate in.

In the systems derived from this work, all ascending paths that led to God were also God in extension. Through contemplation, the soul was transported spiritually into the creative mind of God. The *Sefer Yetsirah* was highly influential on the development of magic in the Middle Ages.

The theory of the paths, linked to the divine names, promised access to higher levels of cognition and power. There is in the *Merkabah* literature, for example, evidence of a specific rite: the putting on, or clothing, of the name. In this ceremonial rite the magician impregnated himself with the tetragrammaton (the holy name of God: Y H W H) by clothing himself in a garment into which the name was woven.

The magician then sought knowledge, such as an explanation of obscure elements of the Law (Torah, which has a prince or archon called Sâr Torah), or other information, such as the secret of heaven and earth. Other questions might concern the dimensions of the Demiurge (sometimes called Metatron) and those secret magical names that were thought to give power over all things.

In his classic *Major Trends in Jewish Mysticism,* Gershom Scholem gave the example of Jacob Halevi of Marvège, who in about 1200 posed "dream questions" *(sheeloth halom)* to higher beings to obtain answers on controversial parts of the Torah. These practices were, like Sufic meditations, frequently accompanied by ecstatic experiences as the magicians left their egos behind them.

As we might expect, conservative minds were not always convinced that it was angelic powers that were doling out the magical goods. Moses Taku, as we have seen above, strongly disapproved, dubbing the practices heretical.

Such criticisms influenced the pioneering kabbalist Abraham ben Samuel Abulafia, born in Saragossa in 1240. Abulafia had led a remarkably adventurous life, traveling to Syria as a youth on a mystic quest to find the legendary stream Sambation and the ten lost tribes of Israel.

He developed a practical Kabbalah, the Path of the Names, employing the seventy-two names of God, the twenty-two letters, the ten numbers, and that array of techniques which constituted the tools of the later kabbalist trade. These techniques were Gematria, the calculation of the numerical value of Hebrew words, combined with their association with other words or phrases of equal value; *Notarikon,* the interpretation of the letters of a word, or reducing whole sentences to key letters; and *Temurah,* the interchange of significant letters.

Abulafia expressly condemned the use of his practical Kabbalah for magical purposes or purposes of an external nature; he regarded magic as a perversion of mysticism. However, the works already mentioned, and indeed those of Abulafia himself (particularly his doctrine of combination, *Hokhmath ha-tseruf*), were used with various degrees of respect by magicians to obtain sensory results in addition to revelatory contemplation.

The reason this temptation was so strong was inherent chiefly in the ascent theories themselves. If the natural universe constituted the expression of inner or occult dynamics, then it was a short step from contemplating those dynamics to actually calling upon their powers to make changes in the manifest world. The essential problem for Abulafia was that the mystical dynamics were already built on gnostic magical systems.

Ancient magical beliefs had profoundly shaped the Gnostic cosmology, and while the process was later interactive, it was impossible to dismiss the magic without dismissing the vitality of the mysticism. Attempting to purify natural or licit magical systems of demonic magic has been an activity of gnostic-influenced theorists and practitioners throughout history—hence, for example, the requirements of moral and physical purification attendant on all initiatic systems. It might be possible to build a high wall about your path, but you could be sure that those old demons were peering over the top to see what you were up to.

ROGER BACON

Fear of those old demons would certainly come to haunt the activities of the "English Leonardo," Roger Bacon. Bacon has been claimed as both a father of modern science and, spuriously, a Rosicrucian Brother, handing on the torch of pristine Egyptian wisdom to succeeding generations.

Bacon was born in about 1215, studied arts at Oxford, and went in 1236 or 1237 to Paris, where he lectured on the *Physics* and *Metaphysics* of Aristotle. While in Paris, he wrote about al-Kindi's translation of Porphyry's Plotinus commentaries, thus fusing Aristotelian philosophy with Neoplatonism. In 1247 he returned to Oxford, where he wrote his *Opus maius, Opus minus,* and *Opus tertium*—respectively, his Greater Work, his Lesser Work, and his Third Work—on which the greater part of our knowledge of Bacon's thought relies.

In 1277 or 1278 he was sentenced to confinement by Jerome of Ascoli, the Franciscan minister general, for "suspected novelties"—a phrase suggesting the whiff of heresy or studies that went beyond the limits of ecclesiastical tolerance. He was certainly suspected of "magic," with all that that suspicion entailed. He died in Oxford in 1292 while writing a theological compendium.

Bacon rejected magic as a religious rite in his *Opus tertium,* using al-Kindi's theory of rays, which offered naturalistic explanations for the power of words, chants, and incantations. As we have seen, many Arabic texts of Aristotelian natural philosophy were favorable to the occult sciences as a kind of applied science.

Bacon joined William of Auvergne, Albertus Magnus, and other contemporaries in interpreting a variety of magical effects as the result of natural causes, part of God's order. While Albertus Magnus boldly used the expression "natural magic," Bacon himself felt obliged to refer to "magnificent sciences" or "marvelous works of art and nature."

Bacon had a unified conception of knowledge and believed in the unity of all sciences (deriving from the One). He argued for a *scientia experimentalis,* an open survey and quest for knowledge based more on experience than on purely received tradition (a dangerous principle from the orthodox point of view), and that brought together different disciplines, including spiritual experience and divine illumination.

Indeed, a thorough knowledge of nature was thought by Bacon to be a path to divine illumination, to gnosis. Thus the study of rays of light could lead to the inner realization of the source of light and the universality, interconnectedness, and mutual dependence of all natural phenomena.

Because the harmony of all things was thought to express the One behind all phenomena, technology should be free to use diverse principles, as well as hitherto unsuspected or hidden powers of nature, to produce new effects. Bacon is credited, for example, with the idea of a flying machine. The study of nature could make humans visionaries.

Bacon was aware that this approach was likely to scandalize the academics of his time but argued that many useful sciences had been needlessly condemned and become illegitimate due to the confusion by early Christian theologians of natural philosophy with vulgar (or demonic) magic. This critique of the theological fathers of the Church challenged the authority of the existing church and got Bacon into deep trouble. However, he could not deny what his eyes revealed to him; he knew he was not alone—others had trod the path before him.

For example, Bacon was deeply inspired by the occult and pseudo-Aristotelian *Secretum secretorum,* a text that contained a vision of a unified knowledge that reflected the unity of the created world. This vision would be passed on to Elias Ashmole and the first endeavors of the Royal Society four hundred years later. (The modern, perhaps less glittering, version of this insight is that of "holistic" theory—the wholeness of mind and explicate nature.)

In the *Secretum secretorum,* the occult sciences of astrology, alchemy, and magic are regarded as integral to this experiential knowledge, due to the belief that the terrestrial world is governed by the celestial and supercelestial worlds. Thanks to this divine sympathy (kindred nature, or holistic medium) or correspondence, this knowledge could be beneficial to humankind—especially since "Aristotle" had made, to Bacon's eyes, the One identical with the Good. Magic for Bacon was a quality inherent in the divine creation. He was one of the first in the Latin West to utilize the *Secretum secretorum,* and he attended more to its occult sections than to its political advice.

Bacon, like the Elizabethan John Dee after him, was very impressed by the special relation of Aristotle to Alexander the Great—the philosopher as guide to the great power—and saw this as a proper role for himself. This undoubtedly made, him contemptuous of academic knowledge for the sake of academe and earned him greater suspicion. The idea that a state ruler should have at his disposal the benefits of science for the good of his rule was certainly an advanced view and looked forward to such ideals as the original (mythic) Rosicrucian Fraternity and the actual Royal Society. Indeed, Bacon was full of ideas that seem to us out of context in the thirteenth century.

For example, the idea of an ancient theology that predated Christianity as an organized church and which went back to the Egyptians and Chaldeans is a view normally associated with the Hermetic impulse stemming from Marsilio Ficino and Pico della Mirandola, among other Renaissance figures.

Bacon associated Aristotle with the tradition of ancient theology revealed by God to Enoch (whom Bacon identified with Hermes, following the Harranian Sabian pattern) and passed on to Aristotle through the Egyptians and Chaldeans. Although the original unity of that ancient theology had been lost, Bacon believed that it could be recovered through study and divine illumination.

Again, like his successor John Dee, Bacon believed that the study of languages was crucial to this aim of restoring the long-gone pristine theology. Bacon stressed the importance of studying Hebrew and Greek as well as Latin and other languages to discover the ultimate grammar and lost Word: the original creative breath, or spirit of God. The Word had made the creation possible; its vestiges could still be seen in the interrelatedness of the natural world and in the divinely natural scheme of rays that for al-Kindi, Grosseteste, and Roger Bacon constituted the created world.

Roger Bacon was certainly caught up in a divine vision of the cosmos, transcending appearances, and he was definitely interested in finding ways of making this vision work for the good of humankind. He stood for the dignity of human beings as active and not passive participants in a magical and orderly universe. To this degree he fulfilled the Hermetic vision outlined in the Latin *Asclepius* of the human as the great miracle whose consciousness may extend from the natural to the divine realms, the two worlds sundered only in perception. The inspired scientist could put this sympathy into practice; he could *operate*. This was new freedom, and it was dangerous.

Bacon stood for freedom of the mind in a world of oppression and ecclesiastical mind control; his work was not forgotten. Nicholas Clulee has shown how much John Dee and the English Renaissance owed to Roger Bacon and to the medieval magical tradition as a whole.[21] In fact, Clulee has demonstrated that Dee's major line of philosophical and magical tradition stems not so much, as had been thought, from Renaissance Hermetism as it does from the earlier medieval practical and operative tradition whose quintessential exponent was Roger Bacon.

In 1557, Dee wrote the *Speculum unitatis: Sive apologia pro fratre Rogerio Bachone anglo* (The Mirror of Unity, or a Defense of the English Brother Roger Bacon), a treatise on cosmic unity that would find its apotheosis in Dee's great *Monas hieroglyphica* (1564).

The work was at pains to defend Bacon's reputation from the imputation that he had been involved with demons and vulgar magic. Dee also suffered from this slander, and he seems to have identified closely with Roger Bacon's quest for a science that brought out the secrets of God's creative mind. God's creative mind (Logos) was reflected in the human being's own mind (nous), which had the potential to go beyond the stars to the incorporeal light Dee believed lay at the invisible heart of all that is.

Dee was as fascinated as Bacon was by the magical manuscripts available in his time. Both men had come to the limits of physical science in their time, and they both felt that this was not enough. Physical science seemed only to skim the surface of reality, while a greater cosmos lay beyond their reach. In attempting to gain a mental picture and operative grasp of the great unknown, they were drawn to the whole range of technical knowledge presided over by Hermes Trismegistus, the prophet of the Sabians.

The Sabians themselves, who had provided the medieval magi with so much literary and technical inspiration, lived in Baghdad as a separate sect until about 1050, seeing out the decline of the golden age inaugurated by the great caliphs (al-Mansur, ar-Rashid, and al-Ma'mún).

Shortly before 950, the Buwayhids took over the
Baghdad; a period of strictly enforced Islamic orthod/
ing until the coming of the Seljuks in 1055. Explicit ɪ.
underground—or perhaps devotees simply changed their hie.
name from Hermes to Muhammad.

It is certainly strange that at the very time the Sabians seem to disappear from Baghdad, the Hermetic documents known to us as the
Corpus Hermeticum appear in Constantinople—after a five-hundred-
year interval—in the hands of the Platonic scholar Psellus. As Walter
Scott (d. 1925), a translator of the *Hermetica,* wrote in his introduction
to that work: "Is there not something more than chance in this?" What
we now know as the *Corpus Hermeticum* may be no more than a
chance collection of what was brought to Constantinople by a Sabian
to escape destruction.

Although conjectural, said Scott, "there is nothing to prevent us
from supposing that it was the arrival in Constantinople of a few such
Sabian Neoplatonists from Baghdad, and the writing which they
brought with them, that first started the revival of Platonic study in
which Psellus took the leading part."[22] Such an occurrence would certainly be strikingly similar to that by which the *Corpus Hermeticum*
arrived in Florence from Macedonia with such epoch-marking
momentousness in 1460, following the fall of Constantinople to the
Turks in 1453.

Can it be complete external coincidence that the disappearance of
the Baghdad Sabians also coincides with the appearance of the first
great Sufi order, in Baghdad, in the form by which the *turuq* (paths) of
Sufi mysticism are now known?

Sufism is the gnosis of Islam.

FIVE

The Sufis

Thou art the sea of knowledge hidden
in a dewdrop; thou art the universe
hidden in a body three ells long.

JALAL-UD-DIN RUMI, *MATHNAWI* 6.3579

he name Sufi first appears in the late tenth century in Mesopotamia. The word seems to be derived from the Arabic *tasawwuf,* usually meaning "to wear wool *(suf),*" pure wool, like the Jewish and Christian ascetics, like John the Baptist, like the Mandaeans of Harran and Baghdad.

A Sufi order or brotherhood is called a *tariqa* ("path"), a path to *haqiqa,* the inward reality. The first great Sufi order to have appeared in the form in which the *turuq* are now known was the Qadiri tariqa, from its founder Shaikh (spiritual master) Abd al-Qadir al-Jilani (1078–1166). This order was an offshoot of the older Junaidi tariqa, the path that stemmed from the great Abu'l-Qasim al-Junaid of Baghdad, who died nine years after Thabit ibn Qurra (A.D. 910).

Among the next to appear was the Suhrawardi tariqa, founded by Shitab ad-Din as-Suhrawardi (c. 1144–1234). Suhrawardi is the only writer in Arabic of the period who we know of to display considerable knowledge of the *Hermetica.* He writes that he "finds himself in agreement" with Hermes, as well as Plato. He says that "it can be proved" of Hermes that he saw "the spiritual world" (τα νοητα, *ta noeta*). This proof almost certainly derives from passages in the *Hermetica* where

144

Hermes Trismegistus speaks of seeing God or things incorporeal "with the eye of the mind" (nous). This stress on the noetic faculty is also typical of Sufic aspiration. In Suhrawardi's work *The Wisdom of Illumination*, we are told:

> Although before the composition of this book I composed several summary treatises on Aristotelian philosophy, this book differs from them and has a method peculiar to itself. All of its material has not been assembled by thought and reasoning; rather, intellectual intuition, contemplation and ascetic practices have played a large role in it. Since our sayings have not come by means of rational demonstration but by inner vision and contemplation, they cannot be destroyed by the doubts and temptations of the sceptics. Whoever is a traveller on the road to truth is my companion and aid on this path. The procedure of the master of philosophy and imam of wisdom, the divine Plato, was the same, and the sages who preceded Plato in time, like Hermes, the father of philosophy, followed the same path.[1]

Suhrawardi was by no means the first to see how the monism of the Islamic revelation could accommodate the Hermetic doctrine. The philosopher al-Kindi (d. c. 873) wrote that he had seen a book whose teaching was accepted by the pagans of Harran, treatises "which Hermes wrote for his son" and which showed "the unity of God"—a key Islamic doctrine.

The Sufis aspire to *baqa* (pure "subsistence," beyond all form), preceded by the extinction (*al fana*) of the individuality or ego. They claim to go back to the Prophet Muhammad by an unbroken chain of initiation. Everything that nourishes them, they say, is justified by the Qur'an. The Qur'an certainly contains the raw materials for a mystical theology:

> He is the first and the last and the outward and the inward. (57:3)

> Verily, We have created man and We know what his soul suggests to him, for we are nigher unto him than the neck-artery. (50:15)

> Allah is the Light of the heavens and the earth. (24:35)

Professor R. A. Nicholson asserts, "It is right to regard the Sufis as esoteric students of the Qur'an, but not, I think, to see in Sufism the pure result of Qur'anic study."[2] It might be said of the Sufis that they believe that whatever initiated the Prophet initiated them, the difference being one of degree.

According to Titus Burckhardt, the Sufis hold "the Lord Jesus (Sayyidna 'Isa) of all the divine envoys *(rusul)* preceding the Prophet to be the most perfect type of contemplative saint. To offer the left cheek to him who smites one on the right is true spiritual detachment; it is a voluntary withdrawal from the interplay of cosmic actions and reactions."[3] In other words, the prophets of God are Sufis.

The Sufis endeavored and endeavor to experience the Prophet's mystical experience for themselves. If, as they claim, the aim or means of Sufism involves *ma'rifa* (gnosis), then it would be logical to suppose, from the Sufic point of view, that the Prophet of Islam's vision must have been, in some sense, gnostic as well.

THE INSIGHTS OF SUFISM

In the first place, the spirit *(ar-Ruh)* and the soul *(an-nafs)* are seen as being in conflict for possession of the essential faculty *al-qalb,* the heart, their common "son." An-nafs, the soul (like the Demiurge or ego of the cosmoclastic Gnostics), mistakenly takes herself to be an autonomous whole, and, through this arrogation of supremacy, can veil al-qalb.

The soul is an accomplice of the world (a negative conception of the Stoic psyche) and is subject to the world's passions and tremors (like the archontic spheres that envelop the pneuma [spirit] of the Alexandrian Gnostic). The spirit, ar-Ruh, is simply above all that. The hope of the Sufi is that the spirit gains victory over the soul, and that the heart be transformed into spirit, while at the same moment transmuting the soul, suffusing her with spiritual light. Then is the heart revealed to be what it really is: a tabernacle *(mishkat)* of the divine mystery *(sirr)* in humans.

Haqiqa, inner truth/reality, is regarded by Sufis as being at the very heart of the Islamic revelation. The Prophet had after all (c. A.D. 620) been taken on a visionary night journey from Mecca to Jerusalem, and thence to the seventh heaven.

In spite of the stress on inner experience, the Sufis nevertheless enjoy a particular vision of the necessity of the *shari'a* (the outward law). They regard the law as the vehicle or expression of the *haqiqa*. While outwardly conforming, they enjoy inward freedom. This view has caused external problems for Sufis. The inward life tends to overflow in ecstasy—and ecstasy and law do not make easy partners. The first great victim of Sufi enthusiasm was al-Hallaj, who, realizing humankind's—and in particular his own—essential identity with the divine principle, declared: "I am the Truth"—*ana'l-Haqq*.

Al-Hallaj was a victim of his success. On the principle that God can be known only when the ego is extinguished before the infinity of God, in accordance with the words "There is no divinity but God," al-Hallaj experienced gnosis. In his work *Kitabu'l-Tawasin,* al-Hallaj conceived of mystical union as union with the Creative Word *Kun:* Be! He had submitted to God and found the victory of the Light. He was crucified in Baghdad in 922. The last words of this saintly man are recorded as follows: "And these Thy servants who are gathered to slay me, in zeal for Thy religion and in desire to win Thy favour, forgive them, O Lord, and have mercy upon them; for verily if Thou hadst revealed to them that which Thou hast revealed to me, they would not have done what they have done; and if Thou hadst hidden from me that which Thou hast hidden from them, I should not have suffered this tribulation. Glory unto Thee in whatsoever Thou doest, and glory unto Thee in whatsoever Thou willest!"[4]

In the words of R. A. Nicholson, the crime of al-Hallaj was "not that he divulged the mystery of the Divine Lordship but that in obedience to an inward call he proclaimed and actively asserted a truth which involves religious, political and social anarchy."[5] Al-Hallaj had written:

Betwixt me and Thee there lingers an "It is I" that torments me.
Ah, of Thy grace, take this "I" from between us!
I am He whom I love, and He whom I love is I,
We are two spirits dwelling in one body.
If thou seest me, thou seest Him,
And if thou seest Him, thou seest us both.[6]

Al-Hallaj had become the "great miracle" that is Man, spoken of in the Hermetic dialogue of *Asclepius*—and he paid the price for speaking out. Had not Hermes prophesied that "the good man will be punished like a criminal"? From the legal point of view, of course, al-Hallaj had simply overstepped the mark. He had permitted his inward truth to overwhelm the outward law. This distinction between outward law and inward truth does not exist in traditional Christianity.

Sufism does share with Christianity the path of love *(mahabba)*, but adds the way of gnosis *(ma'rifa)*. As stated earlier, the essential organ of cognition in Sufism is not the brain, but the heart—a throne for the intellect (understood as the spirit or mind of God, corresponding to the Hermetic nous), which transcends mental or rational forms.

Sufism sees the tragedy of humanity in a way typologically similar to that of the gnosis of the late antique period. The ego, obsessed with the visible, tangible, and apparently objective world, deflects the heart from its true center, rooted in the Eternal. Thus the consciousness of people in their ordinary state is as if imprisoned in a kind of dream state, an amnesia or state of forgetfulness *(ghafla)*. "Wake up!" is the perennial cry of the gnostic prophet.

The Sufi medicine for this state is known as *dhikr,* meaning "recollection" or "mindfulness," as well as "contemplation" or "invocation." *Awareness* would be most succinct.

Starting from *dhikr* as a repetition of the name of Allah, the Sufis worked out a *via purgativa et illuminativa* (path of purification and illumination), predisposing the soul to attain to the gnosis, defined as "knowledge of the attributes of the divine unity, peculiar to the saints who behold God with their hearts."

The mysterious (and legendary) Egyptian Dhu'l-Nun has been held responsible (probably mistakenly) for introducing gnosis into Islamic mysticism. How did Dhu'l-Nun know God? "I know Him through Himself," he asserted, and "God is the opposite of anything you can imagine"; "The more one knows God, the more one is lost in Him."[7]

It is significant that Dhu'l-Nun was Egyptian, for Egypt was to the learned Arabs of this period the birthplace of alchemy. As alchemy became the covert vehicle of occidental gnosis, alchemical imagery was

employed in Sufism to describe the practice of dhikr. In the alch
expression of Sufism, the soul (in its unenlightened condition) is '
The Divine Name Allah works as the philosopher's stone. When the
stone contacts the soul, it transmutes the leaden mass into "gold": a
return to its true but lost nature. The world is full of lost pearls, everywhere to be found but seldom seen.

Alchemists of the Western Middle Ages regarded the *Tractatus
aureus*—a notable alchemical text attributed to Hermes—as being of
Arabic origin. Professor Jung noticed its remarkable resemblance to
"the mysterious happenings of Eastertide," yet clothed in purely
alchemical terms. The humble yet divine stone is found in matter and
psychically redeemed therefrom:

> Our precious stone, that was cast upon the dung-heap, is altogether
> vile. . . . But when we marry the crowned king with the red daughter,
> she will conceive a son in the gentle fire, and shall nourish him
> through our fire. . . . Then is he transformed, and his tincture remains
> red as flesh. Our son of the royal birth takes his tincture from the fire,
> and death, darkness, and the water flee away. The dragon shuns the
> light of the sun, and our dead son shall live. The king shall come forth
> from the fire and rejoice in the marriage. The hidden things shall be
> disclosed, and the virgins will be whitened. The son is become a war-
> rior fire and surpasses the tincture, for he himself is the treasure and
> himself is attired in the philosophic matter. Come hither, ye sons of
> wisdom, and rejoice, for the dominion of death is over, and the son
> reigns; he wears the red garment, and the purple is put on.[8]

The Sufi gnosis makes it necessary to assert that in terms of primacy, the spirit must always gain ascendancy over the letter; morality
is not everything. The spiritual person, when active, frequently finds
himself or herself in tension with external law. The Sufis partially
resolve the conflict by seeing the law as an expression of the spiritual
will of God. Islam means submission to Allah, not to people. For the
Sufi, *submission* means submission to the divinity within, which is held
to be the most sublime exaltation. The law cannot touch a person
whose ego has been conquered by the light of the spirit.

The Persian Sufi Abu Yazid of Bistam developed the doctrine of *fana:* the passing away of the false self (ego), with its positive counterpart, *baqa,* the unitive life in God. Among the sayings attributed to him are: "Creatures are subject to 'states,' but the gnostic has no 'state,' because his vestiges are effaced and his essence is noughted by the essence of Another and his traces are lost in Another's traces"; "I say that I am my own mirror, for 'tis God that speaks with my tongue, and I have vanished."[9]

The working out of this Sufic doctrine of unity was undertaken systematically by the great Sufi master Muhyi-d-Din ibn 'Arabi. Ibn 'Arabi was a thoroughgoing monist whose doctrine was succinctly expressed in the Arabic phrase *wahdatu'l-wujud,* the unity of existence. His doctrine is packed with gnostic dynamics: All things preexist as ideas in the knowledge of God, whence they emanate and whither they will eventually return; the world is merely the outward aspect of that whose inward aspect is God.

The human being is the microcosm in whom all the divine attributes are veiled. In human beings alone does Allah become fully conscious of Himself—a gnostic idea that would reappear in the philosophy of Hegel six hundred years later. Ibn 'Arabi fused Gnosticism, Christianity, Neoplatonism, and Islam into what is essentially a Logos doctrine. Instead of naming the Logos Jesus or the Hermetic Poimandres, the creative mind of God is named Muhammad: the perfect man *(al-Insan al-Kamil)* and cosmic principle by which the world is assimilated and sustained.

According to Ibn 'Arabi, Muhammad's spiritual essence was the first thing God created, being conceived as a celestial light *(nur Muhammadi),* which entered into Adam and into the prophets after him until the light's definitive human appearance in Muhammad himself. According to the Shiites, his light then passed to Muhammad's brother 'Ali and the imams of his house. The Sunnis believe that the Prophet represented the culmination of the process; the Sufis believe it to be immanent in the saints.

Ibn 'Arabi, much like a Christian Platonist such as Thomas Aquinas, identifies Muhammad in his real nature with the "idea of ideas," a phrase used by the third-century Origen of the Logos and identified with the "Active Intellect" (nous) and First Cause of Aristotle. This universalist vision thrusts Ibn 'Arabi into a cosmic conception of humankind and of human potential. He applies the word Kalima (Logos) to both Jesus and Muhammad, although not exclusively, and maintains that even infidels and idolaters are made in God's image and are God's servants. Compassion should override law. Islam for Ibn 'Arabi is intrinsically universalist: "Since evil as such does not exist, hell is only a temporary state and every sinner will ultimately be saved."[10]

Ibn 'Arabi was driven to employ erotic imagery in his poetry to suggest through imagination what reason was unable to grasp. The passion of love bears an obvious analogy to the fits of ecstasy Sufis have always associated with gnosis and with sainthood. This may even have influenced the troubadours. Indeed, the divinization of the erotic would surely have found more fertile ground in the form of Sufi mysticism than among the austerities of the Cathars.[11]

Ibn 'Arabi's vision is far from the philosophically abstract. Flourishing in the heat of Moorish Andalusia during the savagery of the Christian Crusades against the power of Islam, his spirit soared to grasp the transcendent unity of the divine: "My heart has opened unto every form; it is a pasture for gazelles, a cloister for Christian monks, a temple for idols, the Ka'ba of the pilgrim, the tables of the Torah and the book of the Qur'an. I practice the religion of Love; in whatsoever directions its caravans advance, the religion of Love shall be my religion and my faith."[12]

Spiritual Christianity and spiritual Islam would never again be as close as this. However, it is worth recalling that this cultural interchange took place within an alembic of conflict, and today's frustrations in the East may ultimately prove to have been such an alembic, full of magical possibilities for the future. Sufi philosophy teaches that all existence and all action are divine energy made manifest.

SUFIS AND PHILOSOPHY

The philosophical work of the Harranian and Baghdad Sabians had many ramifications. From the ninth to the twelfth centuries,

Neoplatonic philosophy with its Hermetic accretions flourished in the Islamic world, generating both enlightenment and conflict in equal measure, a development that owed much to Thabit ibn Qurra's translation work and to the depth and breadth of his cosmosophical vision. Names such as al-Kindi, al-Farabi, Ibn Sina (Avicenna), and Abu'l Walid Ibn Rushd (Averroës) have become world famous in the annals of medieval and Renaissance philosophy.

Their appearance led to two main tendencies of conviction and subsequent conflict: those relying solely and exclusively on the qur'anic revelation and a school of liberal theologians who, while accepting the authority of the Qur'an, claimed the right to use human reason, regarded as a gift of the spirit. Sufi teaching, in its breadth and divine simplicity, was able both to confound and to clarify arguments between Islamic legalists who were suspicious or hostile to philosophy and those who considered philosophical logic as a significant or even primary tool in the total life of humankind. It is fitting that we find the Sufi on both sides of the debate.

For many thinking Muslims, the tension between the liberal-philosophical and the fundamental-literalist was solved by the Sufi Abu Hamid al-Ghazali (1058–1111). In his book *The Incoherence of the Philosophers,* al-Ghazali recognized that at the root of the debate was the issue of Muslims' personal freedom to interpret their religion in a manner fitting to their conscience and divine gift, thus reconciling God to God's creation—a Sufic insight. At the same time, al-Ghazali realized that human reason alone could not guarantee that liberty.

Al-Ghazali, who began life as a skeptic and spent his first forty years in Baghdad, at the time of the disappearance of the Sabians, sought enlightenment from Islamic philosophers. In place of enlightenment, he found, like many before and since, greater and greater confusion and a torment that drove him to a state teetering on mental collapse. In his anguish he turned to the writings of Harith al-Muhasibi of Basra, the first Muslim to give an experimental analysis of the inner life. "I saw plainly," wrote al-Ghazali, "that what is most peculiar to them [the Sufis] cannot be learned from books, but can only be reached by immediate ecstasy and inward transformation."[13]

To stay close to the truth of himself, al-Ghazali had to give up brilliant worldly prospects, a surrender that caused a breakdown of his health. At last he submitted to God, taking refuge "as a man in sore affliction who has no resource left." He might not have done much for scholastic philosophy, but he did succeed in justifying the existence of Sufism to the conservatives, and, in the process, he made orthodoxy mystical. Fortunately, he did not achieve the reverse process.

Al-Ghazali's greatest challenge came from a brilliant man who was himself highly influenced by the Sufis, but who nonetheless stood up for the necessity of the philosophical enterprise. He was Abu'l Walid Ibn Rushd (c. 1126–98), known to the west as Averroës, an extremely influential and much misunderstood philosopher.

Averroës spelled out his cogent objections to al-Ghazali in his work *Tahafut al-tahafut* (The Incoherence of the Incoherence): "Indeed we can say with the Sufis that there is no reality besides Him and that all things are in God, though this is not a doctrine to be preached to all and sundry."[14] Averroës was accused of arguing that philosophy cannot be used to support the totality of orthodox Islam. What he was actually trying to show was that Islam is not a philosophical system.

He was also accused of denying the resurrection of the dead, whereas what he was actually saying followed from his having isolated Aristotle's teaching from the Neoplatonic structure into which it had become embedded.

In brief, his argument was that since the forms created by the Active Intellect (God's mind or spirit) constituted the principle of *individuation*, then that which died could no longer be individuated. That is, although the individual might have access to the Active Intellect and thus experience divinity of mind—eternal in itself—while in the body, this access could not be individuated on the vanishing of the distinguishable form (that is, the body).

Nevertheless, Averroës accepted the orthodox dogma of resurrection as a fundamental of faith. This may not have been simply to ensure his safety. He may have partially bridged the apparent dichotomy of faith and reason by holding to the concept of a spiritual body, a grace of Allah that permitted individuality within the unbroken whole or unity of the divine mind.

If you find this way of thinking difficult, you can understand the attraction of the mystical solution to the antinomies of experience. There is a distinctively Hermetic tinge to Averroës' philosophy that God creates all things by knowing them. God, in knowing Himself, knows all that can exist. God's knowledge is productive, not representative.

The self-thinking thought of Aristotle, the First Cause, becomes creative thought, or thought and will in identity. To the ecstatic Sufi, all such distinctions as causative thought and thought-caused break down and dissolve as the ego melts and the divine unity is revealed.

MAULANA JALAL-UD-DIN RUMI: SUFI MASTER

Today, Rumi is the most famous exponent of Sufism in the West. His writings are crystal-clear, beautiful; they never cease to illuminate the open or even half-closed mind. They are a treasury of insight and direct experience of God. Thousands every year from East and West visit his tomb in Konya, Turkey, to pay their respects, while once a year the inevitable authorities permit the famous whirling dervishes to perform their wondrous dance of devotion, the dhikr—for the tourists.

Rumi was the founder of the Maulawi *tariqa,* named after the title Maulana (our Lord), which Rumi's disciples gave to him. It is they, the *fuqara* (plural of *faqir,* meaning "poor," "poor in spirit," i.e., *dervish* in Persian), who perform the dance so as to support their dhikr, their invocation or quintessential prayer. They believe that the Sufi saints, with the Quth (Axis) at their head, form the invisible spiritual government of the world—perhaps a precursor of the seventeenth-century Invisible College of the Rose-Cross mythology and its numerous conceptual descendants.

Rumi was one of the greatest mystical poets of all time. Here is his "House of Love":

This house wherein is continually the sound of the viol,
Ask of the Master, what house is this?
If it is the Ka'ba, what means this idol-form?
And if it is the Magian temple, what means this Light of God?
In this house is a treasure which the universe is too small to hold;
This "house" and this "Master" is all acting and pretense.
Lay no hand on the house, for this house is a talisman;
. . . .

Speak not with the Master, for he is drunken overnight.
The dust and rubbish of this house is all musk and perfume.
The roof and door of this house is all verse and melody.
In fine, whoever has found his way into this house
Is the sultan of the world and the Solomon of the time.
O Master, bend down thy head once from this roof,
For in thy fair place is a token of fortune.
Like a mirror, the Soul has received thy image in its heart;
The tip of thy curl has sunk into its heart like a comb.
This is the Lord of Heaven, who resembles Venus and the
   moor;
This is the House of Love, which hath no bound nor end.[15]

INTERESTING TIMES

Jalal-ud-din Rumi was born in Balkh, Persia, on September 20, 1207, and died on December 17, 1273, in Konya (Iconium),[16] the city of his father. Rumi grew to maturity in troubled, indeed for the Islamic world, quite appalling times. The waves of woe came from the West, the East, and, most dangerously of all, from within.

By the thirteenth century, corruption had set in to the vast Muslim Empire. According to Afzal Iqbal, "Comfort and convenience was the rule. The love of controversy had got the better of the love for truth. Islam had been spilt into factions and the wood had been lost for the trees."[17] Such a society was ill prepared to face the twin dangers threatening it: crusaders from the West, Mongol barbarians from the East.

Meanwhile, the Western Roman Church had by 1266 reclaimed all of Spain with the exception of Granada. Nevertheless, the Christian world was rent by its own divisions. In 1228, Frederick II, the Hohenstauffen monarch, made a deal, contrary to the instructions of Popes Innocent III and Gregory IX, with Sultan Kamil and received, by agreement, Jerusalem, Bethlehem, Nazareth, and the corridors to Jaffa and Sidon. The pope put Jerusalem under interdict so long as Frederick remained there.

During the same period, Genghis Khan and his unassailable oceans of Mongol warriors overran Muslim Persia with barely imaginable savagery. After annihilating the border town of Utrar, the Khan's forces moved to Bukhara, a town of academies where the great Neoplatonic philosopher Ibn Sina (Avicenna) had been educated. The town was sacked and all its inhabitants massacred.

In Merv, the city of rose gardens, a veritable "copy of paradise," half a million citizens were slaughtered. The whole Khwarizm Empire, including Afghanistan, Baluchistan, Persia, and Turkestan, was completely overrun amid the deadly dark drumming of hoof on scorched earth. Nor did the horror end with the death of Genghis Khan in 1227. When his grandson Hulagu Khan became governor of Persia in 1251, he heralded his assumption of power by taking that great center of learning, Baghdad, with the killing of hundreds of thousands of Arabs in a week of frenzied bloodlust.

For many, gazing in stunned lamentation at the ruin of a once great empire, it looked as though the end had come, that Allah had abandoned believers to the ferocious force of fate. And yet this same period saw a great flowering of mysticism and poetry. In the West, there was St. Francis, the Cathars, Meister Eckhart, Ramon Lull, Mechthild of Magdeburg, and Kristina af Stommeln; and in the East, the Bhakti (love-devotion) movement, led by Ramanuja in India, Sa'di, 'Attar, and, of course, Rumi himself.

Rumi was twenty-two years old when, amid the carnage, he made his way to his father's house in Konya, the capital of the threatened Turkish Seljuk dynasty. It was a fortunate decision. Konya persisted as an island of peace in a sea of turbulence—and has continued so to this day. Konya's ruler, 'Ala-ud-din Kaikubad, was a patron of learning, and he personally encouraged Rumi. Even when the threat to Konya was intense, Rumi refused to leave. As Ifzal Iqbal eloquently expresses the matter: "His spirit of freedom was far too valuable to be bartered away for personal security."[18] Rumi was not distracted from the path of truth by the threat of violence. In his poetic masterpiece the *Mathnawi,* he wrote of how the evil that people see in others is a reflection of their own: "You are that evil-doer, and you strike those blows at yourself: 'tis yourself you are cursing at that moment. You do not see clearly the evil in yourself, else you would hate yourself with all your soul."[19]

The *Mathnawi* lays an ax at the rotten root of moral corruption.

The basis for doing so is the complete realization that immorality, while appearing to be the road to gain, is in fact the road to self-inflicted pain. According to Rumi, if we loved and understood the root of our selves, we would love God, in whom we exist and in whose life of radiant goodness we may share.

This moral purpose is asserted even in passages describing the emanation of the One Being through every grade of existence. The process finds its epitome in the evolution of the soul. In the form of the universal Logos, it descends to the material world, passes through the mineral, vegetative, and animal kingdoms, and attains to rationality in humans; it suffers probation, undergoes retribution, ascends to the sphere of the angels, and, continuing its spiritual development till it is reunited with the infinite One (of which it is the mirror), realizes that all its experience of separation was merely "such stuff as dreams are made on":

> *Though he is fallen asleep, God will not leave him*
> *In this forgetfulness. Awakened, he*
> *Will laugh to think what troublous dreams he had,*
> *and wonder how his happy state of being*
> *he could forget and not perceive at all*
> *Those pains and sorrows were the effect of sleep*
> *and guile and vain illusion. So this world*
> *Seems lasting, though 'tis but the sleeper's dream;*
> *who, when the appointed Day shall dawn, escapes*
> *From dark imaginings that haunted him,*
> *and turns with laughter on his phantom griefs*
> *When he beholds his everlasting home.*[20]

It would be wrong to deduce from this beautiful poem that Rumi was denying life or promoting a fast escape from the world—nor is he denying the world's reality. He is offering the weary traveler a glimpse of the goal. The magic carpet that takes people to paradise is woven of life's varied experiences, entered into consciously and with as much dignity as may be discovered in the heart.

According to Rumi, turmoil, tribulation, and trial are the lot of our lives until we emerge from the *athanor* of life, ready to let go of the old and put on the new. Rumi employs alchemical imagery with great naturalness: "The purpose of this (severe) discipline and this rough treatment is that the furnace may extract the dross from the silver. The testing of good and bad is in order that the gold may boil and bring the scum to the top."[21] Nor, according to Rumi, should people be dissuaded from the path by the glittering gifts and rewards offered to the apparently successful. They have their reward, and it is flimsy stuff. Logic and intellect, the babble of sharp wits, are extremely short staffs to take on a long journey. People of learning who excel in sharp intelligence have not inspired humanity to great endeavor, counsels Rumi. Neither did kings or the posturing of the powerful so inspire by mere cleverness. It is only by inspiration, revelation, acts of grace from God that illuminate the minds of human beings that they may see the world again anew.

God creates the world by knowing it. It has been the prophets and seers, making no claim to the "authority" of formal knowledge, who have captured the hearts of human beings and raised them to the heights of truly heroic achievement. The tortoise of the spirit beats the hare of reason. It is the holy fool who has conquered the world—and all the armies of the world fail to see him: "The myriads of Pharaoh's lances were shattered by (the hand of) Moses (armed) with a single staff. Myriads were the therapeutic arts of Galen: before Jesus and his (life-giving) breath they were a laughing-stock. Myriads were the books of (pre-Islamic) poems. At the word of an illiterate (prophet) they were (put to) shame."[22]

Rumi recognizes the imprisonment of the soul, and its anguish, as well as any existentialist. But he also knows that the world is a prison in which we find our freedom: "'Tis wonderful that the spirit is in prison, and then, (all that time) the key of the prison is in its hand!"[23]

Rumi's formula for the person who has found his or her role in life is simple:

If you are putting trust in God, put trust (in Him) as regards (your) work: sow (the seed), then rely upon the Almighty. . . . He (God) said: "I was a hidden treasure": hearken! Do not let thy (spiritual) substance be lost: become manifest![24]

Let us leave the last words of this chapter to Rumi's temporary Faridu'ddin 'Attar. His poem "Mantiqu 'l-T
Speech) tells of a flock of birds who set out on a flight to find terious king, Simurgh, only to discover at the end that he and one and the same.

> God said, "I breathed my Spirit into Adam"; and here the name Adam signifies every human individual. The contemplation of those who behold God in man is the most perfect in the world. Something of this vision the Christians possess, and their doctrine about Jesus will lead them at last, when "the Thing shall be discovered as it really is," to the knowledge that mankind are like mirrors set face to face, each of which contains what is in all; and so they will behold God in themselves and declare Him to be absolutely One.[25]

Hermes could not have put it better.

SIX

The Troubadours

The children of this world marry, and are given in marriage: But they which shall be accounted worthy to obtain that world, and the resurrection from the dead, neither marry nor are given in marriage: Neither can they die any more: for they are equal unto the angels; and are the children of God, being the children of the resurrection.

LUKE 20:34–36

PROLOGUE: THE TWO WORLDS

*I*t might be thought today that there could be no more Christian a sacrament than that of marriage. Many who would not attend church as a rule find the idea of ecclesiastically solemnized wedlock appealing. Yet here we have the evangelist Luke, author of what has been called "the romantic Gospel," expressing the idea that those belonging to the kingdom of heaven "neither marry nor are given in marriage," that marriage is for the "children of this world": a world of death.

This notion would not have appeared strange to Valentinian Gnostics a century after Luke's Gospel is thought to have been written (c. A.D. 75). Gnostics were convinced of the duality of the spiritual and material worlds. Nevertheless, they also saw the possibility for romantic love within the Christian tradition: Sex, for the Valentinian Gnostics, could have a sacramental aspect. The followers of the Gnostic teacher Valentinus (c. A.D. 160) emphasized the idea of spiritual marriage as a divine union—a union with God—not as a social contract. They took a distinctive interest in the special relations that their tradition informed them existed between Jesus and Mary Magdalene, and those between the heavenly Christ and the heavenly Sophia (Wisdom). The Valentinian Gospel of Philip (c. A.D. 250), for example, places great emphasis on a sacrament of the Bridal Chamber, a type representing not only Christ's marriage to his church (his body) but also the overcoming of the separation of the sexes.

The Valentinians held the view that the original state of humankind was one of androgyny, and that the fall of humans into matter was intrinsically linked to the heavenly (or archetypal) human's catastrophic division into male and female. A spiritualizing of sex was considered to represent a restoration of the original union of the sexes and thereby a return to God. This idea was open to debasement (orgiastic cults), and such debasement came to be associated with the Gnostics in general by their enemies.[1]

By the fourth century A.D., this idea had been suppressed in the Church at large. The balanced harmonization of the sexes was, from the first, at odds with the conventional Jewish-Christian marital practices that characterized much of the life of the early Church. Furthermore, there had been since the beginning of the Christian Church a tendency to see Christians who remained celibate as constituting something of an elite. The quotation (above) from Luke's Gospel could easily be used to justify this view. Christ himself had praised the eunuch who put the kingdom of God first in his assessment of his needs. A previously muted negativity about sex became ever more doctrinaire as, by the mid-fourth century, leaders of the Church came out of the burgeoning monastic movement with rules that implied or stated that sex was harmful or fatal to holiness, that sex itself was a sin. (There were also Gnostic ascetics of this persuasion.)[2] However, Church authorities had to accept that the vast majority of believers were unlikely to enter monasteries, and so conventional marriage continued to be solemnized. Between elite asceticism on the one hand (Mary's virginity heavily stressed) and approved marriage sacraments on the other (the wedding at Cana), there was no room left for the Valentinian Gnostic concept of the spiritualizing of the sexual union.

The Western Church saw out the Dark Ages in triumph but was largely unprepared for the new cultures that grew out of it. By the twelfth century, conditions had changed sufficiently in the Mediterranean culture of the Languedoc for two extraordinary movements to gain sway. The first movement was initiated by the appearance in the West of the Church of Good Christians, the Cathars.[3] Originally from Bosnia and Bulgaria (but apparently controlled from Constantinople),[4] the Cathars, who had journeyed westward up the Danube, settled in the Languedoc around the early to mid-twelfth century and organized themselves into an impressive preaching church throughout that region. The second movement was that of the troubadours, about whom, as with the Cathars, much romantic material has been written.

The amazing success of the troubadours may be attributed in part to changed social conditions. Chief of these was the emergence in the Languedoc of a large number of feudal lords who were women. These women could inherit property and therefore, to a large extent, regulate their own lives. They married to secure succession, but marriage was seen as a general convention that had nothing to do with love. Indeed, it was not unknown for theologians of the period to assert that if a man made love to his wife for pleasure, he was no different morally from an adulterer, deserving of the judgments meted out for sinners. A very different voice emerged from the lips of the troubadours:

Love is all my thought
Love is all I care about
The malicious gossips will say
that a knight should be occupied elsewhere
But me, I say they know nothing of it,
For it is from Love, no matter what they say,
that the greatest value proceeds,
in folly as in wisdom;
and all that is done through Love is good![5]

Raimon de Miraval, the troubadour who wrote this *canso,* came, along with his fellow troubadours, to the novel and joyous conclusion that since marriage was so fraught with sin, and since the woman was not free to love cordially (since her duties were obligatory), then pure love, the Fin' Amors, the Fine Love—the distinctive love of the troubadours—could be experienced only, and should be experienced only, outside marriage. Romantic love had arrived.

WHAT IS A TROUBADOUR?

We all know the expression "to go courting." That is precisely what the troubadours did. Indeed, their activities form the origin of this and many other expressions and conventions we still associate with love: *courtesy,* for example. The "Fine Love" took place at the courts—that is, the homes—of the nobility of the Languedoc, the Limousin, Provence, Aragon, Castile, and beyond to northern Italy and Portugal. Courtly love became a part of courtly life and its customs, and special forms came to dictate what was expected of a *courtier,* who was usually a knight of lower rank than the seigneur, who might, in this region, be a woman. In the Languedoc, privileged women could enjoy the respect and indeed love expected from a vassal. The basic form of Fine Love is woven into this relationship of vassal to lord: hence the romantic custom of getting on one knee before the loved one. However, the content of the proposition would be rather different from what is heard today. One thing is certain; it would not be a request for marriage, a proposition that would be considered practically disgraceful but was in any case unimaginable. Furthermore, there are not many male lovers today who would refer to their lady as "My lord."

The first troubadour known to history was father to that highly cultured woman Eleanor of Aquitaine. Guillaume IX, count of Poitou, duke of Aquitaine (1071–1127), was, like his daughter, a very clever and witty person. The following canso penned by Guillaume makes a fitting introduction to the movement:

I'll make a poem out of sheer nothingness;
It will not be about me, or about any other;

it will not be of love, or of youth, or
of anything else; it was, rather,
composed while sleeping on a horse.

The last verse:

I've made this poem, I know not of what;
and I'll send it to him who will send it
on for me by another, yonder, toward Anjou,
that he might send back to me, from his own wallet,
the key to it.[6]

Such lyrical inventiveness, so unexpected from a person born only five years after the Battle of Hastings, was developed with inspired vigor by a number of unexpected people; the wordplay, the magic, and the poetry opened up a new world.

Between Guillaume IX and young Raimon de Miraval the art continued to its perfection in the hands of men such as Jaufré Rudel de Blaye, Marcabrun, Bernard de Ventadour, Peire d'Auvergne, and the humorously defiant anticonformist writer Raimbaut d'Aurenja, lord of Orange, Courthézon, and a host of lesser feudal holdings in Provence and Languedoc. Raimbaut was the author of the first surrealist song, "La Flors enversa" (The Inverted Flower):

Now is resplendent the inverted flower along the cutting crags
and in the hills. What flower? Snow, ice and frost which
stings and hurts and cuts, and by which I see
perished calls, cries, birdsongs and whistles among leaves,
among branches and among switches; but joy
keeps me green and joyful now, when I see dried up
the wretched base ones.[7]

This was indeed a new world, and its purpose was single: *Le Joy.* Joy.

Sweet lady, may love and joy
join us, regardless of the base.[8]

The troubadour writes his law on the world and in so doing creates a world: a new and ecstatic dominion of love, *amors e joys,* regardless of the base, the violent, the vulgar, or the "unruly clerics," as another verse puts it. The troubadours did not live in Camelot; though they might desire it, they lived in an age of high spiritual endeavor. They also lived in a country of "vast deserts ruled over by the fury of brigands . . . where there is no law, no tranquility, nothing that does not menace life itself," as a papal legate described his unhappy trip to Languedoc at about the time Raimbaut was writing.[9] Much troubadour writing refers to declining ethical standards, ecclesiastical corruption, and woeful political tremors.

Inspired by the joys and frustrations of love as they were, the troubadours were nobody's fools. They wrote sermons called *sirventès.* There were two classes of these works: the moral sirventès, which were directed against the decadence of morals, the clergy, and women; and the political sirventès, which plunge us directly into mundane reality: political columnists, in twelfth-century style.[10]

Raimon de Miraval employed two *jongleurs* who would travel to welcoming courts to perform his works. Their names were Bayona and Forniers. They would often receive Miraval's new compositions while on their travels, for this was a traveling movement, its exponents journeying all over the known world. While Bayona and Forniers headed for the court of Alfonso II of Castile, Miraval was on his way to his friend and patron Raimon VI, count of Toulouse. While Peire Vidal, the greatest voice of them all, took Fine Love to Tripoli in Syria, Raimon de Miraval offered five years of love service to the famous "she-wolf" of the Cabardès, Loba de Pennautier. This great *dame* was also courted by Peire Vidal, the furrier's son from Toulouse.[11] At some marvelous moment, it must have seemed that the stars were everywhere and the Fin' Amors always in season.

By the many references to "false lovers," it can be inferred that there was something of a bandwagon going on, but reputations were hard to win. The troubadours' principal song genre, *le canso,* was, according to Dante (Occitan poetry's greatest enthusiast), "worthy of the highest honours to those who practise it with success"—and a source of acute embarrassment to those who could not.[12]

The word *troubadour* may derive from the Occitan verb "to find" or "to invent." Certainly the works were original—unlike those of the ecclesiastical world of the time. The literary life of the Church depended to a very great degree on endless copying and the ubiquitous voice of past authority; originality was dangerous. Troubadours vied with one another both for originality and for perfection; their works boast of their superiority to other troubadours—always ready to try out new verse forms, new twists of subject matter, fresh allusions and insights; they seem to have lived in a world of their own. We do know that troubadours would meet and compare works at towns such as Fanjeaux (at one time populated by as many as fifty lords) and at the castle of Cabaretz, down the path some five miles from Miraval, some eight centuries ago.

MIRAVAL

Because everything here is corrupt and returns to nothingness, Miraval never wanted to believe in the God of the Roman Catholics. Because the beauty of women, ephemeral as it is, exalts the man and makes him better, he never wanted to admit that this world was the work of the Demon [as the Cathar Church believed]. He only put his confidence in the supreme love, which is neither of God nor of the devil, but remains the image of the only eternity which nature permitted to men to experience for the duration of an instant.[13]

Miraval is a tiny village in the Cabardès, some twenty miles north of the walled city of Carcassonne. It is an astonishingly beautiful place, set in an intimate valley and bounded by oceans of bright green bushes and trees, full of fragrance and birdsong. Above a small waterfall in the River Orbiel, which has carved out this place, but still in the depth of the valley, is a stone parapet, largely overgrown, part of three surviving walls of the tower of Miraval's ancient castle. It is not the kind of impregnable stronghold associated with kings; it does not need to be. Nature has provided the best defenses for this region. A small plaque in the language of the region, Occitan (hence La Langue d'Oc), placed at the base of the mound on which the castle was built, informs us that here was born

Raimon de Miraval, poet of love and honor. He was born between 1160 and 1165 and died sometime between 1216 and 1229.

According to his Provençal *vida,* Raimon de Miraval was "a poor knight of the Carcassès, who owned a fourth part of the castle of Miraval." The castle was taken by Frankish crusaders against the Cathars in either 1211 or two years earlier, when Béziers was taken and the entire population of the city massacred.

This loss was certainly the coup de grâce for a family whose fortunes had declined consistently over the previous centuries. Deeds show that the family had had to renounce possessions around Castres and cede possessions in Rouergue and feudal rights in the Larzac throughout the twelfth century. Goods situated in the environs of Castres went to the viscount of Béziers and Carcassonne, Rogier II, in 1174, when Miraval was a boy. This demand was made on Guilhem de Miraval as punishment for warlike activity and brigandage.

In stanza 4 of his sirventès "Pos Peire d'Alvergn'a chantat" (Since Peire d'Auvergne Sang), the troubadour known as the Monk of Montaudon scoffs at Raimon's poverty. He refers to Miraval's failure to produce the customary fairs at the beginning of each month due to his attending the courts of the Midi and Spain as troubadour and courtier. Thanks to his castle, Miraval was able to play the role in the courtly love process of vassal-possessor of a fief. He did this by offering his castle to his lady, and this frequently. This symbolic gesture was terribly important to Miraval. Miraval itself was for him more than a place, more even than a home. In a wonderful canso addressed specifically to the lady Azalaïs de Boissézon, he sang:

> *It is a new love which invites me*
> *to serve her in such a manner*
> *that at Miraval let there be firmly established*
> *all the goodness of love and of sincere accord.*

At Miraval his pen would catch fire:

> *At the bottom of my heart is born the flame*
> *which leaves my lips when I sing,*

and with it I set ablaze the ladies and lovers.
And my melodies are gentle and grave,
lovable, gracious and courteous;
. . . .
and that is why one can learn them gladly.
So the one who is slow to love
on hearing my beautiful words
will hurry towards love.[14]

Holding the castle also enabled him to affirm his quality as knight and author. Compared to the great seigneurs of the region, he was indeed a poor *chevalier* unable to equal their obligatory largesse. He still gave much nonetheless, and Miraval, who had a spiritual outlook, might have considered his thoughts the more noble because they were unrelated to material possessions.

Miraval enjoyed the favor of Raimon VI's magnificent court of Toulouse and was, with his few possessions, able to avoid extreme poverty. With the exception of Audiart (his name for the count of Toulouse) and Pastoret (quite possibly Raimon Rogier Trencavel, who at age fourteen in 1199 became the immediate suzerain of Miraval), Miraval was able to address equally the great seigneurs of his own land as well as those of Spain.

Miraval's political role appears to have been discreet, and except for one significant song from 1213, he makes no reference to the ferocious war with the northern crusaders fought by the nobility of the Languedoc and of Aragon from 1209 (the Albigensian Crusade against the Cathars).[15] While his friend Raimon VI was the soul of that resistance, Miraval does not appear to have written sirventès against the crusade. It is possible that Raimon VI did not want outward provocation but instead held out hopes for diplomacy. This may say something of the political and diplomatic weight of the free words of troubadours. According to L. T. Topsfield, it is likely that Raimon VI was against the "inferior" political sirventès (being a politician himself), preferring the troubadour dedicated to the art of courtly love.[16] It was in Miraval's interest to rise above dynastic quarrels, because he could, as a certain Villelmi jibed, have three masters in a year. Miraval had accused Villelmi of moral poverty; Villelmi accused Miraval of being a "goody-goody."

THE LADIES IN HIS LIFE

It is both informative and amusing to look at Miraval's romantic life through the eyes of a critic. A rare work, *L'Histoire littéraire des Troubadours,* was published anonymously in Paris in 1774. This "literary history" is in fact a juicy collection of risqué portraits describing the *vidas* (notes on the poets) and *razos* (commentaries on the poems) revealing the sexual mores of the time. What makes the work particularly entertaining to students of irony is the Catholic moral gloss that intrudes at every possible opportunity, either because the author is shocked or to avoid official censure, or, perhaps, simply for sophisticated amusement. The intended audience would be young aristocrats or rising bourgeois looking for guidance in the ways of love, and of lust. The author appears ignorant of the real conditions of the twelfth century and seems simply baffled as to how the institution of marriage could have been so consistently flouted.

In one sense his account stands as a memorial to how a truly revolutionary culture could be so completely suppressed and trivialized. It is especially ironic that the book appeared only fifteen years before the French Revolution, a series of events characterized by a barbarity similar to that which put an end to the freedom of the troubadours.

The anonymous author begins by claiming that his Provençal sources praise Miraval for his great inventiveness and fine speech, knowing more of love and gallantry "than anyone," possessing to a supreme degree virtuous and pleasant manners. Next we are told that his first passion was for Loba, also much sought after by the seigneurs of Saissac, Mirepoix, Montréal, the troubadour Peire Vidal, and, successfully, by the count of Foix.

LOBA

Raimon de Miraval wrote nine surviving works dedicated to a lady he calls Mais d'Amic (meaning "more than a friend"), who is thought to have been Loba de Pennautier.[17] She imposed upon him a service of something like three to five years, and he adopted the role of defender close to her—defending her merit and reputation. There are numerous allusions to his being cross with her, and perhaps peevish:

> *Also I have longtime been*
> *a faithful lover and without falseness,*
> *for a lady who accordingly keeps me more in doubt,*
> *that I show her more obedience.*
> *And I will do well in seeming to protest,*
> *for she knows well that, as long as I will live,*
> *I could not separate myself from her,*
> *such pain have I undergone from it!*
> *Beautiful lady, soft and charming,*
> *you who are of a nature so noble and so kind*
> *and more gracious than any other,*
> *Why won't you pay me any attention?*
> *The heart burns me like a hot cinder;*
> *I am colder than a stream;*
> *Make me pine no more, since I love you—*
> *and you don't want me to die entirely!*[18]

In spite of his frustrations, Miraval is always ready in the Ovidian mode to engage himself in the melee on her behalf.[19] According to the eighteenth-century commentator, Loba flattered Miraval, received his verses and homage, and permitted him a kiss. This was not only artifice. She loved the count of Foix but kept this affair secret, for the historian tells us that a troubadour counted for lost a woman who took a great baron as a lover: "We have already seen the traces of so remarkable opinion; one can hardly explain the disgrace of the *grands seigneurs* whose morals were extremely disreputable." Meanwhile Miraval, in spite of indifference, pursued Loba but felt "like a Spanish slave held captive by the Moors." It does not appear that he received the kiss for which he had waited so long. A compromise was formed by which he retained his lady's friendship while she gave him the liberty of seeking his happiness elsewhere, whence he addressed himself to the

Marqueza de Menerba—Gemesquia, wife of the count of Minerve[20]—
and to the mysterious "Mantel." Gemesquia was young, pretty, unde-
ceiving, and undeceived. She figures only once in Miraval's cansos.[21]

Returning to our eighteenth-century commentator, we are informed
that not long after Miraval's courting of the Marqueza of Minerve,
Loba's intrigue as mistress to the count of Foix came to light and the
lady was dishonored. The reason for any such dishonor could only have
been that she was considered bound by loyalty to Miraval. Loyalty was
a cardinal value in Miraval's ethic of love and absolutely essential to the
proper conduct of the Fin' Amors. It was, in the troubadour world, a
serious moral issue, and so it is not surprising that Vidal took up the
cudgels and decried Loba in song. Miraval, we are told by our commentator, executed a "more disgraceful" vengeance that "gives a bad
idea of his character." He affected to defend Loba against all the slander, and it is perhaps from this time that Miraval wrote the following
canso—a work that does not give a bad idea of his character at all:

> *Now that the air is so good*
> *and the new leaf comes to life again,*
> *before the cold returns*
> *I would have much need of pleasure;*
> *for the exaltation of love soon dies*
> *and if one lets the summer pass*
> *without any recompense, without satisfaction*
> *It would make it easy for a slanderer to destroy*
> *everything.*[22]

According to the razo, Loba was so charmed by Miraval's zeal that
she told him she had been unresponsive to his love not because of
another passion, but because the waiting would render the pleasure
more dear (essential Fin' Amors refinement technique). Indeed, she joyfully observed that the false attacks made against her had not altered
his fidelity and, furthermore, renounced all other loves for him, abandoning to him her heart and her person, and the right to defend her
always. Miraval, we are told, then exercised those rights she had given
him on her person and left for the countess of Minerve. He went on to

boast of it, saying that it was the only vengeance permitted against ladies. "All honest men today would be shamed by such a vengeance," says our anonymous French author. Somehow this story does not seem to ring true as it stands.

Miraval, after years of concentrated effort, was apparently going through something like a collapse, even a collapse of confidence in the Fin' Amors itself, to which he had dedicated his life. There is a sense of the man's confusion from the first verse of the canso quoted above. Desperately and yet with perfect grace—an extraordinary balance— Miraval with great nobility attempts to shore up the lineaments of his existence. The first line has an almost sublime aphoristic force that rings true for all time:

> Nothing guarantees Love
> There, where Love asserts his strength
> He accepts no other law
> than this: that he must accomplish his desires!
> Thus does he exercise his lordship;
> and those who sulk, resisting him
> Will in the end be obliged to beg mercy of him,
> unless he would renounce Love entirely.

To those then and now who would scoff at the follies of love, Miraval argues:

> That is why the wicked are terrified
> at the idea of running love's adventure;
> but he who concerns himself with his greater glory
> embraces that loving service which makes him more valiant
> and more noble and more proud.
> It is Love who renders a man celebrated
> for his gifts, his courteous manner,
> for his boldness and for his generosity.[23]

In our eighteenth-century commentator's moral judgment, Miraval must be punished: "Two cruel adventures were to provide recompense." Miraval "lost himself" with the lady Azalaïs de Boissézon, *habile coquette,* who wanted to be celebrated by his verses.

Azalaïs was a beautiful lady from Lombers in the Albigeois. In Lombers, from 1165, all the knights were Cathars; it was very soon to become the residence of the Cathar bishop of the Albigeois. It is therefore likely that Azalaïs was a Cathar *croyante*—that is, a lady sympathetic to the Cathar spiritual gospel but who had not undertaken the definitive rite that severed the believer from the power of the material world, the Consolamentum.

Azalaïs is eulogized by Miraval in six works, all of them of exceeding beauty. She must have made an immense impression on him, but, at the same time, she was clearly quite different from Loba; perhaps she was vain. Miraval does not complain. He claims only the privilege of being accepted by her as lover or supplicant. The courteous eulogies that he sings to Azalaïs he sends also to the king of Aragon and to Catalan seigneurs such as Uc de Mataplana. Raimon Drut (possibly Raimon-Rogier, count of Foix) also receives the word. Plenty of allusions, including that of coming out of a recent blow (Mais d'Amic?), enable us to date these songs between 1204 and 1207. There is nothing vindictive in them, but one can detect a certain confusion and definite sadness that it would appear Azalaïs de Boissézon had little capacity to deal with.

> *Between two desires I remain thoughtful*
> *Because my heart tells me "Sing no more!"*
> *While Love will not let me abstain,*
> *so long as I am in this world.*
> *O I have reasons, nonetheless*
> *to compose these songs no longer,*
> *But I will sing because Love and Youth*
> *restore all that Decorum and Reason have made invisible.*
> *And if ever I strove*
> *to be an artful man, courteous and gay,*
> *I must now apply myself with even more eagerness*
> *to saying and doing things which please her;*
> *now that I've put all my hope*
> *in a lady whose precious and cherished favours*

would be unmerited by an ill-mannered man,
whether he be rich, powerful or handsome.
. . . .

Beneath such honour and nobility
I have always shown myself to be a sincere lover,
in spite of sorrow, distress and anguish,
I have never sought escape from the worst of it.
They say that from a hidden love
it is impossible to derive satisfaction,
But they lie! I have known the pleasures and the benefits
As much as I've suffered the shame and deceit of it.[24]

Perhaps Miraval had an inkling of Azalaïs's motives. The following verse is a covert warning, addressed with the greatest concern for her— again, a magnificent balancing act between censure and praise:

In all that matters concerning this noble lady,
I am demanding of her,
lest she do anything which lowers her Merit;
but if it is a lady of small virtue who betrays me,
is that any cause to become party to unpleasant quarrels?
No! She would be too happy
if, thanks to me, she were made the subject of gossip.
The bad ladies of this kind, their faults inflict injury,
and they only feel important when the centre of gossip
and dispute!
. . . .

But my lady belittles the pretentious types
Since her honour increases as she shows it least;
She is like the rose and the gladiolus
which become more beautiful when the summer returns
But my lady is all year in the season of beauty
Because she always knows how to make herself more lovable,
With her charming manners and her gracious gestures
which heighten her Merit and all her ways.
. . . .

My lady Azalaïs de Boissézon
renders her Merit supreme, when it was but good
And God will come to miss some respect due to Him
since she so gently entered my life.[25]

It would be hard to express the rank horror engendered in a Catholic theologian upon reading that final risqué verse. His lady clearly has attributes in his imagination that are, quite directly, divine. Miraval did not fail in his task of amplifying the lady of Boissézon's renown. Razo D not only informs us that Azalaïs was the wife of Bernart de Boissézon (almost certainly a Cathar croyant, appearing in documents dated between 1156 and 1202), but also recounts a fantastic adventure concerning the king of Aragon.

Pedro II happened to be in Montpellier, from where he sent the lady Azalaïs messages and gifts, making it known to Raimon de Miraval that he strongly desired to see the beautiful Azalaïs for himself. This is what Miraval had told him of the lady of Boissézon: "The courtesy and the gaiety of the beautiful Azalaïs, her fresh colours as well as her long tresses, make the happiness of the entire world."[26] Miraval innocently arranged an interview and led the king to her. We might imagine that this event would have caused Miraval acute discomfort, since he had sung to her:

My lady, neither Béziers nor Aragon
would be worth any more to you
than the castle of Miraval
If you would firmly occupy its keep.
It is because her Merit is so precious and dear
that I desire the company of the lady Azalaïs:
I will always be faithful to her.[27]

The king, according to the razo, was well received by the lady, and they spent the night together. The whole court was informed of this the following morning. Our eighteenth-century commentator is keen to describe how Miraval was at once penetrated by confusion and pain and departed from both the lady and the prince. The historian says that

Azalaïs was dishonored by the deception: "These sorts of perfidies were exceptionally common. We shall now see a new example which suggests the strangest depravation of morals."

This new scandal concerned the lady Ermengarda de Castres, neighbor of Miraval and described in razo D as La Bela Albuges. Apparently, Ermengarda told Miraval that while nothing on earth could disrupt their union (she was already sought in marriage by the great baron and patron of Miraval, Olivier de Saissac), the troubadour must repudiate his wife, Gaudairenca,[28] as a proof of his resolve. Breathless, our man in 1774 continues with his story. Miraval takes seriously the demand of Ermengarda that he repudiate his wife, and with blind faith proceeds to execute the project. Gaudairenca, we are told, herself loved a knight called Brémon, the object of her own verses (which, sadly, have not survived). She pretends to be angry and replies that she will inform her parents and friends. She calls Brémon, who arrives at Miraval to be greeted by the troubadour, who is anxious to "shake hands on it" without further ado: "Marriage was counted almost for nothing. The Provençal writer seems to me suspect of untruthfulness or of error and makes me less sure of the details of the adventure. But there is doubtless a foundation in truth, sufficient anyway to characterise the extreme license of morals."

Meanwhile, Miraval hastens to find the beautiful Albigeoise and says that having executed her orders, he now awaits the execution of her promises. She tells him to go and prepare the nuptials and to come when she calls him. Ermengarda then calls for Olivier de Saissac and marries him on the day. The blunt news petrifies Miraval "with astonishment and pain." He becomes the butt of everyone's jokes and spends the next two years "as a man whose reason is troubled." Miraval protests his innocence and charges that an honest knight should abandon a lady capable of corrupting him for the look of money—advice presumably aimed at Olivier de Saissac.

"One would not imagine that a new mistress would offer herself to Miraval. But nevertheless that is what happened," says our chronicler. This lady was Brunissens or Brunessen de Cabaretz. Possibly she was the wife of Peire Rogier, protector of Miraval and co-seigneur of Cabaretz, who had a daughter, Nova, and a son, Peire Rogier—all

Cathar croyants. This lady wrote to Miraval, her friendly neighbor, that he might soon recover his beautiful humor. She cared a great deal for the poet: "If you do not want to come, I will come and find you, and I will make love to you, that you do not suspect me of deception." The literary historian of the troubadours is censorious: "It must be admitted that the ladies here play a role well in line with their character." This is how Raimon de Miraval replied to the lady:

> *As the rose among a thousand branches*
> *is more gracious than the flower of any seed,*
> *So among the false and treacherous posers*
> *does my lady stand within her tent,*
> *None of their false oaths can harm her!*
> *Her Merit has grown under friendly stars*
> *I pray that, due to them, it is not lowered!*[29]

THE RULES OF LOVE: MIRAVAL'S GUIDE TO SUCCESSFUL COURTSHIP

First of all, love is the cardinal virtue; love makes you good. The Fine Love provides the energy for spiritual vision. Thus, regarding Azalaïs de Boissézon, Miraval declares:

> *It's thanks to her that I love the fountain and the stream,*
> *the wood and the orchard, the coppice and the hedge,*
> *the ladies and the wicked ones too!*
> *the wise and the mad and even the simpleton*
> *Of that noble region in which she lives.*
> *My thought is so attracted to this place*
> *that I cannot imagine it ever beholding*
> *another country or another race.*[30]

The world without the Fin' Amors is implicitly vulgar, because it resists the moral of love. This gives Miraval's vision a clear logical parallel with that of the Cathars among whom he spent most of his life. The false God, the Rex Mundi whom the Cathars saw in the figure

Christ called the "prince of this world," the Gnostics' Demiurge (creator of nature), was a symbol of the world-as-object for the Cathars, of all that was alien to the Father of love. The perfected Cathar (consoled one) would have to admit that in Miraval's fragile love there was yet the vestige of the divine source of love. Miraval sang of Azalaïs de Boissézon:

> But her beauty which gives birth to excess love,
> her kind manner of receiving and honouring,
> and her great Merit, superior to any other
> has engaged me on this path which I know is folly;
> But folly, among lovers, has the value of reason
> and reason, of folly.[31]

For Miraval, the agonies of this world can be borne and even redeemed by projecting the inner world upon the state of things about him; love takes him beyond himself. He can love the wise and the mad simultaneously, "the ladies and the wicked ones too"; opposites are reconciled as he and his lady are reconciled. This was his way to wholeness. The Fin' Amors has a religious, or ordering, character that takes it far beyond the mere sexual romanticism that provided the opening key. Troubadours like Miraval did not just dream their way to a better world; they put their law upon the world and lived it out, regardless of the consequences. "One is always right to seek the Love that raises!" as Anne Brenon puts it in her book *The True Face of Catharism*.[32]

What are Miraval's rules of the game?

1. Infidelity is *the* sin, the absolute treason, according to Miraval. In one canso, an infidelity is compared to the treachery of Judas—a betrayal of God. This is a matchless indication of how seriously Miraval took this virtue and explains Miraval's disorder of mind following the debacles of Loba, Azalaïs, and Ermengarda de Castres, offering clear proof that the Fin' Amors was not the careless or pagan moral abandonment of the Dionysiac libertine. The poet is faithful to her who is herself faithful. According to the late Languedocien poet and scholar

René Nelli, "Indulgence for the Lady is always a function of the courtesies he receives from it." Miraval writes of a lady, Na Guilhelma, as a perfect lady; she welcomes criticism and knows how to make the right choice: "I have from her all that I could desire of her." According to Nelli, the *bonnes dames* were for the most part imaginary: "The Middle Ages in fact did not believe much in the sincere adherence of women to pure love. It was difficult to distinguish between ladies who offered platonic love to those they did not love and realistic love to those they did."[33]

There were in the Languedoc, however, a number of exemplary women—from the point of view of the Fine Love. These were the great ladies such as Esclarmonde de Foix (a contemporary of Miraval), the leading "good women" or "good Christians, Friends of God," of the Cathar Church—so the ideals were not wholly unrealized. Nevertheless, there is some indication that Miraval conceived of an ideal lady and sang to her. The references to "her" are enigmatic:

> *Lady, I am so faithful to you*
> *that in all your courteous enterprises*
> *I want Miraval to help you,*
> *but I dare say neither who you are,*
> *nor from what country.*[34]

Is this a kind of "myth of the lady," or simply a blind of some kind, or is she yet the ideal lady within the particular lady he loves? Or even, in himself?[35] Clearly, these very real and characterful women of the Languedoc were internalized and lived in the heart.

2. Jealousy is a prime virtue of the Fin' Amors. Jealousy exacts fidelity from the lady, and from the lover also. Miraval sang: "Jealousy teaches me to consecrate myself exclusively to the service of a lady, so that I want no other and abstain from paying court to them."[36] As Nelli puts it, "It is certainly true that the jealousy of the lover is not that of the husband! Jealousy, exclusive and vigilant attachment to one lady, is a principle of loyalty and fidelity.

On the other hand, in the worldly view, it obliges the poet to show himself reserved, prudent, discreet and, above all, to avoid the vulgar and the indiscreet."[37]

3. The troubadour should not regard a refusal from a lady as being dishonorable. It can even carry much honor to the aspirant, if it is formulated in such a way as to express the highest consideration from her to him. To Miraval the *no* of a loyal lady is worth more than a *yes* from a lady who is faithless and who would necessarily commit fault upon fault against courtesy. Furthermore, the refusal, if accompanied by a sincere and pure feeling of love, has infinitely more value than the carnal recompense of a lady incapable of love and, by extension, faithfulness.

4. What is a troubadour to do if the process of conventional courtesy is cut short—if, for example, he has made a faux pas? In the song "The One to Whom Joy Is Suited," the process has stopped at the second stage of conventional courtesy and the poet has obtained nothing from the lady. He is neither to complain to the lady nor is he to be angry; his only desire must be to serve in all humility. In the song, Miraval does not despair of seeing a return to the lady's best feelings in his regard. The cause of the lady's anger is alluded to in stanza 5. He had gallantly stolen a kiss. Miraval submits in advance to the lady's chastisement. Nevertheless, she must pardon him this theft because he has pardoned all her wrongs, and consents not to take them into account. So long as a lady is loyal, a wooer finds it honorable to serve her, even if in vain:

> If she would turn the theft into a gift
> she would be acting with great Courtesy,
> And if it does not please her, all right:
> Let it be![38]

5. There is a formula for courteous masochism. The lady is wrong, but the lover must support her rigorously as if she were right.

6. Hope in love outlives a break.

7. The best poets sing as if they were joyous even when they are sad.

However, inspiration is primary, for while technical virtuosity makes for success, it is far better if sincere love inspires both composition and courtly behavior. It is true that *le Joy* can be purely carnal. It is also true that courtesy is sometimes conventional and artificial: an exchange of good behavior where each gets what is expected—"obeying the law," as it were, with a necessary exclusion of passion—a fair exchange. This capacity within the Fine Love to simply set up a consistent social order is also part of its demise; the potential for *embourgeoisement* was in fact realized with the fall of the flesh-and-blood lady, when she was forcefully replaced by external votive imagery of the Virgin Mary. It is no accident that bourgeois commentary on the troubadours, when not condemning their morals, has tended to paint them as curious encratites, sexually repressed ("sublimating desire"), socially innocuous virgins weeping about the pains of "platonic love."

8. The troubadour is sold to the lady like a boy-charge (ward) to a guardian; his rights are given over in absolute submission to the lady—but the sum for the "boy" must be paid to the boy-troubadour so long as the lady consents freely to enter the process. At some stage the lady expects and is expected to recompense the service given. As an extension, Miraval himself offers his castle so that he may achieve a symbolic subordination to the lady, who is, with only one exception (Aliénor, sister of Pedro II of Aragon, to whom Miraval wrote in 1213), his social equal. The recompense is in fact made of an ascending scale of courteous responses to the loving troubadour, whose love is refined over a period of time, purification being an essential aspect of the process, with spiritual analogies in both Catharism and alchemy.

9. False lovers are naturally hostile to the "royal art," and the lady must shun them, rejecting their gifts (usually furs and coursers, or horses) and advances. She should accept only beautiful songs that glorify her; she would increase her merit *(paratgé)* if she would listen to the advice of the troubadour-lover in this matter. It is the function of the poet to hinder the diminishing of the Fine Love through vulgarity, banality, or the venality of discourteous women. Miraval constantly complains of the breakdown of

courtesy. He is anguished that ladies, for fear of false lovers, dare not conduct themselves as they would like to. This ties in with Miraval's satires against the decadence of taste that he and other troubadours saw all around them. The courtly system, they maintained, was unable to function perfectly as in days past. There is a strong nostalgia theme.[39]

10. Love is necessarily accompanied by torments, but the good things compensate for the bad with a noble lady. Miraval asks: "What value has Love if one does not suffer evil from it?" Love must be tried in the alembic of experience and time.

11. Regarding that prize, the Good Lady, purely "platonic" love is always preferable to the fleshly caresses of unfaithful women. This idea again has logical affinities with the Catharist sensibility, since it places the passions of the flesh (matter) below spiritual goodness, while a sincere moral choice is enacted in the lofty aspiration. However, the "evil" does not, for the troubadour, lie in the flesh, but rather in the will of the person who inhabits it.

12. Miraval has some interesting ideas of his own. The fault of one lady redounds on all others. This seems to be true, for people are generally treated according to knowledge gained by previous experience. Courtly love is a social, not an individualistic, ethic (the bad conduct of a lady makes her "dead" to society), although the living tenor of the courtly society still depends on the individual. Miraval expresses a curious idea in these words: "The beautiful face she offers another I welcome as if it were destined for me." A lady who does not profit from the advice he offers has only herself to blame if she falls into misadventure. It is ultimately for *her* to distinguish between the real love and the false.

13. Before the absolute fulfillment of the Fin' Amors must come the customary favors of courtesy: affection, kindness, presents, and friendship, the sound basis for recompense after long service— and service could be very long indeed. It was for the ladies to prove, by a thousand means and tests, patience and fidelity. It is this time factor that gives many troubadour cansos an edge of frustration and yearning that is often mistaken for ritual sublimation of sexual desire. It is not unknown to read that the

ladies of the Languedoc were frequently cruel and heartless, as a matter of course; this simply is not true. For example, the following verse from "Blessed Be the Message" (possibly sent to Brunissens of Cabaretz) by Miraval could easily be taken that way were it not for the fact that we know something of what passed between him and Azalaïs de Boissézon:

> I believed that my lady
> was well different from what she is,
> and that her first amazement would last forever!
> But her foolish thought and perfidy,
> her bad faith pursues and traps
> her Merit, already so thin,
> may God diminish it still
> since she has thus plunged again
> my faithful heart into distress![40]

If there were any doubt about the joyfully carnal aspect of authentic troubadour aspiration, one only need read Miraval's canso dedicated ironically to "the one who does not want to hear songs."

> From the beauty by which I am taken
> I desire the embrace and the kiss,
> and to lie, and the total gift of her person;
> and only after the sleeves and the belts,
> and the cordial love I ask of her as a grace.
> But never will I let myself be seduced
> by the joys or the emblems of love
> if I have not first obtained that
> of which I have most desire.

Which is:

> and I ask neither more nor less of Joy
> This is what I want, to stay with her![41]

The theory of Miraval in stanza 2 of this song is that carnal love must precede cordial love. After the permissible caresses, after *le jazer* (lying down together in a voluptuous but chaste manner, to which the ladies consent to prove complaisance and the prudence of the lovers) they are able, if proof had been conclusive and to perfect their love, "to double-gild the gold," to "become total." The greatest value is bestowed to spiritual love. Miraval definitely prefers caresses or le jazer to sordid and unfaithful bedtime adventures. His ultimate aspiration is union absolute of the flesh and the spirit in shared and faithful love. This was the love that raises. This was the love the troubadour never feared to seek.[42]

The spiritual joy can be combined with aristocratic or chivalrous love; Miraval is a knight as well as a troubadour. Embracing, kissing, often completed by caressing, are the carnal maneuvers courtly love permitted to the lover. Le jazer, going to bed, could be probative and chaste (under oath). But if it resulted in sexual communion, and the lady had decided to be in accord with her friend, it was sometimes called le Plus. Miraval differentiates le jazer from le Plus. In adding le Plus he transforms the courtly jazer (chaste in principle) into the realist and chivalrous jazer—that is to say, natural and complete, as it is generally today. The ladies of the Cabardès or Albigeois, Loba or Azalaïs, whose lovers were all great seigneurs, did not refuse them le Plus (*le Sorplus* of Chrétien de Troyes). Azalaïs was not unyielding to the king of Aragon; and Loba had, it appears, an illegitimate child, the celebrated *Loup* (Wolf) of Foix, by Raimon-Rogier, the count of Foix, whose mistress she was for a long time. Miraval wants to play before love and not love before play—an aristocratic approach—but he will never tolerate carnal love alone. And the only proof that can give the carnal love subordination to the love of the heart is fidelity, to which, as we have surely seen, Miraval was very much attached. In short, Raimon de Miraval wants love to be *one*.

WAS THE FINE LOVE A SPIRITUAL LOVE?

The desire of Raimon de Miraval that love should above all be "one," a unity of flesh and spirit, indicates quite clearly the essential spirituality of his approach to the Fin' Amors, an approach that presupposes a particular dualism of matter and spirit. Nor should we underestimate the long suffering, almost the crucifixion, of the spiritual aspiration[43] in the prolonged period of service and extended concentration on the loved one.

It is significant that in Miraval's system, the purely sexual stimulation is to be passed through first, and it seems to be at this point that Miraval often encounters "unfaithfulness" in the actual lady. He is wounded when the lady fails in some respect to conform to his interior image of her, the powerful image that generates his ecstatic songs. Perhaps she intuits that the lady of Miraval's songs is no longer her social self but is in fact a person within Miraval himself. Could it be that the process involves perhaps not only the transmutation of sexuality but also the suppression of herself *as she knows herself to be?* At this point, Miraval's need for wholeness, for oneness, is, he thinks, put in jeopardy.

The troubadour puts his law upon the world; he projects his world in an analogous way to that by which the alchemist projects his unconscious spiritual processes upon chemical transformations. Miraval was bound to be continually disappointed. However, even disappointment fuels his creative efforts, and the human world is changed—and the poet with it. As Miraval himself puts it, "That is why the wicked are terrified at the idea of running love's adventure."[44] Change is painful, yet Miraval knows that the sufferings are ultimately worthwhile. *Le Joy* is his redemption; he is living in touch with his psyche—no wonder he feels a betrayal in this life is a betrayal of God. But it does seem that the spiritual path of woman is not identical: for while the ladies enjoyed the flattery, attention, and amelioration of the worst solitudes by friendship, love, and physical and spiritual warmth, most women know they are not *pure.*

Nevertheless, in Miraval's vicinity there did exist a method by which a woman could be "purified," Catharized—and Miraval himself knew precisely what it was. He never once refers to it, suggesting perhaps that it was not the kind of thing to go singing about to all and sundry in the courts of southern France and northern Spain. That method was the Cathar rite of the Consolamentum, and it may be that Miraval's greatest successes were with ladies who themselves expected someday to complete their induction into the Cathar Church, at which point sexual congress was rejected. Many men and women waited until they had fulfilled their social obligations before joining in the full rite of spiritual baptism. Meanwhile the Fin' Amors was regarded as part of the education of daughters by noble Cathar mothers, because it was seen to refine sensibilities to the point of mature discretion. It is necessary, then, to trace the origins of this spirituality, for it appears to be precisely this dimension that has created a mystique about the troubadours and which has associated them with other heretical (spiritual) movements in the south of France of the twelfth and early thirteenth centuries.

THE ALLEGORY OF LOVE

In his *Allegory of Love,* C. S. Lewis outlines his ideas about the origins of courtly love without a single reference to a single troubadour. It is not surprising, then, that this standard (English) work comes to a number of misleading conclusions. His references are derived almost exclusively from thirteenth-century sources, the *Roman de la Rose,* for example, being composed after—and in the second part, a century after—the Albigensian Crusade had devastated the region and dislocated its religious and cultural life through inquisition and forfeiture of property. Lewis writes that the "erotic religion" shows antagonism to the repressive organization by parodying the official one; that is, it sets up a kind of counterchurch (which is not to be taken too seriously). Lewis quotes from a twelfth-century *jeu d'ésprit* called "The Concilium in Monte Romarici." A chapter of nuns at springtime in Rémiremont hold a mock chapter meeting from which most men are excluded, but for a few "honest clerics"—as many no doubt as could be found:

> *When the virgin senate all*
> *Had filled the benches of the hall,*
> *Doctor Ovid's Rule instead*
> *Of the evangelists was read.*
> *The reader of that gospel gay*
> *Was Sister Eva, who (they say)*

Understood the practick part
Of the Amatory Art—
She it was convoked them all,
Little sisters, sisters tall.
Sweetly they began to raise
Songs in Love's melodious praise.[45]

This kind of ribaldry was doubtless popular in Miraval's time, but it is as far from the authentic Fin' Amors as could be imagined. This mistaken conflation persists today with the banalization of what is mistaken for troubadour culture, not only in pop music but also in more highbrow works such as Carl Orff's version of *Carmina Burana,* which is simply jolly medieval frolicking in a sub-Nietzschean springtime Thule-Fest to great twentieth-century music. Satirical anticlericalism, in spite of relative and continued ecclesiastical censure, does not undermine the established order, because it offers no spiritual revelation and implicitly confirms the power of the Church.

Contrary to Lewis's view, there was in fact alive and visible in the twelfth century a very real organized counterchurch—namely, that of the Cathars. Catharism and the noble culture of the troubadours in a sense needed one another to survive, but it is doubtful if anyone could see it clearly at the time. Ecclesiastics, however, saw the threat very clearly, for it is suspected that honest references to the Cathar Church and to authentic troubadour ideas were systematically excised in the thirteenth century while ersatz versions took their place. There was little room for objection. Between 1209 and 1244, thousands of Cathars were burned alive in the first holocausts of European history—and the burnings persisted throughout the thirteenth and fourteenth centuries. The Cathars' "Lord of this world" had apparently triumphed, leading his sheep armed to the teeth into the once fertile culture of the Languedoc.

C. S. Lewis refers to the thirteenth-century *De arte honeste amandi* (The Virtuous Art of Loving) by Andreas Capellanus, a priest. The title is in Latin; the Occitan language was regarded as subversive after the crusade against the heretics. Capellanus's work gave methodical instruction and moral dialogues on the art of love. It is highly Catholic in its moral tone, a Catholicization of the Fin' Amors. It has wrongly been taken as the authoritative handbook to courtly love—rather like asking General de Gaulle to compose for the Rolling Stones.

According to Capellanus, ordinary piety and reverence for the saints are part of the proper modus vivendi for the serious lover. Most significant, heresy in a knight justifies a lady withdrawing her "love": "And yet some people are so extremely foolish as to imagine that they recommend themselves to women by showing a contempt for the Church."[46] This is a long way from Peire Vidal. Most of Miraval's friends would, according to this stricture, be unable to participate—including the ladies.

The Virtuous Art of Loving makes devastating reading. The work is in fact a hijacked courtly love code, bound, gagged, and bundled up into an orthodox sack. C. S. Lewis seems totally unaware of the Church of Good Christians and furthermore mentions (without seeing the point at all) Andreas's assertion that courtly love is in tune "with natural morality." He condemns "incestuous" and "damnable" unions—possibly a veiled reference to vulgar accusations against the Cathars: namely, that they were homosexuals[47] and that they abolished family relations. It is highly interesting, and should have been surprising, that these activities are mentioned in the context of courtly love at all, since the entire system could not possibly function either within the family or among people of the same sex. As Andreas Capellanus invents a courtly love without the original troubadours, so Lewis, carried along by a fellow orthodox theologian, invents a "ribald left-wing of the courtly world" to account for these references. Already, at the time of the crusade when Capellanus was writing, the genuine troubadour world was being abducted, or rather banished, from its home—as Miraval himself was to be after 1209. As if this were not enough, the ultimate disaster of this so-called courtly love guide comes when the author simply removes the spiritual dimension from courtly love altogether. Thirteenth-century religion must sterilize the Fine Love and make it safe. One of Andreas's ladies puts it this way: Couldn't we "leave the religious side out for the moment"?

Andreas's courtly love is really intended only for youngsters who are not married. He has invented a child's game with a child's religion to go with it. To cap it all, his finale declares that having learned all about this "love," one had better abstain from it and win greater merit from God—who doesn't really like this sort of thing: "No man through any good deeds can please God so long as he serves in the service of love."[48] To this man, *Fine Love* no longer makes you good; it damns you unto eternity. The lid is shut. To destroy Miraval's world it was necessary to drain his love of any reliable spiritual content at all. This happened in direct parallel to the near annihilation of the Cathar Church. Their destinies were linked.

TROUBADOURS AND CATHARS

What, then, was the true relation between the troubadours and the Sancta Gleisa, the Holy Church of the Cathars? In some respects, the relation between Raimon de Miraval and the Good Men and Good Women (as the Cathars are more properly called) was simply a question of "all in the family." Catharism extended from the castles that were the centers of intellectual life in the region. We have already encountered the castle of Cabaretz at Lastours, an hour's walk from Miraval. Here at Cabaretz, Mabilia moved in with Jordan after he renounced Orbria de Durban in the name of renouncing marriage.[49] Mabilia's nieces, Azalaïs and Effante, were *perfecti* who had received the Consolamentum. Anne Brenon puts the matter thus: "The old problem of relations between Catharism and the Fin' Amors need no longer be stated—now we see the intense familial connections—in terms of a secret rapport between religious clandestines from a menacing and mysterious church, and sybilline singers with a coded message destined to ensure the spiritual survival of a Church so pure that Rome would have to extinguish it."[50]

In the Lauragais, the Cabardès, and the Albigeois, Cathars and troubadours frequented the same courts, where the ladies would help the perfecti in the afternoon and listen and be courted by the troubadours and jongleurs in the evening. Raimon de Miraval himself had a perfect[51] relative at Cabaretz, Gauçelin de Miraval. Azalaïs de Boissézon was almost certainly a croyante (rank-and-file member of the Cathar Church). Raimon VI of Toulouse, Miraval's most important protector and friend, was also, like the knights, a protector of the

Cathars. The knights who risked everything to defend and shelter the Cathars during the crusades against them (Ramoun de Perella, for example, gave over the castle of Montségur for Cathar use in 1204) were the same knights of the Fin' Amors who enjoyed hearing Chrétien de Troyes' account of Lancelot and of courtly lady par excellence Guinivere in *The Knight of the Cart*. Later they would enjoy the *Conte del Graal*, commissioned by the granddaughter of the first troubadour, Guillaume IX, duke of Aquitaine.

The troubadour Peire Vidal described in detail, in one of his most celebrated songs, a little paradise of courtesy between Albi and Carcassonne. Every stanza cites a town or castle. Vidal loves at Laurac, loves at Gaillac, loves at Saissac, loves in the Carcassès "because the knights are courteous there, and court the ladies of the country." Around 1200, when Peire was writing, his inspirers at Fanjeaux were still young: Aude, Fays, Raimonde, the wives of knights and co-seigneurs Hélis de Mazerolles, Esclarmonde de Feste, and India de Fanjeaux. All these *belles hérétiques* were destined to wander into hiding or to the stake several years later. In another song, Peire Vidal explains why the "heresy" has spread:

> *Now, how the Pope and the false doctors*
> *have cast Holy Church into such confusion*
> *that God himself is grieved!*
> *It's because they're so foolish and sinful*
> *That the heretics have sprung up;*
> *and since they're the first to sin,*
> *it's hard for one to do anything else—*
> *but I don't want to be their advocate!*[52]

He does not want to be the advocate of the heretics but declares that it is difficult to do anything else. This implicit tolerance of the heretics would, if voiced broadly ten years later, land him in quite serious and possibly fatal trouble. We know only that he died after 1204 in circumstances most probably sudden and obscure. But how could the laughing hostesses of amorous debate receive, apparently without difficulty, the austere voice of the *bons hommes*?

First, the voices may not have been so unfamiliar, because they might be listening to a nephew, uncle, sister, or mother. The message may have been austere, but there is no suggestion anywhere that the Cathars were humorless or colorless, as the archetypal puritan is reckoned (erroneously) to be. Deeper than this, we must consider certain harmonies of logic operating within the Fin' Amors and Catharism. Catharism gave women a spiritual role equal to that of men. The troubadours advocated a mutual cordiality in their relations with ladies. The idea of "putting women on a pedestal" is, however, inappropriate to the troubadours. If the woman was superior to the troubadour, it was only in the sense that she was either—and quite commonly—a social superior or set the conditions of service. The pedestal idea dehumanizes the lady and really belongs to the decadence of courtesy; many women have found that pedestals leave them an awfully long way to fall and that it is difficult to climb down.

The concepts of refinement and purification are very close, as is the generally upward spiritual aspiration, the development of consciousness. Like the Fin' Amors, Catharism rejected the sacrament of marriage, seeing it as an abusive sacralizing of a fleshly act—the Good Men might say the same of Miraval's concept of le Plus in principle, especially as there was always the possibility of producing offspring. This seems to have been rare, however, and has given rise to speculation either on what particular sexual methods were employed or as to whether the herbal lore of the region offered some form of contraceptive. Having said this, the Fin' Amors, unlike marriage, was based on privileged cordial aspiration for something better than what the vulgar world had to offer. (Within Miraval's dualism there is an analogy between the vulgar world and the Cathar suspicion that *this* world was hell, since they knew the light was inside them but trapped in a world of darkness.) We cannot say whether Miraval learned this worldview from Cathar teaching or whether it was merely congenial to his social and religious milieu, or indeed whether Miraval might claim it simply as his own view. It might have been long intuited, even before the Good Men had come from the East with their prepapal primitive Christian rituals. We might see the remnant of late-antique gnosis (Valentinian Gnostics had been particularly widespread in the south of France in the second century) or even a transposition from the Sufi gnosis of nearby Spain, which helped the first Cathar preachers be received and understood. Dualisms of various emphases were very much in the air, especially those of a Neoplatonic character, and this is not surprising in an age of the reassertion of the spiritual and the revolt against the brutality of external material power. As Anne Brenon writes, "It would certainly not be the Cathar Church which would condemn the joy of love as adultery."[53] Certainly there were good grounds for mutual tolerance and understanding, but there was more to it than that.

The interior processes of Cathar faith and practice and the Fin' Amors were parallel within a certain logic—more obvious if your best friends and relations held these views. The signs of a dualism of higher and lower worlds, spirit and matter, light and darkness, are implicit in Miraval's vision of life, but perhaps unlike the *perfecti,* the Fine Love has in itself the power to transform vision from one world to another. Miraval's lofty notions of purity come from within himself rather than any simple external transition of concepts. What we can never say is that the Fine Love was derived from Catharism or that Catharism could be derived simply from Fine Love. What we can say is that each provided a milieu of access to the other and that there is a sensibility, a common aspiration, even, and we have only to look at where Miraval lived to see this—a spiritual atmosphere emanating from the Cathars that almost certainly affected the direction and force of Miraval's *erosophy.*

Miraval does not sing about the religion of the Cathars, perhaps because they are his people. He is trying to work out a place for himself and his own particular gifts. He is not going to speak openly about what is going on. People were burned as heretics before the crusade; the issue of heresy was politically extremely sensitive—and Miraval's songs traveled far. But like Peire Vidal, he did not have to be their advocate—because the Cathars were superb advocates of their own!

The troubadours of the twelfth century all saw Fine Love as the privileged way—to those who surrendered themselves to it without reserve—of becoming better. When the troubadour loved well, when he cultivated within himself the courtesies that refined heart and deed, he ennobled and raised his merit or value and his consciousness. As Miraval sang: "It's thanks to her that I love the fountain and the stream." Troubadour contemporary Arnaut Daniel: "Always I become better and more pure / because I serve and honour the most kind." Miraval again: "Because it is from Love that proceeds the highest value." This love does not simply come from out of the troubadour; rather, everything good in the world comes from love—love is the source. Transcending limitations, yearning for the highest: These were the dynamics shared by Miraval and the Good Men and Good Women.

Above all we must recall that the troubadours were composers and musicians whose immediate task was to eulogize youth, moral courage, beauty, and joy. They were not preachers of the wisdom of age, or of the Ages (although they were, in a sense, prophets). There is little reason to suppose that the troubadours did not sometimes stop to consider that at some time in the future they might also feel the call of that exclusively religious life (as normally understood) advocated by the Good Men and Women. The knight and his family, while not perhaps disposed to look at the minutiae of theology, were yet deeply impressed by the gospel and, above all, the example of the Cathar *perfecti*. The knight could also be tolerant of the troubadour's elevated interest in his wife or sister. He was, after all, in a consistent social and cultural milieu that had the earth for its basis and heaven for its goal—while nobody denied that one essential word, *amor,* was the means from one to the other. The spiritual world was open; particular affiliation was a matter of choice.

The perfecti and troubadours were born in the torment of their age, born, according to Anne Brenon, "from the desire for light, from the desire for spiritual and moral renewal of this first great crisis of conscience—seeking again the Christian consciousness, at the heart of which the quest for feminine identity held so great a place."[54] From the reconnaissance of woman among the poets came a spiritual opening that enabled the Cathars to take their leading place in the general revolt against confusion and materialism. They dared to live, these too frequently forgotten or reviled "children of the resurrection," in accordance with their souls' highest aspiration.

According to Carl Jung, such a movement would simply *have* to exist, given that the "collective dominants of human life had fallen into decay."[55] The Cathars bore witness to the archetype of the numinous Self, the divine being within. The Christ-*Lapis,* or redemptive stone of spiritual alchemy, formerly hidden from consciousness, comes into this world from the dominion of heaven. The stone is a starry messenger of the lost truth concerning humankind. The troubadours, in a period of masculine dominance, bore witness to the numinous divine feminine (reminiscent of the Gnostic Sophia, Wisdom) projected into their very real and characterful ladies, leading through their poetry and music to self-discovery and a higher degree of psychic harmony than had been experienced hitherto. In the process, the troubadours created an entirely new cultural outlook and sensibility that is still, in adapted forms, alive within and without us today—although it does seem time for a renaissance before we are again swamped by the uniformed mass-masculine.

The *mysterium coniunctionis* remains to be achieved in everyone. In liberating the extraordinary and revolutionary vitality and mystery of the feminine—divine and human—the troubadours set a luminous example for their own time, for our time, and for the time to come. The Lady opens hearts and minds; without Her, we are spiritually dead.

THE LAST SONG

It pleases me to sing and appear loveable,
since the air is soft and the times gay,
while in the orchards and the hedgerows
I hear the chirping of the little birds
who sit close together, mocking
amid the green, the white and the violet,
He had better make up his mind—
He who would desire that Love support him—
and take up the manners of a genuine lover![56]

This is how Raimon de Miraval's last song begins. We get little impression of the desperate character of the times. He lives up to his maxim that a troubadour should appear happy even when sad. Then again, he is addressing a great lady: Aliénor, fifth wife of Raimon VI, count of Toulouse, and sister of Pedro II, king of Aragon. The date is

1213, the year when the armed resistance to the northern army collapsed at the battle of Muret. There is no doubt whose side Miraval is on:

> *Song, go speak on my behalf to the king*
> *Let Joy guide it, dressed and nourished,*
> *That there be nothing tortuous to him:*
> *Provided that he recovers Montégut*
> *and retakes his city of Carcassonne,*
> *he will then be Emperor of Worthiness*
> *and the French and the Mohammedans*
> *will dread his crown.*

The Albigensian Crusade had already dispossessed him of his little castle. Simon de Montfort, commander of the first military crusade of Christian against Christian, had taken over from the Trencavel family as viscount of Carcassonne, and Raimon VI of Toulouse was vitally menaced. René Nelli has captured the irony of history very well when he writes of how "after having many times given his castle to the ladies who please him, Miraval is now led by circumstances to offer it a last time—so that she can give it back to him—to the most powerful lady he had ever sung to."[57] Miraval is fully conscious of what is now being played for: the destiny of a civilization, a culture of love and joy.

> *My lady, you who have always supported me so well*
> *It is for you I have begun to sing again,*
> *And although I believed I should compose no more*
> *Before you had redeemed the fief*
> *Of Miraval, which I have lost.*
> *But the king has promised me*
> *that, before long, he will render it back to me*
> *So that, before long, we shall be able*
> *ladies and lovers*
> *to recover the Joy which we have lost!*

These are Raimon de Miraval's last remaining words, rendered even more poignant since we know what will happen. On the eve of the battle,

King Pedro writes to a Toulousain lady to say that he is only there with his army so as to defend her honor. The next day King Pedro is dead, and never more will the ladies and lovers of Languedoc be party to the flowering of joy in the Fine Love.

It is possible that Miraval followed Raimon VI to Lérida in Catalonia, where Pedro's successor Jaime I held court in 1214 and 1218. One manuscript *vida* has Miraval die in the convent of Sancta Clara in that city, but it is unlikely that that convent was yet built in 1216–18, the supposed date of Miraval's death. Louis IX ceded the village of Miraval and its dependencies to the chapter of Carcassonne in 1248. They held it until 1789. The name of Miraval does not figure in the 1262 royal enquiry that examined depositions made by the successors of forfeit seigneurs for the restitution of confiscated goods.

Miraval had gone.

THE JOY THAT WE HAVE LOST

The last troubadour was Guiraud Riquier of Narbonne (c. 1254–92), but by the time he reached maturity, the art was failing, the spirit that had inspired it suppressed. There was a slow process in action whereby religious lyricism aimed at the Virgin Mary was substituted for that of the lady. Consequently, heterodox people since that time have tended to see "Our Lady" not as the Virgin Mother but as Mary of Magdala, Christ's true lady friend. Furthermore, genuine love poetry aimed at real ladies became hidden within the cult of the Virgin, with all the inevitable results for the repression of women entailed in this. Ladies were virgins or safely married; *women* were fallen.

In 1323, a group of merchants, bankers, and clerks got together in Toulouse to codify rules of language and versification to encourage poets to perfect their art, to purify morals, and, in a climate of religious rigor, to edit works to be submitted for the approval of the Grand Inquisitor. The ancient poesy that was above all aristocratic (that is, class-free) became bourgeois. Courtly love had fed the Grail romances, providing the archetypal social context and social rule. With the crusade against the Cathars and the culture of the region in full swing, changes began to appear in the story lines.

One of the most significant changes, usually considered to be a legitimate development, took place in 1210 when a group of probably Cistercian monks from one of the large monasteries in the south of France gathered together their *Queste del Saint Graal.* They decided that Lancelot's sin (loving Guinivere) could be redeemed only at the cost of his personal failure in the quest for the Grail. So Lancelot is tricked into making love to the Grail King's daughter, because he thinks she is Guinivere. The result: Galahad, the "perfect knight," in the spiritual and temporal sense. He is, in fact, not a man at all.

It is given to Galahad to achieve the Grail and redeem the Wasteland: Galahad, the virgin knight who will have nothing to do with women. The courtly ethic is reversed, and we can say that if salvation depended on Galahad, then there is no hope for us; the sterile Wasteland will remain wasted. Virginity was the condition for cultural sterility in the troubadour tradition, and with its dominance the Fin' Amors could "do no more mighty works." Galahad is not a divine man; he is a painful substitute for Christ and the ultimate reason for the insanity of Cervantes' more divine fool, Don Quixote, destined to tilt at windmills while his real opponents laugh at him.

CREATION IS THE PRODUCT OF PAIN

The Cathar gnosis saw humankind as angels who had been called down and tricked by Satan into bodies of sleep and forgetfulness. Since the second century, there has existed a more romantic expression of the tragedy of existence and the redemption from it—namely, the Valentinian gnosis with which we began this chapter. This system describes in psychic terms not only the origin of the cosmos, but also the process of creation itself.

In timeless eternity, within the mysterious mind of the unknowable Father or Depth, Sophia, the divine Wisdom, in her yearning and loving desire to know the mystery of her source, autoconceives a manifest but imperfect cosmos in which the divine spirit is compromised. In this tragedy the human being is caught: a frustrating blend of animal, material, and spiritual. Sophia is brought back to the Fullness or Plenitude (Pleroma) by Christ, and balance is restored within the unfathomable divinity. Humankind (the unconscious Christ) is to embrace the heavenly Sophia, who has been recovered to the Pleroma. She is hidden within the human being and must be activated consciously. Frequently this is accomplished through projection of Sophia upon a woman.

In this quest of wisdom for the unknown and unknowable, we have an analogy for the upward yearning of spiritual aspiration in the love of the feminine spiritual principle. The desire to know God is profoundly involved with the desire to conceive new worlds, to know ourselves. According to this gnostic system, sexuality, once transmuted by the divine word of love that recovers the lost spirit, is an image for the yearning for gnosis, the saving knowledge of human origins. To quote from the Gnostic Gospel of Truth, attributed to the Egyptian Gnostic Valentinus:

> The [G]ospel of [T]ruth is a joy for those who have received from the Father of truth the gift of knowing him, through the power of the Word that came forth from the pleroma—the one who is in the thought and the mind of the Father, that is, the one who is addressed as the Saviour, that being the name of the work he is to perform for the redemption of those who were ignorant of the Father, while the name of the gospel is the proclamation of hope, being discovery for those who search for him.[58]

The characteristic state of the redeemed is joy, and this is also the characteristic ecstasy of the troubadour. In another Valentinian work, the Gospel of Philip, we are told, "Spiritual love is wine and fragrance. But the mysteries of this marriage are perfected in the day and the light. Neither that day nor its light ever sets."[59] This issue of the divinity of the redeemed erotic life is complex and difficult and is easily misrepresented and misunderstood.

There is the view within the Gnostic tradition that duality in the cosmos is the "product" of the fall of the suffering Sophia, to which catastrophe human suffering is psychically linked. It has been considered that this fatal yet necessary duality can be overcome—if only temporarily—through an alchemical concept and practice of sexual communion: an obvious analogy of two becoming one, something fraught with all manner of risks. Some have thought that the root of the purification difficulty could be overcome simply by abandoning altogether the concept of sin, since beyond the opposites, according to theory, there can be no good or evil. This is far from the troubadours, who believed that love made people good. All this is pertinent, since some people believe that the troubadours held a secret sex-gnosis for which they were condemned.

WERE THE TROUBADOURS SEXUAL MYSTICS?

One person who thought the troubadours were sexual mystics was the poet Ezra Pound. In 1910 he published *The Spirit of Romance,* in which he asked, "Did this 'close ring,' this aristocracy of emotion, evolve out of its half-memories of Hellenistic mysteries, a cult—a cult stricter, or more subtle, than that of the celibate ascetics, a cult for the purgation of the soul by a refinement of, and lordship over, the senses?"[60]

Pound, unaware of recent discoveries concerning the Cathars, believed that troubadour poetry involved visionary states of consciousness and probably involved a cult that affirmed the body and senses as vehicles of mystical experience. This theme was taken up by Omar Garrison in a book called the *Yoga of Sex,* in which the author quotes from Guillaume de Poitiers as evidence of Tantric sex practice in twelfth-century France: "I want to retain my lady in order to refresh my heart and renew my body so well that I cannot age. He will live one hundred years who succeeds in possessing the joy of this love."[61] John Kimsey comments on this: "The troubadour emphasis on gazing, extended arousal [?], and intense states of consciousness would seem to resonate with Tantric practices."[62] Ezra Pound reckoned "the Lady serves as a sort of mantram." Pound's peculiar troubadours tell us more about the repressions of the Edwardian era than they do about the twelfth century. Likewise, Garrison's Tantric troubadours tell us more about the "rediscovery" of sex in the 1960s than about Raimon de Miraval and his distinctive Catharized eroticism.

Although it is legitimate to compare the troubadour process with Gnostic imagery as a means of trying to understand the inner dynamics, we must be severely aware that there is no evidence that such typology was current within the troubadour movement. Rather, one is looking at an archetypal poetic process that, while illuminated by Jungian psychology to some extent, is foreign to what was apparently a spontaneous and fertile effusion of people who lived by their own moral, erotic, and spiritual categories. However, if Jung is right in his concept of the "self-regulating psyche"—that the archetypes emerge and possess the conscious mind when the "collective dominants of human life have fallen into decay"—then the process can always be in some respects repeated, given the right conditions.

Miraval died in a heartbreaking downturn of civilized life; his spirit, however, has truly survived, even though the precise details of his way of loving have undergone development. Thus we can find echoes of our man in Renaissance Platonic love poetry, in eighteenth- and nineteenth-century romanticism, and in the best of the rock-and-roll[63] and folk traditions.

The Fine Love was ecstatic but not mindless. Its disciplines were never easy because their aim was an elusive unity of flesh and spirit, requiring a commitment to self-purification alien to exploitable hedonism. Nothing guaranteed love.

SEVEN

The Knights Templar

The men from Brobarz rode up from the whole encampment to gaze at the spectacle of the Templars, who were splendidly arrayed, though their shields were well battered and holed by lance-thrusts delivered at full tilt, as well as gashed by swords.

WOLFRAM VON ESCHENBACH, *PARZIFAL*

*I*t is a common misconception that intellectual contact between Islam and Christianity was a prerogative of the Crusades, beginning around the year 1099, when the First Crusade gave control of Jerusalem to Godfroi de Bouillon, duke of Lower Lorraine, after three years of crusading and 461 years of Muslim rule. But at the time of the First Crusade, Islamic territory bordered on the county of Portugal, the kingdoms of León and Castile, the kingdom of Aragon, and the province of Catalonia. In the Norman county of Sicily, meanwhile, fashionable Christian women had taken to wearing veils like their Muslim neighbors. However, there can be little doubt that the Crusades, while apparently attempting to batter as much of Islam as possible, did accelerate the process of cultural interchange—and most of this cultural interchange flowed in one direction: from east to west. Indeed, the very premise of the Crusades was that there was something in the East worth possessing. Indeed, the crusaders found more than they had bargained for. Within fifty years of the First Crusade, the Latin translation school at Toledo was pouring out works of Arabic origin in a thriving city not twenty miles from the borders of Almoravid territory.[1]

On November 11, 1100, Godfroi's successor, his brother Baldwin, was crowned king of Jerusalem. In the eighteen years that followed, the Holy Land seems to have gone to the heads of the Frankish knights. Baldwin's chaplain, Fulcher of Chartres, asked his readers:

> Consider and reflect, how we, who were westerners, have become orientals: those who were Italian or French have become Galileans or Palestinians; those who lived in Reims or Chartres are now citizens of Tyre or of Antioch. We have forgotten our birthplaces. . . . Some are married, perhaps to a Syrian, an Armenian or even a Saracen who has received the grace of baptism, with children and even grand-children. . . . One man cultivates his vines, another his fields; those who in their homelands were poor have been enriched by God. Why should they return to the west when the east is so favourable?[2]

In the face of a thousand distractions, it must have been clear to some of the knights that, having won the prize, a tendency to recline and "go native" might be thwarted by the erection of a new Christian ideal. Thus were born the Poor Fellow-Soldiers of Jesus Christ, the warrior-monks, Christ's special militia. Their avowed aim was to protect pilgrims who came across the world to see Christ's birthplace and place of crucifixion. The names of the founders of this institution are given to us as Hugh de Payens (from Champagne, and a Holy Land veteran), Godfroi de St.-Omer (a Flemish knight), Payen de Montdidier, Archambaud de St.-Agnan, André de Montbard, Geoffrey Bisol or Bisot, and two men of whom we only know the Christian names: Rossal (or Roland) and Gondemare. The knights were very well connected. André de Montbard's nephew was Bernard de Clairvaux, the mystic, ascetic saint, and popular founder of the Cistercian Order. (He would later preach, with some initial success, against the Cathars and other heretics of the Languedoc in the 1140s.)

The coming together of the Poor Fellow-Soldiers is usually dated 1119, but there is a possibility that the idea first took root in 1111 or 1112. The new king, Baldwin II (cousin of the first), was impressed by their ideals and self-discipline. They had taken vows of poverty, chastity, and obedience and had sworn to defend the kingdom. These vows represented heavy sacrifices for the average knight—even the monk had a cell in which to hide from the world. The knights would be continually exposed to maximum temptation. Baldwin, in consideration of their sacrifice—and their overall usefulness—offered them as a base the so-called Stables of Solomon on the supposed site of the Temple of Solomon, and so the Poor Fellow-Soldiers became the Knights of the Temple of Solomon: the Knights Templar.

On January 13, 1129, an assembly at Troyes, in the county of Champagne, was convened following an appeal made by Bernard de Clairvaux to Pope Honorius II on the Templars' behalf. The job at hand was ratification of seventy-two articles that made up the first Rule of the Temple. This was Bernard's call to a pure and holy life, founded on communal lines at the expense of the individual. Members were to wear white, a surcoat adorned only by a red cross,[3] and, in cold weather, a cloak of simplest wool. They were to show no pride, to tend the Christian sick, and to fight with all possible enthusiasm, beyond the levels normally expected of a soldier. Members were to surrender their property to the order. The rule was very rigorous and idealistic, with a caveat at the end: "All the commandments which are set and written above are at the discretion and judgement of the Master"—the Master, not the pope. Once papal approval had been secured, the Templars set about adding to the rule. Six hundred further articles would appear before the Templars' demise.

The archetypal power of the Order of the Temple was immense. Hundreds of knights flocked to join as word got around. They had everything going for them: a mystery tour of the sacred East, the highest ideals, the abandonment of personal problems, the approval of God and his vicar, social and political status, independence of spirit, the opportunity both to fight *and* to be holy for a living, and, above all, real, unequivocal *meaning*.

The order soon became wealthy as a result of the many donations of land and property from across Christendom, while Templars could enjoy the paradox that they were themselves investing in poverty. The Order of the Temple did not give away its money and became very rich indeed. It lent money at interest to the monarchs of Europe and introduced the "cheque" system, thus assisting the growth of European capitalism. They also fought to the death for Christ. They were brave and disciplined, much feared by their enemies, cultivating a rich soil for legends to grow up in, unchoked by hard facts. They were secretive.

And then it all came to an end. Sixteen years after the fall of Acre removed the Templars from the sacred soil of Palestine (and thus from their primary purpose), Jacques de Molay, master of the Temple of Jerusalem, was arrested, together with five thousand French Templars. They were charged as enemies of humanity by the king of France, the vicious (and broke) Philippe le Bel ("the Fair"). The date was October 13, 1307. The Templars were accused of everything that might shock the vulgar imaginings of the God-fearing Catholic: sodomy, spitting on the crucifix, denying Jesus, kissing each other's erogenous zones, and, to cap it all, worshipping a bearded idol called Baphomet. On the basis of these accusations, not only were the French Templars imprisoned and tortured for seven years, but an entire industry of speculation has grown up that shows no signs of abating. In short, it has not only been suggested, but also stated as a blunt fact, that in its independence from normal feudal constraints, the Knights Templar had become a body of gnostic initiates.[4]

As in most webs of speculation, salient facts tend to be diminished. First, the Knights Templar was a military order, and gnostic belief sees nothing in this world worth going out of one's way to kill for, certainly not bricks and mortar, whether in Jerusalem or anywhere else. The Crusades frequently lunged into orgies of savage bloodletting, and the Knights Templar were certainly party to these atrocities—and an atrocity was still understood as such, even in the twelfth and thirteenth centuries. Second, action against the Knights Templar was taken by the king of France, and was in no way initiated by the papacy—which would have had much to fear from a heterodox military order with bases throughout Christendom. Indeed, the pope did everything in his (constrained) power to forestall and frustrate the mania of the French king against the Templars. The cold-hearted Philippe had, within his own understanding, sufficient reason to destroy the Templars without considering offense to his religion. He had applied to join the order and he—the king of France—had been rejected. Third, there was the simple fact of the Templars' institutional wealth. They even looked after the king's treasury, barely a stone's throw away from the royal palace in Paris.

Let us nonetheless look at the paucity of hard evidence on offer for a heterodox Order of the Temple.[5] On joining the Templars, the knight was made aware that he would suffer expulsion for simony, sodomy, larceny, heresy, conspiring treason, murder of a Christian (Catholic), revealing the secrets of his chapter, retreating from fewer than three enemies, and leaving the house other than by the gate. This is plain enough, but there were ramifications.

On March 29, 1139, Pope Innocent announced to the master of the Temple, Robert Craon, that from that moment onward the Templars had the right to approve their own chaplains (responsible to the master and not to any bishop). They were also granted rights to build their own churches and the right not to pay tithes to any clergyman (including the right to take tithes), and, last, Templars were freed from any authority but the pope's own. The Templars knew that that authority was inclined to waver in proportion to the cooperation the pope could garner from feudal princes. In effect, the order had become a kingdom of its own. Robert de Craon then initiated a curious move: the translation of the rule from nearly incomprehensible Latin to ordinary French. One particular change occurred that cannot be put down to a copyist's error. The original rule forbade any contact whatsoever with those excommunicated from the Catholic Church. To be excommunicated was a dreadful thing to happen to a Catholic Christian. He or she was cut off from God's grace before and after death.

The French rule (the Retrais)[6] states, "In those places where you know excommunicated knights to be assembled, there we command you to go; if there are any of them who wish to join the order, you should not consider the temporal profit as much as the eternal safety of their souls. In no other way should the brothers of the Temple have contact with a manifestly excommunicate man."

This rule was secret and was read only to new members upon their induction to the order. The new measures opened it to a multitude of potential recruits, some of whom might be very rich, and of whom some might have been penitent or even impenitent heretics. The rule shows an astonishing level of independence from ordinary Catholic life—but excommunication was not applied solely in cases of heresy. Barons were excommunicated for the murder of priests or for grossly infringing the temporal rights of the Church. However, the amendment does demonstrate a leniency that might have led to the acceptance of heretics or suspected heretics. Nevertheless, it is clear that the rule was firm on the question of whether a heretic could be a heretic and a Templar. The rule, at least, stated that he could not.

There is the case, for example, of Bertrand de Blanchefort, who became master of the Temple in 1156, and whose ancestral home was in Languedoc, then experiencing a penetration by Cathar perfecti. In their book *Holy Blood, Holy Grail,* authors Baigent, Lincoln, and Leigh state that de Blanchefort was "a nobleman with Cathar sympathies," offering no evidence for this ambiguous assertion, and by a degree of legerdemain link him with "the lord of Blanchefort" who "had fought at the side of Raymond-Roger Trencavel, the Cathar leader."[7]

First of all, Bertrand de Blanchefort died on January 2, 1169—forty years before the first Albigensian Crusade against the Cathars. Second, Raymond-Roger Trencavel was certainly not "the Cathar leader." Nor is there evidence that he was a Cathar. Trencavel's main business was to defend the viscounty of Carcassonne from the twin threats of the count of Toulouse and the crusaders led by Simon de Montfort, among whom, it must be stressed, were authorized Knights Templar. Templars participated in the massacres of perceived heretics.

TEMPLARS AND CATHARS

If Bertrand de Blanchefort *was* sympathetic to Cathars in the 1150s, he was only practiing the courtesy that so many nobles in the region were extending to these mysterious and sincere preachers. Take this, and the spuriously colorful identification of Wolfram von Eschenbach's "Gral castle," Munsalvaesche (in his *Parzifal*),[8] with the Catharist fortress of Montségur, away from the *Holy Blood, Holy Grail* thesis of strong and determinative links between Cathars and Knights Templar, and there really is not much left to argue with.

Why is the identification of Montségur with the fictional Munsalvaesche spurious? First, Montségur was not offered for Cathar use (as a bank) until 1204 and did not become a significant Cathar stronghold until after the second Albigensian Crusade began in 1226, while Baigent, Lincoln, and Leigh themselves date *Parzifal* to circa 1195–1216. Second, von Eschenbach says his story preexisted his telling of it, which again prejudices any historic identification of the Gral Castle with Montségur. Third, von Eschenbach puts "templars"[9] in the castle—highly unlikely, one might think, if that castle were Montségur, considering the Templars' role in the crusade against the Cathars; besides which, we know who was guarding Montségur—and they were not Templars.[10] And fourth, *Parzifal* is not historical evidence; it is literature. Anyone who has read this masterpiece soon realizes how absurd it is to link this tale of knightly fun to the promulgation of secret heresy. Its message is simple: Every knight, no matter how rough he is to begin with, no matter how tempted he is, has the chance to reach his own Gral, his own ideal, and be saved. It might be a recruitment document for a would-be Templar, but never for a Cathar, who would regard its magnificences with amused tolerance. Wolfram von Eschenbach undoubtedly shared the disgust of many troubadours and heretics for the hypocrisy of priests who failed to live up to their own preaching, but he had nothing but respect for the honorable Catholic priest: "You must place your trust in the clergy. Nothing you see on earth is like a priest. His lips pronounce the Passion that nullifies our damnation. Into his consecrated hand he takes the highest Pledge ever given for debt. When a priest so guards his conduct that he can perform his office chastely, how could he lead a life more holy?" (*Parzifal,* chapter 9). Parzifal is a good Catholic; he is also an effective killer.

Further light on the question of relations between Templars and Cathars has emerged from the French historian Raimonde Reznikov. His book *Cathares et Templiers* is something of a scholar's antidote to the wilder extremes of conspiracy-mongering. According to Reznikov, apart from the obvious link that Templars and Cathars were suppressed by mutual connivance between state and church, the only serious sympathetic link came from the imaginations of eighteenth-century Freemasons. Reznikov writes:

> The Templar mythology, fabricated in the 18th century in the bosom of German lodges by the vanity of Freemasons, desirous to join themselves to a pretended tradition more valorous to their eyes than the builders of walls, was then considerably amplified during the religious quarrels of the 19th century. On the one hand, ultra-royalists presented the Templars, allied to the Cathars, as being akin to revolutionaries wanting to destabilise the papacy and the social order by spreading abominable doctrines. While on the other, according to anticlerical republicans, the Templar martyrs, descendents of Cathar martyrs, became "sages indignant at seeing the people oppressed in the sanctuary of their conscience by kings, superstitious serfs and the intrigues of the priesthood [Marquis de Condorcet]."[11]

Today, of course, we have Masonic Templars, whose establishment followed on from Chevalier Ramsay's rousing "Oration" of 1736, which linked Masonry to chivalric orders of the Crusades. Ramsay did not specify the Templars, but the word *temple* worked its own magic and sealed the identification. Nobody ever called their lodge a "hospital," so the Knights Hospitalers of St. John have tended to take second place in Masonic interest to the crimson bloodiness of the Templars. In fact, Reznikov's book shows that the Hospitalers had better relations with Catharist noble families in the Languedoc than the Templars. Reznikov's map shows that the Templars' presence in the region, compared to that enjoyed by the Hospitalers, was relatively slight (the book gives excellent detailed breakdowns of the places and people linked to the Hospitalers, Catharism, and the Templars).

Reznikov's work makes it absolutely clear that there was no concordat or mutual interest between Cathars and Templars, taking it for granted that alleged proto-Masonic links are childish fantasies. Notable with regard to the former statement is Reznikov's fascinating tale of two corpses.

In 1211, while fighting a war begun two years earlier by northern barons led by Simon de Montfort (the Albigensian Crusade) in an effort to exterminate Catharism, Count Raimonde VI of Toulouse gave the defense of Montferrand in the Lauragais to his brother, Baudoin. During the fight, Baudoin switched sides to de Montfort and went on to fight on Simon de Montfort's side at the Battle of Muret (1213) against his own brother's ally, King Peire II of Aragon.

The Aragonese king—the hope of those defending the Cathars— was killed. But in February 1214, Baudoin was himself captured as he slept at Lolmié in the Quercy, whence he was brought to Montauban to the court of Raimonde VI and sentenced to death for treason. It was the Knights of the Temple who would claim Baudoin's body and inter it in the church cloister of their commandery at Villedieu.

This event somewhat mirrors the events of the evening following the decisive Battle of Muret itself during the previous year. With Simon de Montfort's permission, it was the Hospitalers of St. John of Jerusalem (the old rival order to the Templars) who took the body of Peire II of Aragon to their cemetery in Toulouse and thence to their monastery at Sijéna, Aragon. King Peire's mother, Sancha, had founded the monastery for the sisters of the Order of St. John. Peire's surviving son, on the other hand, now a hostage to Simon de Montfort—the proud killer of thousands of Cathars—was given to the care of Guillaume de Montredon, master of the Temple in Aragon.

It is clear from this and other events and accounts of the period detailed in the book whose side the Templars were on. The fact of the matter was that the Templars lived on estates given to them on the express understanding that they would support the Catholic Church— the very deeds of their foundations required that they see Cathars as heretics and enemies of Rome. It had nothing to do with the Holy Grail.

Raimonde Reznikov is quite clear about the nature of the real Templars: "The knights of the Middle Ages did not enter a military order to acquaint themselves with metaphysical or intellectual speculations. The real initiatic knowledge of the era disclosed itself elsewhere, in the scriptoriums of the great abbeys, at Lérins, Saint Victor or Montmajour for the Midi and Provence, at Glastonbury in the British Isles, and at Bobbio in Lombardy." Furthermore, "the esotericism of the 12th and 13th centuries was as scientific as that of antiquity, having nothing in common with the lamentable accusations of the inquisition against the Templars: the old malicious and scandalous themes dragged out against all the adversaries of the Roman church since its birth."[12]

Templar spirituality was a world apart from that of the Cathars: "The spirituality of the Order of the Temple, inspired by that of St Bernard, exalted Marian devotion, glorified the Hebrew Bible [unlike the Cathars] and could not conceive of itself without an unbreakable fidelity to the Church."[13]

So what have they in common? Both groups were victims of alliances between the papacy and the Capetians, and both groups were linked by extra-Craft and fringe Masonry, and the enemies of such groups, each to its own ends. The case for the Blood-Grail-Templar-Cathar connection, diverting as it is, evaporates into thin air. Having said that, the alleged Templar–Cathar link is not the only route to follow in seeking evidence for a religiously heterodox Temple.

For some reason, the last master of the Temple of Jerusalem, Jacques de Molay, after assuming that office in 1293, changed the master's words of pardon and valedictory blessing offered to confessing sinners at the end of Temple services at preceptories all over Christendom. Before de Molay, the words read: "I give you what pardon I may, in the name of God, and of Our Lady, and of St. Peter, and of St. Paul, and of yourselves who have given me the power." De Molay's changes allowed for the forgiveness of unconfessed sins: "I pardon you the faults which, through shame of the flesh or fear of the justice of the house, you have not confessed."[14]

This change may have been well intentioned, and certainly liberal in an illiberal age, but it is nonetheless a profound change and could easily have been taken to mean that all sins, not merely failures in discipline, were absolved. This might have led to degeneration, or even exotic innovation, within an order coming close to the end of two centuries of existence. It could be argued that the (for their time) behavioral enormities confessed after intense psychological and most awful physical torture enacted at the hands of the Dominican Inquisition were, if not pure fabrications, the rare occurrences of those released from confessional obligations, and not characteristic of the order in general. However, there are at least three confessions, one involving the name of Jacques de Molay, that may suggest some doctrinal disorientation within the last master's order.

Godfroi de Gonneville, preceptor of Aquitaine and Poitou, saved his skin (he was sentenced to perpetual imprisonment) before the Inquisition in France by asserting that some unnamed people had said evil and perverse rules and invocations in the Temple, introduced by a brother Ronçelin, formerly a master of the order. Between 1248 and 1250, Ronçelin de Fos was master of Provence, and between 1251 and 1253, master of England. Between c. 1260 and 1278 he was again master of Provence. Provence had been an area rich in Catharist heresy, and it is not inconceivable that he imported or tolerated Cathar ideas and bore witness to these ideas in English temples. The Cathars are generally thought to have repudiated the doctrine that it was the crucifixion of Christ that made salvation possible and resented the image of the cross as a divine rather than a devilish dispensation. This could explain the phenomenon—if such there ever was—of spitting on the cross.

In June 1311, in London, without torture but before representatives of the Inquisition, Stephen de Stapelbrugge confessed that he had been shown a crucifix and instructed to deny "Jesus was God and man and that Mary was his mother."[15] Again, a docetic idea is implied, familiar to Catharism, that Jesus was a wholly spiritual avatar from the kingdom of Light, unencumbered by matter and only appearing to be fleshly.[16] It was, of course, just the sort of thing the Inquisition wanted to hear.

A more interesting confession came out of John de Stoke, formerly treasurer of the London Temple and a man personally known to England's kings Edward I and Edward II. While formerly denying all accusations, he later said that on a visit to Temple Garway in Herefordshire (whose remains may still be seen), Jacques de Molay had claimed that Jesus was "the son of a certain woman, and since he said he was the Son of God, he was crucified." Therefore, he should deny Jesus. He was told to believe only in "the great omnipotent God, who created heaven and earth, and not in the Crucifixion." This is in no way the statement of a Cathar, nor anything like it. It would certainly not be out of place in the mouth of a Saracen (of whom John de Stoke had plenty of experience), or indeed of a Zarathushtrian, Nosairi, Hermetist, or Mandaean.

With regard to the notion that Jacques de Molay was a secret Muslim, one should bear in mind that he had begun his mastership with a determination, based on twenty-eight years of active service in the Holy Land, to wipe out and harass Muslim power wherever possible. He castigated his predecessor for making peace agreements with the infidel. De Molay was even dismayed at the tendency of Templars in the south to take up literary interests.[17] Furthermore, Jacques de Molay had enemies within the order itself, such as Hugh de Pairaud, made treasurer of the Paris Temple in 1307, a man who believed he had been passed over for the mastership as a result of de Molay's intrigue. It might be that John de Stoke was under the impression that if he could pin the blame on Jacques de Molay, the order might be saved in England, or resurrected later. Any hope of that would be dashed the following year.

On April 3, 1312, Pope Clement officially dissolved the Order of the Temple in perpetuity. On March 18, 1314, two old and much abused men, Jacques de Molay and Geoffrey de Charney, the preceptor of Normandy, were roasted alive on an island in the Seine—de Molay having recanted his former confession of guilt and proclaimed his innocence of all charges. Philippe le Bel, a spectator, was cursed by the master as the latter writhed in prolonged death agony, and it is true that both the king of France and the pope he controlled were dead by the end of the year. A period of ignominious defeats then assailed the French kingdom for over a century, a process immortalized in Maurice Druon's dramatic novels *The Accursed Kings*.

In terms of our primary question regarding heterodox beliefs in the order, this really leaves only two main issues: the alleged connection between the Templars and the allegedly gnostic Holy Grail (or, as von Eschenbach spells it, the Gral), and the idol called Baphomet that the Templars were accused of worshipping. In discussing these problems, we are in the position of sporting leaden boots wading through a marshland wondering if we shall ever reach the next hedgerow, never mind the lost horizon.

THE TEMPLARS AND THE GRAL

In 1204 the Knights Templar participated in the sack of Christian Constantinople, all part of a deal struck between Boniface of Montferrat and the doge of Venice, who bore a grudge against the Greeks of that city over matters of trade. The soldiers of the Fourth Crusade duly obliged, satisfied that, as adherents to the Eastern Orthodox Church, the Christians of Constantinople were heretics; and besides, had not St. Bernard himself blamed the failure of the Second Crusade on the treachery of the Byzantines?

Constantinople collapsed in an orgy of blood, iconoclasm, rape, sacrilege, and rioting. Out of all the carnage, it is now suspected that the Knights Templar acquired some rather important relics, such as the True Cross on which the Lord of Life was killed, and that sacred object now known as the Turin Shroud. This, to the mind of the thirteenth-century Christian, was power of a very special kind.[18] In their function as bankers and holders of wealth in trust, while bearing in mind the institutionalized secrecy of the order—not to mention their contact with a Holy Land that to most people of the time must have appeared a semimythical environment—it might also have been speculated that the Templars had acquired the Holy Grail, however that object of knightly aspiration might be understood.

The chief document put forward in favor of such a thesis is Wolfram von Eschenbach's (fictional) account of a celestial Gral guarded by "templars" in his *Parzifal*. Wolfram's account of how he received the Gral story for his *Parzifal* is undoubtedly intriguing, as there is the whiff of some historical actuality underlying the fantasy.

Wolfram states that one of his sources, "the heathen Flegetanis," who left a document in Toledo (famous for its translation school), was an astronomer who was both Jewish and, on his father's side, a heathen (he "worshipped a calf as though it was his god"). Flegetanis had seen the Gral, its name spelled out in the stars, and left on earth by "a troop" that then "rose high above the stars, if their innocence drew them back again." Wolfram states that the document of Flegetanis had been discovered by "the wise Master" Kyot of Provence, thus tying Wolfram's work into the status of the Languedoc troubadours, for whom there was such a vogue in the courts of Germany. In spite of there having been a historical person called Gyot of Provins, a troubadour, the weight of scholarship falls against the idea that Wolfram is presenting a true story regarding his primary source.[19]

Wolfram's sources, other than the highly Catholic Arthurian stories of Chrétien de Troyes, are obscure.[20] Von Eschenbach was exceptionally well read, and alchemical sources cannot be ruled out. For example, his account of the Gral bears little conceptual analogy to the idea of it being the cup in which Joseph of Arimathaea collected Christ's blood—as in Robert de Boron's *Joseph ou l'Estoire dou Graal* (c. 1210). Wolfram's setting for his Gral account is almost wholly alchemical. The Gral is identified with the Stone:

> "It is well known to me," said his host, "that many formidable fighting-men dwell at Munsalvaesche with the Gral. They are continually riding out on sorties in quest of adventure. Whether these same Templars reap trouble or renown, they bear it for their sins. A warlike company lives there. I will tell you how they are nourished. They live from a Stone whose essence is most pure. If you have never heard of it I shall name it for you here. It is called 'Lapsit exillis'.[21] By virtue of this Stone the Phoenix is burned to ashes, in which he is reborn.— Thus does the Phoenix moult its feathers![22] Which done, it shines dazzling bright and lovely as before! Further: however ill a mortal may be, from the day on which he sees the Stone he cannot die for that week, nor does he lose his colour. . . . Such powers does the Stone confer on mortal men that their flesh and bones are soon made young again. This Stone is called 'The Gral.'
>
> "Today a Message alights upon the Gral governing its highest virtue, for today is Good Friday, when one can infallibly see a Dove wing its way down from Heaven. It brings a small white Wafer to the Stone and leaves it there. The Dove, all dazzling white, then flies up to Heaven again. Every Good Friday, as I say, the Dove brings it to the Stone, from which the Stone receives all that is good on earth of food and drink, of paradisal excellence—I mean whatever the earth yields. The Stone, furthermore, has to give them the flesh of all the wild things that live below the aether, whether they fly, run, or swim—such prebend does the Gral, thanks to its indwelling powers, bestow on the chivalric Brotherhood.

"As to those who are appointed to the Gral, hear how they are made known. Under the top edge of the Stone an inscription announces the name and lineage of the one summoned to make the glad journey. Whether it concerns girls or boys, there is no need to erase their names, for as soon as a name has been read it vanishes from sight! Those who are now full-grown all came here as children. Happy the mother of every child destined to serve there! Rich and poor alike rejoice if a child of theirs is summoned and they are bidden to send it to that Company! Such children are fetched from many countries and forever after are immune from the shame of sin and have a rich reward in Heaven. When they die here in this world, Paradise is theirs in the next.[23]

"When Lucifer and the Trinity began to war with each other, those who did not take sides, worthy, noble angels, had to descend to earth to that Stone which is forever incorruptible.[24]

"I do not know whether God forgave them or damned them in the end: for if it was His due He took them back. Since that time the Stone has been in the care of those whom God appointed to it and to whom He sent his angel. This, sir, is how matters stand regarding the Gral."

"If knightly deeds with shield and lance can win fame for one's earthly self, yet also Paradise for one's soul, then the chivalric life has been my one desire!" said Parzifal. "I fought wherever fighting was to be had, so that my warlike hand has glory within its grasp. If God is any judge of fighting He will appoint me to that place so that the Company there know me as a knight who will never shun battle."[25]

Had von Eschenbach's Flegetanis (used here as a cover name for some of Wolfram's alleged Eastern sources) seen Libellus 4.25 of our present *Corpus Hermeticum*, he would have read there the story of a dish or bowl sent down to earth by God. This account, linking this mythical image directly to gnosis, was probably written in Greek in Alexandria (c. A.D. 200–300) and is of course attributed to the mythic sage Hermes Trismegistus.

Hermes: It is man's function to contemplate the works of God; and for this purpose was he made, that he might view the universe with wondering awe, and come to know its Maker. . . . Now speech, my son,

God imparted to all men; but mind [*nous*] he did not impart to all.

Tat: Tell me then father, why did God not impart mind [*nous*] to all men?

Hermes: It was his will, my son, that mind should be placed in the midst as a prize that human souls may win.

Tat: Where did he place it?

Hermes: He filled a great bowl with *nous* [mind], and sent it down to earth; and he appointed a herald, and bade him make proclamation to the hearts of men: "Hearken, each human heart; baptize yourself in this bowl, if you can, recognising for what purpose you have been made, and believing that you shall ascend to Him who sent the bowl down." Now those who gave heed to the proclamation, and dipped themselves in the bath of mind, these men got a share of *gnosis;* they received mind, and so became complete men. . . . As many as have partaken of the gift which God has sent, these, my son, in comparison with the others, are as immortal gods to mortal men. They embrace in their own mind all the things that are, the things on earth and the things in heaven, if there is aught above heaven; and raising themselves to that height, they see the Good.[26]

This amusing account is plainly a gnostic allegory on the theme of free will and spiritual predisposition. Acquaintance with the "bowl" (Greek: κρατηρ, *krater,* origin of our *crater*) is a goal well worth seeking.[27] Are there any grounds for thinking that Wolfram had access to Hermetic sources? Such access might be considered unlikely until the name of Thabit ibn Qurra emerges from Wolfram's text. Thabit ibn Qurra, the Sabian polymath who took Hermes as his prophet and the *Hermetica* as his holy book, is mentioned by name in chapter thirteen of *Parzifal* as a "philosopher" and one who "fathomed abstruse arts." When Wolfram has cause to list the planets, he gives their names in Arabic. Indeed, the whole of *Parzifal* is drenched in Germanicizations of Eastern lore, which, we may surmise, were exactly what his readers wished to be stimulated by—and he makes it plain that the source for such information was Toledo, which indeed it was.

Wolfram says that "Kyot," having learned about the Gral from Flegetanis in Toledo, sought supportive Latin sources to discover whether there was ever a company suitably pure for the guarding of the Gral. He says that he found his answer in Anjou (roughly the modern Touraine). Wolfram was fond of the Angévin dynasty and links it throughout *Parzifal* to his tales of questing knights. Parzifal himself is written up as a scion of the House of Anjou, a family that had produced both Henry II and his son Richard the Lionheart from his marriage to Eleanor of Aquitaine, learned patron of troubadours. Undoubtedly there did exist an Anjou–Templar link. Henry II's grandfather Geoffrey, count of Anjou, joined the Templars in 1125 (giving the order a great deal of property in the process).

Henry II used the Templars in his machinations, whereby he secured the Vexin from the Capetians as a French princess's dowry. He also used the services of the English master of the Temple, Ralph de Hastings, in pursuance of the famous Thomas à Becket case. The master voluntarily went on his knees before Thomas, the exiled archbishop of Canterbury, to encourage the latter to accept Henry's conditions regarding the (Clarendon) Constitution, which Henry wanted imposed on the English church. Under Henry's son John, the king had a Templar master for royal soldier, while the head of the English Temple (acting as papal envoy) was a witness to the Magna Carta (1215).

Henry II's right-hand man, William Marshall, ruled as co-marshal with John Lackland while the latter's brother, Richard the Lionheart, was fighting the Third Crusade, and during the king's subsequent incarceration.[28] Marshall became regent of England from 1216 (on the death of King John) until Henry III attained his majority.[29] He had seen the Templars in Palestine while a crusader, admired them, and was admitted to their company on his deathbed in 1219. He was buried in the Templar church in London. Under Henry III, a Templar brother had control over the king's household finances (the Royal Wardrobe). The House of Anjou placed enormous trust in the Knights Templar.

Once the Gral was deposited on earth, Wolfram's "source" informed him that "a Christian progeny bred to a pure life had the duty of keeping it." This could cover a great deal of ground, but for the suggestion that Flegetanis was an Easterner. If we might speculate further, the origin of these guardians of the Gral (an alchemical but not necessarily heterodox conception) could have been anything from the Sabians of Baghdad or the Mesopotamian Mandaeans to the mysterious Nosairis of northwestern Syria, who may have employed a kind of Grail symbolism. Groups of this kind survive to this day. There were so many different sects operating secretly or otherwise in the Middle East—in northern Syria, Iran, Mesopotamia, Egypt, and Asia Minor—at the time of the Crusades that any Westerner could be forgiven for getting them all hopelessly confused. Syncretism had been a dynamic of Eastern religion from time immemorial.

Nevertheless, the array of talents ascribed to Wolfram's Flegetanis—knowledge of the stars, precise astronomy, material concerning the Gral lodged in Toledo—make it not unreasonable to suppose that behind Wolfram's fiction may lie access (once or twice removed) to the Sabian *Hermetica,* in Greek or in Syriac. The *Hermetica* appeared in Constantinople in about 1050. That epiphany may have been due to the preservation instincts of those Sabians who disappeared from Baghdad at the same time. Constantinople fell to Western knights in 1204, an event referred to in chapter eleven of *Parzifal.*

What Wolfram may have been doing was playing with contemporary myths from the East built around current affairs: news of Christian victories (and disasters) in the East, along with the appropriation of Eastern secrets. His work represents an elevation of the House of Anjou (at the expense of Chrétien de Troyes' patrons in Flanders and Champagne) as protectors of learning and wisdom—even of a mystery beyond the plainly eucharistic mystery of Robert de Boron and Chrétien de Troyes. He may also have been encouraging a fresh crusade based on more spiritual motives that, if honestly adhered to, might have avoided the terrible defeat of crusaders at the Horns of Hattin in 1187. In that campaign, the grand master of the Templars, Gérard de Ridefort, committed two fatal blunders that led to the decimation of both the forces of his own order and those of the Knights Hospitalers.

Readers of the time might have been disposed to compare the high—even supernatural—ideals of the Gral Templars with the low dealings that characterized Gérard de Ridefort's grand mastership. It may be fair to say that behind Wolfram's tale is a sense that responsibility for God's most sacred mysteries has been transposed from the East to the West, and in particular to the great House of Anjou.

BAPHOMET

In looking at the question of the Gral, supposed Catharist practices, and other demonic charges leveled at the Templars, we must keep in mind that these were in the main attached to the Templars by outsiders. When we come to the question of whether the Templars ever worshipped an idol called Baphomet, the issue is more complicated because several Templars did, under torture, admit to some kind of practice involving a head with one, two, or three faces that was said to be responsible for germination. No such head was ever produced as trial evidence, however, and nothing resembling such a head has survived. Sometimes associated with the name Baphomet, that appellation, odd as it is, is just about all we have to go on (unless one wishes to advance the painted head of a bearded man on a door found in Temple Combe as a two-dimensional candidate).

A list of charges submitted by inquisitors on August 12, 1308, accuses the Templars on grounds that:

in each province they had idols, namely heads . . .

Item, that they adored these idols . . .
Item, that they said that the head could save them.
Item, that [it could] make riches . . .
Item, that it made the trees flower.
Item, that they surrounded or touched each head of the aforesaid with
    small cords, which they wore around themselves next to the shirt
    or the flesh.[30]

We know of several belief systems in which a simple head was regarded as a significant object[31]—the most obvious one involving the

;an "green man," whose foliate features have graced many medieval churches and who has been associated with the vestiges of pre- and post-Christian fertility cults. As far as we know, these carved heads were never adored in the manner suggested by the Inquisition charges. Such a head could simply have represented the god Pan (Greek for the All), a conception of nature that might have been of significance to builders building on cosmic principles (the Templars did have their own masons).[32]

According to Peter Partner, Baphomet simply meant "Mahomet" in old French and was used as part of a general demonology current among all classes at the time for the "heathen" Prophet of Islam. Partner quotes from a Provençal poem ascribed to Ricaut Bonomel wherein the poet describes how the Saracens after 1265 "impose new defeats on us: for God, who used to watch on our behalf, is now asleep, and Muhammad [Partner's translation of Bafometz] puts forth his power to support the Sultan."[33] But in a sense, this only raises a question: Why call Muhammad Baphomet in the first place, unless as a general term of abuse—and if so, why would "Bafometz" have been thought abusive?

"Baphomet" does sound like one of the many attempts of Westerners in the Middle Ages to get their tongues around a Semitic or Eastern language. Thus, Abu Hamid ibn Muhammad al-Tusi al-Ghazali turns up in the West as Algazel; Ibn Bajja, Avempace; Abu'Ali al-Hasan ibn al-Haytham becomes Alhazen; and Abu'l-Walid ibn Rushd somehow becomes Averroës. We cannot therefore expect "Baphomet" to mean exactly what it says. Several leading interpretations run as follows. The Arabic *abufihamet* in Moorish Spanish comes out as *bufihimat*, and has been translated as "Father of Wisdom" or "Father of Understanding." If we take the word as a transliteration from Greek, we could sustain βαφη μηθρα *(baphe methra)*, baptism of Mithra. This might tell us something of the confused origin of the word, but not necessarily anything about the particular object to which the word was attached. No student of the subject seems to have thought clearly about what, for example, a "baptism of Mithra" could have involved. The most famous image of the Mithraic cult as it was practiced in late antiquity depicts a youth in a Phrygian cap slaying or sacrificing the "cosmic bull," from whose orifices emerge blood (life), sperm (life), and corn (life). What do all these substances have in common? Water. Mithra is the sender of life.[34] So when Ricaut Bonomel complains that "Bafometz puts forth his power to help the Sultan" (in Partner's quotation above), it might simply be a (then-) understood euphemism for rain or some related climatic phenomenon favorable to the enemy, in terms of either a good harvest (bread for his troops) or thunderstorms that harass the crusaders. There is really no reason to suppose that a more complex rationale underlies the name Baphomet. Furthermore, the Inquisition records themselves attest that the head regarded with respect by some Templars was the bringer or herald of fertility, change, rebirth, new life, and the like.

It may be significant in this regard that Templar confessions suggested the head had two or three faces.[35] The two-faced head speaks immediately of the Roman god Janus, god of the doors between past and future, looking both ways at once: time as a cyclic continuum. Janus is of course the god of January, the first month of the Gregorian new year, the end of the old and beginning of the new. In this regard, a most sensible solution to the age-old mystery of the head "worshipped" by Templars can be found in a recently discovered letter. The letter is from Archdeacon Ralph Churton, fellow of the Society of Antiquaries (1754–1831), to John Brickdale Blakeway, the historian of Shrewsbury, who had inquired of the archdeacon as to the origin of an ancient Christian festival called Relique Sunday:

> I called upon our emigrant priest from France residing in this parish.[36]
> "Pray, monsieur, what is Relique Sunday?" "It is no *saint* in our Church; it is the Sunday after Pentecost, Trinity Sunday. It is no *saint* in our Church; in my country [France] the common people call it Relique Sunday. The Church promotes customs which promote piety; but it is no *saint* of the Church." "Perhaps they show Reliques on that day?" "Oh there be many Reliques! There is [*sic*] the Reliques of St. Peter, *which I have seen;* there be the Reliques of St. Januarius. There had been not a drop of rain for two months; everything was burnt up. All the people, men and women and children, crowded into the street. What now? What is all this? The head of St. Januarius! In

a moment great drops began to fall; they were all wet, could hardly get home! Oh it is wonderful!"

And I think so too, but the good-humoured chattering Frenchman believes every tittle of it, and will, I dare say, swear it through an inch board.[37]

Overleaf, the archdeacon adds, "In the mean time I shall be glad if I can learn how many genuine heads there are of St. Januarius. For I certainly understood my Frenchman to speak only of what he had seen in France; whereas the Neapolitans, as is commonly said, maintain that the veritable wonder-working head of Januarius is in their keeping at Naples."

It would be in keeping with the purpose of the inquisitors of the Templars to present the innocuous as the diabolical.

Nevertheless, there does remain solid evidence of an iconographical link between the Templars and Gnostic symbolism. Sylvia Beamon's fascinating book, *The Royston Cave: Used by Saints or Sinners?* based on her master's thesis on the Order of the Temple, shows a Templar seal (*Archives Nationales*, D.9860 bis, Paris) that she describes as an "abraxus" or secret seal with the words *Secretum Templi* (referring to the Templar treasury) around a figure familiar to Gnostic students. Some of the figure's body is armored, but the chest area sports a "court robe." In place of legs are serpents that terminate in two heads. The figure's head is a cockerel's. The figure has strong Gnostic associations and is identical to magic gems of the Abrasax, or anguiped type, from the Roman period. The figures (with cock's or ass's head and serpent feet) often bear names of Jewish origin found in Gnostic texts as the names of gods or archons, such as Ialdabaoth, Jao, Abrasax, Sabaoth, Adonaios. Abrasax, or Abraxas and has the Greek letters corresponding to the number 365, thus representing the god of the solar year, or perhaps of time itself.

It is striking that the seal depicted in Beamon's book belonged to the grand master of the Templars and was used in a French charter dated October 1214. Following von Hammer-Purgstal, there have been suggestions that the figure represents Baphomet or "Baphometides," the baptism of wisdom; or, alternatively, Bios, Phōs, Metis—Life, Light,

Wisdom. The speculative possibilities are legion because we simply do not know why the grand master of the Templars should have employed such a figure.

And in case we were disposed to consider this an isolated case of fortuitous identification, a metal-detector enthusiast discovered a seal bearing the same figure and inscription in the Lichfield area of Staffordshire in 1997. Most intriguingly, this seal contained within it a tiny piece of woven fabric. The object was sent to the British Museum, where it presumably will languish among many other objects that fit into no currently respectable theory. The matter remains a mystery.

TEMPLARS IN SEARCH OF THE STONES

It must have been an amazing experience for the first Templars to wake up on the Temple Mount in Jerusalem to watch the sun rise over the Holy Land. How could they avoid seeing themselves in biblical colors? Had they not defeated the heathens and established the reign of Christ over the site of the Temple, ushering in a new era for humankind? And yet, perhaps not surprisingly, they sought their spiritual forebears not so much from among the disciples of the New Testament but from among the holy warriors and priests of the Hebrew Bible.

According to Dr. Helen Nicholson, the order developed a pseudo-prehistory based on the Book of Judges. This biblical work describes the military victories of the Israelites over the "heathens" of Canaan. God blessed their efforts as he had those of the Templars. Since there was no Temple at the time of the Judges of Israel, Templars thought of themselves as Levites, the priestly caste in the process of constructing a *spiritual* temple. What is even more astonishing is that these early Templars identified themselves—and were identified by others—with the Maccabees, who fought against the Seleucid king Antiochus IV's troops to cleanse the Temple from heathen profanation (December 165 B.C.) and so purify the religion of Israel.

In 1159, John of Salisbury, in *Polycratus,* his work against hypocrisy, compared the hypocrite with the evidently virtuous Templars who, like the Maccabees, laid down their lives for their brethren. Pope Celestine II's Bull *Milites templi hierosolymitani,* of 1144, accepted the comparison of the Knights Templar with the Maccabees who fought Gentiles in defense of the Temple, and for the land that God had given his people. Before the rout at Nazareth shortly before the Battle of Hattin (1178), Grand Master Gérard de Ridefort gave a rousing speech to his troops, in which he entreated them to remember the courage and example of the Maccabees. After 1215, a work built upon that of Wolfram von Eschenbach, the *Lancelot-Graal,* even called Judas Maccabaeus the first knight. Templars doubtless hurried to read or be read to of their holy forebears' adventures in the apocryphal Books of Maccabees—which, eleven hundred years before, had so nourished the supposed sectaries of Qumran in their quest for a purified Temple. Maccabees contains a little-known mystery regarding the altar of the Temple:

> Then Judas appointed certain men to fight against those that were in the fortress, until he had cleansed the sanctuary. So he chose priests of blameless conversation, such as had pleasure in the law: who cleansed the sanctuary, and bare out the defiled stones into an unclean place. And when as they consulted what to do with the altar of burnt offerings, which was profaned; they thought it best to pull it down, and laid up the stones in the mountain of the temple in a convenient place, until there should come a prophet to shew what should be done with them. (1 Macc. 4:41–46)

Apparently around the year 1125, the first Templars spent a great deal of time clearing out the "stables" (the "Stables of Solomon") beneath their headquarters in Jerusalem.[38] By the middle of the century, construction and excavation work enabled the Templars to keep as many as two thousand horses there. From the discovery of passageways explored at the end of the last century by Charles Warren with the aid of the Palestine Exploration Fund, it is possible to infer that the Templars had, in the process, dug passages right under the El Aksa Mosque. (Entry to these passages is currently forbidden.) While some have speculated that they were searching for the Ark of the Covenant or even the Holy Grail, could it not be that they had simply heard the above passage, and gone in search of the stones—stones with which to symbolically erect a new Temple Order? Certainly, Bernard de

Clairvaux, author of their rule, would have known of the passage. Could he not have played the part of the prophet who would show the Templars what to do with the stones, should they have found them?

Had the stones been discovered, the discovery might even have been regarded as a sign of the Parousia, for which there was widespread expectation in this period. The stones the (Maccabeean) builders rejected (or at least laid aside) would then have become the cornerstones of the new Temple. Although this suggestion is merely hypothetical, it would, again, provide a reasonable solution to a mystery with regard to the Templar presence in Jerusalem that may, of course, not be a mystery at all, but rather the projection of one.

So were the Knights Templar gnostics? They were certainly not accused of being so. They were not even accused of being Manichees, the usual accusation leveled at intelligent dualist "heretics" in the twelfth and thirteenth centuries. The Templars were not accused of being Cathars either. They were accused of apostasy (worshipping idols), heresy, and abominable practices that could not be reconciled to their exalted (and powerful) position in Christendom. In Germany, Portugal, Spain, Scotland, and England, the charges against them were generally held to be spurious. Templars walked free—free, that is, to join other orders, or to retire to monastic quietude—after the pope, under extreme pressure from the French king, announced his decision to suppress the order on March 22, 1312. There is even some reason to suppose that a fleet of French Templars sailed to Scotland and continued their traditions in the Western Isles.

Regarding Baphomet, perhaps the most suggestive idea that Templars were involved in a para-cult to Catholicism, we must bear in mind that even in the thirteenth century, the symbolic use of pagan deities was neither unknown nor proscribed in literate circles (and few Templars were literate). The troubadours, for example, spoke of the god Amor without thinking for a moment that they were transgressing the sacred precincts of the Holy Trinity. Likewise, Baphomet may have meant no more, in terms of contradistinction to the Catholic faith, than Jack Frost, Father Time, Mother Nature, Halloween, the May Pole and May Queen, the Bogey-man, John Barleycorn, the Green Man, and the Lion and the Unicorn have meant to countless Western children. It must also be recognized that the significance of the Baphomet accusation has probably been massively overstated. As evidence it is weak and ambiguous in the extreme—hence, it is open to the most extravagant interpretation.

Baphomet, if it ever existed, may have been no more than either a pet name for what had begun as St. Januarius or something some Templars picked up on their travels. There may have been a private ritual—the word *ritual* need not be overstressed; morning ablutions can be spoken of as a ritual—of pagan origin, perhaps, but that was certainly not regarded as being outside of the general faith in Christ. Formerly pagan practices have often been seen as complementary to or even confirmatory of Christianity. They probably contemplated some kind of head or bust, but the name Baphomet may well have been a "tabloid smear" by their accusers—that is, that the Templars were fifth columnists secretly supporting Islam. Perhaps some Templars *had* picked up something of the theosophical attitude of seeing the names of deities as varying labels for fundamental energies that transcend both language and culture. For those who cared to know the ins and outs, Mithra could be seen as the Christ of the soldier, doing battle, redeeming the world from the dark powers, and promising renewed life on earth and resurrection on the last day. Obviously, there may have been Templars who took such ideas to higher or deeper levels of involvement, but we simply have no concrete evidence to back up such a supposition—and until such evidence appears, we must withhold judgment.

KILWINNING

There is, of course, a longstanding belief that the origins of Freemasonry may be sought among the Knights Templar. In particular, it is still widely held that those origins are most closely bound to Scotland, whither, it is supposed, French Templars fled for freedom from papal jurisdiction sometime after the first attack on the order in October 1307.

One place stands out in Masonic mythology as the epicenter of Templar–Masonic union. That place is Kilwinning, on the banks of the river Garnock, some twenty-five miles southwest of Glasgow.

In December 1999, Kilwinning's Masonic lodge celebrated four hundred years of existence, an event recorded in the Masonic historian Matthew Scanlan's article on Kilwinning for the influential quarterly *Freemasonry Today*. Scanlan wrote of how "numerous myths surround the fabled lodge. After the formation of the first Grand Lodge in London in 1717, the writer and Freemason, Dean Jonathan Swift, published an anonymous letter in Dublin which claimed to have been sent by the Grand Mistress of the Society of Female Free-Masons. In it he linked the 'famous old Scottish lodge of Kilwinning' with 'the Branch of the lodge of Solomon's Temple,' later known as the Knights of St John of Jerusalem and the brother order of the Templars."[39]

The eighteenth century found the story much to its liking. It resurfaced after a Boxing Day Masonic meeting at a Parisian restaurant in the rue du Paon in 1736. "Chevalier" Andrew Michael Ramsay delighted the assembly with his view that the order's great aim was to unite all virtuous, enlightened minds with a love of the fine arts, science, and religion to the end that "the interests of the Fraternity shall become those of the whole human race."

Ramsay had studied under the guidance of the liberal mystical philosopher François Fénelon, protector of the harassed mystic Madame Guyon. Ramsay clearly regarded history as a battle for the revelation of the light. This light had begun to emerge under chivalric patronage in the Middle Ages but had been extinguished by the willful ignorance of wicked authorities. Ramsay's "Oration" continued on the grand theme, likening the Craft to the ancient mystery societies, while claiming their mystic rites concealed traces of the pristine religious consciousness of Noah and the Patriarchs.

Revived during the Crusades, the spark of enlightenment was returned to England by Edward I. Thence it traversed the border to Scotland, where, according to Ramsay, "James, Lord of Scotland, was Grand Master of a Lodge established at Kilwinning in the west of Scotland in 1286, shortly after the death of Alexander III, king of Scotland, and one year before John Balliol mounted the throne."[40]

Ramsay's "Oration" led swiftly to the creation of new Masonic rites built around the myth of a religious-military or chivalric order of knights, not infrequently linked to the name Kilwinning. Students of the Ancient and Accepted Rite of Masonry will be familiar with the

"Heredom [possibly 'holy mountain'] of Kilwinning." Other readers may consult A. C. F. Jackson's history of that rite, *Rose Croix*.[41]

In fact, the first known mention of a lodge at Kilwinning comes from the late-sixteenth-century Schaw Statutes (issued on December 27, 1598). William Schaw, appointed Master of Works by James VI of Scotland in 1583, had jurisdiction over Scottish Masonic practice. According to D. Murray Lyon's *History of the Lodge of Edinburgh*, the regulations confined lodge membership to those who had been tested and who had submitted an essay; charity to brother Masons was required as well as obedience to an elected warden. No master was to work with "cowans," or unqualified Masons.[42]

There was argument about the rules necessitating a second meeting, held on St. John's Day at Holyrood Palace. To this meeting came a commissioner from Kilwinning, begging to know his lodge's status, as it had not been mentioned in the statutes. This omission was rectified in the second set of statutes. Apprentices and craftsmen would be admitted only in the church at Kilwinning; the warden and deacon of Kilwinning should take the oaths of craftsmen. Furthermore, Schaw instructed all "maister massounis" to abide by all statutes made by Kilwinning lodge's predecessors. Wardens should take "tryall of the art of the art of memorie and science thairof." Kilwinning was nonetheless instructed to accept second place to the Lodge of Edinburgh, the principal lodge of Scotland.

In November 1736, the founding of the Grand Lodge of Scotland again raised the issue of Kilwinning's status. Since Kilwinning's minutes were unavailable before 1642, Edinburgh again achieved primacy—a conclusion unwelcome to the brethren of Kilwinning, who seceded from the Grand Lodge in 1743. The lodge would issue charters from their autonomous status to establish other lodges bearing the name, a name jealously regarded, as one might expect. There would be no reconciliation on the issue until 1806, when a happy compromise was reached. From that time on, Kilwinning received the honorary Number 0, to which members today add the rubric: "Mother Lodge of Scotland."

It is clear that Kilwinning's lodge predated Schaw's statutes. However, written evidence is absent, which of course fuels the mystery. Schaw's statutes demanded all lodges employ notaries for making of records—an innovation that explains why evidence is unavailable prior to that time. Furthermore, Kilwinning Abbey's chartulary, which might have assisted us in accounting for the lodge's origins, was lost some time after the Scottish Reformation in the 1560s.

The abbey itself was begun in about 1140 after a group of Benedictine monks from Normandy encountered remnants of Culdees (members of the ancient Celtic Church) at Kilwinning. The abbey gained in wealth and prestige throughout the thirteenth century. It was the abbot of Kilwinning, Bernard de Linton, who, as King Robert Bruce's chancellor (since 1309), recorded Robert's heroic speech before the Battle of Bannockburn in 1314. We do not know if a lodge of Masons continued after the abbey was substantially finished. There was certainly a lodge there after the abbey's destruction by the reformer John Knox's follower, the fifth earl of Glencairn. Indeed, it may have been the effects of Reformation demolition that led to Schaw's statutes in 1598. By 1643, lodge minutes reveal that Kilwinning was calling itself the "antient ludge of Scotland," but there is no mention of Knights Templar.

It would seem that Ramsay's Templar myth may owe its genesis chiefly to the happy confluence of Dean Swift's anonymous letter with an ancient, ruined abbey, a strikingly "ancient" lodge, and the association of that lodge with chivalrous old families (the eighth earl of Eglinton was initiated in 1674). This was all wrapped together with Ramsay's strong desire to find the battle for enlightenment in the misty pages of history and unfolded again for a parched audience thirsty for strong idealistic drink. Where there is a vacuum of knowledge, there is mystery—and vice versa. Of course, it would be decidedly unchivalrous not to note that Chevalier Ramsay—and others—may have known something that we do not.

CONCLUSION: GNOSTICS IN THE TEMPLE?

The Order of the Temple was certainly not a covertly gnostic institution, but some of its members had ample opportunity to acquaint themselves with gnostic experience, and some may have done so. However, the original question itself may mislead us. As stated at the beginning of this chapter, the idea of an institutionalized military gnostic system is simply absurd. In looking for heresy, we may have missed the point. Gnostic thought does not arrive prepackaged with a "heresy" stamp upon it; it is so much a question of interpretation. Much of the knowledge that was moving in the Templar period from East to West was derived from traditions of gnosis. That is a plain fact. But it was *knowledge*. The patron of much of that knowledge was Hermes. The very structures of Catholic Christendom were built on knowledge ascribed to Hermes and any number of other pagan theoreticians. Knowledge itself was seldom banned because of its origin; scientific investigations of origin were not a feature of medieval intellectual life; faith did not require science.

The question with regard to heresy was one of usage and the potential of that knowledge to blend with or coexist with the established ecclesiastical order. The Church of the Cathars, for example, refused to bow its head to the Church of Rome, whereas the Templars accepted the established order. Were it not for the fierceness and duplicity of King Philippe IV of France, the Order of the Temple would probably still be with us—and doubtless the history of the Western world since that time would have been subtly or even overtly different. It is not surprising that since the collapse of Catholic Christendom in the sixteenth century, there have been a number of revivals of the order of questionable legitimacy. However, the great political opportunity of the Crusades (from an orthodox Christian point of view)—seized with such alacrity by the order's founders—seems to have been lost forever.

At Royston in Hertfordshire, below the main street is an extraordinary bottle-shaped cave, cut into the two hundred-foot-thick layer of chalk that lies under the town. Discovered in 1742, the walls of the cave, which encircle an octagonal base, feature enigmatic carvings (once painted) believed to have been made by Knights Templar, possibly following the attack on their order.

The carvings depict the crucifixion, the resurrection, St. Catherine (with her wheel), St. Lawrence (martyred on a gridiron), the twelve apostles, St. Christopher (patron saint of travelers), a troop of saints and martyrs, the remains of what appears once to have been a carving of two knights on a single horseback (denoting poverty, and a traditional seal-image of the Templars), King Richard the Lionheart and his wife, Berengaria, and a number of symbolic hands with the shape of a heart in them. There are also Palestinian-style axes, a *sheila-na-gig* (a

sexually explicit fertility sculpture), a floriate cross, swords, striking figures of indeterminate provenance, and curious concentric circles. The
style and symbolism are closely akin to the peculiarly distinctive style
of graffiti carved into the walls of the Chinon dungeons in the county
of Anjou by arrested Templars awaiting torture and condemnation.

Prominent on the circular relief is the figure of a king, arms
upraised, a finger pointing upward, while his waist is cut off, perhaps
by water. He appears to be drowning. This figure is almost certainly a
representation of King David, author of the Psalms. He is crying for
help. The reference would appear to be to Psalm 69, a terrible lament
sung by a good man in the face of persecution and misunderstanding:

> *Save me, O God; for the waters are come in unto my soul.*
> *I sink in deep mire, where there is no standing: I am come*
> *into deep waters, where the floods overflow me.*
> *I am weary of my crying: my throat is dried: mine eyes fail*
> *while I wait for my God.*
> *They that hate me without a cause are more than the hairs of*
> *mine head: they that would destroy me, being mine enemies*
> *wrongfully, are mighty: then I restored that which I took*
> *not away.*
> *O God, thou knowest my foolishness; and my sins are not hid*
> *from thee.*
> *Let not them that wait on thee, O Lord GOD of hosts, be*
> *ashamed for my sake: let not those that seek thee be*
> *confounded for my sake,*
> *O God of Israel.*
> *Because for thy sake I have borne reproach; shame hath*
> *covered my face.*
> *I am become a stranger unto my brethren, and an alien unto*
> *my mother's children.*
> *For the zeal of thine house hath eaten me up; and the*
> *reproaches of them that reproached thee are fallen upon me.*

The Templars, like so much discussed in the pages of this book, are
still waiting for understanding.

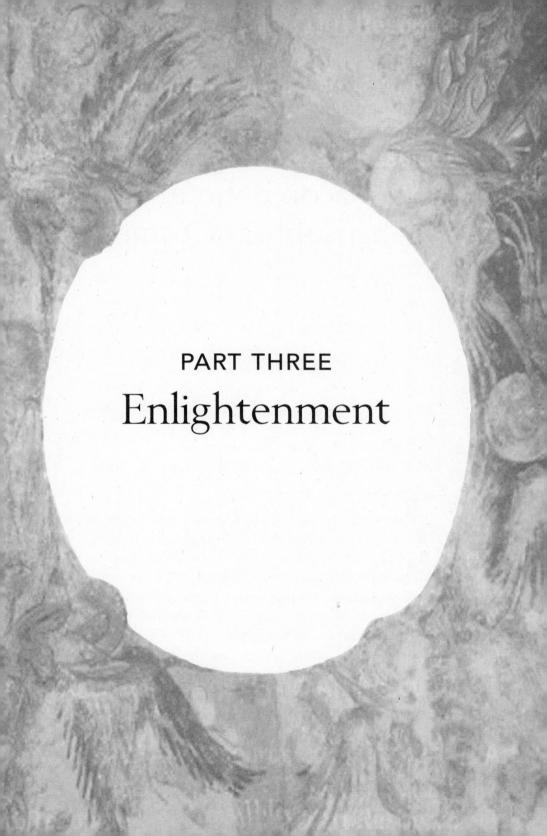

PART THREE

Enlightenment

EIGHT

Jacob Böhme's Theosophick Cosmos

The roaring of lions,
the howling of wolves,
the raging of the stormy sea,
and the destructive sword,
are portions of eternity,
too great for the eye of man.

WILLIAM BLAKE, *THE MARRIAGE OF HEAVEN AND HELL*

According to the twentieth-century theologian Dr. Paul Tillich, Jacob Böhme (1575–1624), the inspired "shoemaker of Görlitz" and "Teutonick Theosopher," has exercised "an astonishing influence on the history of Western philosophy."[1] From the German Romantic philosopher Friedrich Schelling's endorsement of Böhme in his *Of Human Freedom* onward, Böhme's metaphysical dialectics have influenced the works of Hegel, Schopenhauer, Nietzsche, Hartmann, Fichte, Bergson, and Heidegger.

Through Hegel, Böhme's system was passed on to the left-wing radical philosophy of Ludwig Feuerbach and through Feuerbach to Karl Marx, who, being an atheist, made perilous nonsense of the metaphysical inheritance. Nevertheless, Böhme's contribution to the philosophy of the arts of the imagination has been, and still is, enormous. Samuel Taylor Coleridge, for example, in addition to making an enthusiastic study of Böhme's own works, quoted (without reference) whole passages from the writings of the pantheist Schelling in his *Biographia literaria,* begun in 1814. William Blake's fundamental indebtedness to Böhme (along with Emanuel Swedenborg and Paracelsus) is well known.

The style and nature of Böhme's work led to the resurrection of an old word, *theosophy.* The great scholar of the Kabbalah Gershom Scholem defined the word thus: "Theosophy signifies a mystical doctrine, or school of thought, which purports to perceive and describe the mysterious workings of the Divinity. . . . Theosophy postulates a kind of divine emanation whereby God, abandoning his self-contained repose, awakens to mysterious life. . . . Theosophists in this sense were Jacob Böhme and William Blake."[2] Theosophy, then, presupposes the ability of the seer to envision the inward origin of the universe and give an account of the objective being of the divinity.

Böhme frequently attracts and has long attracted those with an irresistibly gnostic cast of mind. When his works first appeared in the seventeenth century, those seeking a theological gnosis (whether that was a word the seeker would recognize as valid or not) could draw on only the *Hermetica* and the condemned works of radical reformers such as Schwenckfeld, Weigel, Franck, and Paracelsus. These latter radical works were often locked into the Reformation debates of previous generations.

What is perhaps most remarkable about Böhme's works is that he integrated the Renaissance science-occult tradition with the growing movement of mystical Pietism and the broad stream of Paracelsianism. His works read like Hermetic dialogues, but their textual sources were predominantly biblical. If you wanted a gnostic sage to deliver the Christian mystical goods, Böhme was probably your man.

Furthermore, his thinking had powerfully liberating elements of intellectual originality, and Böhme lived the life; he walked the walk as well as talked the talk. He was a holy man who dwelt in the real world, a Protestant who did not protest. His thought went back to the mystics of the "undivided Church," broke through the squabbles of the "external Church" to the eternal life of the soul, and looked to the future toward a comprehensive divine science.

BÖHME'S LIFE

Jacob Böhme was born of a prosperous farming family at Altsteidenburg in Upper Lusatia (Ober Lausitz) in eastern Germany, but in his early years he went to live in Görlitz, where he manufactured quality shoes.

Religious life in the city was stimulated by the activities of one Pastor Moller, who had been sensitive to the thought of Caspar Schwenckfeld[3] and who appreciated the theological interests and questionings of his parishioners.

At the age of twenty-five, Böhme seems to have undergone his first spiritual experience, feeling himself to have been penetrated by "the Light of God." He later wrote of how "in one quarter of an hour I saw and knew more than if I had been many years together in a university. . . . I saw and knew the Being of Beings, the Byss and the Abyss, the eternal generation of the Trinity, the origin and descent of the world, and of all creatures through divine wisdom."[4]

Some commentators date his first major experience ten years later, that is in 1610, when, gazing at the reflection of the sun in a pewter dish, he suddenly realized that the brightness was visible only on account of the darkness of the surface from which it was reflected. He grasped in visual form the paradoxical character of light and darkness.

Light and darkness, of course, had long been used as metaphors for divine illumination and spiritual evil, and Böhme was wont to attribute theological value to the physical facts and vice versa. Experience was the keynote of his theosophy; in this he was in tune with the growing spirit of his age. Furthermore, it was something of a "Rosicrucian" principle to obtain illumination by reflection on nature. Böhme's experience was a striking parable of this principle, telling him that if light was to be made manifest, darkness was essential. Since it was obviously good that light should be manifest, then darkness and "evil" had a potential place in the divine will from the very beginning.

According to a follower, Abraham von Frankenberg, Böhme was "according to God's holy counsel . . . stirred up and renewed by God. Whereupon . . . he could not put it from his mind, nor strive against God. These (he) did . . . write secretly for himself."[5] Von Frankenberg dates the pewter dish experience to Trinity Sunday 1600, an experience that introduced Böhme "into the innermost ground or centre of the . . . hidden nature."[6]

Böhme introduced this dialectic in his manuscript *Aurora, or Morning Redness,* composed for his own edification and distributed by Böhme's friend the aristocrat Carl von Ender, of a Schwenckfeldian family; Böhme was encouraged to publish in 1612.

Aurora, incidentally, had a wide circulation among German intellectuals and Continental Symbolists (the art movement) at the beginning of the twentieth century. In 1612, however, circulation was curtailed in Görlitz by Pastor Moller's successor, Gregory Richter. Richter despised the audacious pretension of a tradesman to theological learning and had the magistrates expel Böhme from the city. The magistrates, knowing Böhme a good man, had a change of heart and permitted him to return in 1613, so long as he published nothing more for the rest of his life.

Böhme spent the rest of the decade in publishing silence, while the rest of thinking Europe became excited by the Rosicrucian manifestos (Böhme thought them interesting, but mad). His chief intellectual companions during this period were Carl von Ender, the Paracelsian physician Tobias Kober, Johann Huser (publisher of Paracelsus's works), Johann Rothe (a student of the medieval mystic Tauler), and the devoted follower Balthasar Walter.

By the end of the period, while confusion reigned over the Rosicrucians, clarity had infused Böhme's mind: A metaphysical structure had appeared that accommodated Renaissance schemes of planetary interaction and opposition with the alchemical theme of the transformation of base matter. The alchemical "marriage of the contraries" symbolized in the *rebis*, the androgynous symbol of sulfur and mercury embodying a mutual polar opposition, chimed with Böhme's insights into the necessity of internal opposition in the projection of the divine being. (One immediately thinks of Blake's *Marriage of Heaven and Hell* and his aphorism "Opposition Is True Friendship.")

The Paracelsian influence looms large in Böhme. The title of his work *Mysterium magnum* (1623), for example, is the Paracelsian term for the great matrix of nature—the Mystery, the *prima materia* of all things, whose masculine opposite is the Archeus, or "Separator." The

Archeus is the differentiating aspect of divine mind within the undifferentiated *massa confusa* that extends endlessly throughout creation, like the entwined roots and branches of an infinite, even sinister forest.

Paracelsus' triadic system of salt (matter), sulfur (soul), and mercury (spirit) is deeply ingrained in Böhme's system; the triad is interpreted by Böhme as a dynamic spiritual process of purgation, illumination, and transformation (or union). Indeed, Böhme sees the cosmos as an ongoing dynamic expression of these principles; the process is forever immanent.

Kabbalistic influence is also present. Two of Böhme's basic symbols, the Ungrund, or primal abyss, and the archetypal Man, or original Adam, are consistent in meaning with the kabbalistic Ain Soph (unknowable limitless light) and the figure of Adam Kadmon, whose body contains the universe.[7]

We can see in all this the idea so central to Paracelsian circles that the universe is a divine riddle, encoded with deep secrets awaiting the inspired and pure decryptor. It is little wonder that Böhme himself would come to be so closely associated with the fictional brotherhood of the Rose Cross, even to being seen as a kind of honorary member. For Böhme's most devoted followers, Böhme had apparently "cracked it."

Böhme's works promised a veritable science of God, and some of his followers felt they could no longer deny the world the fruit of Böhme's inspiration. On New Year's Day 1624, they published several of his tracts under the title *Der Weg zur Christo* (Way of Christ). This event precipitated the troubles that would mark the mystic's life's end, or at least his departure from this world.

Pastor Richter stirred up the mob against Böhme and his family; windows in his home were smashed. There was a hearing before the elector, but Böhme was neither condemned nor exonerated regarding his Lutheran orthodoxy.

Until his death in November of that year, Böhme labored hard on works that included the *Table of Three Principles, Theosophical Questions,* and the devotional works *Dialogue Between an Enlightened and an Unenlightened Soul* and the highly influential (in Pietist circles) *Of Divine Prayer.*

Now very ill, Böhme was examined on the Lutheran creed by

Master Elias Dietrich. Dietrich, sent by Richter's successor Pastor Thomas, left satisfied that the dying man was not a heretic.

On the day of his death, Böhme was heard to remark that he could hear the strains of sweet music (as William Blake was also reported to have heard on his deathbed two hundred years later). Böhme blessed his family and murmured quietly, "Now I go hence to Paradise."[8]

ELEMENTS OF BÖHME'S THEOSOPHY

And as the Light hath quite another Property than the Fire hath, for It giveth and yieldeth Itself forth; whereas the Fire draweth in and consumeth itself; so the holy Life of Meekness springeth forth through the Death of SELF-Will, and then God's Will of Love only ruleth, and doth ALL in ALL. For thus the Eternal ONE hath attained Feeling and Separability, and brought Itself forth again with the Feeling, through Death in great Joyfulness; that there might be an Eternal Delight in the Infinite Unity, and an Eternal Cause of Joy; and therefore that which was before Painfulness, must now be the Ground and cause of this Motion or stirring to the Manifestation of all Things. And herein lieth the Mystery of the hidden Wisdom of God.[9]

Böhme's famous starting point is what he calls the *Ungrund*.[10] This is generally understood as a word for God as pure will, without presupposition, without goal or motive, pure divine will beyond all description. And this purity of will is no quality, nor is there a will to do, or a will to will; it is the absence of quality. It is not pure because it contains no impurity, for it contains nothing, nor is the Ungrund a container. This is God as "groundless," unrelated, absolutely nowhere: the abyss, nothingness, timeless, Being before creation, before time—therefore, not being at all: nothing. This Ungrund is nothing because it is like nothing, is impacted by nothing, refers to nothing, is contrasted to nothing; reflectionless because there is nothing to reflect in. It is no thing. Its existence at all is only potential; the Ungrund is actually nothing. To speak of Ungrund is to say nothing. This God does not exist; there is no God where He is.

You cannot pray to the Ungrund, for there is nothing to pray to, nor anyone to pray, neither is there prayer. Nor is there *there*. And the Ungrund is only a word that means nothing but the source of everything.

Welcome to the worlds of Jacob Böhme.

The two contrary worlds of Böhme's theosophy arise from what Désirée Hirst declares to be "the most startling doctrine Böhme developed,"[11] that of the Eternal Nature. Evil does not enter the world through Adam's sin, but was there from the beginning *in potentia*.

Eternal Nature exists, according to Böhme, before creation; it arises from the Abyss, the Ungrund, by God's mysterious will to know Himself. The Eternal Nature is expressed in three principles. The first two principles are defined as "with the stern Fire-world, according to the Father's Property, and according to the Light and Love world is the Sonnes Property; and yet it is, but One only substance undivided, but One God; as Fire and Light is One."[12]

For God to know himself, he required the manifestation of opposites (Father/Fire and Son/Light). Once these opposite principles are manifest, their *contrarium* produces a reaction, a flash like a spark from force of friction, and a third is produced, the Outbirth, with a momentum of its own.

Be it noted, however, that "Light and Darkness are *in* One another."[13] We could not know what the unmanifest nature of light and dark would be, since we would first need to posit the duality. In their manifestation, God "sees" what we cannot, for we are creatures of the duality; at least, from thence we derive our senses.

Böhme chose to illustrate this pattern in a manner akin to other Rosicrucian works of his time, such as those of Robert Fludd, published by Theodor de Bry and illustrated by Matthieu Merian. The iconography of dynamic globes and circles was very much in the air of a world coming to terms with an animated rather than a static universe. Böhme drew a dark circle touching a light one, with a third circle underneath both. The point of contact between light and dark principles is marked by the "lightning flash," the creative spark. This ignited flame of vitality is akin to the belief in an alchemical fire hidden but present in all things, deriving from creation's first birth—the universe derived from a metaphysical combustion.

The subtlety of Böhme's thought did not pass by his contemporaries. Here was a deeply pious image of divine activity—or at least its setting was deeply pious—that avoided the familiar crude divisions into good and evil that continually begged the question of God's responsibility for wickedness and decay. We may also think of the twin pillars of the kabbalistic tradition: the pillar of mercy and the pillar of severity, between which the divine expresses itself. We can be sure that if Böhme had seen a cathode ray tube, with its electrons shooting onto the screen of manifestation and vision, propelled by oppositely charged polarities, he would have delighted in this three-dimensional image of his thesis/antithesis/synthesis dialectic.

To summarize, the Eternal Nature arises from the Abyss, expressing itself in three distinct intelligible principles:

1. The world of Fire and Power: the world of the Father
2. The world of Light and Love: the world of the Son
3. And, as a result of the confrontation of these contraries (the contrarium within the Eternal Nature), the Outbirth, which is the cosmos

As stated, the first two worlds are in reality one, as fire and light are one. So God exists as Father insofar as will is lord of fire and power, and God is Son insofar as will is the bearer of the light-principle.

The being of all being is but a single being, yet in giving birth to itself, it divides itself into two principles, into light and darkness, into joy and pain, into evil and good, into love and wrath, into fire and light; and out of these two eternal beginnings into a third beginning, into the creation itself, as its own love-play between the qualities of both eternal desires.[14]

Through the contrarium of light and dark powers, the self-expression of the eternal will gains life (as we understand it), actuality, definition, and attributes. This process is perhaps familiar to us in the Hegelian dialectic of thesis and antithesis, generating synthesis: the universe as the auto-gnosis or Self-consciousness of the primal One, the formerly unexpressed and essentially inconceivable Ungrund. The contraries of good and evil are transcended in God's essential nature, which nature is ultimately mysterious and not subject to the lower faculty of reason.

The image of a Big Bang, currently favored by some scientists as a good working theory for the origin of the universe, would not be entirely alien to this visualization—the archetypal spark of ignition is there. It should also be observed that there is no Manichaean-type division here between absolute principles of good and evil at source. The whole is an interaction, in the first phase, of different kinds of dynamic good. The absolute essence of that good is not available to ratiocination, however, because, we may assume, rationality is a feature of that which is created, the Outbirth.

Böhme's system, as his disciple Abraham von Frankenberg observed, was very close in principle to that of the Valentinian Gnostics as expressed by Irenaeus in his *Adversus haereses* (c. A.D. 180). Slightly closer to home is the summary of Böhme's essential philosophy made by Edward Taylor in his *Jacob Behmen's Theosophick Philosophy Unfolded* (1691):

Principle 1. The Spring or Fountain of Darkness.

Principle 2. The Vertue (or Power) of Light.

Principle 3. The Outbirth (generated) out of the Darkness by the Power of light.

Represented by Similitudes, *viz*: [here Taylor shows how Böhme's system works from the point of view of the redeemed man]

1. Man's Soul, giving Reason and Thoughts, signifieth the Father.
2. The Light showing the Power of the Soul and how to direct it, representeth the Son.
3. The Mind resulting from this Light, and governing the Body, resembleth the Holy Ghost.

1. The Darkness in us, which longeth after the Light, is the First Principle.
2. The Vertue of the Light, whereby we see Intellectually, is the second Principle.

3. The longing Power proceedeth from the Mind, and that attracteth or impregnateth itself, whence groweth the Material Body, is the Third Principle.[15]

A feature of Böhme's system with Gnostic resonance lies in the place he accords to the heavenly Sophia. It was her ungovernable yearning to know the Depth or Bythos that was, in the Valentinian system (second century A.D.), the cause for dis-ease within the Pleroma or fullness of the godhead, and the indirect cause of the material cosmos.

Böhme added a quaternary principle to the first three: the Virgin Sophia, who acts as a mirror to the uncreated light of the deity. The Sophia is linked to Böhme's conception of the Eternal Nature providing, through mystical devotion to her, an inward access for Böhme's followers to God. The number four symbolizes completion (as Carl Jung has demonstrated) and ensures psychic balance for the mystic, as well as accessibility to Böhme's system for Roman Catholics disoriented by the Protestant tendency to degrade the Virgin.

Among the many subtleties and dynamic developments subtending from the basic scheme outlined above is Böhme's version of the Double Fall, a doctrine that influenced William Blake. According to Böhme—along with gnostic thought in general—Man was originally a spiritual, androgynous being in whom the two sexes were one—sexless, in fact.

This being fell into matter, a catastrophe that involved the division into separate sexes, followed by the sin and disobedience made myth in the Eden story. Put another way, Adam gave way to nature; before that: "Adam was a Man, and also a woman, and yet none of them (*distinct*), but a Virgin full of . . . modesty, and Purity, *viz*. The Image of God: He had both the Tinctures of fire, and light, in him; and in the Conjunction of which, the own Love, *viz*. The Virgineall Centre, stood, being the faire Paradisicall Rose-Garden of delight, wherein he loved himselfe; as we also in the Resurrection of the Dead."[16]

Another contrary relevant to the fate of humankind is that of will and desire. Neither will nor desire is in itself evil. Evil is desire so limited in its focus (on itself, fixated on its relative state of being) that it cuts itself off from Father and Son. A human being must die to self to be reborn in God.

ivine will advances in self-knowledge as it manifests itself as self-consciousness. Ultimately, the human will, itself a manifestation of the divine will, is transformed into the divine will through an ongoing dialectical process. God becomes humanity as humanity becomes God: "The Son of God, the Eternal Word in the Father, who is the glance, or brightness, and the power of the light eternity, must become man and be born in you, if you will know God: otherwise you are in the dark stable and go about groping."[17]

For this magical process to be enacted, humans must rise from self-centeredness, cease babbling, and permit God to be heard in the heart—an organ that has a very special place in Böhme's thought, as we shall see: "*Master*. It is in thee. And if thou canst, my Son, for a while but cease from all thy thinking and willing, then thou shalt hear the unspeakable Words of God."[18]

Redemption comes through the New Man, the appearance of the original type. The New Man is Christ (in whom there was no confusion of human and divine will), and through him humankind is brought back (redeemed) to the original bliss. At the Last Day, Man will rise as Adam was first created.

Adam's essential error was to give way to that part of himself which was reflected in nature: "For the properties of the Creation, which all lay in Adam . . . awakened and rose up in its own self, and drew the free-will into it, and would needs be manifested."[19]

The Double Fall involves the human being in a sleep, unconsciousness, and amnesia. Gnosis in this context means "Wake up!" As long as Man "stood in heaven his essences were in Paradise; his body was indestructible . . . the elements stood in awe of him." Unfortunately, "tired of unity, Adam slept and his imagination turned away from God. . . . He brought will and desire from God into selfhood and vanity; and he broke himself off from God, from his divine harmony. . . . Sleep was succumbing to the world's powers, and Adam became a slave to just those powers which previously had served him. Now the elements ruled him."[20]

In this sleep, Eve was created out of Adam. In Christ the original image is redeemed: Male and female form a new harmony. "Christ has truly, in the body of the Virgin Mary, attracted to Him our human essences, and is become our brother."[21]

The deepest heart of the human being, the conduit where fire and light join, is Christ; Böhme's theosophy is a gnostic theosophy. There can be knowledge only where a real communion exists between the knower and the known.

THE INFLUENCE OF JACOB BÖHME

One of the first English-speaking Böhme enthusiasts was Dr. John Pordage, rector of Bradfield, Berkshire, from c. 1646 to 1647. The son of Elizabeth and Samuel Pordage, citizen and grocer of London, Pordage matriculated at Pembroke College, Cambridge, in 1623 and proceeded to write a number of influential commentaries on Böhme's works.

According to C. H. Josten, Pordage aspired "after the highest spiritual state" through "visible communion with angels."[22] The great Hermetic philosopher Elias Ashmole commended him to Anthony Wood "for his knowledge in, or at least affection to astronomy."[23] Ashmole was in fact lord of the manor at Bradfield when Pordage was accused by a committee appointed by Parliament of being unsuitable for clerical appointment. Supernatural disturbances in the church upset some locals and there were stories of his wife, dressed all in white, carrying a wand, leading dancing followers around the parish boundaries to the accompaniment of folk music. This was quite a heady mix for Oliver Cromwell's sober, Republican England.

There is a cipher note in Ashmole's diary, a horary question inside a horoscope dated October 19, 1650, 1:30 P.M.: "Whether good to let Dr. Por[da]g[e] go to dwell in my house at Bradfield."[24] One wonders what Ashmole's doubts were.

In spite of his downfall at Bradfield, Pordage went on to pen a number of religious, devotional, and mystical works that inspired a large following in England and on the Continent; his *Complete Works* was published in Amsterdam between 1698 and 1704.

In that latter year the colorful English prophetess Jane Lead died, and with her death was extinguished the moving principle of the Philadelphian Society. The Philadelphians appeared at the end of the seventeenth century as an association of pious followers of Böhme, also inspired by the works and example of Dr. John Pordage.

The Philadelphian Society, which took its name from the remnant of true believers at the beginning of the Apocalypse of St. John (the Book of Revelation), gathered around the visionary prophetess Jane Lead. They began with a nonsectarian and interdenominational ideal expressed in public meetings, on the basis that the churches were to be regenerated from within, but sectarian features developed with the passage of time. According to Richard Roach, a contemporary scholar and Böhme enthusiast of St. John's College, Oxford, "They met in Baldwin Gardens in the House of Mrs Joanna Oxenbridg W. whom Mrs A. Bathurst Combined who were Two Principal Persons [sic] in carrying on ye Spiritual Work: and both Enlightened Persons and both having great and Wonderful Experiences & Manifestations from ye Heavenly World."[25]

The meetings were later penetrated by the "French Prophets," the Camisard refugees from persecution in the religious conflict of the Cevennes, people distinguished by violent and ecstatic manifestations: visions of angels from otherworldly realms, bearing messages.

Jane Lead also specialized in rich visions, recorded in works such as her *Enochian Walks with God* and *Fountains of Gardens*. Her experiences convinced many of the immanence of the spiritual world and the interest of a number of its denizens in human welfare.

One follower was the German Platonist Dionysius Freher (1649–1728), who came to England to find Jane Lead and formed an association with the editor of the Philadelphian Society's *Theosophical Transactions,* Francis Lee. Freher later built up an influential theosophical circle of his own.

Meanwhile, a greater circle of Böhme interest crystallized about the person and works of the Anglican divine William Law.

WILLIAM LAW

William Law was the greatest representative of Böhme's thought in eighteenth-century England. He attracted followers dismayed at the state of religion in that country, at least two of whom would become very famous indeed: Samuel Johnson and the founder of Methodism, John Wesley. Both these men, in their own respective ways, were concerned at the lack of heart, vitality, warmth, sincerity, and, above all, spirituality in contemporary religion and intellectual life.

Law was born at King's Cliffe, Northamptonshire, in 1686, the son of a gentleman grocer. He entered Emmanuel College, Cambridge, in 1705 to study classics, philosophy, mathematics, and Hebrew. Law became a fellow of Emmanuel in 1708 and took holy orders in 1711. In 1714 he refused to accept the Hanoverian George I as head of the Church of England and thus became one of the "Non-Jurors" who believed that the Stuart dynasty was favored by God. As a result, Law had to surrender his Cambridge fellowship, with its accompanying academic responsibilities. He concentrated instead on purely religious writings.

In 1727 he became private tutor to Edward Gibbon's son, the father of the man who would write *Decline and Fall of the Roman Empire*. Law worked with Gibbon for ten years at Putney. In 1740 he established a semimonastic household at King's Cliffe and was joined by Hester Gibbon and Elizabeth Hutcheson. Their charity was great; they established schools, a public library, and almshouses. King's Cliffe became a destination for paupers. The almshouse survives to this day.

Law had read the works of Dionysius Freher as well as those of the editor of the *Theosophical Transactions* of the Philadelphian Society, Francis Lee (though Law himself did not approve of the Philadelphian Society, considering its members addicted to visionary experiences for their own sake). This disaffection did not prevent him from embracing a theology deeply imbued with the thought and spirituality of Böhme.

Law's works *A Serious Call to a Devout and Holy Life* (1728) and *Practical Treatise upon Christian Reflection* were widely influential, leading many to look again into the deeper implications and spiritual possibilities hidden within the Christian tradition. Law refuted the deism of Matthew Tindal. Deism was, for many, the religious principle most at ease with Enlightenment thinking. God had made the universe, and the job of the universe was to function according to God's preestablished Law. God was outside the system. A person who had absorbed the works of Böhme, who believed that the divine being was active in the lower world as much as in the higher, could hardly tolerate this fashionable religious outlook. As Blake would later write, "God is in the lowest effects as well as in the highest causes." For

Böhme followers, the universe was a divine system waiting to be discovered and fully participated in.

Böhme believed that deeper vision and transformation was better than mere argument. His books *The Spirit of Prayer* and *The Spirit of Love* explored the farther reaches of Christian spirituality; it was Böhme who had helped Law to get there. Not, however, with ease.

When Law first encountered the works of Böhme, he was brought to a "perfect sweat," as many might be today. But Law persevered and came to see Böhme as an "illuminated instrument of God"[26] to whom the mysteries of creation, fall, and gradual redemption and reunification of the human and natural worlds were revealed. Sacred reunification leads inward: "Though God be everywhere present, yet he is only present to you in the deepest and most central part of your soul."[27]

Law asked his readers to distinguish between the written word and the cosmic Word; real knowledge involves "the communion of the knowing and the known." The disciple must overcome egocentrism and aim for the religion of the heart (the essence of the Pietist movement): The "one true way of dying to self . . . [is] the way of patience, meekness, humility, and resignation to God." He encouraged men and women to believe that the spirit of love could yet triumph, "for great as the power of the world is, it is all built upon a blind obedience, and we need only open our eyes to get rid of its power."[28]

The contents of Law's library bear witness to his devotion to the gnostic spiritual tradition. It contained not only works by his master Böhme, but also works by Ficino, Pico della Mirandola, Agrippa, Dr. Everard, Ashmole, Maier, Paracelsus, John Pordage, Thomas Vaughan, and the Cambridge Platonists (Ralph Cudworth and Henry More), together with a worthy selection of the great Catholic mystics. It was perhaps this devotion to works that were not generally regarded as being in the mainstream of orthodoxy (especially the Renaissance Christian occult tradition) that may have led Wesley (who was fascinated by Law) to think that it was impossible to be "half a Christian."[29]

Law was no evangelical in the modern sense, and like his spiritual descendant William Ralph Inge, dean of St. Paul's (d. 1954), he preferred to be engaged in the work of the "Spirit of the ages, rather than the spirit of this particular age." He was, in short, unworldly, engrossed in a higher calling, dwelling in the divine mind as much as possible. This approach went against the grain of Wesley's activist, robust, and lively creed, which stirred and still stirs the hearts of many hundreds of thousands on both sides of the Atlantic.

Law, Wesley wrote, "does not see any meaning in the actual business of life."[30] This is a familiar accusation aimed at the gnostic frame of reference. Nevertheless, Wesley was still fascinated by the approach, and after debating in a friendly fashion with another Law and Böhme follower, the preacher Ralph Mather, Wesley asked himself what he had been doing for "the past thirty years."

For Law, God was in the deepest marrow of the human soul: "The essences of our soul were a breath in God before they . . . lived in the created soul, and therefore the soul is a partaker of the eternity of God and can never cease to be."[31] Humankind's original creation is a spiritual one: "Our Fall is nothing else, but the falling of our Soul from this celestial Body and spirit into a bestial Body and Spirit of this World."[32]

Law was no inflated ego, arrogantly bestriding the sick world. Humility was for him the gateway to love. Humility is answered by divine love, answered and met. According to Désirée Hirst, "It was around the figure of William Law while he was alive, and round his works when he was dead, that those who clung to an earlier and more spiritual way of thought in reaction to eighteenth century materialism, grouped themselves."[33] This influence of William Law and Jacob Böhme spread all over England, offering a picture of the country quite different to that which a superficial history of the Age of Reason might suggest.

Ralph Mather's *Account* of his very extensive journeys around England reveal a widespread preoccupation (in the 1770s at least) with mysticism, mystical literature, visionary experiences, and theosophy. These interests were enjoyed among a broad cross section of English society—a minority, no doubt, but a well-distributed minority of very lively people from artisan, middle-class, and genteel families. Indeed, the situation may not have been so very different from that which obtains today, more than two hundred years later. But how many today would warm to the following quotation from William Law's masterpiece, *The Spirit of Love?*

If Christ was to raise a new life like His own in every man, then every man must have had originally in the inmost spirit of his life, a seed of Christ, or Christ as a seed of heaven, lying there as in a state of insensibility or death, out of which it could not arise, but by the mediatorial power of Christ. Unless there was this seed of Christ, no beginning of Christ's mediatorial office could be made.

For what could begin to deny self, if there was not in man something different from self? Unless all the commandments had been really in the soul, in vain had the tables of stone been given to man. And unless Christ lay in the soul, as its unknown, hidden treasure, as a seed of life, a power of salvation, in vain had the holy Jesus lived and died for man.[34]

As William Ralph Inge, dean of St. Paul's, paraphrases the above in his *Studies of English Mystics:* "The redeeming work of Christ is to raise the smothered spark of heaven out of its state of death, into a powerful governing life of the whole man."[35]

Inge, it should be noted, was one of the small number of serious writers who were not already members of esoteric societies who would revitalize the study of mysticism within the Catholic churches at the turn of the twentieth century. A prolific and highly readable author, Inge also had an impact on the popular mind, applying spiritual principles to the affairs of his lifetime with simplicity, extraordinary wit, and intellectual penetration.

Inge ended his treatment of Böhme and Law with the following quotations from the former mystic.

If you behold your own self and the outer world, you will find that you yourself, with regard to your external being, are that external world.

He that findeth love findeth God; and he that findeth God findeth nothing and all things.

The soul hath heaven and hell within itself.

> The body of a man is the visible world, and the visible world is a manifestation of the inner spiritual world; it is a copy of eternity, wherewith eternity hath made itself visible.[36]

ROMANTIC PHILOSOPHY

According to Harriett Watts's fascinating essay "Arp, Kandinsky, and the Legacy of Jacob Böhme," "The question of mystical revelation through nature leads beyond the Romantic movement itself, back to Jacob Böhme . . . whose dialectical vision of the universe incorporated the most important components of Renaissance occult science and laid the foundations for Romantic aesthetics and metaphysics."[37] Watts recommends Alexandre Koyré's *La Philosophie de Jacob Böhme*[38] as the "best introduction to Böhme in the history of science" while drawing attention to a famous diagram that Böhme designed for his *Forty Questions of the Soul*. The diagram contains the essentials of his system and has two titles ("The Philosophical Sphere" and "The Wondrous Divine Eye of Eternity"), both suggesting the significance of ocular vision as dependent on the mind of the perceiver. "We receive—in perception—but what we give" is a central Romantic tenet; the primary imagination is creative of reality.

Böhme explained how the divine eye—a circle—must be split into two, with the two resulting arcs placed back to back and rotated in opposite directions. Being Böhmistically opposite, the arcs form a kind of perpetual motion system driven by equal and opposite energies. One eye becomes two eyes, propelling each other through their mutual opposition. One of the arcs issues from the corrosive fire eye of the Father, the other from the loving eye (warmth/illumination) of the Holy Spirit. At the center point of contact between the two arcs is the Heart, or the Son.

While the circle that contains the two arcs has a center focal point, this center is in fact engendered by the two foci of the opposing arcs, which project their respective arcs to the point of contact. The point of contact of the two arcs is the spark of ignition. The circle that contains the entire system can be engendered only when ignition takes place at this center point, created by the touch of the two arcs. (We are reminded of an axiom of Cusanus, "God is an infinite sphere whose center is everywhere, circumference nowhere.")

This diagram, containing two foci within a circle, caught the attention of German Romantic philosophers and poets at the start of the nineteenth century. Romantics such as Franz von Baader, Friedrich von Schelling, Ludwig Tieck, and Friedrich von Schlegel sought a symbolic representation of a unity that could embrace diversity and even polarities, because they felt in their different ways oppressed by monistic rationalism, the tyranny of one-dimensional logic. As Watts puts it, "Böhme was the western philosopher to whom they looked for suggestions." They took his "Wondrous Eye" and turned the two foci into the basis for a closed elliptical curve generated by two foci rather than one central point.

Occult iconography reached an advanced level in the late seventeenth and eighteenth centuries. The Heart in Böhme's diagram received a rich alchemical or "Rosicrucian" rendering in works such as the frontispiece to the 1730 edition of Böhme's *Christi testamenta*. There, the Heart is doubled, converted into a circulatory system that might have been mistaken for a biological textbook were it not for the striking upper arc of divine light and the lower arc of corrosive fire. This circulatory system ensures a perpetual interchange and interaction—an infinitely creative variation on the divine perfection of the circle—once, that is, that circle is divided. Again the division, the polarity, the opposition is creative. Furthermore, it vouchsafes the spiritual notion of two worlds interacting with lower reasons and higher reasons: logic and divine inspiration.

And the Heart is seen as central to the system. The human heart with its feeling and devotion has its counterpart in the central principle of the divine system—a gift to Pietists and Romantics alike. Indeed, the Heart of the divine system exists in the human heart, as it does everywhere. As Watts notes: "The heart is first the Hermetic vessel in which the marriage of contraries takes place and then the womb, nurturing the sublimated manifestation of base matter, achieved if the alchemical process is successful."[39]

The left/right opposition of the divine bipolar eye in Böhme's original diagram has in the 1730 engraving been rotated 90 degrees to the left into a vertical opposition. The trunk of the tree/cross sinks its roots/veins into *prima materia*—the *magnum mysterium*—and the lifeblood of the system is conveyed by alchemical transmutations into the Heart of the upper realm. At the point of intersection of the horizontal and vertical of the cross, the blood with its source in base matter is converted into the wine/blood of the Son. The tree, rooted in the devouring flames, becomes the tree of Eternal Life.

Harriett Watts observes how the "circulatory system is so constructed that there need be no end to this process of alchemical transmutation."[40] For a Romantic artist or philosopher, here was revelation indeed! Eternity kissed the natural world; organic beauty could save and be saved. The first step was to push away the cold stone of reason and reveal the open heart, a door and cave into the mysteries.

The Romantic philosopher Friedrich von Schelling constructed a similar model of the heart in which he envisioned the universe as a divine heartbeat. Its source was the pulsating point between Böhme's first two principles: "The whole spatially extended universe is nothing but the swelling heart of the godhead. Held by invisible powers it persists in a continual pulsation, or alternation of expansion and contraction."[41]

The language of contraction and expansion is derived from Böhme's seven-step progression, which is in turn derived from alchemy. According to the late Dr. Kathleen Raine, "To Böhme [alchemy] was a symbolic language purely and simply; his theme was the divine essence, good and evil, Heaven and Hell."[42] This is not entirely the case. Böhme was also envisioning the universe as being itself a vast spiritual-alchemical operation with sparks, fire, and combustion.

Böhme's seven-step progression, marking the dynamics of divine creation, was to him one simultaneous step, although human understanding could not see it as such. Again, the idea of instantaneous combustion is strong.

Steps one to three concern the prima materia. First, contraction and concentration: the sour source. Second, expansion/dispersion: the sweet source. Third: agitation caused by the conflict of sour and sweet. This conflict generates the bitter source that is pulled toward both contraction and expansion, each working against the other. Step four involves the base matter now in its agitated state. The agitation generates an ignition—a critical stage wherein matter is projected into the fire source, at which stage the fire can either return to tormented prima materia or attain sublimation in the paradisiacal realm of divine corporeality.

If the latter, the sublimated fire moves to step five, love: sustaining light and warmth. Stage six is that of the *Mercurius,* or the *Logos,* as the differentiating, spoken word, the holy vibration that makes possible form through sound.

The seventh stage is that of realization and participation in embodied divinity—the holy Sophia—wisdom.

The essence of the Romantic life is a spiritual process made possible by contrariety and the life of the heart. The Ungrund must pass through the materialized conduit of the heart to manifest its undifferentiated infinity as the infinite richness and diversity of divine corporeality. The unknowable pure spirit is made manifest in matter. The forest of matter is a mystery, but the questor must find a path through it in search of the Beloved.[43] Here we have the fundamental itinerary of much Romantic fiction, including the Gothic horror story.

We also should see clearly why the Romantic movement was in such open revolt against the Deism of the Enlightenment. The Deist had, as it were, drained God out of the universe, leaving nothing but bare bones and cranking machinery—no longer a heartbeat, merely an incessant, deafening tick-tock *ad infinitum* with no glimpse of the eternal. Little wonder, then, from the Romantic point of view, that humans would eventually come to cry out that God was dead. As Böhme might have remarked, humans had become dead to God.

THE NEO-ROSICRUCIANS

During the late eighteenth and early nineteenth centuries, curious legends surrounding Rosicrucians reached England. These were not the Rosicrucians of Robert Fludd and Elias Ashmole's longing; nor were they the genial physicians of John Pordage and the Philadelphians' imagination. The Rosicrucian had somehow metamorphosed into a considerably darker, more baroque figure. The Victor Frankenstein of

Mary Shelley's famous novel, as an imaginary and symbolic figure, owes much to the mythology of neo-Rosicrucianism. The doctor even attends Ingolstadt University, where he is castigated for his addiction to the works of Paracelsus and Cornelius Agrippa.

Mary Shelley's husband, the poet Percy Bysshe Shelley, dedicated the subject of his first novel, *The Rosicrucian* (1811), to the story of a weird adept called Ginotti who comes to a bad end through his devotion to Faustian powers. What had happened to the good old Rosicrucians?[44]

What had happened to the good old Rosicrucians was that some less-than-perfect goings-on had been taking place in the *name* of the Rosicrucians. Orders claiming or suggesting links with the Fraternity of C.R. emerged as Freemasonry spread to the European continent, offering a structure and ideological format conducive to the elaboration of Rosicrucian mythology. These orders we shall examine in more detail in chapter 9. For now, it is worth mentioning that neo-Rosicrucian orders and individuals in the eighteenth century seldom came into being without a good strong dose of the theosophy of Jacob Böhme. Böhme opened up a mystical cosmos to the hard heads of the Enlightenment. Böhme represented a crack in the rationalist universe.

WILLIAM BLAKE

William Blake (1757–1827) is sometimes revered as an autodidact, a man of such vivid imagination that he created from scratch a system of which he was sole autarch. Kathleen Raine (author of the important work *Blake and Tradition*)[45] regarded Blake as nothing less than her "Guru." But it was Kathleen Raine herself who was one of the first scholars to delineate precisely what many of the sources of Blake's visionary works actually were.

Then again, Blake had himself made the matter of his early intellectual development clear. In his *Marriage of Heaven and Hell* (1790), Blake declared that "any man of mechanical talents" might from the writings of Paracelsus or Jacob Böhme "produce ten thousand volumes of equal value with Swedenborg's." In a verse letter to his friend the sculptor Flaxman, Blake recalled his early masters:

Isaiah and Ezra, Shakespeare and Milton, then
Paracelsus & Behmen appear'd to me, terrors appear'd in
The Heavens above
And in Hell beneath.[46]

As Désirée Hirst writes in her own pioneering book *Hidden Riches*, "Böhme's particular presentation of material creation as a fall into matter seems to have caught Blake's imagination and haunted his mind all his life."[47] This is perhaps no exaggeration.

Once the reader has grasped the linguistic and visionary world of Böhme, many of Blake's apparently most highly idiosyncratic works come over as a kind of protracted argument, questioning, elucidation, or even jocular dialogue with the old German master. It is sometimes as though they are playing with each other on an exalted and joyful plane; the arguments, though, are serious.

Understanding Böhme is one of the vital keys for understanding Blake. If the reader should find a study of Blake with Böhme's name hardly mentioned in the index, it is probably wise to discard it; the author has not done his or her homework.

Blake does not imitate Böhme, but Böhme is never far from the structure of Blake's thinking. The pair can be read like a mystical double act. What had they most in common—apart from being self-educated craftsmen? Both men brought a gnostic cast of mind to their mutual appreciation of the Bible.

As we have seen, in Böhme's system the fire principle is the Father, source of nature, and the abyss of hell. From the fire proceeds light, the Son and principle of heaven. Fire and light springing from a single root: "the God of the holy World, and the God of the dark World, are not two Gods; there is but one only God."[48]

Böhme armed Blake with his critique of the commonly understood sense of the Bible. So Blake could write of the Jehovah of the Bible as "no other than he who dwells in flaming fire." The flaming fire is Böhme's first principle of divine essence expressed. As Blake put it, it is "Energy, call'd evil." In these fires dwell devils as "living spirits in the Essences of the Eternal Original";[49] angels live in the principle of light, and each spirit must be confined to its principle. Blake always had some sympathy for the devils.

We can feel Blake enjoying a joke at Böhme's expense in his "Memorable Fancy": "I [Blake] was walking among the fires of hell [the natural world in one aspect], delighted with the enjoyments of Genius, which to Angels look like torment and insanity."[50] The angels can only see their side of the contrarium; Blake feels free to "walk" in the energy of desire: the fire principle. And to Blake, of course, "Energy is Eternal Delight." The phrase "Eternal Delight," which sounds so Blakean, is Böhme's. In "Voice of the Devil," Blake says, "It indeed appear'd to Reason as if Desire was cast out; but the Devil's account is, that the Messiah fell, and form'd a heaven of what he stole from the Abyss."[51] This Messiah is Lucifer, the Light-bringer: the dim light of nature, once blazing.

Most readers of Blake will be familiar with the poem "The Tyger," which describes so vividly the creation of the tiger's "fearful symmetry." The unresolved question haunts the believer: "Did he who made the lamb make thee?"

In his *Aurora,* Böhme wrote that evil beasts were never intended in the divine plan, originating in Lucifer and his fallen angels' corruption of the world. Without their fall, there would have been no snakes, toads, or venomous insects. But Lucifer focused his admiration on his selfhood, exalting himself and so poisoning the fountains of creation. The life principle took on evil forms, "as a fiery serpent, or Dragon, and imaged and framed all manner of fiery and poisonous forms and Images, like to wild, cruel and evil Beasts." According to Böhme, Lucifer "half killed, spoiled and destroyed the source of life"; so the beast that had most of the fire, or the bitter or the astringent quality became also a bitter, hot, and fierce beast.[52]

> *Tyger, Tyger burning bright*
> *In the forests of the night,*
> *What immortal hand or eye*
> *Could frame thy fearful symmetry?*[53]

And what are these "forests of the night"?

Adam, who might have lived on the "fruits of life" (a Böhme phrase used by Blake), chose the earthy nature of the tree. In "The Poison

Tree" (*Songs of Experience*, 1794), we find the words *wrath, poison,* and *anger*, highly reminiscent of Böhme in his treatments of the Double Fall. Böhme asks, "Why did God suffer this Tree to grow [in Eden], seeing Man should eat it? Did he not bring it forth for the fall of Man? And must it not be the Cause of Man's destruction?"[54]

Kathleen Raine observes, "From this 'deadly root' of poison and wrath the Mystery [Nature] branches and extends endlessly."[55] The extended branches and infinitely twisting roots are the dark forests of fallen nature, all about us. *Yes!* Blake seems to say, the Tyger *is* magnificent, awe-inspiring—but doesn't he make you *think*?

Kathleen Raine relates "The Tyger" to Böhme's "wrath fires" of the Father in one of Blake's "Proverbs of Hell" *(The Marriage of Heaven and Hell)*: "The tygers of wrath are wiser than the horses of instruction."[56] Blake turns Böhme's meditative theosophy into the ammunition for prolonged battle cries in a war against abstracted reason and sexual repression, military and corporate stateism and industrialization. But his greatest fight is with materialism, the worship of mere nature in its outer aspect, the quantifiable and measurable universe, the external world as seen by the cold eye of abstracted science—what he calls "Newton's sleep." And as his war is against external vision, Blake knew that the struggle that mattered was not through external politics and laws but rather through spiritual transformation and freed energy.

Blake famously saw the hidden energy, the vast eternities in the apparently microscopic:

> To see a World in a Grain of Sand
> And a Heaven in a Wild Flower,
> Hold Infinity in the palm of your hand
> And Eternity in an hour.[57]

Now hear Böhme, though not as succinct: "If thou conceivest a small minute circle, as small as a grain of mustard seed, yet the Heart of God is wholly and perfectly therein: and if thou art born in God, then there is in thyself (in the circle of thy life) the whole Heart of God undivided."[58]

Blake seems to have derived his whole notion of movement, velocity, force, change, and momentum from Böhme's dynamic theosophy.

Everything is forced into a change and transformation. Morality and physics jump and dive and dig and cut together.

In the poem "The Poison Tree," the Poison Tree grows from "wrath" and the "apple bright" from anger. For Böhme, this tree is also nature: "it grew out of the Earth and has wholly the Nature of the Earth in it" and "as the Earth is corruptible, and shall pass away in the End, when all goes into its Ether."[59] Kathleen Raine, commenting on this parallel, exclaims how Böhme "might be paraphrasing Paracelsus."[60] Of the two trees in the legend—the Tree of Life and the Tree of Good and Evil—Böhme holds that they are one tree but manifested in two different principles: the light of heaven (Son) and the fires of hell ("the wrath of the anger of God," the Father).

The ambivalence of the divine "wrath" preoccupied Blake. The issue surrounding this fiery and decidedly unliberal issue reaches its apex in the famous question provoked by contemplation of "The Tyger": "Did he who made the Lamb make thee?" Kathleen Raine wondered if we should consider an answer through the prism of Böhme's words: "The God of the holy World, and the God of the dark World, are not two Gods; there is but one only God. He Himself is all Being. He is Evil and Good; Heaven and Hell; Light and Darkness; Eternity and Time. Where his Love is hid in anything, there His Anger is manifest."[61]

Raine comes to the conclusion, "This is the god of the Alchemists, beyond the contraries."[62] "Too great," Blake might add, "for the eye of man."

NINE

Germany 1710–1800: The Return of the Rosy Cross

Mein Leib ist ein Schal, in dem ein Kuchelein
Vom Geist der Ewigkeit will ausgebrütet sein.

My body is a shell, in which a chicken will be
hatched from the spirit of eternity.

ANGELUS SILESIUS, GERMAN PIETIST AND POET

As in England, a reconnaissance of discreet societies operating in Germany after 1710 belies the eighteenth century's image as an era of widespread, dry rationalism, an Age of Reason dominated by the Aufklärung (Enlightenment). Historians who have observed the great proliferation of Pietism, Freemasonry, and neo-Rosicrucianism in Germany in this period have in the main tended to see the latter two movements especially as anti-Aufklärung, constituting an obscurantist counter-Enlightenment: nostalgic, traditionalist, even repressive.

Dr. Christopher McIntosh's important book *The Rose Cross and the Age of Reason* has demonstrated that this picture is deeply inadequate. There were progressives on the conservative side and conservatives on the progressive side. Indeed, much of the time such labels had little practical meaning. This was due partly to the multifaceted implications of the word *enlightenment*. To a gnostic-type mind, the word means spiritual enlightenment, regarding the light that enlightens as substantial, more than a metaphor. For the rationalist-type mind, the word suggests an escape from a superstitious and unscientific past: the *dark* ages.

In a sense the real question—from the point of view of the Enlightenment—was whether an ordered, scientific, rational society, free from religious conflict and tyrannical government, was more likely to be obtained by spiritual or by scientific means. Reason can operate effectively only on a knowledge base of certainties and high probabilities, as Descartes fully established in the mid-seventeenth century in his *Discourse on Method*. It is clear that in the eighteenth century, among thinkers such as Voltaire and Pope, following on from Locke and Descartes, there was something of an overconfidence regarding the imminence of total knowledge. This gathering hubris was itself partly a result of a secularization of the apocalyptic and original Rosicrucian hope.

There was certainly a frustration among Enlightenment thinkers, akin to that felt by a sentient beam of light on being refracted by denser material. As Christopher McIntosh puts it: "The obstacles that the Enlightenment wished to clear out of its path were ignorance, superstition, prejudice and blind faith in authority and tradition."[1] On the Continent, this invariably meant opposition to the Roman Catholic Church and frequently to traditional religion in general. The reduction of religion to first principles (deism/brotherhood) also meant that Masonic orders could easily accommodate Enlightenment; Voltaire was a Freemason.

According to Max Weber, Aufklärung meant the "de-mystification of the world," and its aim was simply (!) to emancipate human beings from the world of historical tradition—all authorities, teachings, systems, allegiances, institutions, and conventions that could not withstand critical examination by the "autonomous human faculty of reason."[2]

The idea of the world being under great illusion and in need of emancipation, even in its secularized sense, would also have appealed to those of a gnostic cast of mind who were yet concerned for the fate of human society. The difficulty lay chiefly in the primacy given to reason as the chief and indeed only arbiter of approved action.

Counter-Enlightenment figures may have shared the ultimate ideals of the rationalists, but they differed as to the means. Most opponents were unimpressed by the ends as well. Not all counter-Enlightenment figures were reactionary and repressive exponents of tradition. While counter-Enlightenment thinkers shared the general view that faith rather than reason constituted the more reliable approach to the world, there were also people who were generally pessimistic about human potential on earth.

Giambattista Vico, for example, saw evidence to support a sad cyclical view of history: the recognition of a central human tragedy that prevents the ultimate terrestrial progress for which humankind frequently cries out. His cycle saw an "age of gods" succeeded by an "age of heroes," subsequently degenerating into an "age of men." The age of men sinks inevitably into barbarism and destroys itself. The survivors turn back to divine guidance, and the cycle begins again.[3] The problem exposed by this view is that of the nature of humankind.

The Enlightenment enjoyed an extremely optimistic view of human ability to do good on seeing good. All you had to do was remove the debris of past ignorance, and the light would shine for all to see. Result: progress. It is not particularly astonishing to see this cozy view still advanced by people who regard themselves as progressive social anatomists. The gnostic view suggests that humankind must undergo a radical inward regeneration, must recover the divine image, before any great (magical) strides may take place.

Gnostics seem to be divided equally between those who are optimistic about human potential in the world and those who regard the world and its destiny as merely a temporary dwelling through whose stricture purgation and release may be achieved. The world as material-world is at best just part of the process. The dialectics cannot be argued away in the world. Positive and negative polarities are of the world's very nature. The wise person steers a midcourse between (as the kabbalist has it) mercy and severity. The direction is upward—to more spirit.

More-optimistic gnostics put great store in humankind's intermediate position between the worlds of matter and spirit. Its task is to marry these worlds to liberate the world from itself. If the world is a prison, it is a prison in which we find our spiritual freedom.

According to the alchemical theory implicit in the first Rosicrucian manifestos,[4] social good, prosperity, and general harmony are the *par-*

ergons, or by-products, not the single aim, of the spiritual process. For a person who favored this view, those rationalists who fundamentally doubted the spiritual life were in danger of leaving themselves—and the rest of the world—cut off from all but their own immediate faculties. For the neo-Rosicrucian, reason is not enough. For the radical Enlightenment thinker, it is all we have. Visionaries and their followers took the view that if reason constituted the ultimate emancipation, humankind was, practically speaking, better off before it appeared as a new demigod. In other words, the Enlightenment was not enlightened enough.

There were in Germany in the eighteenth century three main groups or currents operating that might find a home for the mind: the established churches; Enlightenment optimism; and those in favor of, as McIntosh puts it, the "expansion of human possibilities that could not be satisfied within the confines of traditional, mainstream religion . . . a spiritual thrust that could not be quenched by rationality."[5]

This third group included theosophists, mystics, Pietists, neo-Rosicrucians, and magical and alchemical enthusiasts. They represented a distinctively Germanic phenomenon, encouraged by the great lack of centralization in German culture. It should be understood that Germany in this period was a collection of nearly two thousand sovereign or semi-independent entities.

One movement that found representatives across the board, but especially in Silesia and in the north, was Pietism, and Pietism constituted a central pillar of German neo-Rosicrucianism. At first sight, this might appear strange. However, the thought of the chief founder of the Rosicrucian literary experiment, Johann Valentin Andreae (1586–1654), and that of his friends Christoph Besold and Joannes Arndt moved in a strongly pietistic direction, toward a combination of social goodwill and deep inwardness along the dynamics of spiritual alchemy.

Jacob Böhme was as popular with German Pietists as he was with English groups such as the Philadelphians and some of those people favorable to Quakerism and Methodism (and in France, Jansenists and Quietists). Pietists stressed the feeling and emotional side of religion, and it is difficult here to resist noting the view of S. T. Coleridge that really deep thought is most accessible to those of deep feeling.

By 1700, Pietists greatly influenced the thought of about thirty-two

German cities, but its relation to the Enlightenment was ambiguous and complex. On the one hand, Pietism shared with "Enlighteners" egalitarian ideals and concerns for social justice, as well as opposition to coercive religious ideologies; on the other, punitive opposition to the Enlightenment was also possible. The great Enlightenment thinker Christian Wolff was expelled from the University of Halle in 1723 under pressure from Pietists.

When pietistic influences dominated the religious policy of Prussia fifty years later, extensive efforts were made to keep Enlightenment influences out of the Lutheran Church, efforts that included intellectual "means testing" and censorship.

THE GOLD UND ROSENKREUZERS

The precise origins of the German neo-Rosicrucians, in particular that organization known as the Gold and Rosenkreuz, with its distinctive alchemical stress, are unknown. One thing is certain. Its ideology was not in tune with that which informed the original Rosicrucian manifestos. McIntosh expresses the difference in these terms: "Those who espoused the new Rosicrucianism did so in a very different spirit from that of their seventeenth century precursors. The latter had seen themselves as promoting the advent of a new age and a new kind of society, and they saw no conflict between religion and the advance of science. The neo-Rosicrucians, on the other hand, saw themselves as upholding an ancient tradition of wisdom and piety which, although strong in Germany, was to find itself increasingly marginalised."[6]

The first suggestion that a working Rosicrucian order had been created came from a work that appeared in Breslau in 1710: *Die wahrhaffte und vollkommene Bereitung des philosophischen Steins der Brüderschaft aus dem Orden des Gulden und Rosen Kreutzes* (The True and Perfect Preparation of the Philosophical Stones of the Brotherhood of the Order of the Gold and Rosy Crucians). The author, Sincerus Renatus, was in fact the Protestant Pietist pastor Samuel Richter, a native of the intensely pietistic region of Silesia, home to the Bohemian Brethren refugees from the Thirty Years War (among whom had once moved the great figure of Comenius). Rosicrucianism had become part of their ideological tradition, and Richter was no exception.

It is not known whether Richter's document denoted an existing movement or whether, as seems likely, it formed the basis for creating one. Its rules were rather different from those put forward by the Rosicrucian enthusiast, doctor, and alchemist count Michael Maier nearly a century before (*Themis Aurea,* 1618). The order permitted Roman Catholic members. There was a new alchemical emphasis. Members were to receive a "portion" of the philosopher's stone at their initiation, doubtless a great incentive to join.

Richter's account of the order's greetings and rules reappeared later in many different neo-Rosicrucian documents. Richter was a follower of Paracelsus and of Böhme. He studied theology in Halle and was there accused of supporting the "blasphemous [gnostic] doctrines of the Manichaeans" under the Pietist-dominated regime of August Hermann Francke, principal, Halle University. Richter's thought was certainly imbued with Gnostic tendencies, as can be discerned from his foreword: "How can we recognise the true separation of the blessing from the curse or of the light from the darkness if we do not even rightly know how light and darkness are distinguished and indeed have not perceived the true separation of light and darkness in our souls nor recognised the difference between the old and the new birth? And how can we recognise these things in outward nature? . . . For that is the purpose of true chemistry."[7]

A number of German alchemical texts, following that of Richter and signed by various "Imperators," suggest that some kind of neo-Rosicrucian organization existed by the late 1730s. There is the example of Imperator Johann Carl von Frisau's *J. G. Toeltii, des Welt-berühmten philosophi Coelum reseratum & hymnicum* (J. G. Toeltii, the World-famous Heaven Unlocking and Praising Philosophers) published in 1737,[8] as well as the *Ms Testamentum der Fraternitet Roseae et Aureae Crucis,* acquired in 1735 by Johann Adalbert, Prinz de Buchau, and now in the Austrian National Library, Vienna.

In the latter work, the writer states that the Mysterium originated with the patriarch Noah and then passed through the Jews, the ancient Egyptians, the Chaldeans, the Romans, and the Arabs—the more-or-less *prisca theologia* viewpoint (pristine or original theological revelation): "From the prophets and beloved ancient ones it came down to us Germans through our father Theuth [Thoth-Hermes] and it has been preserved by us until today, often in a miraculous way."[9] This "Testament" of a neo-Rosicrucian order is in favor of complete religious toleration but is wary of all religious orders (such as the Jesuits). From the late 1730s onward, the neo-Rosicrucian movement is mostly to be found situated within the general development of Freemasonry in Germany.

MASONRY IN GERMANY

The first Masonic lodge in Germany was established under English influence in Hamburg in 1737, the basis for what later became the English Provincial Grand Lodge for Hamburg and Lower Saxony.

In 1731 Francis, duke of Lorraine, later to be Holy Roman Emperor, was made a Mason in The Hague. This event doubtless gave impetus to the acceptance of Freemasonry on German soil. In 1738, the crown prince of Prussia, later Frederick the Great, was initiated at Hanover. In 1744 a lodge was established for Braunschweig (Brunswick), followed by a steady growth of lodges throughout Germany.

In the 1760s, the Strict Observance Rite of Karl Gotthelf, Baron Hund, made great progress in establishing the mythology of a Knights Templar origin for Freemasonry, and neo-Templarism caught on in lodges across Europe.

Rival to the Strict Observance Rite was that of the Clerks Templar, founded by Johann August Starck, who claimed that it was the Clerk and not the Knight Templar who was the guardian of Masonic secrets. The clerk, lacking the archetypal power of the knight, was not as successful a mythology for attracting new Masonic adherents.

The Braunschweig lodge Zu den drei Weltkugeln (To the three Globes; The Three Globes) adopted the Strict Observance and later became a nerve center for the Gold und Rosenkreuz. Between 1761 and 1780, during the great period of German Masonic expansion, some two hundred sixty-five lodges were founded in the north and about twenty-eight in the (overwhelmingly Catholic) south. By 1800 there were in existence about four hundred ninety lodges in the north and about sixty-seven lodges in the south.[10] There are three degrees in Craft Freemasonry, of which the third is the last and most celebrated, that of

Master Mason. Advance in Freemasonry in some jurisdictions requires initiation into further explanatory degrees, sometimes called "higher," "other," or "side" degrees, which rise in number using the geometrical division of the degree. These further degrees emerged—especially in Europe and America—after 1730.

The first two degrees, Entered Apprentice and Fellow Craft, existed in the seventeenth century; the third degree emerged by 1725 after the loss of control by the Freemasons' trade of Accepted Freemasonry between 1720 and 1730. "Acceptions" occurred before the first record of them in London in 1638. The higher degrees were the most popular, promising occult as well as moral mysteries. In the 1780s, there were between twenty to thirty thousand active Masons in Germany.

The lodges provided welcome homes for exponents of the Enlightenment, due to Masonry's universalist and egalitarian principles, as well as offering the simple opportunity to meet men of like mind and to discuss ideals and beliefs in a tolerant setting. The lodges were conducive to moral, intellectual, and artistic progress. Masonry undoubtedly influenced Frederick the Great of Prussia's tolerant social beliefs and encouragement of new science and thought.

In Austria, the composers Haydn and Mozart were Masons. (Mozart's character Sarastro in his *Magic Flute* was based on fellow Mason Ignaz von Born.) The great legal reformer Joseph von Sonnenfels was a Mason. Masonry brought in a whole spectrum of thought, from spiritual idealists to exceptionally radical social and intellectual revolutionaries. Some wanted the best of both worlds, radical progressive thinking and a privily guarded gnosis, men such as Adolf, Freiherr von Knugge, who was to become the chief collaborator of Adam Weishaupt (founder of the radical Illuminati), but who, unlike Weishaupt, retained his spiritual and esoteric interests.

Furthermore, the figure of the knight sallying forth against oppressive thought and rule represented a vital moral contribution to the culture, effecting a rebirth of an idea of chivalry that had perished in the Thirty Years War if not long before. Templar Masonry answered a pressing social need: an idealist standard of conduct in a milieu of intellectual adventuring that for some threatened the basis of morality. Masonry was for many of its adherents a higher religion, offering a privileged oversight above the countless religious and ideological divisions that had sundered Europe into armed camps. Masonry at its best could be a liberating influence.

The genesis of an organized Gold und Rosenkreuz movement may be from the strivings of one Hermann Fictuld, the author of a number of alchemical and magico-cabalistic works, among which is the *Aureum vellus* (1749), a document that refers to a *Societät der goldenen Rosenkreuzer*.[11] According to Fictuld, this society constituted the body of initiates pledged to preserve the mysteries of the Golden Fleece.

From the linguistic coincidence that *fleece* in German *(Vliess)* is cognate with the verb *fließen,* "to flow," Fictuld draws the conclusion that the Golden Fleece symbolizes philosophical gold, a liquid fiery substance said to flow from the planetary spheres. The substance was also known as the essence of the *anima mundi,* or soul of the world, supporting the general phenomenon of growth and the infinite potential for life.

Fictuld seems to have believed that the Gold und Rosenkreuz owed its origin to the Order of the Golden Fleece, a chivalric order founded by Duke Philip III of Burgundy in 1429. Fictuld's fundamental outlook was, even by the standard of the dominant currents of his time, archaic; he stood against his age, and his role in the founding of the Gold und Rosenkreuz is at best ambiguous.

The earliest solid evidence for a working Gold und Rosenkreuz Order dates from 1761 and was discovered in Hungary by the Masonic historian Ludwig Abafi among the archives of the Festetics family.[12] The work he discovered was that of a member of the Prager Assemblée, the *Aureum Vellus seu iunioratus Fratrum Rosae Crucis* (The Golden Fleece Being the Younger Brother of the Rosy Cross).

This document of the Prague group of neo-Rosicrucians contained rituals and a list of members. The members included moneychangers, an artillery captain, and a Polish lieutenant colonel. The account of the order's founding was apparently taken from Fictuld's *Aureum Vellus*.

The order had seven grades of membership: Juniores (Juniors), Adepti exempti (Exempt Adepts), Philosophi minores (Philosophers Minor), Philosophi majores (Philosophers Major), Philosophi majores primarii (Primary Philosophers Major), and Magi (Magi). Describing a substantial body, the document refers to there having been as many as seventy-seven magi. The framework was universalist and at ease with the Aufklärung: "Members can be masons from all lands and nations; for the universal Good knows no boundaries but must benefit those who are worthy of it wherever it finds them."[13]

Members should celebrate a mass before entering but, out of respect for the Jewish Law, Jews may also enter. Members of religious orders may enter "with difficulty," kings and princes seldom. Alchemy was an important part of order activity. Since a reform was written into the rules as having to take place at ten-year intervals, and since we know there was a reform in 1767, it is to be presumed that the order was founded in 1757 (the year declared by Swedenborg to be the beginning of the new spiritual age, and the year in which William Blake was born).

The order was closely linked to Freemasonry. The Prague circle bore the name Zur schwarzen Rose (The Black Rose) and certainly included some members from the Masonic lodge Zu den drei gekrönten Sternen (The Three Crowned Stars).[14]

In 1761 the Prague circle was officially dissolved during an outbreak of anti-Masonic policy stemming from the fears of the Catholic queen Maria Theresa; three of its members were sentenced to six years in prison. Two papal bulls had been issued against Freemasonry (one in 1738 and another in 1751) and two general decrees were subsequently issued banning Masonry from Hapsburg lands (1764 and 1766). After 1764, Masons were obliged to work in secret.

In spite of suppression, neo-Rosicrucianism spread and founded centers of activity in Prague, Regensburg, and Frankfurt-am-Main, radiating outward to Vienna, Saxony, Berlin, Hungary, Russia, and Poland. It was particularly popular in the mystico-pietistic lands of Silesia.

The 1767 reform began to push the spiritual roots of the movement to the outer limits. There were now nine grades: Junior (Junior), Theoreticus (Speculative), Practicus (Active), Philosopher (Philosopher), Adeptus minor (Minor Adept), Adeptus major (Major Adept), Adeptus exemptus (Exempt Adept), Magister (Master), and Magus (Magus). Members of the ninth grade were now to be regarded as superhuman: "From them nothing is concealed. They are masters of everything, like Moses, Aaron, Hermes and Hiram Abiff [the Temple-building hero of the Masonic third degree]."[15]

A year after a gathering of twenty-six German nobles for a Strict Observance Congress at Braunschweig, some leading members of the Strict Observance journeyed to Wiesbaden at the invitation of Baron von Gugomos. Claiming to be the "emissary of the True Superiors of the Order" whose headquarters were, he said, in Cyprus, he declared he would hasten there to obtain more secret writings.[16] Gugomos, however, was exposed as a charlatan; he had forged titles and charters. (This is an almost exact parallel to the debacle that enveloped the British Hermetic Order of the Golden Dawn in 1900.)

Confidence in Templar Masonry slipped, leaving the way for the two extreme wings of esoteric Masonry to emerge: the Gold und Rosenkreuz (Christian-mystical) and the Illuminati (radical enlightenment) paths. Splits and recriminations followed, and new alignments were formed.

In 1777 the Gold und Rosenkreuz underwent another reform. Behind this reform was the circle about Duke Frederick August of Braunschweig (a descendant of Johann Valentin Andreae's patron; many of Andreae's manuscripts are now to be found at Braunschweig Castle at Wolfenbüttel). Great hopes were projected onto the duke for a divinely guided reformation of the world's happiness, to be directed by a figure containing within himself the roles of monarch, sage, and hierophant. These hopes were eventually to find concrete expression when Crown Prince Friedrich Wilhelm of Prussia was initiated into the Gold und Rosenkreuz on August 8, 1781—an event fraught with unexpected consequence, as we shall see.

The Gold und Rosenkreuz began to attract interesting people whose position with regard to the Enlightenment was open-ended, a phenomenon that boded ill for the order as its leaders became evermore doctrinaire with respect to the secular Aufklärung.

The scientist Georg Forster, for example, a man who accompanied his father on Captain James Cook's second voyage around the world in 1772, kept his Enlightenment sympathies and joined the Gold und Rosenkreuz, but later turned against it. He had joined the Paris lodge Des Neuf Soeurs (Lodge of the Nine Sisters), founded by the astronomer Lalande and dedicated to Enlightenment. The lodge's members also included d'Alembert, Condorcet, and, notably, the American ambassador to France, Benjamin Franklin.[17] Forster left Paris for Cassel, joined the Strict Observance, and then entered the Gold und Rosenkreuz. He may have been attracted by the promise of firm alchemical knowledge.

Alchemy spread fast in Germany in the 1770s and 1780s. All kinds of substances were collected, since traditional alchemical texts regarding the prima materia, or first matter of the Work, were vague as to its nature. The common thread was that the prima materia was itself so common that nobody bothered to notice its potential. For those who found the idea of the soul too abstract an inference for the purpose, great efforts were made to gather dew ("the sugar of the stars"), semen (containing the life force), urine, and feces as being suitable elementary material for transformation.

Forster was also greeted by the promise of hidden gnosis, hinted at in the admission questions put to him. He was asked not only how Christianity was to be restored and how true alchemy was to be practiced, but also, "What is the spirit of God in man, and how does one become aware of it?"[18]

The beginning of the answer was the assertion that humankind must be free of the "animal and mundane nature" to which we cling.

Gnostic tendencies were also strong in the Gold und Rosenkreuz's peculiarly pietist understanding of life and religion. Pietist writers such as Gerhard Tersteegen were appreciated. In Tersteegen's poem "Pilgrim's Thought" are lines that would easily have found congeniality among the books of the Nag Hammadi library:

My body and the world are a strange dwelling place for me.
I think: Let it go; you will soon be leaving.
He who lives here as a citizen busies himself with great matters;
He calls me wretched and stupid but is himself a fool.[19]

The corruption of the world—a theme both pietist and gnostic—became ever more an attack on the corruption of morals, social order, and religious and secular authority. This tendency grew to somewhat paranoid proportions in the order's battle with Adam Weishaupt's Illuminati.

What else could an adherent of the Gold und Rosenkreuz expect to be told when joining the order? Christopher McIntosh has unearthed some interesting correspondence in this regard.[20] The correspondence took place between the nobleman von Maltzahn, from his estates in Mecklenberg, and his "most Worshipful Master" von Röpert.

Following a request for admission (November 2, 1782), von Röpert writes to inform von Maltzahn that he will be able to admit him soon. However, he stresses in a concluding sermon that, since the tragic fall of Adam, the image of God, which formed the whole perfection of Adam, has been lost. Fortunately, not all is lost. The "highest Creator" in his gentle mercy cares enough for the lost creatures to show them directly on earth the way to restore the lost happiness (was this the "happiness" that the American Constitution guaranteed its citizens the right to pursue?). Even in the flesh, it may yet be possible to understand what might have been thought of as having been reserved for eternity.

The order's intention is that von Maltzahn be "reborn." This situation was certainly not in line with essential Enlightenment principles. Rather than rely on his own understanding (as the philosopher Kant, a contemporary, would have suggested), the neophyte places his faith in a chain of supposed revelation emanating from the mysterious upper echelons of the order.

Von Maltzahn was enjoined to keep his membership a life secret and to communicate regarding the order work with no one except his "immediate superior and leader."

In March 1783 von Maltzahn received a circular warning him of the activities of the Illuminati. He should beware and inform if possible. The Illuminati were seen as a dangerous threat to the order's purpose and existence.

The attack on the Illuminati had begun.

RADICALS UNDER ATTACK: GOLD UND ROSENKREUZ VS. THE ILLUMINATI

The Order of the Illuminati was created in Bavaria by a twenty-eight-year-old professor of canon law and practical philosophy at Ingolstadt University, Adam Weishaupt (1748–1830). Weishaupt and his Illuminati have gained a significantly dark reputation, a product of deliberate misinformation and ill-informed modern conspiracy-mongering. The order has come to embody, for conspiracy theorists, the archetypal evil, subversive institution *par excellence,* desperate and ruthless gnostics hellbent on bringing Europe into the pit of hell from which the order sprang.

Much of this kind of thing stems from a century of anti-Masonic Jesuit propaganda and the tendency of conservative minds to regard the call for just reform, egalitarianism, humanism, and enlightenment as evil. The outer fringes have even advanced the view that Weishaupt and his followers were in the grip of those ubiquitous demons of paranoia the Men in Black, some kind of extraterrestrial cosmic subversives dedicated to the downfall of all that is natural, familiar, and good. Whether such beings might exist beyond the fertile imaginations of those who fear their existence, I cannot say. One thing is clear: Adam Weishaupt was not among them.[21]

The circumstances by which Adam Weishaupt's ideas rose to prominence may not be unfamiliar to us. The original Enlightenment depended for its success to a large extent upon enlightened despots such as Frederick the Great of Prussia, and frustration naturally grew when this kind of general benevolence was replaced by conservative rule.

In Bavaria, for example, Elector Maximilian III Joseph, who had encouraged the founding of the Bavarian Academy of Sciences (1759), was succeeded by Karl Theodor, an accession that signaled the return to narrow-minded clericalism. The Aufklärer began to feel the chill winds of the anti-Aufklärung. Not without reason, this was soon attributed to a conspiracy of Jesuits, neo-Rosicrucians, and other conservatives. (While the pope had officially dismissed the Jesuits in 1773, they still retained a widespread network of teaching posts.)

Karl Theodor's chief adviser was the Jesuit Ignaz Frank—also said to have been leader of the Munich Gold und Rosenkreuz.[22] All this aided Weishaupt's recruitment program. Weishaupt was a radical reformer who had seen the (ideologically) revolutionary potential of Freemasonry. At this time Freemasonry was, as we have seen, a powerful reforming force in Germany and in France. Weishaupt read all he could find on the subject and conceived of a secret society with radically enlightened aims.

In 1777 Weishaupt joined the Munich lodge Zur Behutsamkeit (Cautious Lodge; affiliated with the Strict Observance) and began to use Freemasonry for recruitment. He felt the urgency of so doing, incensed as he was by the attempt of the head of the Burghausen-based Rosicrucian circle to recruit Ingolstadt students to the cause of alchemy and to what Weishaupt regarded as the follies of Rosicrucianism.

By March 1778 Weishaupt's secret order had nineteen members. Four years later there were three hundred members, the poet Goethe and the distinguished Sonnenfels among them. Weishaupt had really put something together, and it is difficult to resist admiring a man who was in fact taking on a colossal system of Continental oppression. It is also pertinent to ask—or will be—who was closer to the revolutionary essence of gnosis: Weishaupt or his opponents within the Gold und Rosenkreuz?

Influenced by the social ideas of the French *philosophes* Rousseau, Morelly, and Mably—and by the scientific writings of Holbach and Helvetius—Weishaupt held the view that through education, science, reason, and the rejection of superstition and obscurantism, it would be possible to erect a free, happy, egalitarian society by peaceful means.[23]

From a collection of his writings intended to damn him (the *Originalschriften*)[24] we can see some of his ideas in close-up. Weishaupt believed that after a primitive state of equality and pleasure, the human being "began to take second place to being the citizen of a nation, and nationalism took the place of philanthropy." Humankind comes from the state of equality and freedom—and we shall return to it. This is, of course, a completely secularized and materialized gnosis, a progenitor of the ideas of Feuerbach and his follower Marx.

A "state of general *Aufklärung* and security makes princes and states unnecessary." Weishaupt wrote that Jesus had cloaked his essential doctrine in a religious form "and cleverly linked it with the ruling religion and customs of his people in which he concealed the inner essence of his teaching." Weishaupt clearly saw Jesus as the precursor of his own method. He saw that people do not in general take the simple truth in its simplest form. People fall for the wrapping, the image, the appealing decoration, the wish fulfillment. His method was to begin with the popular wrapping of Masonic secrets and then—in direct contradistinction to the method of Gold und Rosenkreuz initiation—remove the shells one by one.

What would be revealed at the end might be, for some, a platitude, but a platitude that, when seen through logical process, would appear as itself for the first time. The essential difference between great revolutionary orators such as Martin Luther King Jr. and the ersatz political bigmouth is that the former not only know inwardly what words like *truth, dignity, peace, brotherhood, justice,* and so on actually mean, but they are also gifted with the ability to evoke the knowledge in their hearers. In a sense, this is a form of magic: revealing the holiness of the word.

The structure of the order of the Illuminati was established as follows: Complex rituals were divided among three stages, all requiring much study. The first grade was that of Novize (Novice), demanding knowledge of the works of Adam Smith (author of the classic work of politico-economics *The Wealth of Nations*), Lessing, Goethe, and Wieland.

The second grade, that of Minerval (Minerva was the Roman goddess of wisdom and science), required the reading of classics by Seneca, Epictetus, and Plutarch, as well as the works of Sallust. The third grade, Illuminatus (the Illuminated), was essentially atheistic and materialistic (in the philosophical sense). Works by Holbach and Helvetius were required reading.

At the head of the order was the highly secret Areopagus, membership in which was granted to those who had fully grasped the order's subversive and revolutionary aims. People were frequently recruited in terms of their ability to infiltrate the political establishment: people of wealth, position, and real ability. Weishaupt himself was known by the code name Spartacus after the famous slave-leader of the first century B.C. who took on the Roman army and for a time shook the foundations of the imperial order.[25]

Adolf, Freiherr von Knugge, who had toyed with the Rosicrucians, joined Weishaupt as his deputy and set about strengthening Masonic ties and adding a mystical element to the grade process. He even got Weishaupt to agree to become part of the ruling oligarchy rather than supreme head of the order. (It is a compliment to Weishaupt's integrity that he assented.) Nevertheless, von Knugge's esoteric leanings clashed with Weishaupt's ideas, and von Knugge left the order in 1784. This can only have increased Weishaupt's hostility toward the neo-Rosicrucians.

Spartacus was extremely well informed and sharp on the subject of the Brotherhood of the Rosy Cross and seems to have better understood the mind of Johann Valentin Andreae than did the latter's ostensible followers:

> It is now well enough known among enlightened men that the Rosicrucians have never really existed. Rather, everything contained in the *Fama* and the *Allgemeine Reformation der Welt* [Boccalini's extract in the first published edition of the *Fama*, 1614] is a fine allegory composed by Valentine Andreae, and that subsequently an attempt was made, partly by charlatans (and Jesuits), partly by fanatics, to realize this dream. No one who is conversant with philosophical history is unfamiliar with this cobbled-together system of Hermetic philosophy.
>
> From the writings of the German Rosicrucians, however, it is abundantly clear that these good people have not even rightly understood the sense and spirit of this system, and it is no longer any secret that the aforementioned society, which includes very worthy men, has been cunningly led astray by a number of ignorant charlatans . . . who wish to bring all Masonic lodges under their control.[26]

This is very precise. Needless to say, the two organizations hated one another—although, and this must be stressed, this cannot be said of individual members. Some neo-Rosicrucians wanted nothing to do with unseemly internecine Masonic conflict, so contrary to the spirit of brotherhood.

The campaign against the Illuminati got under way in 1783. Gold und Rosenkreuz leaders accused the Illuminati (correctly, in a sense) of having set themselves "the soul-destroying task of tearing away the light of belief and our Lord and World-Redeemer as well as his eternal healing Word from the already too-benighted children of humanity."[27] This language, compared to that of Weishaupt above, conveys as much about the temperamental and philosophical gulf between the two orders as anything else could.

The fall of the Illuminati was ensured when a plan backed by the

Illuminati was revealed. It had as its aim Joseph II Hapsburg's acquisition of Bavaria, while Karl Theodor would be given Belgium in return. Duke Karl Theodor's wife, Duchess Maria Anna (a member of the electoral house of the Holy Roman Empire and a Bavarian patriot), was strongly opposed to the plan. The duchess Maria's secretary, one Utzschneider (who had left the Illuminati), informed Karl Theodor of the Illuminati's part in the plan. The influential Rosicrucian author Karl von Eckartshausen further informed Karl Theodor (von Eckartshausen was his archivist) that certain documents had gone missing from the ducal archive and that Illuminati infiltration was suspected.

On June 23, 1784, Karl Theodor signed an edict against secret societies. This act was followed on March 2, 1785, by the condemnation of all "lodges of the so-called freemasons and Illuminati in our country as traitors and hostile to religion."[28] Other rulers followed in banning the Illuminati, including Joseph II of Austria, who also put restrictions on regular Masonic lodges.

It is perhaps not surprising that the Gold und Rosenkreuz enjoyed immunity from harassment. The latter order could add this victory against the radical Aufklärung to the program of anti-Enlightenment laws then currently being enacted in Prussia, which, so far as religious matters were concerned, the Gold und Rosenkreuz effectively ruled until 1797. It does seem that Weishaupt's deep suspicion of the leadership of the Gold und Rosenkreuz had a point. There followed a general pogrom against the Illuminati, in the course of which Weishaupt himself was forced from his chair at Ingolstadt and had to escape to the protection of Ernst, duke of Saxe-Gotha.

A REAL ROSICRUCIAN KING (ON THE THRONE OF PRUSSIA)

Before the death of King Frederick the Great of Prussia (1786), a faction emanating from the circle of Masonic enthusiast Duke Friedrich August of Braunschweig emerged around the figure of Crown Prince Friedrich Wilhelm. The faction included Masonic theosophers, Templar Masons, followers of illuminism (the French variety), and, later, neo-Rosicrucians.

Taking advantage of some kind of illumination experienced by Friedrich Wilhelm, they persuaded the crown prince to join Strict Observance Masonry. The heir to the Prussian throne was duly initiated in the autumn of 1778. In the meantime, the Gold und Rosenkreuzers were making great strides in interesting the duke of Braunschweig in neo-Rosicrucianism.

According to Johannes Schultze, "We have only scanty information concerning Friedrich Augustus and his intellectual world, but he appears early on to have become inspired with a plan to realize certain practical religious aims and to found a kind of theocracy in Prussia. In view of the attitude of the king, this was only possible if the heir to the throne could be counted on as a willing tool."[29]

It fell to two men of the Gold und Rosenkreuz to transform the crown prince into such a willing tool, Johann Rudolf von Bischoffswerder and Johann Christof Wöllner. Von Bischoffswerder was of noble Thuringian parentage and an army officer. He joined the Strict Observance in 1764 and the Gold und Rosenkreuz on December 24, 1779. Wöllner came from peasant stock in Mark Brandenburg and was described by Frederick the Great (when Wöllner was trying to marry a noble heiress) as "a deceitful and scheming parson"—although this may have had more to do with the rigid class structure of Prussia than a fair character assessment. Originally a member of the Strict Observance, he moved over to the Gold und Rosenkreuz after the Gugomos affair and was initiated in January 1779.

Wöllner rose quickly through the grades and was soon made Oberhauptdirektor for northern Germany with authority over twenty-six circles, consisting of about 235 members. These two men became Friedrich Wilhelm's closest advisers.

Their plans reached the first stage of success when the crown prince was initiated into the Gold und Rosenkreuz on August 8, 1781. Wöllner did not let the matter rest there. He regularly besought the crown prince to improve sermons and guidance.

The crown prince was known to be somewhat eccentric and was certainly promiscuous. Perhaps he regarded Wöllner as a kind of benevolent but firm uncle—quite a contrast to his real uncle, the Great Frederick. Wöllner drew attention to the superhuman powers that would be at

Friedrich Wilhelm's disposal when he—*if* he—reached the grade of Magus. He also encouraged the heir to the throne to seek guidance not from the example (pro-Enlightenment) of his uncle, but from his grandfather Friedrich Wilhelm I, whose Christian piety had, he was told, ensured victory in the Seven Years War. Subsequent immorality and impiety was the direct result of "enlightenment religion." A new ruler would surely have to intervene to stem the evil tide. The crown prince must make himself ready—one day he would find himself in the presence of the Superiors in all their greatness.

In September 1785 the crown prince received from Wöllner the latter's *Abhandlung* (Treatise) *der Religion* for deep consideration and study. It was the first step to ensuring that the new king's religious policy would be in line with the intentions of leading Gold und Rosenkreuzers. Religious toleration was to be encouraged, but the basis in principle for loyalty to the king was held to reside in his subjects being good Christians: "On the whole of God's earth there is nothing more unfair, more unjust, more debasing to the freedom of the soul and more deplorable for the whole of mankind than religious intolerance or the attempt of one group of people to coerce another against their convictions in religious matters. . . . If a person errs I should try to persuade him, but if I fail I must let him go his way in peace, be tolerant and not infringe his beliefs. . . . I must not infringe God's role as judge."[30]

Nevertheless, Wöllner was strictly against those who would disturb the peace with ideas such as that reason was the only test of a thing being true: "Human nature remains a mystery to us, which we cannot explain without the Bible and divine revelation." Wöllner went so far as to blame Frederick the Great for the laxity that encouraged unbelief, along with the rationalist principles of Voltaire, Diderot (the encyclopedist), and the scientist Helvetius. (It is an interesting question whether William Blake, who was so against the primacy of reason, would have sided with Wöllner in this respect.)

The treatise further recommends good Sunday observance with a ban on military maneuvers on that day. The crown prince is also encouraged to choose an "honest man" to head the Department of Religious Affairs—that is to say, Wöllner himself.

In the following year (1786), Friedrich Wilhelm II came to the throne of Prussia. Wöllner was given responsibilities in public works (including a part in the commissioning of the architect Langhans as designer of the famous Brandenburg Gate in Berlin), but Wöllner's dream finally came true when on July 3, 1788, he replaced Zedlitz as head of the Department for Religious Affairs. Wöllner lost no time in setting his stamp on religious policy. Six days after moving to the new post, the Department of Religious Affairs issued the "Edict Concerning Religion."

While all confessions were forbidden to proselytize, religious toleration was built into Prussian legislation for the first time. Section 7 attacked the latitude of Protestant pastors. They would have to refrain from Deism, nominal belief, and ideas connected with the Aufklärung ("so-called")—on pain of dismissal. When a person chose to look at the label on the bottle called Lutheranism, that was precisely what he had a right to expect. In good Prussian style, the point was put forward that as a judge cannot change the law, a pastor cannot invent the faith he teaches.[31] New pastors would be closely examined for doctrinal felicity. This edict was followed by the "Edict of Censorship" on December 19, 1788. Books on religion would have to be submitted to government censors before they could be published. Admittedly, Wöllner had misgivings about this, but von Bischoffswerder had his way.

Bischoffswerder's preferred method of influencing the king was to expose the monarch to demonstrations of spiritism and clairvoyance. It was as a result of one such experience that Friedrich Wilhelm was introduced to the character of Hermann Daniel Hermes, the provost of the church of St. Maria Magdalena in Breslau, Silesia.

"Spiritual messages" conveyed to the king the necessity of employing the strict Pietist Hermes as a censor and general helper in the struggle against the Aufklärer. All clergy were to be tested as to their orthodoxy. This suggestion from Hermes led to the establishment of the Immediat-Examinations-Kommission, with powers to set up religious surveillance throughout the kingdom. Measures were enacted, for example, to ensure that passages of the Bible objectionable to rationalists would be preached.

The following year saw the crowned heads of Europe in a state of alarm over the French Revolution (1789), a panic that resulted in the breaking down of the connection between Enlightenment and enlightened despotism. Five years later, the philosopher Immanuel Kant fell foul of the Wöllner clique when he published "Religion Within the Limits of Pure Reason," part of which had been rejected by the censor (Hermes) when submitted for publication in the *Berliner Monatschrift*. Kant was obliged to submit an apology and a promise to keep his religious thoughts to himself in future.

In 1797 Friedrich Wilhelm II died, and with him neo-Rosicrucian power in Prussia. His successor, Friedrich Wilhelm III, dismissed the entire clique. Bischoffswerder retired on a full pension to the pleasures of a Polish estate given to him by the late king. Poor Wöllner retired without an annuity to an estate he had bought with his wife's money in 1790. He died embittered in 1800.

The combination of events surrounding the attack on the Illuminati and the religious policy of the Prussian king did the Gold und Rosenkreuz no good at all. Defections had grown throughout the 1780s. Not everyone who had joined the Gold und Rosenkreuz wanted to be a pietist or to sever relations with progressive thought in the fields of science and philosophy. Georg Forster, for example, the man who had sailed around the world with Captain Cook in 1772, became convinced that the Rosicrucians were nothing less than Jesuits in disguise—and this view developed into a widespread suspicion among the Aufklärer.

In 1786, members of the Moscow Gold und Rosenkreuz accused Wöllner of having cheated them out of money sent to obtain promised (but undelivered) secrets. Something was rotten in the Gold und Rosenkreuz. Toward the end of 1787, the Unknown Superiors announced that a General Convention would be held. This paved the way for the pronouncement that a Silanum (a silence) was to be observed. All lodge work was to be suspended until further notice.

While Wöllner and his circle of neo-Rosicrucians continued their Rosicrucian activities, the Silanum was really the end of the road for this particular manifestation of the Gold und Rosenkreuz. On April 7, 1792, the Superiors issued a final declaration that the order had ceased to exist. This announcement appeared for public scrutiny the following year in the *Wiener Zeitschrift*: "We are withdrawing. We are destroying the building at the same time as we are eliminating the cleft in it." The editor of the paper, Leopold Aloïs Hoffman, in a neat twist to the story, was convinced that the Gold und Rosenkreuz had in fact been destroyed from within by the Illuminati.

For those seeking alchemical knowledge, the establishment four years later (1796) of the Hermetische Gesellschaft may have provided some kind of haven. The founder of the society, Friedrich Bährens (1765–1833), also started the *Hermetisches Journal,* which ran for one issue in 1801. Karl von Eckartshausen[32] is known to have contacted the Hermetic Society and established a correspondence with Bährens. In 1805, the leadership of the Hermetische Gesellschaft passed to Baron von Sternhaym of Karlsruhe, who resurrected the journal, called it *Hermes,* and attracted new interest in Rosicrucianism and alchemy.

ROSICRUCIANS IN POLAND

Poland contained an idiosyncratic commingling of Enlightenment, counter-Enlightenment, rationalist, mystical, humanist, and theosophical strains of Freemasonry. The last Polish monarch was a Mason, King Stanislas Augustus Poniatowski (1732–98). In 1777 he joined the German-affiliated Masonic lodge Karl zu den drei Helmen (Karl and the Three Helmets),[33] led by Reichsgraf Aloïs von Bruhl. The king took an interest in high-grade Masonry, was promoted to Chevalier Rose-Croix, brother of the twenty-first degree, and became some kind of Rosicrucian. He may have become an adherent of the Bon Pasteur (Good Shepherd) system that coexisted in Poland with the Gold und Rosenkreuz.

It is possible that the king's friend Toux de Salverte founded the Bon Pasteur system in about 1750. There were lodges of this system in Warsaw and in Wilna.[34] They operated an idiosyncratic mystico-kabbalistic system of twelve degrees, which were confined to Poland. Since to be a member it was first necessary to have gone through the three Craft degrees (Apprentice, Fellow-Craft, and Master Mason) as well as the Rite of Scottish Master, the Bon Pasteur degrees begin at:

5. Chevalier du Soleil
6. Chevalier de la Rose-Croix (Knight of the Rose Cross)

7. Prince Chevalier de la Croix d'Or (Prince Knight of the Cross of Gold)
8. Maître Intérieure du Temple (Interior Master of the Temple)
9. Erhabener Philosoph (Exalted Philosopher)
10. Ordre des Chevaliers Hospitaliers de Christ et du Temple de Salomon (*sic*) (Order of the Knights Hospitaller of Christ and of the Order of the Temple of Saloman)
11. Architect Souvérain ou Philosophe du premier Ordre (Sovereign Architect or Philosopher of the first Order)
12. Frater Operator (Brother Operator)

The religious outlook of the Bon Pasteur system expressed a pietistic and gnostic-dualist sensibility. An extract from the "Instruction to Candidates" asserts that "the light must rise out of the darkness, and our souls, having received and recognised the true light, must allow themselves to be led by the heavenly spirit. . . . Thus the fruits of the spirit are life and purity, while the fruits of the body are earthly death and destruction."[35]

The system was not anti-Enlightenment. Reason was credited with bringing humankind out of darkness and superstition, but reason needed to be divinely enlightened. The lodges featured the familiar Masonic pillars of Jachin and Boaz, and these were interpreted kabbalistically as the twin opposites that (as in Böhme) make the All possible. The order regulations were almost certainly based on those of Sincerus Renatus (Samuel Richter), published in 1710 at Breslau, Silesia. We do not yet know what became of the Bon Pasteur lodges.

RUSSIA

Freemasonry reached Russia in 1731, its growth proceeding initially out of the English Provincial Grand Lodge, based in St. Petersburg. In 1775, the philanthropic journalist and publisher Nikolai Ivanovich Novikov was initiated, beginning a great Masonic-Rosicrucian career. Novikov was a supporter of the Enlightenment in Russia and worked tirelessly against bureaucratic corruption and the oppression of the serfs in Russia's feudal economy.

Martinism (followers of Louis-Claude de St. Martin) also flourished in Russia, as did Jean-Baptiste Willermoz's Chevaliers Bienfaisants de la Cité Sainte (Benificent Knights of the Holy City), or Lyons system. (Willermoz, like St. Martin, was a disciple of Martines de Pasqually, founder of the Order of Elect Cohens in 1760.) Novikov also became an initiate of Willermoz's Beneficent Knights of the Holy City.[36]

After the Wilhelmsbad Masonic Congress of 1782, Russia became the Seventh Province (of Masonic jurisdiction), with Novikov as president and fellow Mason Johann Georg Schwarz, a Transylvanian German friend of Novikov, as chancelor.[37]

It also appears that Schwarz was the head of the Gold und Rosenkreuz in Russia. He persuaded Strict Observance members of the superiority of the Rosicrucian system. Schwarz also gave Sunday lectures in Moscow on such doctrines as the emanations of God and the spiritual hierarchy. His greatest influences were Thomas à Kempis's *Imitation of Christ,* Joannes Arndt, Angelus Silesius, and Jacob Böhme. His spirited promotion of German literature contributed greatly to Russia's receptivity to the Romantic movement, a movement that was to bear astounding artistic fruit. He died at the home of his patron, Prince Trubetskoi, at Ochakovo in February 1784; he was thirty-three.

Novikov, meanwhile, echoed Pico della Mirandola's seminal treatise, the *Oratio* (1486; Russia, it should be noted, had missed out on the Renaissance), in his article "On the Dignity of Man in His Relations to God and the World," published in his own journal, *Morning Light.*

Novikov advanced the Hermetic view of Man as "lord of the universe," the link between matter and spirit. On the basis of this vision, he argued that all human beings deserved respect, regardless of origin or social status. Every individual should work for the common good as an individual, and joyfully so.

Novikov next took the step of forming a highly significant publishing syndicate along with other publishers, such as I. P. Turgenev and the Rosicrucian I. V. Lopuchin. The Typographical Society published works by Böhme, Silesius, John Pordage, the mystic Madame Guyon (1648–1717, whose works so pleased William Law), St. Martin's incredibly influential work *Des érreures et de la verité* (Of Errors and Truth), as well as works of Paracelsian alchemy and works of

Rosicrucian provenance. Novikov himself favored Hermetic and alchemical works, while Lopuchin's publishing house preferred mystical and pietistic works, proving that people of different preferences can work together for a common aim.

Through the efforts of the Typographical Society, the (reading) Russian public was introduced to a whole range of mystical and esoteric writings. The society, amazingly, produced 893 titles between 1779 and 1792—that is more than thirty percent of all works printed in Russia in that period. This was a most remarkable achievement. The society also involved itself in charitable activities, establishing both a hospital and an apothecary shop for the poor. During the famine of 1787, Novikov and fellow Rosicrucians were out on the streets, active in poor relief.

The great heyday of Rosicrucian lodges in Russia ended when the commander in chief of the Moscow militia, Yakov Bruce, took advantage of an impending state visit of Catherine II to declare that the Moscow lodges were subservient to Berlin, a not uncharacteristic attack of xenophobia from the perennially suspicious militaristic brain.

Inspections and false witness led to the closure of all Rosicrucian lodges at the beginning of 1786. In 1792, Novikov was condemned without trial to fifteen years in prison. He was released, happily, four years later when Paul I came to the throne, a man friendly to Novikov and appreciative of some of his ideas.

In 1786, secret teachings for which much had been paid failed to materialize from Berlin, and Wöllner was accused of cheating. Schröder, the Moscow leader of the Gold und Rosenkreuz, was suspended, and in 1787 the Silanum was announced. Russian Rosicrucians continued the good work in loose association and exerted a liberalizing influence on the cultural atmosphere, which touched both Paul I (d. 1801) and his successor, Tsar Alexander I.

Paul I liked the theocratic ideas brought by the Martinists and Rosicrucians. The conception of the Holy Tsar, mediator between heaven and earth, was promoted by Novikov. He believed that the prince should be a mystical initiate drawing on spiritual and supernatural virtues and sanctified by the Inner Church (a conception voiced roundly by the sixteenth-century radical reformers Sebastian Franck and David Joris, influential on the young Johann Valentin Andreae). Novikov's 1783 novel, *Chrysomander,* featured a magus-king, Hyperion, who used alchemy to relieve the hardship of his subjects.[38]

After Bonaparte's retreat from Moscow (1812), Tsar Alexander I— who regarded the retreat as an act of divine grace—turned to the writings of Böhme, Swedenborg, and St. Martin and the works of Karl von Eckartshausen (which had been appearing since 1793). Alexander I was particularly impressed by Eckartshausen's *Die Wolke über dem Heiligtum* (The Cloud upon the Sanctuary, 1802), published in Russia in 1804, the year in which William Blake released his beautiful poetic prophecy "Jerusalem" to an uncomprehending English public.[39]

Eckartshausen's work is a most eloquent treatment of the theme of the invisible body that perpetuates the true, esoteric Christian message. It was presented to Tsar Alexander in 1812, probably stimulating his interest—along with the influence of Baroness Julie von Krüdener, who helped the tsar to understand Eckartshausen's work—in the political realization of the Holy Alliance. The alliance was promulgated in September 1815 (three months after Waterloo) in an attempt to realize the dream of a Christian theocratic order in Europe.

It was not to be. The Russian Orthodox Church, like the Roman Catholic Church in its intolerance to competition, worked hard against the mystical influence. In 1824 Archimandrite Photius declared the "new religion" of illuminism was that of the Antichrist and a fomenter of revolution. Alexander moved back to orthodox conservatism, and another great Rosicrucian dream died.

THE ASIATIC BRETHREN

One other German order of this period deserves mention. In the early 1780s there emerged Die Ritter des Lichts (the Knights of the Light; 1780 or 1781), later called Die Brüder St. Johannes des Evangelisten aus Asien in Europa, the Asiatic Brethren of St. John the Evangelist in Europe. The founder was Hans Heinrich von Ecker und Eckhoffen, a former member of the Gold und Rosenkreuz.

Initiates of the highest of the five grades of the order, the grade of Melchisedeck, were known as Royal priests or True Rosicrucians.[40] The uniqueness of the Asiatic Brethren lay in their permitting (for a time) Jewish members, while the order itself was steeped in Jewish esoteric lore. How had this come about?

Ecker had met a Franciscan monk in Vienna called Bischof, an aficionado of alchemy who had been in a monastery in Jerusalem, where he had met kabbalistic Jews, and in particular a singular kabbalist called Asaria, who claimed to represent his order throughout the Old World. Asaria initiated Ecker into mystical Jewish knowledge.

The Order of Asiatic Brethren was conducted according to a loose Masonic framework, with the unusual caveat that no one who had been initiated into a regular Masonic lodge was admissible. The rituals bore the alchemical character of those enjoyed by the Gold und Rosenkreuzers. The Masonic Star was represented as standing for Aesch-Majim (Fiery Water): "the watery fire or fiery water, which we know how to obtain from our substance."[41]

The Temples of the Asiatic Brethren were decorated with ornaments of a strongly Hebraic character. In keeping with the Jewish atmosphere, the Supreme Council was known as the Synedrion (Sanhedrin); its officers bore Hebrew titles. Within the order there appears to have been the interesting intention of bringing about religious unity by leading Christianity back to its Jewish form. Jewish festivals were celebrated, and the order began to attract members of the Haskalah, the Jewish Enlightenment, who seem to have been happy— given the give-and-take spirit of the order—to celebrate Christian festivals as well as their own.

The order claimed to have been founded by Freemasonry's favorite saint, John the Evangelist, in A.D. 40 (John's Gospel has been called a "half-way house to Gnosticism"), and they consequently used a calendar system that subtracted forty from the calendar year.

The dominant ideas of the system were those of Paracelsus, the Christian theosophy of Böhme, and a number of kabbalistic doctrines. With Vienna as its base, the order spread to Prague, Innsbrück, Berlin, Frankfurt, Wetzlar, Marburg, and Hamburg—in spite of the Austrian anti-Masonic Freimaurerpatent (Freemason Law) of December 1785.

Wöllner did not like the Asiatic Brethren and opposed their appearance at the 1782 Wilhelmsbad Convention. A letter survives written to

Duke Ferdinand von Braunschweig, grand master of the Strict Observance, alleging that Satan was threatening: an order called the "Knights of the True Light, has been created and is divided into the following 5 grades: Novices of 3, 5 and 7 years, Levites and Priests. All is said to be conferred free of charge with acts of the blackest diabolic magic."[42]

Needless to say, there is no evidence for the diabolical nature of the brethren, and Ecker continued to reside in Vienna in 1784 without Satan's companionship. In the following year he reorganized the order with Joseph Hirschfeld. The longer title was dropped, and they became known simply as the Asiatic Brethren.

Another collaborator in Ecker's dream was Baron Thomas von Schönfeld, a follower of the cult of the seventeenth-century kabbalistic pseudomessiah Sabbatai Zvi. Schönfeld incorporated some Sabbatian doctrines into the order's teachings. His efforts were cut short on the Paris guillotine during the Reign of Terror. Prince Ferdinand von Braunschweig ignored warnings and became Generalobermeister of the Brethren in 1786.

Ecker needed patronage to establish the order, and soon supreme headship was granted to, and accepted by, Landgraf Carl von Hesse-Cassel. This latter lord spent a great deal of his time looking for "hidden superiors," "the true secret," and so on. He constructed an alchemical laboratory according to the guidance of the highly mysterious French alchemist the Comte de St.-Germain. The legendary alchemist continued to be harbored on the Landgraf's estates for the last years of his life. (Anthroposophists today take the view that the Count of St. Germain was a reincarnation of Christian Rosenkreuz.)

In the late 1780s, Ecker was furiously opposed by writers who asserted that Jews should not be admitted, on the basis that Jesus was the cornerstone of Masonry.

Meanwhile, Friedrich Münter, later to be bishop of Seeland, a Dane of German origin and eminent Freemason, theologian, and Aufklärung supporter, feared that philosophical theology and enlightened science would disappear in fifty years if Rosicrucianism was permitted to spread any further.[43]

In his 1787 *Authentische Nächricht von den Ritter- und Brüder-*

Eingeweihten aus Asien, zur Beherzigung für Freymaurern (Authentic Report Concerning the Knights and Initiated Asiatic Brethren, for the Attention of Freemasons), Münter advanced the hysterical notion that the Asiatic Brethren were secret Illuminati and disclosed rumors that its initiates held secret ceremonies in a cave at the monastery of Monte Senario near Florence. This was a cave, mark you, formerly used by the ancient Etruscans for diabolical sacrifices! Even rationalists could be quite irrational on the subject of unrational orders; the same obtains today. Münter's work also shows what a bête noire Rosicrucians had become to some Aufklärer.

Meanwhile, things were not going well for the Asiatic Brethren. To repair the split over the "Jewish issue," Carl von Hessen proposed a compromise whereby the Jewish Asiatic Brethren would form a separate Melchisedeck Lodge, but in Hamburg the Jewish members rejected the proposal and left the order.

Appalling anti-Semitism poisoned the whole enterprise, and the Asiatic Brethren collapsed in a vortex of mutual recrimination. Heinrich von Ecker got into protracted litigation with Hirschfeld but died in August 1791, the matter unresolved. As late as 1817, Hirschfeld was still dreaming of resurrecting his life's greatest achievement.

ROMANTICISM

When the doors of perception are cleansed, then we shall see things as they really are, Infinite.

WILLIAM BLAKE

When the Romantic movement came as a long-awaited reaction to the Enlightenment, and feeling, intuition, spiritual idealism, and—above all—imagination returned to the philosophical and artistic forefront, there was a renewed interest in the worldview represented by the neo-Rosicrucians: new interest in Hermetism, magic, alchemy, and Kabbalah.

In Blakean terms, Albion, formerly pinned down to the rock of reason, arose to greet his "lovely emanation" Jerusalem—and spiritual liberty went abroad once more. Gnostic tradition has been traced in the works of Novalis and found in the mystical ideas of the Romantic philosopher Schelling. Samuel Taylor Coleridge popularized German Romantic ideas in England and had a tremendous influence, especially after his death, making a major impact on English philosophical, poetic, and religious life. His was the philosophy that helped inspire the famous Oxford Movement of religious revival (1833–45).

Coleridge's theory of creative imagination has stood the test of time—the human mind is not a blank screen on which the material world imprints itself. The mind is creative of reality: "[W]e receive but what we give." No wonder one scholar has dubbed the leaders of the Romantic movement "the Avatars of the Thrice-Great Hermes."

TEN

Freemasonry in France

The ancients called practical magic the sacerdotal and royal art, and one remembers that the magi were the masters of primitive civilisation, because they were the masters of all the science of their time. To know is to be able when one dares to will.

ÉLIPHAS LÉVI, *THE KEY OF THE MYSTERIES*

Freemasonry was established in France between 1725 and 1730. It grew rapidly, due partly to a fashionable interest in English institutions among the French educated classes. While the Parisian Grand Lodge dominated French Masonry in the 1730s, more exotic forms of Masonry began to proliferate across the nation.

There is an implicit contradiction in eighteenth-century Continental Masonry, and this contradiction contains within it the dynamic for two broad Masonic currents. The contradiction lies in that while on one hand all men are brothers, united as a species under the Great Architect, on the other hand, secret wisdom embodied in symbols is revealed exclusively to privileged initiates. Depending on the extent to which the concept of brotherhood might reach, Masons can go either way: toward Enlightenment with its broad social itinerary or toward more esoteric and personal Masonic expressions. It is also possible to combine the two.

In France, there was (and is) a far greater enthusiasm than in England for chivalric themes with mystical tendencies. Chivalric

Masonry was influenced by the Scots emigré to France Andrew Michael Ramsay, who in 1737 published a speech claiming that Freemasonry began during the period of the Crusades. Other enthusiasts picked up the idea and attached the chivalric mythology to the condemned order of the Knights Templar—those who fought and suffered for the Temple.

Largely as a result of Ramsay's efforts, chivalric and mystically oriented Masonry, with its high grades beyond the three Craft degrees, became known in France as Scottish Masonry. Some Scottish rites make use of the mythology of the "chosen masters" *(maîtres élus)* sent by Solomon to arrest the assassins of Hiram Abif.

Myths are not difficult to generate when legend and history are drunk from the same cup. We have only to think of Wolfram von Eschenbach's fictional "templars," for example. In *Parzifal* (c. 1210), these fantastic knights ride out from their literary mountain fastness of Munsalvaesche in the service of the mystical Gral. Think now of the actual knights (not Templars) who attempted to preserve the gnostic Cathars at the mountain castle at Montségur and other castles of the Languedoc in the early thirteenth century. Throw in the curse that the last Templar master, Jacques de Molay, is said to have put on the French monarchy for its vicious attack on the Templars in the early fourteenth century, then add the papacy's objections to Freemasonry from the eighteenth century onward. Grind in the Vatican's frequent persecution of spiritual heretics, scientists, and gnostic philosophers (Galileo and Giordano Bruno, to name two), and mix thoroughly with the fear of philosophical rationalism, social liberalism ("the halfway house to atheism"),[1] and the yearning for transcendental personal meaning. The result: a spicy, nourishing dish called Masonic neo-Templarism.

First you conceive of your ideal (and ancient) order of things, and then you invest the knights with the duty to protect it. The mythology can be applied to almost any appropriate circumstance. Becoming a knight of such an order solves, in the first instance, the pressing problem of human identity and purpose for its adherents. Medals of service and attainment proliferate, as do grandiose titles—the latter, incidentally, despised by Johann Valentin Andreae, for one; he favored simplicity, honesty, and sincere directness.

Nevertheless, it must be said that people need a sense of the past, of their ancestral roots, of their essential beliefs—and mythologies of knighthood help to bring forth precisely this sense. Romanticism is a great motivator, necessarily ill at ease with rationalism and logic-chopping; we cannot live on bread alone.

THE ELECT COHENS

Interacting and overlapping with the world of eighteenth-century French Freemasonry were a number of organized esoteric and mystical currents. In 1754, Martines de Pasqually, a man said to have traveled the East in search of wisdom (the Rosenkreuz archetype), set up an order called the Scottish Judges in Montpellier. Six years later, in Bordeaux, he established the Order of Elect Cohens, of which order Pasqually was grand sovereign.

The Elect Cohens practiced a form of ceremonial magic: a combination of the Catholic mass with the works of Renaissance occultists such as Henry Cornelius Agrippa. Pasqually claimed to be in contact with unearthly beings. He held an animist conception of the universe, a universe pulsating with life on many planes or in dimensions ulterior to those ordinarily experienced by human beings. His ceremonies were regulated by astrological considerations. According to Pasqually, "The bodies of the universe are all vital organs of eternal life."[2] The moon and the sun figured prominently in his system. Equinoxes were chosen as propitious times for important rituals, to encourage the operation of good spirits.

There was a daily invocation wherein the Elect Cohen would trace a circle on the floor, at the center of which was inscribed the letter *W* below a candle. The Cohen then stood in the circle and, holding a light to read the invocation, would begin: "O Kadoz, O Kadoz, who will enable one to become as I was originally when a spark of divine creation? Who will enable me to return in virtue and eternal spiritual power?"[3] The purpose of the invocations and evocations was ultimately to open communication with what Pasqually described as the "Active and Intelligent Cause."

In 1772, Pasqually sailed to Santo Domingo in the Caribbean, leaving the organization in the hands of his followers Bacon and Jean-Baptiste

Willermoz. Pasqually never returned, dying in Port-au-Prince in 1774. Bacon then joined the Grand Orient, the mainstream French Masonic order (founded in 1772), while Willermoz not only joined the Strict Observance Rite (founded in 1754 by Baron Hund) but also founded several influential orders of his own. The high-degree Masonic order of Chevaliers Bienfaisants de la Cité Sainte, also known as the Rite Écossais Rectifié, we encountered in the last section, on Rosicrucianism in Russia— Novikov was an initiate of it. The Chevaliers de l'Aîgle Noir et Rose-Croix performed a rite containing strong alchemical and neo-Rosicrucian themes.

Another significant follower of Pasqually at Bordeaux was Louis-Claude de St. Martin, initiated into the Elect Cohens in 1768. St. Martin was known as the Philosophe Inconnu, the Unknown Philosopher—for what reason is not exactly clear, but an unknown philosopher would go very well with an invisible fraternity.

In 1774, the year of Pasqually's death, he began writing his very influential work *Des Érreures et de la verité* (published in 1775), the book that, together with Eckartshausen's *Cloud upon the Sanctuary*, made such an impact on Tsar Alexander I, and which was read widely across Europe. St. Martin's greatest influence was the ubiquitous Jacob Böhme.[4] St. Martin also had a great social dream: a "natural and spiritual theocracy" governed by men chosen by God, men with demonstrable "divine consciousness."

St. Martin's dualistic outlook is reminiscent of Gnosticism. In spite of the advantage of reason, human beings cannot, according to St. Martin, by their own faculties light the torch to guide them in the darkness. Physical existence is a state of continual suffering (whether we are immediately conscious of it or not). In their misery, humans are cut off "from the one source of light and the only aid for living beings."[5] The system of the materialists "reduces human beings to a lower level than the beasts."[6] In the view of the Unknown Philosopher, theocratic monarchy offers the only solution capable of bringing into the temporal world "the functions of a true and infinite Being."[7]

Eighteenth-century France was a very fruitful field from the point of view of gnostic advocates. In 1716 was born Antoine-Joseph Pernety, the founder of the Illuminés d'Avignon, often confused with the Illuminati, with which phenomenon Pernety's order had practically nothing in common.

In 1732, Pernety became a Benedictine monk, with unusual interests. He became fascinated by alchemy when he read *L'Histoire de la philosophie hermétique* by the abbé Longlet-Dufresnoy (1741). In 1765 he dropped the habit but was still referred to as Dom Pernety. He went to Avignon and became a Freemason. He wrote his own rite, the *rite hermétique,* based on alchemical principles, which was adopted by the lodge Les Séctateurs de la Vertu. The rite had six degrees:

1. Vrai Maçon (True Mason)
2. Vrai Maçon de la Voie Droite (True Mason of the Right Path)
3. Chevalier de la Clef d'Or (Knight of the Golden Key)
4. Chevalier de l'Iris (Knight of the Iris)
5. Chevalier des Argonautes (Knight of the Argonauts)
6. Chevalier de la Toison d'Or (Knight of the Golden Fleece)

The dom later added the grade Chevalier du Soleil (Knight of the Sun), whose ritual, he claimed, contained a complete course in Hermetism and *gnosis*.

In 1738, escaping from a papal bull against Freemasonry, he went to see Frederick the Great. The Prussian king made Pernety a member of the Royal Academy of Berlin with the post of curator of the Royal Library. Pernety contacted Berlin occultists.

He was, he said, guided by the angel Assadai. Assadai helped him in the accomplishment of the Great (alchemical) Work, the transformation of the soul. (This kinship with his angel Assadai is reminiscent of Aleister Crowley's trust in his holy guardian angel, Aiwass, whom he first encountered in 1904.)

In November 1783 Pernety left Berlin, as instructed by the angel Holy Word, to return to Avignon. At the estate of Bédarrides, near Avignon, he formed a new people-of-God community (as predicted by Holy Word in Berlin) called the Illuminés d'Avignon. All members were Masons. The order had two grades: *novice* and *illuminé majeur*. The leader was simply called *mage*. There was a temple there, and alchemy was practiced.

The glorious French Revolution persecuted illuminist sects. In 1793, Pernety was arrested. He was later released, and died in Avignon in 1786, aged eighty, guided to the end by the angel Holy Word. By 1800, the Illuminés had declined to only fifteen circles. (After Pernety's death, his Chevalier du Soleil grade was turned into the twenty-seventh and twenty-eighth grades of the Ancient and Accepted Scottish Rite.)

The rite of the Philalèthes (Lovers of Truth) was founded by the keeper of the Royal Treasury, Savalette de Langes, in 1775. This rite combined ideas from Swedenborg and Pasqually. There were twelve degrees. The ninth degree, Unknown Philosopher, was the name of a spirit familiar to Pasqually's rituals—and this is perhaps whence St. Martin's pseudonym derived.

In the years before the Revolution, all kinds of Masonry flourished. One of the most exotic forms was that of the Sicilian Alexander, Count Cagliostro (Joseph Balsamo), founder of the so-called Egyptian Rite of Freemasonry, purportedly dating back to the time of the ancient Egyptian hierophants from whose descendants Cagliostro claimed initiation.

Cagliostro gathered devotees from all over Europe, claiming to be in possession of miraculous occult powers. He certainly appears to have been not only adept in the art of fascination but no mean hand at numerology as well. His brilliance in selecting winning numbers for the royal lottery of France made him a darling of Parisian society, for a time.

In 1785 he founded the Temple of Isis in the rue de la Sondière in Paris, which, notably, admitted women. He was later falsely implicated by his enemies in the scandal of Marie Antoinette's diamond necklace and was thoroughly and quite unfairly disgraced. He had brought joy and a measure of understanding to thousands. He later went to Rome, where he was arrested by the Inquisition, and died alone in prison—a rotten fate for a wonderful human being.

By 1789 there were some six hundred and thirty lodges in France with something like 30,000 members. Many lodges were explicitly political, while a number had been infiltrated by the followers of Adam Weishaupt. Many Masons helped create the conditions for and the desirability of some kind of social revolution in France: the philosophical rationale. Members of the Grand Orient of France, for example, included Voltaire, Bailly, Danton, and Helvetius.

At the great Masonic Congress at Wilhelmsbad (1782), the rationalist and revolutionary Masons, led by Bode, were defeated by the moderates. Bode and his followers allied themselves with the Bavarian Illuminati. Some Masonic lodges in France had the definite knack of turning philosophical principles into political action. When in the critical year 1789 Louis XVI summoned the States General to meet the impending crisis, the coherence of the *cahiers de doléances,* the list of grievances that were submitted to the king for redress, showed a high level of organization for liberty and equality. As things turned out, Freemasons were unable to check the storm that overtook the country. Esotericists rarely distinguish themselves in politics, being concerned with fundamental, timeless principles ("My kingdom is not of this world").

In the wake of the suppression of the Catholic Church, strange and frankly absurd revolutionary cults developed, with all the thematic incongruity of a painting by Miró. One of the most famous was that of the cult of the goddess Reason, whose aesthetic abomination of a statue was erected in Nôtre-Dame de Paris. If, as Lenin observed, ethics will be the aesthetics of the future (and doubtless vice versa), then God help us.

Worshippers at the throne of Reason were greeted by a girl dolled up in red, white, and blue with young nymphs performing a spot of ballet around her presence—and this was reason for Reason's sake! The main propagator of this cult, Anaxagoras Chaumette, succumbed to the logical chop of the guillotine in 1794.

The cult of Reason was swiftly followed by Robespierre's cult of the Supreme Being and the Immortality of the Soul, again observed with theatrical rites.

Some people make a mess of the moment, and some seize it. In 1799 Napoleon Bonaparte seized power and reinstated orthodox Catholicism, as he saw it. Occult movements continued underground. Bonaparte left them alone. He had been raised in a household full of occultism. (I have seen a handwritten manuscript copy of the magical *grimoire The Key of Solomon the King* that belonged to Napoleon's father.) Bonaparte was not a rationalist. He believed in destiny and heroism. And many believed in him.

ÉLIPHAS LÉVI ZAHED: A GREAT SOCIALIST MAGICIAN AND OCCULT REVIVALIST

Alphonse-Louis Constant (born February 8, 1810) was a man who kept his sense of humor and mental liveliness to the end of his life, when the old bores tend to flag into terminal criticism, sclerosis of the conscience, and self-pity.

Alphonse-Louis Constant spent a dreamy and very religious childhood on the Left Bank of the Seine. Later he recalled how he "stood apart and meditated vaguely or tried to draw; I became easily enthused by a toy or picture, which afterwards I broke or tore up; the need to love intensely was already tormenting me; I did not know how to explain my malaise."

Here we find the perennial cry of the young outsider: excluded from the daily drift and lost in wondering why. His mother sensed his spiritual inclinations and was proud to send him to the seminary of St. Nicholas du Chardonnet, Paris. There his curiosity was aroused by mysterious subjects like animal magnetism (as had been, not so long ago, promoted in Paris by Franz Anton Mesmer—the founder of mesmerism, or hypnosis).

Constant's teacher, the abbé Frère, who was to be ousted from his teaching position, believed Christ had inaugurated the Age of the Holy Spirit. Alphonse took this to be the essential and genuine message of Christianity, not realizing that his teacher was a heretic. The rough treatment of the abbé made the boy doubt his teachers.

He next entered the seminary of Saint-Sulpice to a wave of personal disappointment: "Art and poetry were regarded as dangerous things," he later wrote, adding, "Theological text-books take the place of spirit and heart."[8] Thus speaks the natural romantic. The curriculum included attention (for moral purposes) to the *Golden Verses of Pythagoras*—a work that contained passages of genuine magical thinking. Constant picked them up. His mind moved toward the magical conception of the universe: "hidden forces" bound the material order together.

In 1835, he was ordained deacon. All seemed set for a priestly career, when he was visited by Adèle Allenbach, separated from a Swiss army officer, extremely poor, fervently pious, and in fear for her daughter's religion. Alphonse-Louis suddenly experienced human sexual love. He abandoned the priesthood at the last moment. His widowed mother committed suicide. "It seemed at that time as though all belief and all hope had abandoned me,"[9] he wrote.

Constant became a political radical after encountering Flora Tristan, a great anarchist, socialist, lover of people, and trade union organizer. She received the love of thousands in return. Constant set to work to write *La Bible de la liberté,* a social polemic, along with the ecstatic prophet Ganneau, known to his disciples as Mapah. Constant spent eight months in prison in 1841 for this work and read Swedenborg in his cell. On his release, Constant became famous with the left wing.

In 1843 he changed his name so that he could acquire a teaching post without harassment. He became the abbé Baucourt, an auxiliary priest at Evreux, with the right to give sermons. He was a great success until he was exposed in the *Écho de la Normandie* newspaper, whereupon he was obliged to leave the seminary. The bishop of Evreux offered him priesthood but he refused, feeling that he could not bear the responsibility.

Returning to Paris, he found that Flora Tristan had died (1844). He published her women's emancipation manuscripts in 1846 in a work entitled *L'Émancipation de la femme, ou testament de la paria* (The Emancipation of Woman, or the Pariah's Testament). In 1845 Constant had published, anonymously, a pacifist manifesto, *La Fête-Dieu, ou le triomphe de la paix religieuse* (The God-Feast, or the Triumph of Religious Peace). Alphonse-Louis Constant had become that rare thing, a spiritual socialist.

On July 13, 1846, he married Noémi Cadiot, aged eighteen, a pupil from the Evreux Girls School. Six months later he was tried before the courts, accused of provoking scorn and hatred between the classes and against the government of Louis-Philippe. He spent a year in prison. A daughter, Marie, was born in September 1847. Noémi Constant made a passionate appeal to the judges and was able to win her husband's release six months before the end of his sentence.

In 1848, the year of revolutions, Louis-Philippe fled. There were widespread riots in Paris. According to Constant, the deadly Paris riot was begun by one Sobrier, a delicate and nervous disciple of Mapah, who worked himself into a state of enthusiasm and strolled through the streets calling for supporters. Magically, they arrived, and a revolution of sorts began. Constant wrote articles for the left-wing press and composed revolutionary songs. The same year saw his last political writing, *Le Testament de la liberté* (The Testament of Liberty): "Now the fourth stage of the revolution is in preparation: namely, that of love. After forms come passions; after passions, thought; after thought, love. And it is thus that the reign of the Holy Spirit, proclaimed by Christ, will be realised on earth. . . . The great heretics have burned the dead-woods; the revolutionaries, axe in hand, have cut down and uprooted the old stumps; everywhere the socialists are sowing the new word, the word of universal association and communal property."[10]

Constant began to find himself more and more attracted to the Kabbalah, Christian mysticism, Hermetism, Böhme, Swedenborg, St. Martin, and the occultist Fabre d'Olivet. The catalyst for the change was the arrival in 1852 of the Polish emigré Hoene Wronski, who had a military background.

Wronski's march to gnosis had begun when he had met the astronomer and advanced mathematician Lalande in Marseilles. Lalande had been the founder of the lodge Des Neuf Soeurs in Paris, the lodge joined by Georg Forster (later Strict Observance and Gold und Rosenkreuz), and of which Condorcet and Benjamin Franklin were members. Wronski's life was one of unrelieved poverty. Constant wrote of him, "A man whose mathematical discoveries would have intimidated the genius of Newton has placed, in this century of universal and absolute doubt, the hitherto unshakeable basis of a science at once human and divine. He has dared to define the essence of God and to find, in the definition itself, the law of absolute movement and universal creation."[11]

Wronski showed Constant a synthesis of rationalism, religion, and belief in human progress. He also made perpetual-motion machines and three-dimensional demonstrations of the paradoxical union of human and divine knowledge. Commenting on one of Wronski's machines—a kind of mechanical version of the early-fourteenth-century mystic Ramon Lull's moving tables of divine attributes and terrestrial correspondences—

Constant declared, "Man can explore the entire sphere of the sciences; but never will he meet God, who always seems to retreat before his researches and who is always hidden by the globe, that is to say by the thickness of material things. The globe [a concept borrowed from Böhme, meaning a combination of condensing and materialization] symbolising divine knowledge can be dismantled [a model of Wronski's], and on it is written: ALL THAT HAS BEEN, IS AND WILL BE."[12]

Under Wronski's influence, Constant began his first magical treatise, the *Dogme de la magie*. In 1853 Noémi left, never to return, for the Marquis de Montferrier, for whose journal, the *Revue Progréssive*, she had written. Lévi immersed himself in the *Dogme* as therapy and transliterated his name into Hebrew. He became Éliphas Lévi Zahed, or plain Éliphas Lévi. The same year his wife left him, his friend Wronski died.

In the spring of the following year, Lévi went to London, staying at a hotel at 57 Gower Street. In London he met Sir Edward Bulwer-Lytton, author of the Rosicrucian novel *Zanoni*. The two men became friends. This visit also saw the famous evocation of the spirit of Apollonius of Tyana, the first-century theurgist, performed for the pleasure of a bizarre and mysterious lady who invited Lévi to her home for the express purpose of a touch of necromancy. The evocation was only partially successful—something caused Lévi's arm to be temporarily paralyzed. Lévi was shaken, and he returned to Paris in August.

Back in Paris, he met Count Alexander Braszynsky, a man with a passion for alchemy, and Lévi visited the count's laboratory at the Château de Beauregard at Villeneuve-Saint-Georges, Madame de Balzac's home. Both were friends of Lord Lytton, to whose house at Knebworth in Hertfordshire Lévi was invited on his second visit to London in 1861.

Lytton had a very loose connection with the founders of the British Freemasonic Societas Rosicruciana in Anglia. Perhaps this explains how it came to pass that the young Englishman Kenneth Mackenzie, one of the founders of the S.R.I.A. (founded officially in 1866—and from which the Hermetic Order of the Golden Dawn directly derived), came to visit Lévi at his apartment at 19 avenue de Maine on December 3, 1861.

The visit, a fascinating one, was recorded in the journal *The Rosicrucian and Red Cross* in May 1873.[13] At this meeting, "the

Professor of Transcendental Magic" showed Mackenzie a manuscript prophecy attributed to Paracelsus. The prophecy predicted the rise of Napoleon, the downfall of the papacy, the restoration of the kingdom of Italy, and the ultimate ascendancy of the occult sciences "as a means of restoring general harmony in society."

Regarding Lévi's following, he told baron Spedalieri that he had twelve disciples, among whom four (including Spedalieri) were devoted friends. One was a doctor in Berlin, two others were Polish noblemen. Of the four, Lévi told the baron that he was the most advanced in theosophy; the Berlin doctor had made the greatest progress in Kabbalah; one of the Polish nobles was a first-rate scholar of Hermetic philosophy; and the other had turned from pleasure to science. The two Poles were Count Alexander Braszynsky and Count Georges de Mniszeck. The Berlin doctor's name was Nowakowski.

Lévi was scornful of charlatans and those who allowed themselves to be misled. He himself lived a warm-hearted, sober, and calm life—and in the 1860s, in the Paris of Napoleon III, that was remarkable by itself.

In 1870 the miseries of the Franco-Prussian War made Lévi sad—but he had seen it coming. He pondered on what it meant: "If everything is but force and matter, as Dr Buchner would have it, then Prussia is right. But if force is only the manifestation of the universal intelligence, right exists over and above force, and France is right. . . . Force can for a time be put at the service of stupidity, but real and lasting power belongs to reason alone, for *complete reason* [my emphasis] is the same word as God."[14]

Lévi addressed public meetings and went out at night (he was sixty) to encourage the patriotism of the citizens.

On May 31, 1875, Éliphas Lévi died.[15]

LÉVI'S LEGACY

Much of the content of Lévi's books today seems to be obscure, tame, irrelevant, or contradictory. His Catholicism, for example, intrudes in all sorts of unexpected and often unwanted ways. But those who have studied his works in depth, and realize the extent to which Lévi used paradox and suggestion to hide ideas that he thought in the wrong hands could be misleading or dangerous, have found much of value. Even to the cursory view, there is an undoubted fund of simple practical wisdom and observation. The following passage, for example, dynamites in a few sentences those very ideals still regarded as cornerstones of French political orthodoxy: "Liberty, Equality, Fraternity! Three words which seem to shine are in fact full of shadow! Three truths, which, in coming together, form a triple lie! For they destroy one another. Liberty necessarily manifests inequality, and equality is a levelling process which does not permit liberty, because the heads that rise higher than others must always be forced down to the mean. The attempt to establish equality and liberty together produce an interminable struggle . . . that makes fraternity among men impossible."[16]

Lévi's recognition of the importance of science and scientific method is also useful, as is his realization of the limitations and indeed futility of a science that divorces itself from spiritual life. He recognized that scientific advance relies on going from the known to the unknown. Between the two (known and unknown), within the step itself, Lévi recognized a definite need for faith. When the cavern is dark and the torch is dim, human beings need courage, faith, and a transcending ideal to go onward if their eyes are to remain open. The source of reason is absurdity to the rational mind.

Lévi's account of the magical or (in its original sense) scientific nature of religious miracles is instructive and subtle (the issue of miracles was hot in his day, for their supposed existence was a chief pillar of the church's argument against absolute mechanical determinism in the universe): "All so-called miracles are caused by perfectly explicable phenomena. And these phenomena can be manipulated by anyone who knows the techniques of magic. Therefore, to the initiated, magic is a marvellous demonstration of the unity of all religions; but for an uninitiated person, it could lead to rejection of his own particular creed. Therefore it is prudent for the adept not to reveal the innermost secrets of magic to the public."[17]

Lévi's multifarious ideas owed much to Trithemius, Paracelsus, and Agrippa. He attempted to integrate micro-macrocosm theory, the inner correspondences that support the universe and are believed to make it possible to contact other planes through signs and talismans, with his own understanding of Kabbalah. He adapted kabbalistic ideas in many kinds of idiosyncratic ways. In respect of the great sephirotic tree, he regarded Daath (knowledge/science) as a reflection of all the sephiroth.

Lévi also seems to have been the first to connect the Kabbalah with the Tarot (in his *Doctrine et rituel de la haute magie*). He believed it was profitable (and many occultists would be happy to agree with him) to see the twenty-two trumps of the Tarot as correspondent to the twenty-two letters of the Hebrew alphabet: the four suits with the four letters of the Tetragrammaton and the ten numbered cards of each suit with the ten sephiroth. Modestly, perhaps, he believed that the Rosicrucians and the Martinists were in touch with the true Tarot.

Another characteristic concept of Lévi's (although probably derived from the theories of Mesmer) was his theory of the Astral Light or Universal Agent:

> The primordial light, which is the vehicle of all ideas, is the mother of all forms. . . . Hence the Astral Light, or terrestrial fluid, which we call the Great Magnetic Agent, is saturated with all kinds of images and reflections.[18]

The Astral Light is a term representing a plastic medium on which thoughts and images can be imprinted. Its purely material counterpart might be thought of as celluloid: "The soul, by acting on this light through its volitions, can dissolve it, or coagulate it, project it, or withdraw it. It is the universe of the imagination and of dreams. It reacts upon the nervous-system and thus produces the movements of the body. . . . It can take all forms evoked by thought, and, in the transitory coagulations of its radiant particles, appears to the eyes; it can even offer a sort of resistance to the touch."[19] Lévi, at the end, seems to be reflecting on his experience in evoking the spirit of Appolonius of Tyana.

By use of the imagination, the Astral Light can be manipulated— that was and is the essential theoretical basis of most Golden Dawn magic. In magic, imagination must work by established rules; to make contact with forces in the Astral Light, it is recommended to use well-known signs—as with any form of successful journeying. Lévi stressed the essential requirement of rigid—and flexible—disciplining of the will: "The empire of will over astral the Light, which is the physical soul of the four elements, is represented in Magic by the Pentagram. The elemental spirits are subservient to this sign when employed with understanding."[20]

Magic for Éliphas Lévi was power over self, how to direct will. The magician must strike a balance—or be swept away by the ebb and flow—between opposite currents, the most easily accessible image of which is that of the feminine and masculine poles, or light and darkness, or "positive" and "negative."

Lévi was perhaps the first writer in the West to attempt to popularize Self-realization on the grand scale: drawing the will through certain channels and turning the magician (the active human being in tune with the creator) into a more fully realized planetary citizen. Such a process is deeply desirable, and travelers on the path might well take note of the qualities needed for the voyage, the personal characteristics of the mature Lévi: courage, honesty, warmth, and compassion.

Lévi left a last prophecy. After the appearance of the Antichrist, "Enoch will appear in the year 2000 of the Christian world; the Messianism of which he will be the precursor will flourish on earth for a thousand years."[21]

MAGIC REVIVES IN FRANCE

Beyond the influence of the works of Éliphas Lévi, which was considerable, we can trace the revival of occultism and practical gnostic life by looking at the activities of Dr. Gérard Encausse.

Encausse was born in Corogna in Spain in 1865 and died in 1916. His first major taste of gnostic thought was through the influential Theosophical Society, founded by the great-spirited Madame Helena Petrovna Blavatsky in 1875 and dedicated principally to the "All religions are one" approach to comparative spirituality.

She and her assistants attempted to make Westerners aware of the spiritual benefits to be gained from an understanding of Hinduism and Buddhism. Those assistants included Colonel Henry Steel Olcott, Charles Leadbeater (the odd Anglican clergyman who through his peculiar clairvoyance established to the satisfaction of many the existence of the aura), and the curious and energetic Annie Besant.

The ideas of the Theosophical Society attracted many intelligent people to the realization that forgotten wisdom was there for the taking and that matter is not the end of the matter. Activities were combined with a heavy freight of fantastic evolutionary and "root-race" theory, along with a strong interest in such paranormal activity as table-tapping and dubious seances. Those were the days!

In 1888 Encausse left the Theosophical Society, tired of its insistence on the superiority of Eastern wisdom. He looked into the Western esoteric tradition and found satisfaction. It is significant that his first glimpse of the magical world came through his early scholarly devotion to science—in particular, the practice of medicine.

He had come to see, contrary to the "selfish gene" theory (a typical product of a selfish age perhaps), that the progress of organisms is dependent on progressive sacrifice of the lower organic constituents to the higher. This process, which he observed through his microscope, made the realm of spiritual values come alive in his mind, and he became a seeker after understanding.

After parting company with the Theosophical Society, he formed his own Groupe Indépendant d'Études Ésotériques. His chief occult mentor was Saint-Yves d'Alveydre, whose real name was Joseph-Alexandre Saint-Yves, a pupil of Antoine Fabre d'Olivet (author of *Les Vers dorés de Pythagore, expliqués, et traduits . . .* , 1813).

Saint-Yves, or the Marquis, as he was also known, promoted the idea of a utopian occult-political society ruled by an intellectual elite. Not unlike Madame Blavatsky, he claimed to be in telepathic communication with the Grand Lama of Tibet. (It had now become normal to place the Unknown Superiors within the mountains of Tibet—see also James Hilton's version of Shangri-La in his novel *Lost Horizon,* where the geography suited the ideology.) Saint-Yves also claimed to be grand master of the Martinist Order.

From 1891, Encausse preferred to be known to his followers as Papus. The number of Papus's lodges multiplied. In the same year, Papus had a meeting at No. 29, rue de Trevisé, Paris, to establish a supreme council for his Independent Group of Esoteric Studies. Papus was elected grand master; he was already involved with another order, the Cabalistic Order of the Rosy Cross, headed by the marquis Stanislas de Guaïta and by Joséphin Péladan.

De Guaïta was born in 1861 and lived for only thirty-six years, dying in the year of Queen Victoria's Diamond Jubilee. As a young man, he had written poetry in the Symbolist mode, some of which was published (for example, "Rosa Mystica" in 1885). It was suggested to him that he read the works of Éliphas Lévi. He did so and found the experience revelatory. His short occult career had begun.

Joséphin (christened Joseph) Péladan (1858–1918) was a most surprising figure. He was a Bohemian, a symbol of the Décadence. With his great round eyes, he was something of a joker. Occasionally glimpsed breezing through Paris in a monk's habit or medieval doublet with velvet breeches—topped off by a great sponge of wild black hair—Péladan was the Jimi Hendrix of the Naughty Nineties.

Péladan liked to be known as Sâr Mérodack Péladan, a name based on Assyrian and Israelite mythology (Sâr being Assyrian, he said, for "king"). He wrote a number of novels that mixed occultism with eroticism, a winning combination in that great fin-de-siècle period with its wild artistic optimisms and underlying sense of psychological foreboding. Péladan was obsessed by the image of the Androgyne. This figure appears in his novel of 1886, *Curieuse.*

De Guaïta read the first volume of Péladan's series of novels *La Décadence Latine, le vice suprême.* The Sâr, with his great talent for showmanship, self-advertisement, and no mean ability to make his novels exciting, impressed de Guaïta greatly. Awestruck, he wrote to Péladan, requesting a chat about Hermetism.

The two met, and relations developed quickly. They both adored the music of Wagner—Péladan had met Wagner in Florence and astonished the great Romantic with his opinions about Wagner's work. For a time, de Guaïta suited Péladan's need to sort out some of his ideas on occultism, in which he had been drenched as a child in Lyons. He was always on the lookout for new stimulus, and de Guaïta provided it. De Guaïta himself grew in self-confidence—what a circle he had entered!—and began signing himself Nébo (a name reminiscent of the Babylonian—of course!—god associated with Mercury).

De Guaïta professed that he preferred the Western mystical tradition to that of the hidden Mahatmas of Madame Blavatsky. Péladan liked what he heard. Western culture was what interested him—especially the new culture that he, Sâr Péladan, was about to enact. The order created between them was, one suspects, more of de Guaïta's imagining than of Péladan's.

The Cabalistic Order of the Rosy Cross (founded in 1888) consisted of a supreme council of twelve: six known and six unknown (in good old Rosicrucian tradition). It is unlikely that the "six unknown" actually existed. The main participants of the order (in addition to de Guaïta, the supreme chief, and Péladan) were Papus, Marc Haven, the abbé Melinge (a curate in the diocese of Versailles and a religious author), the writer Paul Adam, and François-Charles Barlet. Barlet was a minor civil servant who had tried alchemy and whose real name was Alfred Faucheux.

There were three grades: *baccalauréat,* licentiate, and doctor of the Cabala. As is not uncommon in awestruck relationships when the dominant person does not meet the criterion of seriousness worshipped by the original supplicant, de Guaïta and Péladan fell out. That would have been all right in the normal course of events, but de Guaïta took the whole business very seriously indeed.

In the June 1890 edition of *L'Initiation,* an occult journal, Péladan departed from the Cabalistic Order of the Rosy Cross, pronouncing, "I refuse to rub shoulders with spiritualism, masonry, or Buddhism." He was a good Catholic—always had been. Péladan had been building up to his life's real objective: an artistic revolution. He seized the moment, just as the Symbolist painters were increasing in morbid, pained, subversive beauty; strange spiritual idealism—and popularity.

To further his aims, Péladan, with a shot in the eye to his former colleague, founded the Order of the Catholic Rose-Cross, the Temple, and the Grail. Péladan said that he wanted to bring occultism back (?) under the wing of Catholicism to accomplish works of mercy, and to prepare for the reign of the Holy Spirit—the coming kingdom of the Paraclete.

For Péladan, his aesthetic was his ethic. Failing to read the wind, de Guaïta tried to get Péladan to return. Péladan was now deeply into his "thing": setting up a nucleus from which would emanate a whole set of religious, moral, and aesthetic values.

He declared the Artist to be the authentic priest and magician of the new culture—very prescient. The Artist was the hierophant in touch with the deeper wells of soul. Péladan proposed annual salons of anti-realist, anti-Impressionist, pro-spiritual or visionary art, Symbolist and abstract, as well as "idealist theater" and the promoting of concerts of "sublime" music. He was tremendously successful.

In opposition to the official Salon, the first Salon des Rose + Croix was opened in 1892 at the Durand-Ruel Gallery to the sound of Erik Satie's trumpets and financial backing from the comte Antoine de la Rochefoucauld. There were six salons between 1892 and 1898, and they had a very great influence. The first exhibition contained one of the first characteristic works of Art Nouveau, *Les Ames deçues* (The Disappointed Souls), by the Swiss artist Hodler, a considerable influence on painters as different as Toorop, Maurice Denis, Munch, and Klimt.

Strange themes emanating through the British pre-Raphaelite aesthetic emerged from the unconscious, often disturbing, sometimes transcendental: sexual, doomed, decadent, romantic, such as Séon's *Le Désespoir de la Chimère* (The Despair of the Chimera), for example— the end of an era in the form of a femme fatale joined to a voluptuous, bored, yet paradoxically ecstatic winged sphinx, stuck out on a rock like a siren, guarding a cave entrance to a new, vivid, and ambiguous darkness.

The salons brought a great number of artists to public attention, artists such as Jean Delville, painter of *Portrait of Madame Stuart Merrill,* a very magical work, and the extraordinary *Le Trésor de Satan,* whose incredible draftsmanship suggests an Albrecht Altdorfer of the unconscious. Manifesting such a genuinely mystical sensibility, he became, not surprisingly, a theosophist.

The appropriate music to hear when seeing these works, or thinking about them, is *Péléas et Mélisande* and *Clair de lune* by Debussy (after Maeterlinck's Symbolist-spiritual fantasy), and Satie's *Gymnopédies* and *Gnossiens.* The sculptor to admire in this strange Rosicrucian garden is, of course, Auguste Rodin.

In 1894 Péladan wrote *L'Art idéaliste et mystique:* "From year to year the Rosicrucian idea wins over both artists and the public. Aesthetically, the cause is won."[22]

Péladan was quite brilliant at precisely dissecting artistic movements and reconstituting them to serve his spiritual vision. He was one of the first to see that abstraction was a form of Platonic idealism and could be a vehicle for genuine spiritual expression—an idea that clashes with our notion of what modern art is supposed to be, but something that great abstract and Abstract-Expressionist artists have well understood.

Péladan wrote, "The artist should begin with the abstraction of his subject; that is to say by fixing the abstract plane which it occupies; then he will imagine the soul most consistent with this abstract plane; finally he will choose the forms most characteristic of this soul."[23]

Péladan was also a theater impresario, playwright, and director. His company, Le Théâtre de la Rose + Croix, performed plays with an occult and mystical message: *Orphéus; Le Mystère du Graal; Le Mystère des + Rose Croix,* and *Les Argonautes.*

In 1893 de Guaïta issued a full-scale attack on Joséphin Péladan: "We, Brothers of the Rose Cross, declare the said M. Péladan to be a schismatic and apostate Rosicrucian; We denounce him and his so-called Catholic Rose Cross before the tribunal of public opinion."[24] And so on. Papus signed but later regretted it.

Three years after the death of de Guaïta, Papus wrote in his article on Péladan in *Les Sciences maudites* (The Accursed Sciences) in the year 1900: "For his part, Joséphin Péladan—that admirable artist to whom the future will render justice at the final reckoning, in judging him apart from the perhaps too original aspects of his work—took the head of a movement to spiritualise aestheticism, whose fruits are only beginning to be apparent and which will have profound repercussions on contemporary art."[25]

This was an accurate assessment. As Papus was writing it, a young poet calling himself Aleister Crowley was also in Paris, being initiated into the Inner Order of the Golden Dawn and obtaining "plenipotentiary" authority from Samuel Liddell "MacGregor" Mathers, head of that Hermetic order.

Crowley, aged twenty-five, was to return to London to sort out a major dispute that had arisen among Golden Dawn members (among whom was the poet W. B. Yeats). The Golden Dawn's founding charter was suspected of being a forgery.

On April 12, 1900, Edward Alexander Crowley wrote in his little book of Magical Rituals: "I, *Perdurabo* [I shall endure], as the Temporary Envoy Plenipotentiary of *Deo Duce Comite Ferro* [Mathers] and thus the Third from the Secret Chiefs of the *Order of the Rose of Ruby and Cross of Gold,* do deliberately invoke all laws, all powers Divine, demanding that I, even I, be chosen to do such a work as he has done, at all costs to myself. And I record this holy aspiration in the Presence of the Divine Light, that it may stand as my witness.

"*In Saecula Saeculorum.* Amen!"[26]

What a strange way, you may think, to enter the twentieth century.

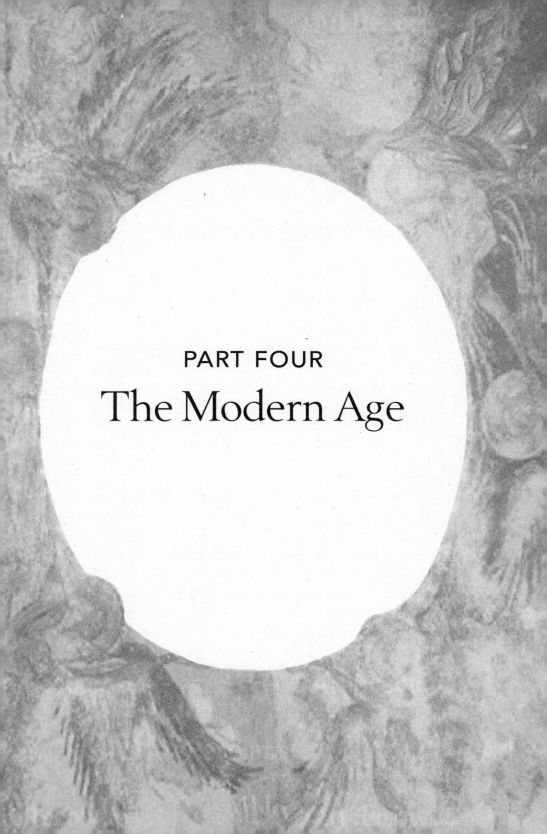

PART FOUR
The Modern Age

ELEVEN

A New Aeon:
Aleister Crowley

*I don't know why everyone takes me for an absolute
No 1 B.F. [bloody fool]—do I look like one? I sometimes
think that it's because they don't believe in Magick, and
knowing that I do (though they don't understand what I
mean by it) suppose me credulous and gullible.*

ALEISTER CROWLEY TO LOUIS WILKINSON, AUGUST 1, 1942

The night of May 6, 1944, rocket-propelled bombs are falling
on London. Aleister Crowley, the Great Beast 666, the Word
of the Aeon, Outer Head of the Ordo Templi Orientis
(OTO), is residing at the Bell Inn, Aston Clinton, Buckinghamshire.
The old magician is writing to his friend Gerald Hamilton: "The Duke
Street-King Street bomb not only damaged 93, but caused diversion of
traffic through Jermyn St. At times one had to wait five minutes or
more to cross! Racket quite insupportable, work totally impossible; so
I drifted out here for a while . . . my object is to go on with my work
on the Yi King . . . I hope all is well with you, and that you have a quid
to spare to square. Love is the law, Love under will. Yours A.C."[1]

Aleister Crowley, broke as usual, is busy on his interpretation of the
Chinese classic better known to us as the I Ching, or Book of Changes.
He has become something of a Taoist sage. Later in that summer of
1944 he will be visited by his old friend Nancy Cunard, unsung hero-

ine of the century: poet, publisher, 1920s avant-garde star, determined campaigner for racial, social, and sexual equality—and discoverer of Samuel Beckett. In a letter to Nancy dated July 22, he calls her his "Beloved Dream Woman" and "my own strange fellow-traveller in monstrous worlds!": "How delightful to get a letter—and such a letter! from you, who have always played so great a part in the life of my imagination! Many thanks for the war-poem; so fine in rhythm and expression, with such powers to make one visualise as well as experience your reaction."[2]

Crowley had met Nancy Cunard in the late 1920s. She had written to him seeking astrological advice concerning her financial relations with her mother, Lady Emerald Cunard, who, Nancy feared, was about to cut her allowance because she was living with the black American jazz pianist Henry Crowder. In the spring of 1933 they met again. Nancy was organizing interracial dances in Notting Hill and the East End of London as well as a major appeal for the Scottsboro Boys.[3] Crowley signed Nancy's appeal as follows: "This case is typical of the hysterical sadism of the American people—the result of Puritanism and the climate.—Aleister Crowley, Scientific Essayist."[4]

On August 18, 1944, Crowley wrote from the Bell Inn to thank Nancy for her visit—quite a trek in wartime conditions: "My own adorable Nancy, Do what thou wilt shall be the whole of the law. How too angelic a visit! But let it not be so 'far between' next time! I cannot remember so few hours packed with so much rapture."[5] This from the man the vulgar press had dubbed the "King of Depravity," the "Human Beast," "The Man we'd love to Hang," "the wickedest man in the world."

On October 24, 1954, Nancy Cunard sent these letters to Gerald Yorke, Crowley's old friend and preserver of his manuscripts, with an accompanying letter:

> What a galaxy of people he did offer himself to! This particular point seems practically the pivot of the man—man or magus—does it not? I should have hated all the "hoolie-goolie" stuff, but that seems to have been long before. I can well imagine him absolutely terrifying many people—serpent's kiss[6] and all (I have had the honour; no

trouble whatever, it lasted about 10 days, very pretty, on my right wrist).

. . . La! What a picture it evokes, even this short sequence: there he was, in an excellent inn, see how well fed, with plenty of coupons &c. . . . It has been a pleasure to copy them for you, but alas that none of us will see him again.[7]

"The greater the artist, the more frequent and atrocious his failures; for 'tis his greatness to attempt impossibilities,"[8] Crowley had written twenty years before Nancy's last visit. Sitting alone in that inn in 1944, the Beast had ample time to contemplate his frequent and atrocious failures. His failures were failures in the world; his successes were in art and in the spiritual life. Like Elias Ashmole (whom Crowley included as a saint in his *Gnostic Mass*), Edward Alexander Crowley was an English Mercury Lover.

When he was a young man, Crowley had desired the laurels of fame in the conventional sense: as a poet, a mountaineer, and a daring explorer. However, he was torn between this desire and the knowledge (which came to him early on) that a truly lasting memorial would need to be written in stuff more permanent than a plot in Poet's Corner or an honorable entry in *Who's Who*. He would have to be a magician. Yet Aleister never lost for very long that thrill and delight in fame, notoriety, and significance whose promise is the opiate of youth.

"Did you see the Daily News? And the others? I am on ten pinnacles of fame all at once. And K.P. [Kegan Paul Publishers] go out of their way to tell me that Tannhäuser (I have the proofs here now) is miles ahead of any of my other work. And we know Orphy [his poem 'Orpheus'] will be better still!"[9] This from a letter to his best friend, the painter Gerald Kelly, when Crowley could be found at No. 34 Victoria Drive, Kandy, Ceylon, in 1901. He was studying and experiencing, with enormous self-discipline, the high Buddhist trances, attaining vision of the Golden Dawn of the Inner Sun by the technique called *dhyana* on October 1 of that year. Crowley's delight in the *Daily News* was due to a review of his poetic work *The Soul of the Osiris* by none other than the famous G. K. Chesterton. It looked like Aleister Crowley's career as a twenty-five-year-old poet and public mystic was well under way. How had he got so far?

Twenty-five years before his first sojourn in Sri Lanka, Edward Alexander Crowley had been born into a well-off family of Christian fundamentalists, members of the Exclusive or "Plymouth" Brethren in provincial Leamington Spa, Warwickshire. Young Edward's education was entrusted to the care of a coterie of oddly sadistic Brethren, whose efforts at indoctrination intensified after Edward's beloved father's death in 1887.

Crowley called his education at the hands of his mother's family "A Boyhood in Hell," and the many privations led to a collapse of his health. He began to hate (in the form of biting wit) what he knew as Christianity, sympathizing with "the enemies of Heaven." Good and evil, the absolute and sundered values of Christianity, became open to question. Questioning the roots of one's culture was not as common then as it is now, and in his loneliness and deep isolation, Crowley began to seek a solution to the problem that might transcend not only these apparent opposites but also the miseries of life in general. His youthful rebellion against the established religion of the West is expressed succinctly in several passages of his *Confessions,* of which the following is most apposite:

> I was trying to take the view that the Christianity of hypocrisy and cruelty was not true Christianity. I did not hate God or Christ, but merely the God and Christ of the people whom I hated. It was only when the development of my logical faculties supplied the demonstration that the Scriptures support the theology and practice of professing Christians that I was compelled to set myself in opposition to the Bible itself. It does not matter that the literature is sometimes magnificent and that in isolated passages the philosophy and ethics are admirable. The sum of the matter is that Judaism is a savage, and Christianity a fiendish superstition.[10]

The fact of the matter is that Crowley was, among many other things, a very religious person—not religious in the ordinary sense of the word, but one with an intense drive to the highest possible aspiration. In 1913 he would describe himself as an "HIMOG," a Holy Illuminated Man of God—and he meant it. Meanwhile, he decided to overcome his physical weakness and the taunts of his peers by developing amazing skill in the discipline and adventure of mountaineering, a haven for many solitary young people and an area in which Crowley more than distinguished himself.[11]

In 1895 Crowley matriculated at Trinity College, Cambridge, a most able scholar who preferred his own voluminous reading to that prescribed by his tutors. Coming from a wealthy family of entrepreneurs in the brewing trade ensured that money was for him, at this stage, no object.

Returning from St. Petersburg the following year, Crowley experienced his first mystical awakening. He received an "intimation" of the magical control of phenomena (while in Stockholm) and began to study the scattered masterpieces and not-so-masterful pieces of occultism with even greater avidity than hitherto. In particular, he was fascinated by Karl von Eckartshausen's *The Cloud upon the Sanctuary,* in which the author spoke of an invisible *ecclesia* of gnostic initiates whose task was to guide humankind through its development toward the fulfillment of the Hermetic Great Work. The Work can be summed up as the liberation of the spiritual from the material. The optimistic Crowley, like Elias Ashmole two and a half centuries previously, fervently aspired to come to their attention.

The year 1898 proved to be an *annus mirabilis* for this recondite endeavor. He not only saw his first printed poem, "Aceldama" (in the Shelley-Swinburne mode), privately published, and graduated from Trinity, but he was also introduced to George Cecil Jones following a casual conversation on the subject of alchemy in a Zermatt hotel.

Jones was an initiate of the Hermetic Order of the Golden Dawn and recommended the anxious Crowley to this highly influential British Masonic offshoot. In spite of initial disappointment—the Golden Dawn did not seem to reveal either the exalted saints of Eckartshausen's sublime Sanctuary or the humor and breadth of vision of Rabelais's Abbey of Thelema[12]—Crowley began his magical training with characteristic singlemindedness, thoroughness, and discipline. He was also now a dashing man-about-town with a powerful interest in romance, sex, and good living generally. Because of these qualities, combined with his sturdy good looks, fine physical condition, great intellect, and talent for robust and risqué amusement, he encountered not a little envy and soon came under the suspicion of other more prosaic, bourgeois, and cautious order members.

In 1899, he met his fellow asthmatic and brother in the order, former electrical engineer Allan Bennett, and together they pursued a more intense magical program; Crowley turned his flat in Chancery Lane (where he lived as Count Zvareff) into a serviceable magical temple. He also met the chief of the Golden Dawn, translator of *The Key of Solomon the King* and *The Sacred Magic of Abramelin the Mage,* and Samuel Liddell "MacGregor" Mathers, Celtic enthusiast and fan of the French Occult Revival.

According to Crowley, Mathers had "that habit of authority which never questions itself and so, inspires respect." This double-edged description might also apply to his mother, Emily Bertha Crowley, née Bishop, who her son believed never loved him, although, in spite of statements that might imply the contrary, he did himself love her.

The same year also saw him acquire a country residence befitting his own fading Celtic revivalist enthusiasms: Boleskine House, Foyers, near Inverness. From there that year, he wrote a letter to a brother of the order. In it already one can detect his predilection for the role of teacher (his father had been a Plymouth Brother evangelist), on his way to becoming a master:

Care Frater,

Agrippa [Henry Cornelius Agrippa of Nettesheim, author of *Three Books of Occult Philosophy,* 1651] is very useful. It is practically the source of Barrett [Francis Barrett, author of *The Magus,* 1801] and is much fuller in the same style. . . .

You can only curse a spirit because you have conjured him by the Great Names of God the Vast One, and he obeyeth Them not. You cannot use these Names unless you are yourself in accordance with His Will. . . .

My First magical Operation was devoted to the Invocation of That One whom Abramelin calls the Guardian Angel. As also it is written: So help me the Lord of the Universe and My own Higher Soul! And without the Aspiration to, and in a little measure, the grasp of this: no White Magic is possible. "In myself I am nothing: in Thee I am All-Self." Therefore, you are not of a position to act as Master: for you are not yet Master of yourself, nor even in communication consciously with That One who hath made of you His Habitation.

Therefore, it is necessary First to reach unto your own Kether [Crown; the higher mind of the Kabbalist]: that the influence of the Most Holy Ancient One descend upon you: and then "all things will appear easy to you."

. . . As to Abramelin, he is a quite different bird. You devote six moons to the purification of your sphere or "aura." Then you can invoke the Angel with complete success. Then you can compel the Forces of the World—the "visible Image of the Soul of Nature" to your service. This Operation is so Awful that I cannot find any words to tell you of it. I may now say that I have devoted my life since our fortnight at Folkestone to the Beginning of it. And the oppositions on every plane have been tremendous. Even now, the copying of the symbols is so terrible a task that I can barely finish a dozen daily. After that my brain seems to reel, the characters dance around me, and it is useless to proceed. And this while avoiding putting any magical force into them in the making. If you wish to try Abramelin, God forbid I should hinder you. But I warn you that for all its apparent simplicity and ease, it will be a bigger job than anything you ever tackled in your life.

. . . The part about the Angel and my intention of doing Abramelin is very secret—not from obligation standpoint, but from its extreme sacred character. To no other person inside or outside the Order, would I have spoken thus plainly. But as I said above, what will not paternal affection do?

Yours fraternally,

Perdurabo [Crowley's magical motto, "I will endure"][13]

Magical orders, like religious sects, are highly prone to schism, and the Golden Dawn was no exception. The reasons were of the usual kind: interpersonal relations, familiarity breeding contempt, ego versus order, moral disaffection; the inevitable inequalities of perception; differing aims and expectations; and, above all, that old bugbear: the question of authority.

It was rumored—and rumor turned to inquiry, and that to accusation—that the origins of the Golden Dawn might be less than preternatural, as had been supposed; foundation documents might be—God forbid—forgeries. Alleged links with the Hidden Masters or Secret Chiefs might be fraudulent or misinterpreted—and anyhow, Mathers was beginning to behave strangely, like a general who has finally got his full complement of tanks but has forgotten who paid for them.

Crowley did not give a sou for democracy, realizing with his accustomed clarity that an order without a central spine of wise autocracy would soon become a talking shop; and so, with typical logic, he put all his resources at Mather's disposal, dedicating them all henceforth to the Great Work, as he understood it.

Mathers, for his part, rewarded Aleister Crowley with initiation into the Inner Order of the Golden Dawn in Paris, much to the disgust of order members back in London. These included the poet W. B. Yeats, who, distrustful of Crowley, asked whether a mystical order ought to become a reformatory—a clear attack on Crowley and his worldly habits. Crowley himself (with how much seriousness it is difficult to fathom) attributed Yeats's antipathy to consciousness of the latter's poetic inferiority—a view with which contemporary literary criticism has not yet caught up.

Crowley's friend Allan Bennett, about to embark on a life as a Buddhist *bhikkhu* (novice monk), surrendering Western magic, had at one point reckoned that Crowley was too interested in evoking demons. This suggestion seems to have stopped Crowley short in his magical tracks for a while, and he eventually decided to head for Mexico with his friend and fellow mountaineer Oscar Eckenstein to reassess his priorities and generally sort himself out. Abramelin magic, for the pursuance of which he had purchased Boleskine, would have to wait. The mountains and the promise of adventure were calling him.

A red Moroccan-bound notebook in the Warburg Institute gives us some idea of what Crowley was up to in Mexico from January to April 1901, apart from scaling the great peaks of that country in double-quick time. On the cover of the notebook, next to a sketch of the *Monas Hieroglyphica* of John Dee, are the words: "Feb 2. My 2 ½ years work crowned with success."[14]

What precisely this success entailed we shall probably never know, but we may imagine it was some kind of spiritual attainment. Perhaps it was connected with Crowley's initiation by an old man named Don Jesus Medina, a chief of Scottish Rite Freemasonry in that country, who raised Crowley up to the thirty-third or last degree of Don Jesus's rite.[15] Crowley returned the service of Don Jesus by making the latter "first High Priest" of an order he founded himself: L.I.L., the Lamp of the Invisible Light. In his *Confessions,* Crowley makes some most suggestive comments about this project, which surely warrant further investigation:

> The general idea was to have an ever-burning lamp in a temple furnished with talismans appropriate to the elemental, planetary and zodiacal forces of nature. Daily invocations were to be performed with the object of making the light itself a consecrated center or focus of spiritual energy. This light would then radiate and automatically enlighten such minds as were ready to receive it. Even today, the experiment seems to me interesting and the conception sublime. I am rather sorry that I lost touch with Don Jesus; I should like very much to know how it turned out.[16]

These were practices that should not have been out of place among the pagan Hermetists, or Sabians, of ninth-century Harran or Baghdad. Crowley seemed to have jumped across the centuries with very little interest indeed in what might be termed the wisdom of his age. His rejection of the values of his own era was quite astounding to many contemporaries, who, lacking the requisite historical and philosophical knowledge, simply did not know where to place him.

Whatever became of the Order of the Lamp of Invisible Light is a matter for conjecture and, possibly, further research. Crowley's strong wish to "know how it turned out" does suggest that there was a continuity following his departure from Mexico. The contemporary diary record reads as follows:

In Nomine Dei
Inspiret Naturae Regina Isis
At the End of the Century

At the End of the Year:

At the Hour of Midnight:

> did I complete and bring to perfection the work of L.I.L. in Mexico: even as I did receive it from him who is incarnated in me: and this work is to the best of my knowledge a synthesis of what the Gods have given unto me, so far as is possible without violating my obligations to the Chiefs of the R.R. et A.C. [Ruby Rose and Cross of Gold: the Golden Dawn, Inner Order]. Now did I deem it well that I should rest awhile resuming my labours in the G.W. [Great Work], seeing that he, who sleepeth never, shall fall by the wayside and also remembering the two-fold sign: the Power of Horus, and the Power of Hoor Par Kraat.[17]

Crowley left Mexico for San Francisco and from there he set sail, via Hawaii, for Japan. A diary entry for June 18, 1901, reveals a hankering for the life of a Buddhist monk, a withdrawal from the absurdity, stupidity, and illusion of the world: "Shall I go to Kamakura and live a hermit's life in the Temple?"[18] A Tarot divination advised against it, as well as proffering a piece of advice the meaning of which will soon become apparent: "Be wise in avoiding quarrel if Alice be obsessed."[19]

From Yokohama Crowley wrote to his friend, the aspiring painter Gerald Kelly:

> You are a good boy and I am a good boy and I am right and you are right and everything is quite correct. . . . Japan is a fraud of the basest sort. . . . To change the key. This in strictest of all possible confidence. I have had the greatest love-affair of my long and arduous career (arduous is good). Her name was Mary Beaton. Think of it! Absolutely the most beautiful woman I have ever seen, of the imperial type, yet as sweet and womanly as I ever knew. Moreover, a lady to her finger tips. I call her Alice in the poems you will read about her, as she preferred that name. She was travelling for her health in Hawaii where we met. We loved and loved chastely (She has a hub. & kids— one boy with her) I made her come here with me. On the boat we fell to fucking, of course, but—here's the miracle! we won through and fought our way back to chastity & far deeper truer love. Now she's

gone & forgotten but her sweet and pure influence has saved my soul. (Heb: *Nephesch*). I lust no more—What, never? Well—hardly ever!

. . . I wish you'd buck up with occultism so that I didn't have to talk with all this damned reticence. I have done none myself lately— there's been love and poetry going on. Also my ideas are changing and fermenting. You will not recognise my mind when I get back.[20]

Crowley was certainly capable of deep love, but a certain adolescent machismo would bring him back from the brink of anything remotely like a life commitment that might override or threaten his essential and nagging sense of mission.

> *So the last kiss passed like a poison-pain,*
> *Knowing we might not ever kiss again,*
> *Mad tears fell fast: "Next year!" in cruel distress*
> *We sobbed, and stretched our arms out, and despaired,*
> *and—parted. Out the brute-side of truth flared;*
> *Thank God I've finished with that foolishness!*
>
> FROM *ALICE: AN ADULTERY*[21]

I want to serve God, or as I put it, Do My Will, continuously: I prefer a year's concentration with death at the end than the same dose diluted in half a century of futility.[22]

Alice: An Adultery was published by Crowley's own Society for the Propagation of Religious Truth, Boleskine, Inverness. No doubt he found it funny that a poem describing "an Adultery" should come out of such a society. The *Glasgow Herald* was certainly bemused: "We confess to being so dense as to miss the essentially religious purpose of the book. . . . But the power of many of the sonnets is undeniable. . . . For the perfect art of these lyrics, for their tender music, we have nothing but admiration."[23]

It would not be too long before Aleister Crowley began to see that love in tune with the True Will was indeed highly "religious" and a pathway to God, thorny as it might be. He had much maturing to do.

At this stage in his career, he only dimly glimpsed the meaning of his own paradoxes, reveling a little too much in the balm of his own jokes—either his cure for the Universal Sorrow or his constant self-defeating rebelliousness.

Parenthetically, one should add that this poem, like many others, received good reviews in the prewar press. He really was a poet, and he was seen as such. However, for Perdurabo, poetry was not enough. There was too much unresolved conflict in his psyche. That strange and sometimes uncomfortable combination of masculine, active vigor with a distinctively feminine insight, sensitivity, and passivity shows how much he loved and hated the woman he called "a brainless bigot of the most narrow, inhuman and logical type": his mother. It was she who gave him his name, the Beast, little realizing she was merely echoing Charles Darwin's estimation of human origins.

Leaving behind Mrs. Beaton to her household management, Crowley headed for Sri Lanka in the hope of annihilating the universe that was his troubled mind. From Colombo, he wrote to Kelly: "I have chucked all nonsense, except a faint lingering illusion that anything exists. This (with my breathing practice [*pranayama*]) should go soon."[24] Crowley, for a season, became something that perhaps had never been seen before: a combination of neo-Egyptian novice-hierophant and a Buddhist. The Buddhist asserted the illusion of the very world the Egyptians deified.

The Writings of Truth. 1901. Sri Lanka.

To thee be Glory

I exist not: there is no God: no time: no place:

wherefore I exactly particularise and specify these things.

August 1, A.D. 1901

I succeeded in causing a Chinaman of high rank to believe that there was an insect on his left cheek. Instant success

. . . the eyes are drawn up to behold the 3rd eye without conscious volition of the Yogi.

August 10. Sound as of a broken bell in my head.

Aug 11 Recakram—Voice of Mantra is terrible and tremendous.

Pacakram—Voice is still and small.

Aug 27, 28, 29. Under following conditions: Vow of silence: reduced food: constant muttering of Pranava Mani Padme Hom with meditation on Buddha and Anahata [Heart chakra]: I lost consciousness when meditating Buddha: Voice of Nadi [meditative equivalent of "background noise"] became "Aum" alone, sounding like far-off solemn song.

Meditation Buddha—a great luminous gold Buddha appears. Will & Control become weakened after some 24–48 hours of constant Yoga . . .

Sept 5 With Pranayama [breath control to lose body-consciousness] one may get confused—dizzy—and unable to see clearly eg the second hand of the watch. Definitively heard the Astral Bell—not mine but M's [the Master's?].

Dharana [gathering all the powers of the mind and getting them to focus on a single point] on Nose gives a clear understanding of the unreality of that nose: its difference from "Me." An hour after this Dharana, lying in bed, I felt hot breath on my arm and asked "What can this be from?"

. . . As before, but muttering "Namo Shivayana" &c. I was (a) conscious of physical background seen after nose had vanished (b) conscious that I was not conscious of these things. These (a) and (b) were simultaneous. This seems absurd: is inexplicable: is noted in the Buddhist Psychology: yet I know it.

Sept. 8 The Ajna Câkkra [pineal gland] is misty blue-grey texture of fine hair. Flame-cone in shape. At intervals it opens out like a flower. Heard my own Astral Bell. [Madame H. P. Blavatsky, founder of the Theosophical Society, had heard the ring of an "astral bell" when she felt the Hidden Masters had wished to communicate with her.]

Oct. 1.

Blessed be Thou, O Bhavani,
O Isis my Sister, my Bride, my Mother!
Blessed be Thou, O Shiva, O Amoun,
Concealed of the Concealed. By thy most
Secret and Holy Name of Apophis be
thou Blessed, Lucifer, Star of the Dawn,
Satan—Jeheshua [Jesus], Light of the World!
Blessed be Thou, Buddha, Osiris, by
Whatever Name I call Thee Thou art nameless

to Eternity . . .
Blessed be Thou, O Day, that thou hast
risen in the Night of Time, First Dawn
in the Chaos of poor Aleister's mind!
Accursed be Thou, Jehovah, Brahma,
unto the Aeons of Aeons, thou who didst
create darkness and not Light! Mara,
Vile Mask of Matter!
Arise, O Shiva, and Destroy! That in
destruction these at last be blest![25]

"Never dull where Crowley is!"[26] he once said (truly) of himself. Not many can find humor in dharana. "The Mystery of Sorrow was consoled long ago when it went out for a drink with the Universal Joke," he would write in 1920.[27]

> Marlborough. Kandy Ceylon 1901
>   Dear Gerald,
>   You should be starving in the Latin Quarter not getting fat with what Allan would call a "camel-kneed prayer-monger" in some unknown part of France. A slut for your mistress, a gamine for your model: a procurer for your landlady and a whore for your spiritual guide. This is the only way to become a great artist.[28]

Crowley droned his mantra while back in England the nation mourned the passing of Queen Victoria. Another late Victorian, also blessed with a highly individual cast of mind, as well as being dean of St. Paul's in an era when the Church of England could boast first-class men, was the Very Reverand William Ralph Inge. In a now unjustly forgotten work, *Mysticism in Religion,* published shortly after World War II, the dean wrote:

> We all know that our civilisation is in great danger, and most of us agree that our only hope is in a revival of spiritual religion, with a recognition of absolute values, and a devotion to whatever things are true, just, noble, and of good report. But where shall we look for our prophets? It

is not the clergy but laymen and free lances who are taking the lead, and more and more they are turning to the wisdom of the East.

. . . The fundamental doctrine of Indian religion is that the self-conscious ego, the subject of rights and duties, is not the real self. Consciousness is never more than a mirror of reality; it creates nothing.[29]

Inge and Crowley should have had a chat sometime.

Crowley must have had some intimation by the end of 1901 that he had a role to play in the new century. There is ample evidence that he was deeply aware that a breakdown in Western civilization, as he knew it, was imminent. In February 1903 he was in Nice, trying to have a good time. He wrote of his efforts to Gerald Kelly, in his typical no-nonsense style:

I am beginning to doubt whether Nice is dull after all. Today I began very badly: playing billiards in despair, I cut the cloth—first time in my life! I sneaked away unperceived, luckily, went to the reading-room, and tore a newspaper. In disgust, I went out, met a charming girl and had a real good old-fashioned face fuck in the grounds.

I returned to tea; fearful of the fatal third tearing, I ripped up the tablecloth with my penknife, and made a successful evening of it by preaching the Good Law to Humphreys, winning 5fr at the Little Horses, meeting the girl I'd been hunting ever since the Masked Ball; meeting a 3rd girl and getting another v.g. o-f f.f.[30]

This is one of many letters to Kelly covering the years 1899–1904—all of them very funny, light, eccentric; and they give a marvelous picture of the expansiveness of the early Edwardian era—twilight of the old civilization.

They also give a picture of a strange outsider hanging on to reality, with all the bravado in the world, by the skin of his teeth. Six months later, he wrote to Kelly a letter full of suppressed guilt feelings, unsure of himself, frustrated. He had just met Kelly's very beautiful but, by the standards of the time, wayward sister, Rose—a woman whom he would marry (to her family's initial dissatisfaction) within the month, in a fit of youthful impetuosity—in order, he thought, to get her out of an unwanted liaison:

> I have been trying since I joined G.D. in '98 steadily and well to repress my nature in all ways. I have suffered much, but I have won, and you know it. . . . Did your sister want to hear the true history of my past life, she should have it in detail; not from prejudiced persons, but the cold drear stuff of lawyers. And English does not always fail me. If your worst wish came true, and we never met again, my remembrances of you, with or without beard would, as you say, be good enough to go on. But I am ambitious. I hope one day to convince you that I am not only a clever (the 4tos have "mentally deformed") man but a decent one and a good one. Why must 9/10ths of my life ie: the march to Buddhism, go for nothing; the atrophied 1/1,000,000 always spring up and choke me, and that in the house of my friends? . . . All luck, and the greatest place in the new generation of artists be yours. So sayeth Aleister Crowley, always your friend whatever you may do or say. Vale! till your Ave![31]

The nature that he had been "trying to repress" would come upon him with all the mighty power of psychic projection eight months later, during his honeymoon in Cairo in March–April 1904.

AIWASS: MESSENGER OF THE GODS

The extraordinary business began when Crowley's pregnant wife told him that "they" were waiting for him. Crowley sometimes wrote of this startling and somewhat offhand declaration as if he did not really know what she was talking about. But there can be little doubt that a great bell would have been struck in Crowley's mind.

Crowley had been anxious to make contact with his Holy Guardian Angel, his Genius or Augoeides, since at least 1899, when he wrote the letter quoted earlier on the subject of Abramelin magic to a brother of the order. Furthermore, the suspicion that Mathers had flunked his contact with the Secret Chiefs of the Hermetic Order of the Golden Dawn had grown into a firm conviction. Crowley certainly felt it was necessary to somehow get into contact with these beings, should such beings exist. In fact, he had been trying to come to their attention for years. He could never found an effective order of his own without such authoritative contact. The L.I.L. episode clearly demonstrates Crowley's desire to do so and further throws that episode itself into a greater mystery. What was he really up to with Don Jesus Medina when he was still undergoing training in Golden Dawn magical procedures?

The day after Rose's announcement, she added that it was "all Osiris" and "all about the child." Crowley invoked Thoth, presumably in an effort to understand what was happening. By "invoking Thoth" (Hermes)—Egyptian god of magic and the intelligent arts—we are to understand a ritual performed to obtain the powers of Thoth: wisdom, insight, understanding.

Crowley wrote in his "Book of Results," a contemporary record, that these powers then "indwelled" the two of them.[32] The following day, Rose, in a state of clairaudience probably encouraged by sex and alcohol, revealed that the one who attended on her husband was "Horus, whom thou offended and ought to invoke." Crowley later thought that the power of "Horus, the avenger" with his character of "Force & Fire" (very much like Blake's Orc, child of freedom and rebellion) was precisely what he had been trying to avoid or suppress. He associated it with the martian tendencies of Mathers, whom he had been obeying in an almost masochistic fashion—and this obeisance went against his true nature, a nature that years of Plymouth Brethren conditioning had made him repress. Horus, of course, is the avenger of his father's murderer; Set, the sun in the south: symbolically speaking, the dark or hidden aspect of the unconscious.

A small Japanese vellum notebook written in red ink and beautiful copper-plate handwriting contains the "Invocation of Hoor," written in 1904, composed to enflame the spirit and direct the will of the magician. Crowley, in robes, read it out the window of his upstairs hotel room in Cairo on Saturday, March 19:

> By thy name of Odin I invoke Thee, O warrior of the North,
> O renown of the Sagas!
> By thy name of Jeheshua [Jesus], O child of the flaming Star, I invoke thee.
> By Thine own, Thy secret name Hoori, thee I invoke.[33]

That Saturday's invocation achieved, Crowley wrote, "little success."[34] But Sunday's invocation was a real mind-blower. It was revealed that the Equinox of the Gods had come, "Horus taking the throne of the East and all rituals being abrogated. . . . I am to formulate a new link of an order with the solar force."[35]

Crowley was determined he would not be taken in by the rush and thrill of psychic phenomena, as he believed to be too frequently the case in the world of occultism. He devised a number of tests for Rose, in order to discern how she could be so sure that the god Horus, whom she was "speaking for," was the real thing.

One of the tests was to take her to the Boulak Museum and pass by the many inscriptions that depicted the god in his many aspects. He smiled to himself when she passed by one after another without comment. Was this just another occult blind alley? Suddenly, Rose pointed down a corridor to a stele, the image of which she could not see, and announced, "There he is!" Crowley, intrigued, approached the stele and saw the funerary inscription of the priest Ankh-f-n-Khonsu.

On the latter's left, enthroned, was Horus in his form called Ra Hoor Khuit, the solar aspect of Horus. Arched over the scene was the body of the goddess Nuit, and below her the winged globe of the god Hadit. Below the stele, Crowley was astonished to observe that the catalogue number of this otherwise undistinguished exhibit was 666, a number for the sun, and a number he identified with himself as being in revolt against the Christian era.[36] After a fruitless Tarot divination on March 23, he made the following notes in his "Book of Results": "There is one object to complete the secret of wisdom—or it is in the hieroglyphs [of the stele]. (perhaps or Thoth) GD [Golden Dawn] to be destroyed ie: publish its history & its papers. Nothing needs buying. I make it an absolute condition that I should obtain samadhi, in the Gods' own interest. My rituals work out well, but I need the transliteration [of the stele]."[37]

Crowley had the assistant curator of the museum (M. Brugsch Bey) make a transliteration of the stele's inscription into French, which he then transposed into verse. According to Crowley's *Confessions*, Rose then told her husband to enter the room where the transliteration had been made every day at noon on April 8, 9, and 10 for one hour.

It is interesting to note at this point that the "Book of Results" and the notebook containing the "Invocation of Hoor" contain notes revealing that a fortnight before Crowley entered the room, he was already thinking about turning the image of the stele into a ritual. He was also making inquiries about the nature and origin of the stele.

In the Tarot divination of March 23, we find the words and symbols: Mars in Libra = the ritual is of sex; Mars in the house of Venus exciting the jealousy of Saturn or Vulcan.[38] Crowley had been thinking deeply already about how to turn the Horus invocation and its message into a working magical system. He could not fail to see the image of Nuit bending over Hadit, witnessed by Horus, as a sexual image of magical potency. This is especially surprising, for it is usually held that Crowley took no serious interest in sexual magic until after 1913.

The Invocation of Horus was the key event, proving for Crowley that he had come to the explicit attention of the Secret Chiefs and was thus empowered to create his own magical order.

The next stage of what came to be called the "Cairo Working" introduced Crowley to someone he had been wanting to meet for some considerable time. Crowley entered the room at noon, as instructed, on the three appointed days "to write down what I heard," for an hour each time.

"In these three hours were written the three chapters of the Book of the Law."[39] The interpretation of the *Book of the Law* taxed Crowley's mind for the rest of his life, and since he was its authoritative interpreter, it is presumptuous for this author to attempt to do any more than examine what Crowley himself believed to be its meaning and import, and to attempt to clarify some of its contents for the interested reader, with due reference to Crowley's work on the subject.

THE *BOOK OF THE LAW*

The *Book of the Law*, whatever its provenance, is neither more nor less than a call to spiritual revolution at the very core of human existence. Its three chapters contain a radical ethic of conduct: "Do what thou wilt shall be the whole of the law" (an extension of Rabelais). They also contain a fresh spiritual cosmography, much prophecy concerning the world at large (especially the life of Aleister Crowley), a large number of mathematical and kabbalistic conundra, poetic prose of great incantatory beauty, blasphemy against the dominant religions of the world (especially materialism), a general call to magical arms for those who would survive the coming cataclysm—and five verses from Crowley's poetic rendering of the inscription on Stele No. 666.

The style varies from that of English translations of the Qur'an, to the Authorized Version of the Bible, to ancient Egyptian inscriptions, to the works of Aleister Crowley, and to a most peculiar, sometimes goatish and newly liberated voice that in fact breathes through the whole work. This is the voice of Crowley's Holy Guardian Angel, his unconscious Self, heard by him, apparently, for the first time.

The angel's name is given as Aiwass, the Minister of Hoor Paar Kraat (Harpocrates, an integration of spiritual powers within the god Horus), and Crowley expects him to be thought of as a complete individual, of whom "the scribe" Crowley is but a projection in three dimensions. It should be remembered that Crowley, by this time, had had his personality disintegrated on several levels in order that he might better understand its contents.

We can say, then, that the *Book of the Law* is certainly the product of the essential phenomenon known on this plane as Aleister Crowley. Crowley has found his god, and he speaks in a voice somewhat alien to his conscious self—because Crowley has not yet grown into "who he is."

Never does Crowley say of the experience that he was terrified, as if meeting an alien from Planet X—quite the reverse, in fact.

He put the essence of the experience quite clearly in a "Commentary on the Book of the Law," written at the Hotel du Djerid at Nefta in Tunisia in September 1923: "The Secret was this: the breaking down of my false Will by these dread words of mine Angel freed my True Self from all its bonds, so that I could enjoy at once the rapture of knowing myself to be who I am."[40]

The question of identity had plagued Crowley as much as it has many adolescents; but, as we have seen, Crowley could never be satisfied with the "caps" that society places on the individual's head, especially in an age of conformity in dress and outlook.

More to the point, it is necessary to consider why Crowley's undergraduate account of his childhood should be called *The World's Tragedy*. Why not simply his own? The fact is that Crowley had felt the burgeoning presence of cosmic identity from a quite early age. That is what led him to the study and practice of magic. Magic recognized Man as microcosm; society does not. Crowley felt his life and his struggle were nothing less than a microcosm of the struggle of the free spirit in the West: He would be to all intents and purposes Everyman—and that meant he would have to experience what every man (and where possible, every woman) experiences.

It is worth noting that when in 1900 Crowley took the Adeptus Minor grade and entered the Inner Order of the Golden Dawn under Mathers's aegis, the ceremony included his being tied by cords to a cross. There, Mathers instructed him: "If ye be crucified with Christ, ye shall also reign with Him."

The aspirant was encouraged to see himself as a participant in the mystical crucifixion and resurrection of Christ, understood not as historical events but as stages in the alchemical process of purification—the uncovering of the Stone of the Wise, God "within."

The mystical death of the ego and resurrection of the hidden God would also be characteristic of the birth of Crowley's New Aeon. So Crowley believed that his problems were also the problems of the culture in which he was suffering. If he overcame them, it follows that he and anyone else who had attained this would be empowered to be an authentic mouthpiece for a new culture. Aiwass-Crowley, the hidden and formerly repressed god of the West, thereby became the Logos (Word) of the Aeon—and the Word was *thelema*—will.

Crowley claimed that in his ordinary day-to-day consciousness as an English gentleman (or whatever other role he chose to play), he could not have cared less about the title Logos of the Aeon. Why should he? The responsibility implied by the title was "simply a nuisance." He found out time after time, certainly to his own pained satisfaction, that when he ignored his True Will, his hidden Angel, things always went wrong.

Crowley always maintained with sincerity that the last thing his conscious self would ever desire would be the responsibility of leadership for a New Aeon, and he evaded this responsibility at every opportunity. The

Cairo Working over, Crowley tossed the manuscript of the *Book of the Law* into a packing case and virtually ignored it until a fortuitous rediscovery in the attic at Boleskine in 1909.

The mental preparation for the rediscovery seems to have occurred during March 1906, two years after Crowley received the *Book of the Law*. A series of powerful invocations sustained internally while walking and riding across southern China with his wife and baby daughter left him profoundly disturbed. Crowley's Buddhism had already been severely undermined by the message of Aiwass that existence was "pure joy" and that sorrows pass.

Now it was time for his intellect to undergo a severe attack. As Blake had realized that reason is only one faculty of mind and should never be permitted to unbalance the harmonious *mens* and rule the roost alone, now the essence of that conclusion smashed into Aleister Crowley's mind with sudden violence. A letter of March 28, 1906, sent from Hong Kong to his friend Clifford Bax, reveals something of the change that had come over him:

My dear Bax,

your letter reached me here on my arrival from Burma via Yunnan-Fan with the wife and child. We had a fine time—about 4 months on the road . . .

It is very easy to get all the keys (invisible and otherwise) into the Kingdom; but the locks are devilish stuff—some of them hampered.

I am myself just at the end of a little excursion of nearly 7 years into Hell. The illusion of reason, which I thought I had stamped out in '98, was bossing me. It has now got the boot.

But let this tell you that it is one thing to devote your life to magic at twenty years old and another to find at 30 you are bound to stay a Magus. The first is the folly of a child; the second the Gate of the Sanctuary. It's no good, though, my writing indefinitely like this—only as a magical act can it be justified (ie: the Masters may operate the coincidence that it should fit the case). By rights you should get ordeals and initiations and things. A really good student can make it all up himself; and if he has really the wit to interpret all right he needs no teacher.

Solve et coagula said some ass. *Solve*—volatilise the fixed by a firm resolve to interpret everything in life as a spiritual fact, a step on the Path, a guide to the Light. An old disciple of mine put it more clumsily, thus: "Whatever ye do, whether ye eat or drink, do all to the Glory of God." I may add that in my own experience failure to do this has given me a bad time. Every time you interpret anything whatever materially you go a buster, worse than a motor-car smash. . . .

Coagula—the volatile—means what you had better find out for yourself. If you do, write and tell me. I haven't an idea. So shall take some pretty drastic steps to discover. . . . Register magical letters, unless your soul is worth less than twopence.[41]

Seventeen years later, his thoughts on the limitations of reason had coalesced into a firm grasp of the problem. This from a commentary written at the Hotel du Djerid in Tunisia on Aiwass's declaration that "Reason is a lie":

When Reason usurps the higher functions of the mind, when it presumes to dictate to the Will what it desires ought to be, it wrecks the entire structure of the star. . . . The Will should only take its orders from within and above. It should not be conscious at all. Once it becomes conscious, it becomes able to doubt; and having no means of getting rid of this by appeal to the Self, it seeks a reason for its action.

The reason, knowing nothing of the matter, promptly replies, basing its judgement not on the needs of the self, but on facts outside and alien to the star. The will having stopped in doubt goes on again in error. The will must never ask Why. It ought to be as sure of itself as the Law of Gravity. Aiwass now leaps to the supreme stroke—Reason itself is a lie. . . . It can never be sure of being right unless its knowledge is complete, which of course can never happen. There is always a factor infinite and unknown.[42]

Crowley's god moved in mysterious ways. He attributed the rediscovery of the *Book of the Law* in 1909 to a series of synchronicities, which, he was convinced, must have been considered in advance by preternatural intelligence. Providence?

In spite of these super-rational or, better, unrational goings-on, Crowley never lost his intellect. He simply learned not to take its constructions and conclusions as being necessarily of the nature of truth, nor to allow it to interrupt the voice of inspiration. Crowley had a message for the smart priests of our contemporary cult of the rational and for its crooked sister, the apparently pragmatic: "There is a factor infinite and unknown." Niels Bohr would have agreed with him.

To fall out of your cultural fictions is not necessarily to fall out of nous, but it will almost certainly entail appearing to be mad. Crowley was not bothered about this. "Attainment is insanity," he said.

The laws of the unconscious are not the laws of the conscious. Awareness of this made it easier for Crowley to embrace the *Book of the Law*. From 1909 onward, the "Cairo Revelation" would come to be both the yardstick of his entire teaching and the arbiter of psychological, spiritual, and philosophical conflict. It should also now be absolutely clear why Crowley declared himself to be the sole and final judge of its contents. Not only did he not want it to be center of theological conflict and disputed readings—as the Bible had become—but it was, in the profoundest possible sense, his work.

He knew that if he did not ring it about with safeguards and prohibitions, it would become a playpen for idiots and hysterics. Purchasers were advised to burn their first copy after reading it. That would be a book you would never forget.

Very few people really want to listen to their "true will": the will of the god in the human being, of whom the personality is an expression. It always seems too difficult. The ego is compromised by the admission of a Higher than itself. Aleister Crowley rebelled against his Angel almost as much as against his parents and his culture. It would take fifteen hard years before he became permanently identified with Aiwass, his own very Self: a Secret Chief, an Ipsissimus—the highest grade of the Golden Dawn system.

Nevertheless, on the earthly plane, the awareness would require constant reinforcement. In July 1926 he would write in his diary: "To Mega Therion 666 [the Great Wild Beast] consecrateth himself anew by this rite to establish the Law of Thelema by each and every way conceivable. Aum. Ha . . . I praise the immortal Gods. My will is to clean up affairs here, and answer the call of the three mountains to save the world from destruction, of the outworn formula by recreating it through the Word and according to the Law of Thelema."[43]

So what is this Law of Thelema, and how is it relevant? In a letter to the head of the German Ordo Templi Orientis, Heinrich Tränker, written in 1925 when Tränker was considering Crowley for the outer headship of that order, Crowley expressed his conviction regarding the necessity of the Law.

THE CRISIS

Those who came to me in 1904 E.V. [vulgar or Christian era] told me that They chose me for the Work in question on account not of my spiritual or magical attainments (which were and are, small indeed) but for (a) my loyalty and steadiness. (b) my knowledge of comparative occultism, especially my comprehension of the essential unity underlying sectarian differences. (c) my perception that the Great Work was as strictly scientific as Chemistry. (d) my command of language.

The urgency, they told me, was this. There was to be a general destruction of Civilisation. . . . We are on the threshold of the New Aeon. The death of the formula of Osiris is marked understandably to any student of the affairs of the planet, with the complete breaking-up not only of all the religions but of all the moral sanities. The result is constantly increasing anarchy feebly stemmed here and there by reactionary movements which are merely brutal, containing no firm elements because of the lack of any principle to which reasonable men can appeal.

. . . The only Word which can unite Mankind is "Do what thou wilt" for this asks no man to distort his personality to serve a fixed ideal of conduct. At the same time, the injunction is most austere; for it permits no man to go beyond the aim appointed by his nature. The real opposition to the Law of Thelema lies just here. The base understand by instinct that this Law must destroy the whole machinery of the civilisation which assumes that the greatest good of man is the possession of material means of enjoyment.[44]

On January 27, 1941, Crowley wrote to his friend Louis Wilkinson: "The world needs revolution in the root of life. This is already well at work, but must be brought up into consciousness so that the apparatus of intellect may be applied to it."[45]

The *Book of the Law* does in fact go "to the root of life," for it came from the very root of Aleister Crowley, in spite of his frequently stupid, frequently selfish, and frequently delightful magical self. The Cephaloedium Working (Cefalu, Sicily, 1920–21) produced a "Commentary on the Book of the Law" that represented much of his mature consideration on its import—although, in a sense, his entire life subsequent to April 1904 was a living commentary on the book and its perils.

The Cefalu "Commentary" contains enlightenment, rhetoric, and disciplined synthesis. We learn, for example, that the Greek kabbalistic numbers of Agape (Love) and Thelema (Will) are both 93, as is Aiwass, spelled *Aiwaz,* the name of the god of the Yezdis: "Our work is therefore historically authentic, the rediscovery of the Sumerian Tradition . . . (the earliest home of our race)."[46]

It is also suggested that the principal deities of the *Book of the Law,* Nuit and Hadit, correspond to Anu and Adad, the supreme Father and Mother deities of the Sumerians.

It may also be added that Nuit corresponds not only to the Gnostic Sophia (Wisdom), the Lady of the Stars, but also to Sabbaoth, the starry sky goddess of the Sabians. In late antiquity, and even after the Islamic Hejirah, the Sabians took the *Hermetica* as their scripture in the city of Harran.

The *Book of the Law* is divided into three chapters, being the respective expressions of three cosmic concepts personified in the form of three Egyptian deities: Hadit (motion), Nuit (infinite space), and Ra Hoor Khuit (the martial aspect of Horus and archon for the Aeon).

Space is motion-concealed, and by motion, space is made manifest, at the center of every atom in the cosmos. These dynamics also correspond to the Shiva and Shakti of the Hindu pantheon and to the Tao and Teh of Chinese philosophy. The conception is profound and has many intriguing correspondences. Crowley wrote: "It is cosmographically, the conception of the two Ultimate Ideas, Space, and that which occupies Space. . . . These two ideas may be resolved into one, that of Matter: with Space its 'Condition' or 'form' included therein. This leaves the idea of 'Motion' for Hadit, whose interplay with Nuit makes the Universe. Time should be considered as a particular kind or dimension of Space."[47]

As space is filled with stars, so humankind is to think of itself likewise. Chapter 1 reveals a perception that, if taken seriously, might put Hollywood out of business: "Every man and every woman is a star"; "each human being is an Element of the Cosmos, self-determined and Supreme, co-equal with all other Gods. From this Law 'Do what thou wilt' follows logically."[48]

Crowley's comments on Hoor-paar-Kraat, for whom Aiwass is a minister, are both revealing and beautiful:

> Hoor-paar-Kraat or Harpocrates, the Babe in the Egg of Blue, is not merely the God of Silence in a conventional sense. He represents the Higher Self, the Holy Guardian Angel. . . . He is the first letter of the Alphabet, Aleph [Hebrew], whose number is One and his card in the Tarot is the Fool numbered Zero. . . . In his absolute innocence and ignorance he is "The Fool"; he is "The Saviour," being the Sun who shall trample on the crocodiles and tigers and avenge his father Osiris.
>
> Thus we see him as the "Great Fool" of Celtic legend, the "Pure Fool" of Act I of *Parsifal,* and, generally speaking, the insane person whose words have always been taken for oracles. But to be "Saviour" he must be born and grow to manhood; thus Parsifal acquires the Sacred Lance, emblem of virility. He usually wears the "Coat of many colours" like Joseph the "dreamer"; so he is also now Green Man of spring festivals. But his "folly" is now not innocence but inspiration of wine; he drinks from the Graal. . . . Almost identical symbols are those of the secret god of the Templars, the bisexual Baphomet, and of Zeus Arrhenothelus, equally bisexual, the Father-Mother of All in One Person. (. . . Tarot Trump XV, "The Devil.") Now Zeus being Lord of Air we are reminded that Aleph is the letter of Air. As Air we find the "Wandering Fool" [the Troubadour] pure wanton Breath, yet creative. . . . He is the Wandering Knight or Prince of Fairy Tales who marries the King's Daughter.
>
> . . . Thus once Europa, Semele and others claimed that Zeus-Air had enjoyed them in the form of a beast, bird or what not; while later

Mary attributed her condition to the agency of a Spirit, Spiritus, breath of air,—in the shape of a dove.

But the "Small Person" of Hindu mysticism, the dwarf insane yet crafty of many legends in many lands, is also this same "Holy Ghost," or Silent Self of a man, or his Holy Guardian Angel. He is almost the "Unconscious" of Freud, unknown, unaccountable. "Blowing whither it listeth, but thou canst not tell whence it cometh or whither it goeth." It commands with absolute authority when it appears at all, despite reason and judgement.

Aiwass is then . . . the "minister" of this Hoor-paar-Kraat, that is of the Saviour of the world in the larger sense, and of mine own "Silent Self" in the lesser.[49]

A key aspect of Horus is that of the "Crowned and Conquering Child." The Child is a most significant archetype for our times, redolent of the march of youth that ever gathers pace across the planet: "The Concealed Child becomes the Conquering Child: the armed Horus avenging his father, Osiris. So also our own Silent Self, helpless and witless, hidden within us, will spring forth, if we have craft to loose him to the Light, spring lustily forward with his Cry of Battle, the Word of our True Wills."[50]

Was it instinct that led the Beatles to make Crowley a member of their Lonely Hearts Club Band? "Love is the law, love under will" shouts the *Book of the Law:* "Come forth, O children, under the stars, and take your fill of love!"

Crowley's comment: "'Come forth'—from what are you hiding? 'under the stars' that is, openly . . . above all, be open! What is this shame? Is Love so hideous that man should cover him with lies?" Thelemites are extroverts in a world of cant and can't. Directly associated with the liberation of sex, the *Book of the Law* openly predicts the successful revolt of Woman, whose body is the door to the manifest world that should on no account, according to Aiwass, be closed. Away with false modesty:

"Let Mary inviolate be torn upon wheels: for her sake
let all chaste women be utterly despised among you!"

We do not fool and flatter women; we do not despise and abuse them. To us a woman is Herself, as absolute, original, independent, free, self-justified, exactly as a man is. . . . We do not want Her as a slave; we want Her free and royal, whether her love fight death in our arms by night . . . or Her loyalty ride by day beside us in the Charge of the Battle of Life.

It is we of Thelema who truly love and respect Woman. . . . For I, the Beast, am come; an end to the evils of old, to the duping and club-bing. . . . Once and for all in vain will bully and brute, and braggart man, priest, lawyer, or social censor knit his brows to devise him a new tamer's trick; once and for all the tradition is broken, vanished the vogue of bowstring, sack, stoning, nose-splitting, belt-buckling, cart's tail-dragging, whipping, pillory-posting, walling-up, divorce court, eunuch, harem, mind-crippling, house-imprisoning, menial work wearying, creed-stultifying, social-ostracism marooning, Divine-wrath scaring. . . .

. . . She, agonised, ridiculous and obscene; gave all her beauty and strength of maidenhood to suffer sickness, weakness, danger of death, choosing to live the life of a cow—that so Mankind might sail the seas of Time. . . . She hath been trampled through all the ages, and she hath tamed them thus, her silence was the token of her triumph.

But now the word of Me the Beast is this; not only art thou Woman, sworn to a purpose not thine own; thou art thyself a star, and in thyself a purpose to thyself. Not only mother of men art thou, or whore to men; serf to their need of Life and Love, not sharing in their Light and Liberty; nay, thou art Mother and Whore for thine own pleasure; the Word to Man I say to thee no less; Do what thou wilt. Shall be the whole of the Law![51]

Aleister Crowley reformulated his entire philosophy and personal practice around the *Book of the Law*. It remained a virtually inex-haustible treasury of inspiration, insight, and not a little mystery for him.

However, the notorious third chapter contains promise of the utmost savagery and inhumanity: antidemocratic and antiliberal, antire-ligious and antiwelfare, anticommunist and anticapitalist: "Mercy let be off: damn them who pity! Kill and torture: spare not: be upon them!"

It is the sound of Lidice, Auschwitz, Katyn Wood, My Lai, Hiroshima, Dresden, Vietnam, Pol Pot, the Gulf War, Bosnia. It is the voice of our times. It is also the voice of Crowley in 1904, contemptuous of the mush and mire of Edwardian sentimentality and idealism, so soon to be crushed in the blood-soaked trenches from the Dardanelles to the Somme. It is the voice of every place where the True Will is silenced, where the individual walks in fear of the mass.

And all this came to Crowley in 1904.

ALEISTER CROWLEY: SEX MAGICIAN

On June 28, 1930, Crowley reflected in his diary, "Spiritual attainments are incompatible with bourgeois morality."[52] The morality Crowley is referring to is based on the restriction of natural impulse: a concatenation of fear of disease, fear of self, fear of poverty, fear of truth, and ultimately fear of life itself.

To get around the possible judgment of God, it is necessary to ring life about with a large regiment of laws indicating what is right and what is wrong. Crowley was obviously not alone in his revolt against the moral conventions of his time—for a while it seemed that everyone from the Bloomsbury Group to D. H. Lawrence and the vast panoply of the emergent Hollywood was hell-bent on destroying those constraints associated with the Victorian Age.

In 1913, Crowley wrote a characteristic letter to a Dr. Graham of Cambridge on the subject of marriage:

> I should have supposed that any mind could see that the finest possible thing is the indissoluble union of the whole of two personalities. Such union would be Samadhi [union with Brahman] and in accordance with the One Great Law through whose operation we get back to God.
>
> I should also have thought even the conventional mind could see that this union was not secured by marriage, and owing to this failure, marriage has today become certainly to the young a symbol for the association of all that is vile and degrading with all that should be most pure. . . . It has consequently already been replaced by hazardous unions between economically independent people. That such unions are not open and respectable prevents them from developing into

unions which would be marriage in all but name. Respectability, as always, defeats itself.[53]

Today, some ninety years later, such unions are indeed respectable, and the laws have been adapted to accommodate the change—but it has taken a long time and maybe two world wars to get there. Crowley was on the forefront of the change.

However, we are wrong to suppose that the so-called sexual revolution is in any sense complete. Crowley regarded the sexual life of his time as a mass of hypocrisy that stirred up something akin to an international neurosis that could find satisfaction only in conflict of the destructive kind. On the outside, a crisp, sugary coating of sentiment, lush, romantic, and dreamy; on the inside, a craven desire for satisfaction of a blind urge with the reward of a relief redolent of defecation.

The organs of reproduction: dirty, dangerous, unspeakable, deadly. Young girls placed in mental institutions because they had "gone too far." Men skulking in fear of the admission of syphilis; an entire underground culture of prostitution, titillation, pornography; brown envelopes, cash-in-hand, dirty raincoats, moral terror; the police ready to pounce. We don't want to know that. Kindly leave the stage. Ladies, please leave the room so the gentlemen can talk.

Crowley cut through the whole morbid morass with a sharpened scalpel in an attempt to clean out society. His efforts, as we might expect, earned him the kind of innuendo, police harassment, tabloid character assassination, and widespread denunciation that would later be meted out to another sexual pioneer, Wilhelm Reich. It was not society but Aleister Crowley who was King of Depravity, living on immoral earnings, debauched, diseased, and demonic.

Crowley refused to be ignored. In October 1930 he was in Berlin, reflecting on the vaunted gains for liberty of the Jazz Age: "The 'chief advance in morals' in the last generation is that people keep on being dirty little boys and girls instead of growing up."[54]

Crowley went a lot further than simply delineating the hypocrisy of the time with regard to sexual mores and morals. He divinized sex—he wanted to drag it out of the gutter and make people see what Blake meant when he said, "The Lust of the Goat is the Bounty of God" and

"Everything that lives is Holy."[55] By 1912, Crowley had commenced a full investigation of sexual "magick."

Sexual "magick" is the use of sex for magical purposes. Since magick (Crowley's idiosyncratic spelling) may be defined as "the art and science of causing changes in nature in conformity with will," we may conclude that sexual magick enables this process to take place.

Crowley justified the use of sex succinctly: "The close connection of sexual energy with the higher nervous centres makes the sexual act definitely magical. It is therefore a sacrament which can and should be used in the Great Work. The act being creative, ecstatic and active, its vice consists in treating it as sentimental, emotional, passive."[56]

Crowley (along with all nature) had been using sex for magical purposes for years. The *Book of the Law* (like the Song of Solomon) is full of sexual typology in its expression of cosmic dynamics (e.g., Nuit and Hadit; the Beast and the Scarlet Woman).

Crowley's theory of sex departs from the conception that ecstasy is a mystical state and that orgasm represents not only the condition whose sublimation is laughter but also, more important, the temporary annihilation of the ego-bound consciousness, thereby permitting in principle the unveiling of the unconscious. That sex involves such a possibility ought to be evident from the extreme trepidation and tremor that characterizes the virgin at the Gate of the Holy of Holies in adolescence, the aching longing of the romantic, and the trauma of the botched attempt.

Crowley recommended to his students *The Divine Pymander* by Hermes Trismegistus as being "invaluable as bearing on the Gnostic Philosophy."[57] He would doubtless have been delighted to discover that the following fragment of Hermes' dialogue with Asclepius turned up in a Coptic version in the Nag Hammadi library two years before his death, but was not published until thirty years afterward:

And if you wish to see the reality of this mystery, then you should see the wonderful representation of the intercourse that takes place between the male and the female. For when the semen reaches the climax, it leaps forth. In that moment the female receives the strength of the male; the male for his part receives the strength of the female, while the semen does this.

Therefore the mystery of intercourse is performed in secret, in order that the two sexes might not disgrace themselves in front of many who do not experience that reality. For each of them [the sexes] contributes its [own part in] begetting. For if it happens in the presence of those who do not understand the reality, [it is] laughable and unbelievable. And, moreover, they are holy mysteries, of both words and deeds, because not only are they not heard, but also they are not seen.

Therefore such people [the unbelievers] are blasphemers. They are atheistic and impious. But the others are not many; rather, the pious who are counted are few. Therefore wickedness remains among the many, since learning concerning the things which are ordained does not exist among them. For the gnosis of the things which are ordained is truly the healing of the passions of matter. Therefore learning is something derived from gnosis.[58]

Music to the Beast's ears: sexual intercourse, a holy mystery; those who do not recognize it as such, blasphemers. True knowledge of the sexual mystery, a gnosis for the few. For Hermes, the mystery of sex lies in its being a sacramental image of the larger truth that "God eternally generates the cosmos, and that the cosmos possesses generative power, and thereby maintains all races that have come into being." Sex is God's way with All.

Crowley had also begun to see what was for him a satisfying realization of the identity of free will and determinism, in the divinity of the true will freed from error, partiality, and illusion. Since the fact of the universe represented "Love under Will," it was not in a sense such a great step to particularize the macrocosmic within the microcosmic for the purpose of cosmic consciousness.

The promise of sexual magick was, Crowley realized, implicit in all the world's esoteric theories. He had glimpsed what he regarded as the essential esoteric secret within the tradition of the Rosy-Cross and in alchemy, in the type of the Hermetic or Alchemical Wedding that joins these traditions.

In fact, it is precisely at this point that Aleister Crowley offended the "(physical) virginity is white/asceticism is good" tradition of Western esotericism and orthodox religion—an outrage that persists to this day.

Aleister Crowley never reckoned that the sexual magick as taught in the ninth degree of the Ordo Templi Orientis was something to be entered into lightly. He tried to make it absolutely clear to his pupils that sex magick is not for the "animal human" but concerns the subtle body projected by the divine Self incarnate—that is to say, the human as a spiritual being, a being endowed with the cosmic force of life itself.

Contrary to the classical ascetic or Gnostic encratite position, Crowley's concepts of purity and virginity belonged to the new world of relativism. In that world, what was right was that which was in tune with the True Will, and therefore in conformity with the express purpose of the Great Work: the experiential union of human and God. Any deviation from this was considered to be black magic.

Orgasm as normally experienced is not at issue, but rather the subtle energy behind or hidden within orgasm. The aim is expressly not pleasure for its own sake; indeed, sacrifice of pleasure and uninterrupted concentration on what is willed is, he taught, vital to effective sex magick: "Thou hast no right but to do thy will."

Due to the repressive laws governing sexual material—as well as many other things—in Crowley's lifetime, in addition to the (necessarily) initiatic character of Crowley's teaching, much of his writing on the subject is expressed in symbol, metaphor, euphemism, and humorous plays on words from the old occult tradition. "Bloody sacrifice," for example, does not denote something out of a horror novel but refers to the expenditure of semen (= life = "blood") for magical purposes other than reproduction of the species, and "child sacrifice" meant, cheekily, masturbation or contraception.

Crowley was confident that genuine sex magick could not be abused without great danger to the abuser or inept practitioner—since it dealt with "the will of God": the truly free will.

Beyond the positively and negatively charged particles exists the subatomic—or shall we say unatomic—level where, as the *Book of the Law* puts it, "there is a factor infinite and unknown." This factor guarantees free will by the principle of paradoxical randomness, or uncertainty, and where all motion is universally reciprocated and known (i.e., not ultimately reducible to the categories of terrestrial logic).

Those seeking kicks of the sensual kind, selfish power, or ego gratification will do well to steer clear of sexual magick—indeed, they should steer clear of magick altogether. As dictators find to their cost time after time, unbalanced force brings a retribution that is usually swift and always certain. As severity must be balanced by mercy, the reverse is also the case. There are no shortcuts. As Crowley himself noted in his diary on July 9, 1930, "I think knowledge of the IX° has quite upset Frater E.N.C. [?]. It is too much like a short cut; and is very dangerous practice indeed for one untrained by long years of ceremonial. My success, and immunity, may well be due to the fact that I did not know it till after 14 years hard work."[59]

How did Crowley come to place so much emphasis on sexual magick, virtually abandoning much of the ceremonial methods that he had acquired in the Golden Dawn? In a letter written in 1925 to Heinrich Tränker, in response to the dying wish of Dr. Theodor Reuss that Crowley succeed him as outer head of the order (Crowley was already head of the British Ordo Templi Orientis), Crowley gives an account of his first acquaintance with the OTO's "supreme secret":

I came to great public notice in London in March 1910, E.V, when Mathers attempted to prevent the publication of Number III of the *Equinox*. In this Volume as instructed by the Chiefs who had come to me in Cairo in 1904 I published the rituals of 5°=6° of RR et AC. London talked for 9 days of Rosa Crucians & my studio was besieged by authentic chiefs of that order in great multitudes. Among them was Brother Reuss who tried to bully me into—well nothing in particular. I was simply bored and got rid of him. Some time later however he came to see me again in an entirely different spirit; he was the Grand Master of Germany under Brother Yarker who had given me 90-95. Reuss claimed that the OTO combined all the secrets of all degrees soever. His reason for coming to me was that I had published the secret of the 9° in plain language in one of my books [possibly chapter 36 of *The Book of Lies*, published in 1913—three years does not seem like "some time later"]. I denied this and he then told me the secret, which was entirely new to me. He then took the book in question from the shelves and showed me to my complete astonishment that I had published it in the simplest words. The passage in question had been written under inspiration derived from an important magical invocation; but I had refused to accept it myself as of any value. He now explained the great importance of this method of working. I did not take him very seriously but from time to time made experiments. My personal reaction against Reuss was always very strong. His overbearing aggressive manner was offensive. Although morally obliged to work with him, I kept him at arm's length and was careful not to compromise myself. His business in London seemed to me to be of a highly suspicious character. He had a number of accommodation addresses under different names. . . . I felt reasonably sure that he was employed by the Prussian Secret Services as when the war broke out he left England among the [members?] of the German Embassy. With regard to my experiments of the 9° I had a reaction also against this so that I did not even trouble to record them.[60]

In a letter dated June 3, 1913, Crowley wrote to Don Isidore Villerino del Villar, Puissent Sovereign Grand Commander of the Rite of Memphis in Madrid, informing Don Isidore of the death of John Yarker and the need for an electoral college meeting "for the purpose of electing a new Grand Hierophant 97° and I have much pleasure in proposing Don Isidore 96° to that post. My proposal is seconded by the Most Illustrious and Puissent Brother Theodore Reuss 96°—the Sovereign Grand Master General of the German Empire."[61]

It is clear that Crowley was cooking up something with Reuss. In April he had written to Grantwood, the Most Worthy Supreme Magus of the Societas Rosicruciana in America: "Please accept my thanks for the honour you have done me, and the diploma duly received. The death of the Most Illustrious Brother John Yarker 33° 90° 97° leaves me the sole Custodian of the authority to work the Memphis & Mizraim Rites in Great Britain and Ireland; but as I think I told you in a previous letter, I am proposing to concentrate the whole teaching of all these Rites in the 10 degrees of OTO and M.M.M [Crowley's own order, the Mysteria Mystica Maxima]."[62]

The letter earlier referred to makes it plain that the OTO was effectively to absorb Yarker's rite and become a vehicle for Thelemic teaching: "With regard to the New Supreme Council I should explain that the real secret to which all Masonry only forms a veil is in the keeping of the OTO to which our Supreme Council is subject."

Perhaps this was what Reuss had been trying to bully Crowley into doing in the first place, but he did not wish to admit this to Tränker in 1925. It should also be added that Crowley found all this to-ing and fro-ing with one or another Masonic organization a great joke—it was like acting. Crowley had a lot of fun with pretentious titles all his life. He knew they really counted for nothing at all (unless, that is, they marked some definite magico-spiritual attainment).

There is also the possibility that Crowley's move toward the OTO was somewhat opportunistic, for the following reason. In April 1911, Crowley had refused to defend himself against the imputation of homosexuality with Allan Bennett in the *Looking Glass* trial, where that scandal rag was taken to court by Crowley's friend George Cecil Jones (who had introduced Crowley to the Golden Dawn).

The *Looking Glass* had misrepresented Crowley's Rites of Eleusis public presentation held in Caxton Hall in 1910 as a scandalous riot of debauchery presided over by an "abominable and loathesome creature" (Crowley). Jones was implicated with Crowley, and reputations were at stake. Crowley's unwillingness to come forward as a witness lost him the friendship of Captain J. F. C. Fuller (later Major General Fuller, genius of modern tank tactics) and George Raffalovitch, who had helped finance *The Equinox*. This must have been a great blow to Crowley. Having been divorced from Rose in 1909 (she had been diagnosed as a "dipsomaniac," or alcoholic, and was certified insane in September 1911) and thereby lost any respect he might have had from Gerald Kelly, Crowley was rapidly losing his social base. He had long been on a collision course with society.

Furthermore, June 1909 had seen his rediscovery of the manuscript of the *Book of the Law,* which laid out a very distinctive role for Crowley and warned of problems if he was untrue to "himself" (Aiwass). It might become necessary to give up everything dear to him. It should also be borne in mind that Crowley was an artist, and this shaving off of unnecessary interests to uncover the pristine and essential idea is a key stage in any serious artist's life. Thelema was the only idea that mattered to him.

This general situation may very well have made him look again at the possibility of making a commitment to the OTO—on the condition that its rituals would serve as new vehicles for his radical Thelemic ideas. This scenario might explain the gloss over Crowley's involvement with Reuss and his making light of that connection. Reuss might very well have remarked in 1913 that the secret of the OTO was enshrined in chapter 25 of *The Book of Lies,* but that this was only one factor in his commitment to Reuss's OTO and the working of the ninth degree. Indeed, as will be seen later, Crowley was making notes for OTO rituals in 1912.

It seems to me that Crowley was embarrassed by his inability to cope with the full implications of the *Looking Glass* trial—embarrassment being a sensibility that he always suppressed. (Hence: "Bourgeois morality is incompatible with spiritual attainment." To be embarrassed is to forget that you are a spiritual star.) If you cannot embarrass a middle-class Englishman, then you lose control of him—and from 1912 onward Crowley became practically uncontrollable and, therefore, an embarrassment to those who did not share his deepest, most uncompromising convictions. His greatest support from then on would come from Germany and America, whose inhabitants are not generally sensitive to what embarrasses the English.

Eleanor Marx, of the Socialist League, described Reuss (also a member of that body) as a vulgarian and a filthy fellow—the sort of thing that was said of Crowley. Crowley might very well have found Reuss objectionable. He was often disgusted by himself, tending, as most of us do, to project his own unacceptable qualities onto other people; such was the extent of his hypertrophied ego. Crowley hated the idea of being seen to be manipulated by anyone, but circumstances may have forced the day in Reuss's favor. Reuss's own motives are beyond the scope of this study.

It is not surprising that it is around this period that many occultists lost contact altogether with Crowley, and suppositions of madness, derangement, addiction, possession, and so on entered in. If "freedom is just another word for nothing left to lose" (as Janis Joplin sang in

Kris Kristofferson's "Me and Bobby McGee") then Crowley's bottom line was the *Book of the Law*: the revelation, as he saw it, of himSelf to himself, and of himself to a deaf world.

Occasionally he would don his good-fun, in-for-a-laugh English gentleman persona, but from now on, remoteness would be an essential and visible feature of his being, like a mountaineer who has reached the peak of Everest but, to the bemusement of his fellows, just keeps on climbing. Is he imagining that the mountain goes on ever upward, or are his former companions imagining him? Crowley's deepest motives become ever more difficult to assess. He would rarely stop to assess them himself. He was a Star, rolling on through the cosmos.

Regarding purpose in life, he would come to declare that "only a human being would have such a thing." Would he ever return? In spite of saying that he "did not give a pack of cards for the whole human-race," he still felt obliged to save them. It was his oath and really his only reason—if reason were necessary—for being here. In order to succeed, Crowley began to stir things up in the whole world of esoteric orders and secret societies. To protect himself, he had his reputation—as when he turned on his bullies at school by developing his body through mountaineering—and people were now afraid of him. Those who knew would know.

It is a reasonable supposition that Crowley's intention was to persuade all extant esoteric organizations, wherever possible, to the Thelemic cause and that he had decided the OTO was one of the best means then available for doing so. The letter of 1925 to Tränker was an attempt to get complete control of the OTO on the death of Reuss. Reuss obviously had contacts and influence that Crowley saw as valuable. The process of uniting the scattered bodies of Western esoteric knowledge behind the banner of Thelema was never finished in Crowley's lifetime.

A letter to Herr Krumm-Heller, a grand master of the OTO, dated December 28, 1936, throws light on an organization, the Ancient Mystical Order Rosae Crucis (AMORC), which still advertises in Western periodicals and newspapers. It concerns the founder of AMORC, H. Spencer-Lewis:

Lewis was never a disciple either of Reuss or myself. He had [in 1918] been knocking about for years trying to run a fake Rosicrucian Order.

He cast about everywhere for authority and when I first met him in New York in 1918 E.V. he was showing a charter supposed to be from French Rosicrucians in Toulouse. . . . This ridiculous forgery . . . Lewis didn't know French! In the last 2 or 3 years . . . Reuss was sick, impoverished and desperate. . . . He accordingly handed out honourary diplomas up to the 95° and sometimes very foolishly the 96°. That is how people like Spencer Lewis and Tränker got their standing. It is particularly stupid because Reuss had got into great trouble through Yarker's giving the 95° to Wedgewood. . . . If he [Lewis] had none [authority] he can be prosecuted, if he had mine [a charter from Crowley as Sovereign Inspector General of Yarker's Rite] he must account for the 900,000 dollars odd which he had accrued in the last few years. Unfortunately, my people in California, although most devoted and intelligent, are not precisely men of the world and do not understand how to handle big affairs. It is imperative that I should go over there and put the screws on Spencer Lewis.[63]

Crowley was prepared to go to virtually any lengths to unite esoteric bodies behind his system, whether it was recommending that Krishnamurti be brought into the OTO (Rudolf Steiner had been a member) or, as in the following letter to the German OTO G.M. Herr Hopfe, urging contact with Adolf Hitler, written on January 20, 1936:

Under the present circumstances, if I understand them aright, the only means of propaganda is to address the leader himself [Hitler] and show him that the acceptance of these philosophical principles is the only means of demonstrating to reason instead of merely to enthusiasm the propriety of the measures he is taking for the rebuilding of the Reich. Unless he does this, the Churches will ultimately strangle him; they have an almost infinite capacity for resistance and endurance for this very reason that their systems are based on a fundamental theory which enabled them to survive attacks and restraints. They bow as much as they are compelled to bow by force and they subsequently excuse their yielding on the grounds of expediency. If the Fuehrer wishes to establish his principle permanently he must uproot them entirely and this can only be done by superseding their deepest conceptions.

> Enthusiasm for a man or an outward system dies with the man or with the circumstances which have brought the system into being. The Law of Thelema being infinitely rigid and infinitely elastic is an enduring basis. Love is the Law, Love under Will.[64]

Hitler's will was already irredeemably perverted, and its duration was consequently short, overpowered as he was by unconscious forces that he was utterly unable to balance under the point of crisis. His ego simply grew and then cracked under the strain of those reactionary forces he had himself evoked and that manifested themselves all over the planet. In magick as in nature, equilibrium is all. Should a country ever lose grip of the Golden Mean, we shall know what to expect.[65]

The key to equilibrium may lie in a consideration of sexual magick: balanced forces of male and female, right and left, Jachin and Boaz, sun and moon, positive and negative, the duality whose apex is the unknowable One, projected in creation. Crowley denied the ascetic, encratite, and Buddhistic view that duality must mean evil. According to Crowley, "Love is the uniting of opposites": Subject and object are separated "for the sake of union." In a letter of May 27, 1913, to George Macnie Cowie, Crowley wrote: "I have just got back and have read *Transcendental Universe*. It is rather interesting but I think of no great value. This alleged contest between intellect and spirit makes me tired. It shows a totally wrong conception of the nature of the cosmos. It is just as bad as the alleged antagonism between mind and body."[66]

Sexual magick undertook to obliterate any such perceived duality. Its source was in the East, and that is where Crowley, like the mythic hero Christian Rosenkreuz, headed in search of wisdom.

The Hindu macrocosm is based on the primordial recognition that the god of the day is the sun and that of the night, the moon. The sun symbolizes the creative aspect of God and is hailed daily in the Gayatri mantra across India, and by the birds in England. The moon is seen as the receptive principle, so that in the microcosm the sun corresponds to the phallus (lingam) and the moon to the womb (yoni), and as such these organs are worshipped.

As the Christian declares that "the sun and moon bow down before Him," the Hindu holds to the view that the God of which the cosmos is an expression (Brahman) has no attributes and can be considered to be absolute zero (the philosophical Nothing). While some of the early Gnostics postulated theories as to how 0 came to generate 2, the Hindu is satisfied that such things are beyond thought; from Brahman came an egg that divided into two, male and female, and their uniting created the universe in which we move. The Vedantic Vaishnava and Shivite sects worship the male principle; the Shakti sects worship the female principle. Some schools assert the necessity of remarrying the opposites and merging into the resultant union (samadhi, and the meaning of Crowley's "stars separated for the sake of union").

Tantrics do in flesh what others sublimate in symbol. Tantric sages believe that the process of creation (reflected in the microcosm) must be reenacted in reverse, before the practitioner may become free *(mukta)* and be reabsorbed into God (Kether, the Crown, in Kabbalah). The first stage of the journey is realized in the Muludhara, an imaginary center (chakra) at the base of the spine (Malkuth, the Kingdom, in Kabbalah). There sleeps the Kundalini, symbolized as a coiled serpent, the creative principle at rest.

When awakened through spiritual intercourse, Kundalini is sent up the spinal cord *(sushumna)* to the Sahasrara (Kether) in the top of the skull. She there meets Shiva. In sublime orgasm, sun and moon mingle, resulting in the subtle body being flooded with Amrita, the Elixir of Life. On the physical plane, the flow of semen *(bindhu)* constitutes the gross form of a subtle essence called *ojas* (the alchemical "white eagle," according to the OTO).

Amrita is not normally present in the human body but is the result of the marriage of the white and red eagles (red eagle here meaning the female sexual fluids) and is vital to a final union of spirit (atman) and God (Brahman—see chapter 1). The OTO derived its knowledge, according to Gerald Yorke, a good friend and onetime pupil of Crowley, from the Kaula circle of the Bhairavi Diksha, a fraternity of Indian Tantric yogis observed by Yorke. Tantra becomes sexual magick when the will of the magician is projected consistently into the union of atman and Brahman, followed usually by the ingestion of resultant sexual fluids that Crowley calls (with technical correctness) the sacrament.

Sexual magick is exceedingly dangerous to the minds of those who have not been through thorough training learned how to disassociate mind and senses—hence Crowley's rigorous Yoga training within his magickal system. In India, Tantrics undergo many years of probation. Tantric worship may take place in marriage, where the male partner honors his wife as the divine mother; this is called the left-hand path (*vema marga;* frequently given sinister overtones by the uncomprehending). In this form, there is no ritual, but the practice is characterized by realizing ideas such as worship, self-sacrifice, and gratitude to God. Sex in this context is regarded as holy and the sinner one who despises it.

This brings us briefly to the question of Aleister Crowley's alleged Satanism. Crowley regarded Christianity as hostile to sex, associating it with sin, the work of the devil, immorality, and so forth. His experience of Kundalini convinced him that sex was a manifestation of the archetypal creative power of God. It is such a simple idea that it beggars belief how sex could ever have been seen as wrong.

Nevertheless, Crowley was intrigued by the association of Satan with sexual energy, and with darkness. He came to the conclusion that Satan or Shaitan, the Hebrew being derived from the Egyptian god Set—the sun in the south that blackens everything (and becomes to the physical eye invisible or occult)—had acquired his evil overtone from a war between rival solar priests in Egypt. Osirian priests, taking the myth of the murder of their god by his brother somewhat literally, eventually triumphed, and Set's followers went underground.

Crowley sometimes identified Shaitan with Aiwass, his unconscious self—or the self of which he was largely unconscious. The Hebrews had simply taken over from the Egyptians this idea of Satan, the Adversary (as he appears as God's servant, the one that tempts, in the biblical Book of Job). In time he became the actual and cosmic adversary to their more Osirian (or in Greek mythology Apollonian) god, with the result that Set/Shaitan became ever more the receptacle for ideas of evil, anti-God or antihuman, and so on.

Persian dualism simply intensified a process that would result first in the cosmic warrior cult associated with Qumran and the Zealot Armageddon, and then in Satan as Antichrist with poor, sinful, sexual humankind his woeful dupes. Crowley was also aware of the classical

Gnostics' view of the serpent in Eden (coiled about the Tree of Life) as the bringer of gnosis. Many are familiar with the devil in his aspect as Lucifer the Light-Bringer—which, of course, was Set's role as he took the light about the earth, ready to be assumed as Osiris resurrected in the morning.

A similar range of ideas can be seen in Nietzsche's *Birth of Tragedy,* in which the German philosopher pits the Apollonian (sun god) virtues and classical Greek theater against the earlier demonic and instinctive, chthonic and unconscious life, symbolized as Dionysus. Dionysus is the energy of the Bacchic revel that tears the ego to pieces (as the body of Osiris was found in pieces and reconstituted by Isis, the Earth Mother).

We are accustomed to thinking of the artist (magician) as being driven by his demon, careless of the values of the world. All this explains why dominant Western culture has had such a problem with the bohemian (Bohemia had been the home of Hermetic alchemy in the sixteenth and early seventeenth centuries). The artist, the reveler, the Falstaffian figure, the rock-and-roller—all have been treated with contempt until contained and the joy or ecstasy controlled. Materialist culture is fearful of what Crowley was and stood for. It is the urge for order over what is perceived to be chaos—and repression by almost any means is the tool.

Apollo is inevitably a materialist in this context, clinging to the hope of the solid, the visible, the stable, while the whole universe (ignoring Newton[67] and praising Bohr) is crying out that things just ain't that way! This is what Blake means when he sees the sun not as "a golden guinea" but as a host of angels crying out "Holy! Holy! Holy!" Apollo here corresponds to the Gnostics' Demiurge or Blake's Old Nobodaddy, the archrationalist, the divider, the cosmic account-ant—likewise the disrespect of Gnostics for the God of the Law. But it happened, according to Crowley's way of thinking, that the Osirian and Jehovistic wing got hold of the Christian Church, linking it up to the legality and force of the Roman Empire.

Crowley believed that this old conflict between Osiris and Set was exploded in April 1904 when Horus, Crowned and Conquering Child, came to reign over the destiny of humanity. This helps explain, perhaps, why Crowley was anti-Christian,[68] seeing himself as the Beast (the solar man) of the apocalypse whose coming heralds a new age.

Beyond that, it is difficult to see that he was more or less evil than the rest of humanity. Yes, he was an egotist; yes, he mistreated some of his friends and acquaintances; yes, he was sometimes paranoid; yes, he was as irresponsible as a naughty youth; yes, he could be spiteful, aggressive, and petty. But has it not occurred to his detractors that the Satan of their personal mythology would find it more appropriate to infiltrate quietly, subtly, stealthily, under guise of being something else? In the Hermetic scheme of things, the real darkness comes from repressed energies, mangled, regrouping, and then overwhelming the psyche. It is the unrestrained Apollonian total-control, total-order, total-law states that have generated the greatest evil. The worst murderers have been found to be cool, orderly, calm, often distinguished by the ice of intellect that has frozen out the Love under Will that is, according to Aleister Crowley, the agent of the world's salvation.

In short, Crowley knew and confessed he was an "arsehole"; he was as surprised as anyone that such a wild card could be used for a higher purpose beyond enjoying himself at the devouring world's expense.

SEXUAL ALCHEMY

The great secret of the OTO consisted in the integration of Tantric theory and practice into Rosicrucian and alchemical typology, a viewpoint that was further claimed to have been in the possession of the Knights Templar, hence the name of the OTO. Ordo Templi Orientis, the Order of Oriental Templars, was a romantic conceit developed within German Freemasonry. Of course, there is no a priori reason to suppose that certain Knights Templar were ignorant of something like Tantric theory, but no link has been established despite great efforts and a good deal of romancing.

Just how this integration sounds can be gathered from Crowley's notes in a small Japanese vellum notebook that survives from 1912. It contains, among other things (such as "The Lesser Mass of the Gnostics"), "The Book of the Unveiling of the Sangria," wherein it is spoken of the Wine of the Sabbath of the Adepts.[69]

The cover of the book bears Crowley's seal as Baphomet, head of the British OTO, and the opening page of the "Book of Unveiling" bears a hand-drawn Templar cross with MERLIN in capitals beside it. Merlin was the name Reuss took as a brother of the order. We may then suppose that the work is the product of Crowley and Reuss getting their heads together, Reuss relying on Crowley's extraordinary gift of language—what better than to have a published poet write your rituals for you? The notes begin with a preliminary prayer couched in the language of Christian Masonic conventions:

> From Thine Hand, Oh Lord, cometh all Good. . . . Greeting and peace in the Most Sacred & Mysterious Name of the True & Living GOD Most High, and in the Word, and in the Holy Ghost. . . . Seek thou, and see; discover the inmost will of each thy knight and bind him to thee by an oath. Further, thou shalt test him through the last of the Ordeals. . . . For in this secret and in this alone resident the Godhead; yea, he that possessed it, is no more man, but GOD. . . . The favour of God, and the grace of Our Lord Jesus Christ, and the abiding of the Holy Spirit be with you now and evermore Amen.[70]

That done, we may "hear now the Secret of Secrets, the Key of all Magick, revealed unto me for your instruction and behoof by the loving kindness of the OHO [Reuss]."[71]

We now see Crowley's subtle reworking of Christian apocalyptic language into a strictly gnostic and sex-magickal interpretation. This method had been a favorite conceit of Crowley's for years, and he was expert at it. He had, for example, found that a poem (in the collection *Amphora*) in praise of Isis with the name Mary substituted for that of the goddess could be picked up and published by a Roman Catholic publisher (Burns and Oates, submitted anonymously to Wilfrid Meynell in 1912).

> I am the A and the Ω, the beginning and the end. I will give unto him that is athirst of the fountain of the water of life freely. He that over- cometh shall inherit all things, and I will be his GOD, and he shall be my Son. . . . Wherefore this is the Great Work, to attain into the Godhead . . . the way of attainment, the Gnostics and the Manichaeans

preserved it in their most secret assemblies as they had received it from the greatest of the Magi of Egypt; Our Lord Jesus Christ expressly established it through the mouth of the Beloved Disciple [St. John]: nor were the Ophites ignorant of this mystery, nor did the men that did [worship?] Mithras.

1. The secret hidden in the fable of Samson. This was the inmost secret of the knights of the Temple, and the Brethren of the Rosie Cross concealed it in their College of the Holy Ghost. From them and their successors through the Hermetic Brothers of Light have we received it directly and here declare it openly to you.[72]

The first hearers of this speech must have been enthralled:

This is the True Sacrament by which ye are partakers of the very body and blood of Our Lord Jesus Christ, not in His death, but in His resurrection. By this are ye made Children of Light, Fellows of the Holy Ghost, perfect pure, companions of the Sangraal, illustrious knights of the sacrosanct Order of Kadosh. . . . Come! . . . to take the water of life freely. . . . To thee do we entrust the arcanum Arcanorum, the Hidden treasure of the wise. Without it all is cold, inertia, death, with it Fire, Energy, genius, Creation. This is the Key to every door in the Kingdom of Heaven, this is the sceptre of all the Realms that Are. . . . DEUS EST HOMO: AS ABOVE, SO BELOW AS WITHOUT, SO WITHIN. There is no part of man that is not GOD and there is no part of GOD that hath not its counterpart in man. . . . Now learn also this, that God is never to be known by thee for all that thou knowest is but thy creation as truly as thou art his. . . . Our Lord and Saviour Jesus Christ, in His death who gave us the Spirit the Water & the Blood, as St John beareth witness in his Evangel. Hence is Jesus Christ Alpha and Omega, the symbol of the union of God and man.

Here then is a second Trinity. God, God-man, man and to this God-man our ancient brethren have given many names. And though this Name of Jesus Christ hath been universally blasphemed by Christians, yet this Name hath been acknowledged by the true Brothers of the Rosie Cross and that which is written of Him in the

Evangels and in the Epistles and in the Apocalypse is true, if it be interpreted in light by the adepts of the Stone. For in God-man is our salvation, in this we are both God and man.

. . . Therefore for their ill guarding of the secrets have the adepts been persecuted these 2000 years. Trust not a stranger; fail not of an heir![73]

We are now led into a description of Amrita in terms of the Christo-Hermetic mystery and a description of the sexual union in terms of conventional alchemy. We see drawings of two figures from the Altona Secret Symbols of the Rosicrucians (1785): Sun and Moon together in a tub, the open rose (yoni) on the cross (lingam). There is a drawing of an athanor, heated by a Bunsen burner (the symbol for Leo, the Lion, within it) ready to extend into a cucurbite flask in which is the symbol for Aquarius (water-bearer, the womb). The resultant is depicted as a flask on the top of which is the Hebrew letter Shin.[74]

Take an Athanor and Cucurbite and prepare a flask for this Wine of the Holy Ghost. Thou needest also a flame for the distillation. In the Athanor is thy Lion, in the Cucurbite is thine Eagle. Use first a gentle heat, increasing, at last a full flame until the Lion passeth over. Pour immediately the distillation into the flask prepared for it. . . . For this is the arcanum of the hierophants of old that in this cult of the Sun in Heaven and of the Phallus on Earth all men can unite, for that then these mysteries are reasonable and true, and no man can deny them. This is that which is written "Peace on Earth. Goodwill toward men!" and this is the true and final secret of Freemasonry.—Sun is it not the Great Architect of the Universe, the Father of the System, the Eidolon of the Macrocosm? and this Phallus, is it not the Great Architect of this other universe of Man, the Father of the Race, the Eidolon [image] of the Microcosm?[75]

Adjacent to a drawing of the vagina, Crowley has written: "Nuit is all that may be, and is shown by means of any one that is."[76] It ought to be obvious how the cosmogony of the *Book of the Law* fits in comfortably with the cosmosexual viewpoint, where Nuit is the womb and Hadit the seed, and the resultant universe the essence or elixir of life itself. In the Djeridensis "Commentary on the Book of the Law," Crowley wrote further on this identification of Nuit with Pan, the All:

> The Book of the Law shews forth all things as God. . . . I am the Point of View (as of the Artist) from which Nuit may be seen by all; for I am her inmost thought, her sense and her voice. The essence of a Man & Woman—each being a Star or sovereign God poised in Space by its own act. . . . This essence is all-worthy; adore it, and the light of all that may be shall be shed upon you. . . . Those who adore and love all things alike, for that they of Truth, are yet but few, and are not known of man. Yet being free of fear and lust their power controls the many whose souls are subject to limit, the limit of knowledge which is always two, and can be counted. Men adore Naught, although they deem Naught God and Man; thus the Pure Fool rules them, and saves them from base knowledge which is false. All acts are in truth acts of Love. Fulfill all Loves that may be, to the full. . . . Nuit is formed into an Image of a Woman, that she may be the symbol of all ways of Going in Love. She is our Goal and our own heart's essence of Will. She is Nature, who is glad at the birth of all that cometh forth. The Soul of Man floweth forth in Love unto the utmost spaces of the Stars, and hath his joy with all of them.[77]

Aleister Crowley's experiments with sexual magick did not really get going until he went to America in 1914, where he spent the war years, becoming a magus and very poor. As the heavy guns fired hundreds of thousands of shells from trench to trench across the western front of northeastern France, blowing countless young lives to smithereens, wasting the flower of a generation for no particular purpose that anyone can properly remember, Crowley expended hours on sex magick. The contrast makes for a disturbingly surreal juxtaposition.

He recorded the salient details of his operations in the best traditions of Baconian science, always with good humor and dedicated to ends consistent with his concept of the Great Work: the establishment of the Law of Thelema, the unveiling of the "company of heaven." This company celebrated humankind's hitherto occult potential, his divine identity, and the breaking down of all the mental bonds that had broken the will and bound humankind to millennia of misery and ignorance. He wrote to John Symonds on June 25, 1946, a year before his death, from his last home in Hastings, "The mainspring of my life is my Oath in the Order of A.A. [Astrum Argentium] to devote myself wholly to the uplifting of the human race. It is fair to say that any other motive which might influence my actions is no more than subsidiary to that great affirmation."[78]

Right through his diaries from 1914 to his death in 1947, there are countless operations to obtain success for his writings, for money to promote his ideas, for the establishment of the Law of Thelema, to acquire energy and magical power for himself and his pupils. Many he wrote up as being unsuccessful. He was quite plain about his failures. Frequently, the operations were simply overtaken by the pleasure of ecstasy and the point abandoned.

It is pertinent to ask why, if so much energy was expended on promoting his work by this method, he was not more successful. It may be early days yet. One thing is clear: There are now more works by Aleister Crowley on sale than there have ever been before, and his following grows consistently, in spite of enemies both outside the gate and in the court. But whether we can count this success or not is difficult to say. We may also doubt whether this is due in much part to sexual magick or to simply the inherent strength, clarity, humor, and truth of his point of view—or, of course, to the weaknesses of those who have taken an interest in him.

Crowley did not want slavish followers, so he said. He could be deliberately obnoxious simply to prevent some people from becoming obsessed with him. His ego undoubtedly craved attention (doesn't everybody's from time to time?), but he wanted people who had the guts to find their own path.

Often he was encumbered with people who were just lost with no real belief in themselves. He complained at one point that his pupils were not selfish enough; they did not really want to succeed, or believed from the outset that they could not. He once said, "You cannot teach the people who need to be taught." He preferred to help those who were already on their way. He did not consider that the full panoply of Magick was for everybody—artists at their best are natural magicians—but he never doubted that it could be useful for everybody, while some people would simply waste their potential without application of its disciplines. It should be remembered that he preferred to spend his time with artists, thinkers, literary people, prostitutes, and scientists.

Augustus John, signing off a letter to Crowley of June 24, 1946, wrote: "Do what thou wilt shall be the whole of the law. How right you are!"[79] Nancy Cunard wrote this to John Symonds (Crowley's literary executor and biographer) in 1949:

> He just could not stand fools and bores! He certainly was an artist and had due respect, and wonder for things of the senses (and they are many!). [When he died] I was in Mexico at that moment [December 1947] and revolted by the inevitable rubbish and muck and spite vented in "Time" and wanted to write and protest, and didn't for of course they would not have printed what I would have, succinctly, sent. . . . He was simply a DEAR with me. . . . I'm glad that I did know him later, after his Cefalu days. He signed my protests and came to anti-Nazi meetings and was admirable with an African. . . . That was the time that I began to like him, that summer of 1933 in London. . . . I don't know how I should sign otherwise than "Do what thou wilt." Obviously, if and when one can.[80]

A certain Andrew Green wrote to Symonds in July 1949: "He was wasted in England. In Persia, or India or Japan millions would have followed him."[81] And Alexander Watt, a pupil from Canada: "Were all these people [who followed his teaching] dupes? . . . the Wine was GOOD! . . . Such a bottle was Crowley."[82]

I shall leave the last word to Crowley himself, sitting in his flat at 93 Jermyn Street, London, on May 31, 1943, writing a letter to his friend Karl Germer's wife, Sascha:

> When you are wholly concentrated on your True Will, personal woes and worries tend to assume their real place. Everything that happens is all part of the plan; and when you can really see it as such, you become

indifferent to circumstances. For instance, all the ostracism and persecution which has been my lot for so many years appears to me as part
of the necessary condition for the historical view of me in times to
come. Of course it is very difficult not to react in an ordinary human
way to things that go wrong. In fact you ought to react according to
your nature; but there should be a city of refuge far removed from all
these tribulations, where you can see the battle in perspective.[83]

TWELVE

Light in the Jar

*It is not profitable to think about the Pleroma, for to do
that would mean one's dissolution.*

CARL JUNG, *THE SEVEN SERMONS TO THE DEAD*

The year in which Hiroshima and Nagasaki played guinea pig
to a desperate experiment in warfare also saw the discovery
of a group of texts that could revolutionize our understanding of religion in the West.

In December 1945, Muhammad Ali al-Samman and his brothers,
while digging for bird lime on Jabal al-Tarif near the village of Hamra
Dum, three hundred miles south of Cairo, came upon a jar about
twenty-four inches (60 cm) in height. Sealed by bitumen, the jar was
probably intended to be the last home for fifty-two books, bound into
thirteen volumes. This collection, now called the Nag Hammadi library,
was not published in its entirety in English until 1977, following a
checkered history of being passed piecemeal from one scholar to
another.

It is a curious coincidence that a library of predominantly Christian
Gnostic works (including several pagan works attributed to Hermes
Trismegistus), testifying to the fundamental vision that absolute reality
is spiritual, should come to light in an age characterized by intense
materialism. There is also an uncanny sense of the completion of a great
temporal cycle.

A river of gnostic influence had flowed both under the surface and in the open veins of Western culture since the day the jar was buried in about the year A.D. 367. At the head of that river stood a man under whose auspices a number of the texts were to be shared with scholarship. The scene was akin to a son meeting a long-lost father. In this case the son was Carl Gustav Jung (1875–1961), the founder of the Bollingen Foundation, which agreed to purchase Codex I of the Nag Hammadi library in August 1951.

CARL JUNG

In 1916, Jung had written an extraordinary work called *The Seven Sermons to the Dead* under the name of the Gnostic teacher "Basilides in Alexandria, city where East and West met":

> Hear ye: I begin with nothing. Nothing is the same as fullness. In the endless state, fullness is the same as emptyness. The Nothing is both empty and full. One may just as well state some other thing about the Nothing, namely that it is white or that it is black, or that it exists or that it exists not. That which is endless and eternal has no qualities, because it has all qualities.
>
> The Nothing, or fullness is called by us the PLEROMA. In it, thinking and being cease, because the eternal is without qualities. In it there is no one for if any one were, he then would be differentiated from the Pleroma and would possess qualities which would distinguish him from the Pleroma.
>
> In the Pleroma there is nothing and everything: it is not profitable to think about the Pleroma, for to do that would mean one's dissolution.[1]

When Carl Jung was handed the codex that contained the Gnostic Gospel of Truth in 1952, he said that all his life he had worked to know the secrets of the psyche "and these people knew already." Escaping from the dismal attic-unconscious of his former colleague Sigmund Freud, Jung's penetrating insight led him to a conception of the unconscious that he identified with the Gnostic Pleroma: an everlasting fountain of life-giving symbol, the divine plenitude, and projection of the unknown Father.

Jung's conception has been typified as the "self-regulating psyche," a somewhat mechanical description embodying the discovery that the unconscious plays the central role in the healing of the conscious mind. Jung discovered that many of his patients encountered numinous symbols in their dreams that, while often disturbing, were found to contain keys for effective psychoanalysis. These symbolic images partook of what Jung called the archetypes, a conscious application of gnostic archetype theory.

When the human being is faced with the unknown, archetypal material flows into consciousness through the medium of dreams, visions, and art. Thus could Jung explain that works of art had the power to bring humankind to a truer knowledge of the self than rational processes ever could: "The central ideas of Christianity are rooted in Gnostic philosophy, which, in accordance with psychological laws, simply had to grow up at a time when the classical religions had become obsolete. It was founded on the perception of symbols thrown up by the unconscious individuation process which always sets in when the collective dominance of human life fall into decay."[2]

Jung collected vast quantities of Hermetic books and manuscripts, particularly those connected with the symbolic world of alchemy. For him, Hermetic alchemy provided key after key for making a start in understanding the human psyche. Psychological concepts such as individuation, projection, and notions of the healing and integrity of the psyche in general he found prefigured in the obscurities and long-since-dismissed annals of the followers of Hermes.

Like John Dee before him, he could see that the Protestant Reformation of the sixteenth century had cut off many Westerners from their soul, and, in following a doctrinaire bibliolatry, had removed believers from the contents of their own authentic experience, breeding confused behavior and what were called neuroses.

Materialism in philosophy had turned the rich world of the soul to ice, and Jung believed that a revived and refreshed understanding of the way of Hermes—the uniter of estranged opposites—could bring the lost sheep back to themselves and their "right mind."

It is interesting that one of the first English writers to recognize the importance of Jung was Aleister Crowley. While approving of Jung's work in sending a torch beam into the unconscious, Crowley wryly observed that modern scientists were constantly stumbling on concepts that had been commonplaces of the enlightened magical tradition for centuries. Arrogant nineteenth-century historians and scientific theorists had condemned them to the pit of intellectual no return in the jubilee of Progress. Crowley observed the same phenomenon in the world of physics, which, as he and others predicted, finds itself ever closer to spiritual interpretations of humankind's place in the universe.

Jung did not regard it as his province to prove the existence of God. All he could say as a natural scientist was that since the word *archetype* contains the idea of something imprinted on the psyche, then one was at liberty to suppose an imprinter. When asked by John Freeman in 1961 whether he believed in God, Jung said, "I do not need to believe. I know."

Finding much in his psychology in tune with the ideas of the gnostic Jacob Böhme, Jung recognized that the unconscious contains a dynamic interrelation of light and darkness. To ignore the activity of the unconscious generates what Jung calls the shadow: repressed unconscious material that, if persistently ignored—that is, not brought to consciousness—may overwhelm and literally possess both individuals and whole peoples. A quotation from the Gnostic Gospel of Thomas both encapsulates and prefigures Jung's point of view: "That which you have will save you if you bring it forth from yourselves. That which you do not have within you will kill you if you do not have it within you."[3]

Jung was a kind of shaman who, in exploring spiritual worlds, came back to the Euro-tribe with healing knowledge. He foresaw, for example, how the manipulation of the shadow by demagogues like Adolf Hitler would result in cataclysmic events that we now recognize as evil—but which so many lost souls at the time utterly failed to perceive and were, overcome as they were, incapable of perceiving.

In the postwar period, intelligent and sensitive people owe a debt of gratitude to Jung, whose life and works have brought many to the light of spiritual being. Jung has shown satisfactorily that the isolated self is an ego-based fiction that denies that the individual has roots in the Pleroma and drinks from the ocean that Jung called the collective unconscious. Jung's insight has made it possible to see that the psychological determinants of all humankind share in one humanity; anything less than wholeness is a sin against the truth. We find our Self by losing our selves. For Jung, the gnostic Christ as the archetypal philosopher's stone is for Western people the symbol of complete individuation.

Jung's concern for wholeness in the psyche and projected worlds (his idea of projection is akin to gnostic alchemical emanationism) enabled him to rescue the alchemists from obscurity and to see in their conception of the *mysterium coniunctionis*[4] the path to wholeness. Jung's psychological holism (both whole and holy), combined with a spiritually based conception of ecology allied to the holistic cosmos revealed by quantum physics, has provided not only the blueprint for all that is good in the New Age movement but also the outline for a new cosmos. Many now believe that humankind must embrace the new paradigm if we are to avoid some of the catastrophic errors of the last four hundred years—rationalism, nationalism, dogmatism, and materialism.

Spirit, mind, and matter are interpenetrating realities that converge in cosmic humanity as we reach our highest level in the heroic return to the One. Jung has shown that this process must be enacted within the person before any attempt is made to externalize the process through religion or politics.

Shortly before his death, Jung informed his assistant of his "last dream." He dreamed of a huge block of cut stone in a landscape, a symbol of wholeness and, he declared, a promise for the future.

Jung, too, had been hit by the Stone.

THIRTEEN

Gnosis and the New Physics

Throughout the world the news will be trumpeted that you are engaged in labours, the purpose of which is to ensure that human knowledge and the empire of the human mind over matter shall not for ever continue to be a feeble and uncertain thing.

COMENIUS, *VIA LUCIS* (THE WAY OF LIGHT)

*I*t was inevitable that sooner or later physics would return to metaphysics. That is, after all, how it began: with the gnostic search for the One behind all phenomena. The desire to understand and master matter; the quest for the spirit imprisoned in matter; the chasing of the light diffused throughout nature in divine signatures; the central role of humankind, the Great Miracle, as bridge between the visible and the invisible—all are gnostic themes. And they all influenced the quest for science.

From the time of Friar Bacon to Michael Maier's *Atalanta fugiens* (1617) and beyond, the scientific effort has been characterized by the appearance of spectacles: instrumental apparatus to aid the carnal eyes in making a theory of nature. This effort was predicated upon Christ's dictum "The truth will make you free." Investigation of nature's laws was thus regarded at the outset of the sixteenth-century scientific endeavor as a Hermetic pursuit. Know nature, know the creator; know thyself: ergo, become free of nature. It was in a sense a quest for virginity; scientists wear white for their chemical nuptials.

The quotation from Comenius that begins this chapter also contained a warning to the youthful Royal Society of 1668. Should the spiritual ends of knowledge be subsumed beneath the purely material, then the work might well degenerate into "a Babylon turned upside down, building not towards heaven, but towards earth."[1]

This transpired to be prophetic. State and privately funded scientific knowledge has come for many to represent not a liberation but a threat. It seems the more power over nature we have attained, the more critically dependent on nature we have become. Resources dwindle, and Mother Nature is unwell. The blame has been placed, somewhat unfairly, at the door of the mechanistic philosophies embodied or deduced from some of the works of Newton, Bacon, and Descartes and of rationalist philosophers such as Locke, Hume, and Mill. But human beings find it difficult not to see the world in terms of their own ideals and, more especially, thoughts.

It was especially difficult for them to resist deifying their rational constructs and even the rational principle itself when faced with the enormous practical success of reason's application. Machines worked. It was difficult not to see the universe as an objective, mechanistic system, external to mind and indifferent to the spiritual. Likewise today, it is a popular idea to see the brain as a computer and to eulogize the advantages of artificial intelligence while eschewing the abiding value of the real thing.

The scientific revolution represented a wonderful opportunity not only for craftspeople of unbelievable ingenuity, but also for every moron who would like to rape all mystery out of existence. The objective, the visible, the tangible, the observable: These represented the real universe of science. Away with angels and subtle forces and the whole panoply of magic and the (organically) invisible spirit; matter was real, vital, all-inclusive. Numbers were firm, solid, reliable. Intellection was masculine.

The Hermetists with their organic doctrines of mind *in extenso* were out of date; theology had nothing to do with practical, realistic science. God the demiurge-mechanician, the bored Hephaestus of the stars, had created the cosmos and had handed over the reins of the cosmic chariot to an evolutionary, mathematical process whose "selfish genes" were destined to give birth to man the toolmaker, separated surveyor of all he saw and an idol unto himself. So we see the symmetrical inversion of the truth. In short, matter was real. Spirit was a matter of opinion.

Although this mentality still dominates most Western thinking and commerce and is trundled out thoughtlessly in our places of education, the triumphal ecstasy of materialist science had begun to wane even before World War I, at the very height of what has since come to be called "classical" physics. "Classical" was a suitably pretentious name for an era of gathering humanistic certainties.

Everything in the cool materialist garden looked more or less rosy until around the turn of the century, at which time were born a number of people destined to become physicists. They were Werner Heisenberg, Wolfgang Pauli, Max Born, Pascual Jordan, and Paul Dirac, born to build with and build on the work of Max Planck, Ernest Rutherford, Erwin Schrödinger, Niels Bohr, and Albert Einstein. Their minds opened upon an unexpected world: the world of the atom, the elementary building block of what was then conceived to constitute matter— that is, as far as mainstream science was concerned, reality.

A year after Aleister Crowley received the highly relativistic *Book of the Law* (1904), promising revolutionary children and an era of force and fire, Albert Einstein published his general theory of relativity, in which he proved mathematically that space and time were relative, not absolute, conditions of the universe—relative, that is, to the speed at which the observer or observing apparatus was traveling.

Einstein identified mass with energy and showed that nothing could be expected to travel faster than light (an idea highly suggestive to gnostics). Beyond 186,000 miles per second, the idea of traveling anywhere collapsed. Putting it another way, if two photons (from the Greek, light-beings), or light-energy particles, were traveling in opposite directions at the speed proper to light, and if one were to affect the other, we would need to postulate a fourth dimension, even the rupture of linear time. A photon "knows" no time. Such theories were unsettling. The machine rattled.

If mass was energy, what did this energy consist of? Energy, in physical terms, is a measured effect—to be precise, the effect of activity associated with and within atoms. Since atoms release energy at measurable (but not necessarily consistent) intervals, it was reasonable to assume that unlike the atoms of Democritus, they are not irreducible solids—as if the creation was the work of a three-dimensional *pointilliste*—but hide within them a world of their own. This world is called the subatomic world, beyond the senses and, to some extent, the logic of sense, and is the particular province of quantum physics.

Quantum physics has to do with quantities of energy (called quanta) emitted from atoms under certain conditions. In particular, energy registers as light, called photons, as well as electrons, particles bearing electrical charges loosed from proximity to the nuclei of atoms, interacting with other subatomic particles (variations of which are still being discovered and given tentative names like quarks and gluons).

In spite of what we were taught in physics at school—the famous atom of Bohr (a mini-nucleocentric cyclic universe, wrapped in a spherical shell)—we should not picture the atom in this fashion, except for general visual appropriation of indeterminate phenomena. We can have no solid picture of the atom at all.

What appears to be the atom is a dynamic set of relationships so small that were we to remove manually each atom from a spoonful of carbon in reverse time, we should still be scooping them at the time when the universe is currently thought to have originated. That's fifteen billion years ago.

An atom is to be regarded as a set of statistical probabilities, indefinite knowledge of whose behavior has been found to have useful applications, from lasers and microchips to DNA and holograms. In fact, the atom has been described as being more like a cloud than an object, a cloud of electromagnetic activity—a description highly suggestive in gnostic parlance.

In gnosis, the cloud is a regular symbol for the illusory or gross body, the idea behind which has to do with the veiling of the sun. When, for example, it is written that "a cloud received Him [Christ] out of their sight" (Acts 1:9), we may take it to signify that the Logos (creative Mind) incarnate became imperceptible to carnal sense.

Likewise, the world of subatomic physics is imperceptible to the senses, except through apparatus cleverly designed according to preconceived types and ranges of measurable phenomena. The beauty of quantum physics is that observations suggest from within themselves the experimental shortcomings of the process of observation itself. We can now join in qualified assent to William Blake's assertion that the atom is "a thing that does not exist," something he observed without recourse to external apparatus, but in keeping with the vision granted him by what he called the Divine Imagination. It may be said that the impact of that imagination is now being observed by scientists.

Carl Jung, when examining the thought-world of gnostic alchemy, came up with a formula of perception pertinent to this study. Jung recognized that on confronting the unknown, when the conscious mind is at a loss to ratiocinate the mysterious phenomenon before it, the unconscious mind projects images and ideas from an interior well of archetypes onto the external phenomenon, uniting the subject to the object. The mind makes matter meaningful—not surprisingly, if we see matter as a manifestation of mind. Thus, the alchemists saw the chemical process as embodying a spiritual or at least psychic process and perceived themselves to be united with it.

After Newton, we can broadly say that where the study of physics was concerned, rational cause-and-effect, linear mathematics proved adequate to explain a whole range of natural phenomena, from the planets to plastic. Come the advent of quantum physics, reaching its first high-water mark in the late 1920s, Jung's formula comes back into play. As scientist and author of *The Tao of Physics,* Fritjof Capra, said in 1982: "I now believe that the world view of mystical tradition is the best and most appropriate philosophical background for the theories of modern science." In this setting it would be most surprising if we did not find ideas familiar to the history of Hermetic thought, when theorizers attempt to interpret the sub- or even nonatomic world. What had quantum physics to assert that could lead to such a conclusion?

THE COPENHAGEN INTERPRETATION

At first sight the association does not look too promising. A meeting of physicists held at Lake Como in Italy in September 1927 saw Niels Bohr reveal what has since become known as the Copenhagen interpretation of quantum mechanics. (Bohr was in Denmark when he worked it out.) The theory runs as follows: When a choice is made to measure precisely the position of a particle (such as an electron), the process of measurement forces the particle to develop more uncertainty with regard to its momentum. The reverse is also the case. Science will have to be content with the knowledge that precise measurements of momentum and position of particles is impossible—only probabilistic formulas can be applied.

These formulas are, nonetheless, highly useful. Among other things, this apparent block on knowledge means that the future cannot be statistically predicted, which, in classical physics, was always a theoretical possibility in the context of a universe consisting of separate components obeying fixed laws. These features of quantum theory also contributed to Heisenberg's uncertainty or indeterminacy principle.

This has been expressed by Professor David Bohm as the discovery that "even if one supposes that the physically significant variables actually exist with sharply defined values (as is demanded by classical mechanics) then we could never measure them all simultaneously, for the interaction between the observing apparatus and what is observed always involves an exchange of one or more indivisible and uncontrollably fluctuating quanta."[2] This was quite a blow to the old school.

Furthermore, in quantum physics the observer participates in the system of observation to such an extent that the system cannot be viewed as independent. That meant, at least in the quantum context, *au revoir* to the Cartesian notion of an external universe, independent of cognition. Most significant, it had been discovered that the energy we call an electron may become manifest both as a wave and as a particle, depending on the measuring conditions.

In the famous (idealized) two-slit experiment, we are asked to imagine a wall seen from above, with two holes spaced apart. In front of the wall is an electron gun and behind it, a detector. When a single electron is aimed at the wall, the pattern displayed on the detector indicates wave interference. This extraordinary phenomenon suggests that the electron has gone through both holes at once, in the form or function of a wave, and interfered with itself.

The electron "knows" that both holes are open. Yet, if observed, an electron is seen to go through one hole or the other, and is registered on the detector as a particle. It is as though the electron experiences or even creates a parallel world in which it is in two places at once—a process that can never be observed directly, for the moment an attempt is made to do so, the wave function immediately collapses. The particle "knows" it is being watched! It also behaves as if it knows what other particles are doing. In this context, objective knowledge of a supposed material world is simply impossible.

We are currently unable to know how an electron particle can suddenly function as a wave and what, if anything, happens in between. In the words of Professor John Gribbin: "It is interesting that there are limits to our knowledge of what an electron is doing when we are looking at it, but it is absolutely mind-blowing to discover that we have no idea at all what it is doing when we are not looking at it."[3]

No wonder Niels Bohr was moved to declare, "Anyone who is not shocked by quantum theory has not understood it." Going farther down the metaphysical road, Gribbin asserts in his book *In Search of Schrödinger's Cat* (1984): "Nothing is real when we look at it, and it ceases to be real as soon as we stop looking." Not only has the Machine fallen to pieces, but the pieces are not pieces anymore as well.

Einstein for one was most disturbed, and he (and others) spent years trying to fill in the gaps left by the collapse of linear, classical logic, with the formulation of what are called hidden variables to account for the illogical and uncertain character of the quanta.

In the quantum world the left hand always knows what the right hand is doing. In physics, this idea is called the theory of complementarity. Complementarity involves compensations in energy made "between" separate photons traveling apart at the speed of light with no known three-dimensional medium joining them.

Yet in spite of the fact that nothing we know can travel faster than the speed of light, one photon can indeed affect the other. According to Einstein, "No reasonable definition of reality could be expected to permit this."[4] The theory of complementarity was proved decisively in the summer of 1982 in a series of experiments conducted at the University of Paris-South by a team led by Alain Aspect.

John Gribbin concludes: "The experiments prove that there is no

:lying reality to the world."[5] It is difficult to see precisely what the .mably unreal Gribbin means by this astonishing statement. If quantum effects are real (and human perception is a valid approach to the real—a big *if*), they cannot demonstrate themselves out of existence.

I understand him to mean that a world of three dimensions cannot sustain itself alone. The idea of a relatively material universe has broken down—but then it could be suggested that such a world is only an idea after all! This will come as little surprise to students of gnosis, in whose domain matter has long been symbolized by water. Water—or clouds—represents energy in flux whose ultimate basis is ultimately unknowable by ratiocination: the Ungrund of Böhme; the Ain Soph of the kabbalists; the Bythos of the Valentinians; the cosmic Nothing of Pico and Crowley; the Hermetic Good, source of Mind.

In the gnostic conception, All ($\pi\alpha\nu$) is projection from source into greater complexity and obscurity. The human being, with a foot in both worlds, is understandably perplexed. However, the Buddhist notion of the world as maya (whose root is shared by the Sanskrit *matra,* measure), or illusion, can be, and frequently is, taken to the extreme that the world does not exist.

It might be more illustrative to say that the world bears an illusory character if we take our sense of it at any point to be absolute (the essence of materialism). The world constantly breaks down into partly chaotic activity the more we analyze it—that is, take it as the real by breaking the whole into parts. As Dean Inge observed, "A journey through the unreal is an unreal journey,"[6] and it is not only the first Gnostics and last existentialists who have held the view that this journey, though vexatious to the soul, may not be totally in vain.

Those who have explored other dimensions of consciousness have seldom returned to say that this one is a complete waste of time. The positive aspect of the Hermetic vision invites us to explore the mind of God, in whose projection we may be conscious participants, having experienced gnosis. We can, if we so choose, go along for the ride; we can follow the Law of Thelema: Do what thou wilt!

Nearly two thousand years ago, a writer of a Hermetic dialogue pondered the problem of what it was that bodies or, in our case, photons, moved in:

Hermes: All movement then takes place within something that stands fast, and is caused by something that stands fast. . . .

The movement of the cosmos then, and of every living being that is material, is caused, not by things outside the body, but by things within it, which operate outwards from within; that is to say, either by soul or by something else that is incorporeal.

. . . I have now explained to you what is that by which things are moved, as well as what is that in which things are moved.

Asclepius: But surely, Trismegistus, it must be in void that things are moved.

Hermes: You ought not to say that, Asclepius. Nothing that is, is void; it is only that which is not, that is void.

. . . Is not air a body? . . . And does not that body permeate all things that are, and fill them by its permeation? . . . Hence the things which you call void ought to be called hollow, not void; for they are full of something that exists.

Asclepius: There is no gainsaying that, Trismegistus.

Hermes: Now what was it that we said of that Space in which the universe is moved? We said, Asclepius, that it is incorporeal.

Asclepius: What then is that incorporeal thing?

Hermes: It is Mind, entire and wholly self-encompassing, free from the erratic movement of things corporeal; it is imperturbable, intangible, standing firm-fixed in itself, containing all things, and maintaining in being all things that are; and it is the light whereby soul is illuminated.

Asclepius: Tell me then, what is the Good?

Hermes: The Good is the archetypal Light; and Mind and Truth are, so to speak, rays emitted by that Light.

Asclepius: What then is God?

Hermes: God is He that is neither Mind nor Truth, but is the cause to which Mind and Truth, and all things, and each several thing that is, owe their existence.[7]

Because gnosis is concerned with the elementary character of consciousness, we should not be surprised to find unprejudiced attention to matter throwing up classically gnostic features; the wave/particle duality is an obvious example. Duality is the character of creation from a primal unity in all gnostic systems, and emphasized at the core of the I Ching, Tantra, and, indeed, all rational intellection (thesis/antithesis—synthesis, or, more properly, thesis/antithesis—annihilation of thought).

The core of the Gnostic Anthropos is alien to this duality, and from a purely gnostic perspective, it is no surprise that the once godlike objective observer of nature has, in quantum studies, "fallen" into matter and been united with his observations—like that fatal aesthete Narcissus. He thinks he is investigating nature but finds instead that he is exploring some of the contents of his own creative mind. No wonder he is entranced! This possible confusion is what seems to have irritated Einstein so much. How could there be science without absolute objectivity? To which one might respond: How could there be objects without absolute rationality?

This process of projecting ideal archetypal unconscious contents onto the findings of quantum physics is most noticeable in the influential works of David Bohm, late professor of theoretical physics at Birkbeck College, London. Bohm's interpretation of quantum physics suggested to him that the cosmos bears inherent continuity, a universe of co-inherent extension, the whole (including mind and matter) enfolded at all possible points with wholeness or "holomovement" (the essence of holistic theory) governed by a universal holonomy as its essential nature: "undivided wholeness in flowing movement," he called it.

"In this flow mind and matter are not separate substances," Bohm wrote in his striking book *Wholeness and the Implicate Order,* which reads very much like a description of the Stoic world-soul, the *anima mundi,* the grainy god of paganism and of its corollary, pantheism. There are also strong suggestions of pre-Socratic concepts deriving from Anaximander and Heraklitos: All is Flux. Bohm's vision also bears many remarkable similarities to that of the gnostic Giordano Bruno: the universe as a total energy system of infinite potential, "a synthesis of infinite relativity,"[8] expressing nous rooted in other dimensions.

For Bruno, an infinite universe is the only possible expression of an eternal God.[9] Where Bruno sees infinity in the extension of space, Bohm sees it in an unending enfoldment of reality, the holomovement.

Likewise, we are reminded of Nicholas of Cusa's use of the Hermetic geometrical apotheosis: God is an infinite sphere whose center is everywhere, circumference nowhere.

Bohm could have taken as his text Christ's saying that if a house be divided against itself, it cannot stand, for he deduces an ethical imperative from the quantum survey. He believes that the physics of his holomovement has immediate practical consequences, providing a noetic basis for the struggle against fragmentation of the world and its resources (ecology), fragmentation of the mind (psychology and psychiatry), fragmentation of the body (medicine), and the painful fissures throughout human society (politics).

What difference will acceptance of this truth make? As Johann Valentin Andreae found in the seventeenth century, the truth—whether from science or from any other quarter—is mostly despised and her followers shunted into cloisters. We need more than thoughts to sustain us; something like an active principle of complementarity would do the trick. These photons seem to love one another as themselves.

Samuel Taylor Coleridge had a similar vision to Bohm's, calling it the One Life, which his famous Mariner transgressed in a moment's thoughtlessness. This is the *unus mundus* of the alchemists (that which is above is like that which is below; to work the miracle of the One Thing), Blake's marriage of heaven and hell, a baby in a backyard stable in Bethlehem—the Hermetic romance.

In answer to those who would see such a vision as an idealistic goal still to be achieved, we have the assertion of John Lennon (a man who had had a bellyful of the illusion of the world) that it is not that we want the world to be one. It is One, hence "One World One People" appeared on the run-out groove of his last record. Elias Ashmole's armorial motto says much the same thing (with a suggestive construction denying simplistic monism): EX UNO OMNIA—certainly more practical than the somewhat premature *E Pluribus Unum,* on which the United States and other social idealisms have foundered.

This all ties in with the gnostic vision that duality and the accompanying phenomenon of separateness, isolation, and alienation represented the central problem in the nature of consciousness in three dimensions (the hylic hell). The gnostic goal was to participate in the restoration of the Pleroma, the fullness of God as a dynamic, equilibrated whole.

Three-dimensional consciousness represented the fall from a protean unity, with its fixation on the illusion of real objects and accompanying desires and pains. This is important, since gnostics are too frequently called dualists. In their consistent (Hermetic) form, gnostics were and are—when properly understood—antidualists. To communicate to the world-fixated being the gnostic message that materialist perception leaves us in a prison without light, it was perhaps necessary to concretize the idea that immersion in matter was a terrible thing and should be resisted and overcome. Materialist consciousness is a very hard nut to crack. It is in all of us and is everywhere about us. The real difficulty is that it is relatively true!

The Hermetic gnosis is weighted very heavily against the idea of creation as evil, while Aleister Crowley was adamant that dualism of matter and spirit was anathema, since matter may be seen as a manifestation of mind. The ideal gnostic state, which Raja Yoga calls samadhi (union with God), is expressed by the Logos incarnate in St. John's Gospel as "I and my Father are one"—a statement anathematized in its turn by those who believe in an external God, separate from an external material world. The classic illusion of low-level human perception thus turns God into a materialist.

Lama Govinda, a modern Buddhist scholar, expresses union with God in these terms: "This experience does not dissolve the mind into an amorphous All, but rather brings the realisation that the individuality itself contains the totality focalised at its very core."[10] This compares interestingly with Aleister Crowley's dhyana experience in Sri Lanka in 1901, which brought him a vision of the divinity of the human archetype, itself akin to Ezekiel's vision of God in human form in his famous prophecy (1:26), so like Blake's glorious Albion.

Other facets of quantum theory abound in suggestive parallels with familiar gnostic themes. As stated earlier, a photon moving at the speed of light does not know time. A light particle emitted at the time of the Big Bang (a demiurgical image, as Hans Jonas has observed) and traveling outwardly ever since would, at the end of time, be back where it started: both alpha and omega, beginning and end. Does this not indicate a phenomenon akin to Plato's description of time in his *Timaeus* as "the moving image of eternity"?

The experience of timelessness that characterizes the essential gnostic experience is thus shown not to be the delusion of an overheated brain but rather *less* illusionary than the average consciousness.

The principle of complementarity suggests that everything in the universe, past, present, and future, is connected to everything else. Each thing somehow holds an image of everything as a whole within it. Spare a thought for the limitations of language! Everything is connected within a web of electromagnetic radiation that functions as if it were omniscient, omnipresent, and even omnipotent (bringing particles forth seemingly *ex nihilo* and transcending linear time when occasion demands).

These features, normally associated with an external deity, appear to function in the nature of . . . things (?). Thus the Hermetic axiom so important to a practical mystic like John Dee: *Mundus imago dei* (the world is the image of God) is to believers a valid inference from the results of experimental physics.

There is much in quantum physics to suggest a kind of pantheism. That is to say, if you see the universe as interweaving matrices of energy, then is this energy in toto, GOD? It is a tempting thought.

However, this idea of God as a binding intelligence, or even a blind force working on automatic mathematical pilot, reads very much more like the Gnostics' crazy Demiurge (identified by Blake with the rational faculty in mournful isolation), whose work is that which can be bound and measured (Law), than the unknowable Father who can, paradoxically, be known in the spirit. It very much depends on whether you conceive of the universe as a spiritual system in sensible manifestation or as a statistical system of abstracts in which we find ourselves.

The inevitable tendency of physics, when we consider the premises of experimental observation in the Baconian mold, is toward the latter. But in spite of Stephen Hawking's amusing tease that science will show us "the mind of God" (especially when the reverse might equally be the case), it is doubtful if we know enough about the universe to be anything like conclusive on this question.

The prodigious mathematician Kurt Gödel's incompleteness theorem, formulated in the 1930s, not only seems to presage some aspects of current chaos theory but also, according to Larry Dossey, M.D., writing about the primacy of nonlocal mind, shows that nature's laws, if they are consistent as we believe them to be, must be of some inner formulation quite different from anything we know[11] and which, at present, as Bronowski put it, "we have no idea how to conceive."[12]

Personally, I find the term *panentheism* useful: the concept that God is in the All, and the All is in God—but that the All is not God. This view leaves more rooms in the many mansions of the divine house open for inspection. And like those electrons that seem to keep freedom of direction open to the very, very last instant—and may alter course or even form when observed—this formulation (and that is all it is) seems to guarantee freedom from being dominated by matter. This is what the Hermetically influenced Comenius hoped would characterize the work of systematic science in the Royal Society.

Furthermore, we may doubt that spirit—or, more particularly, mind—is an activity of what is called electromagnetism on the same basis that we doubt the nineteenth-century paraphysical speculation that God was embodied in the supposed medium of ether. We may just end up with another phlogiston: a nonexistent substance dreamed up to fit a preconceived formula.

St. Paul said that "spiritual things are spiritually discerned"—and when we grasp the meaning of this, we may see a renewed theology once more become the reigning queen of the sciences—so long, that is, as theologians do not become the reigning queens. God, Blake tells us, is not a spiritual diagram.

We may also wonder how it could possibly be that such ideas as the primacy of mind (apprehended in the Hermetic nous); the plurality of multidimensional worlds; the human being as microcosm (reflecting and creating the macrocosmos, the whole present in the parts—a deduction of Bohm from quantum theory); the interpenetration and (mainly) orderly correspondence of all things in the astromagical doctrine; the effectiveness of willed magical gestures (note the "butterfly effect" in chaos theory); the significance of randomness in guaranteeing freedom and extradimensional guidance (from the Urim and Thummim to the Tarot and I Ching); precognition; the illusion of matter; the creation of the universe as a consequence of a disturbed prior equilibrium (the universe as a result of vacuum fluctuation and asymmetry, a deduction from quantum theory); the idea of a nonlocal mind affecting matter—and indeed the whole idea of God and eternity—could have arisen without humankind possessing faculties superior to sense perception for thousands of years (at least). All these ideas arose long before systematic physics had even found its way out of Plato's cave. If humans lacked such faculties, it is difficult to see how physics itself could ever have emerged.

We can only conclude that contrary to the materialist delusion, humans, in their essential being, are, as the Hermetic philosophy asserts, superior to their senses in ways we have hardly begun to grasp. It seems that our only obstruction is ourselves.

In this context, it would not be going too far to say that physics, along with the other sciences, is advancing "back" toward her glorious status as the practical and applied aspect of spiritual gnosis.

In the words of the quantum physicist Erwin Schrödinger: "We may, or so I believe, assert that physical theory in its present stage strongly suggests the indestructibility of Mind by Time."[13]

The British physicist Paul Davies has remarked that physicists "have learned to approach their subject in totally unexpected and novel ways that seemed to turn common sense on its head and find closer accord with mysticism than materialism. . . . Science has actually advanced to the point where what were formerly religious questions can be seriously tackled."[14]

If all this appears to some minds to be antiscientific, this is far from my intention. It is simply to say that there is a persistent tendency to use science as a proof for religious ideas and, less frequently, vice versa. This must, ultimately, be as vain as supposing that archaeology could prove that Moses was who the Bible says he was, or that the Turin shroud could prove to be as miraculous as the resurrection of Christ is supposed to have been.

"First comes the bread, then the morals,"[15] as Brecht put it. The archetypes create us, not we them, as (the gnostic) Jung has shown. The mind that observes nature is—at its highest point, synthesis, or evolution—gnostic, seeking knowledge of its freedom. Undoubtedly such a mind, even if it is as maimed by the overdependence on sense or reason as ours are, will discover a gnostic universe, for it is an article of knowledge in gnosis that the mind that creates the universe is shared among us, should we choose to be participants in it.

We all go back before the Big Bang, and what we uncover in its extension is nothing more nor less than ourselves.

"Now fix your thought upon the Light." he said, "and learn to know it." And when he had thus spoken, he gazed long upon me, eye to eye, so that I trembled at his aspect. And when I raised my head again, I saw in my mind that the Light consisted of innumerable Powers, and had come to be an ordered cosmos, but a cosmos without bounds. This I perceived in thought, seeing it by reason of the logos [spiritual mind] which Poimandres had spoken to me, "You have seen in your mind the archetypal form, which is prior to the beginning of things, and is limitless."

Thus spoke Poimandres to me.[16]

In perception, as in love, we receive but what we give.

FOURTEEN

Gnosis Today: A Personal View

The Oriental once experienced the world in himself, and in his spiritual life he now hears its echoes; the western man is at the start of his experience and has set out to find his way in the world. If he wished to become a yogi, a westerner would have to become an out and out egoist, for Nature has conferred on him that consciousness of self that to the oriental was no more than a dream experience; if the yogi, like the westerner, had sought to discover himself in the world, he would have taken his dream experience with him into unconscious sleep and would have been like a drowned soul.

RUDOLF STEINER, WRITING ON THE OCCASION OF
THE EAST-WEST CONGRESS IN VIENNA, 1922

RUDOLF STEINER

The world that emerged out of the rubble of World War II has been fortunate to witness the continued development of the ideas and practical dreams of Rudolf Steiner, a man whom Aleister Crowley considered to be an adept of high attainment and whose spiritual system, called Anthroposophy, is of undoubted gnostic provenance.

Steiner was born in Kraljevec in Austria in 1861. At the age of twenty-one, after having taken his degree in mathematics, physics, and chemistry, he was invited to edit a prestigious edition of the scientific writings of Goethe. Goethe's romantic vision coalesced with Steiner's peculiar spiritual consciousness. He came to realize the terrible future awaiting humankind should we continue to disregard the spiritual dimension and source of life. Furthermore, he believed that the claims of spirituality needed to be tested scientifically, an attitude that led to the concept of "spiritual science," which could test spiritual claims by direct experience and would not outrage the sense of reason.

In 1902, Dr. Steiner joined the Theosophical Society and became editor of its journal *Lucifer-Gnosis,* but he grew to doubt whether the Theosophical stress on Eastern philosophy was appropriate for the Western mind. He had also come to see the central importance of the incarnation of Jesus Christ in human spiritual evolution—whereas many Theosophists saw Jesus as one among many avatars and tended to depersonalize his message.

In February 1913, the Anthroposophical Society was instituted. Steiner said that Anthroposophy meant, quite simply, "awareness of one's humanity." He saw his system arising from Rosicrucian foundations and believed that Christian Rosenkreuz was the name of an adept being who periodically incarnated through history as a spiritual guide. He derived this idea from the old Rosicrucian tradition of the Hidden Masters. He wrote, "By way of our stream it is possible to penetrate into true Rosicrucianism, but our way must not be designated as 'Rosicrucianism' because our stream encompasses a far broader realm than that of the Rosicrucians, namely the whole of Anthroposophy."[1]

Steiner himself was always careful to avoid the pitfall whereby Anthroposophy would become a narrow sect. His desire was to make esoteric wisdom the common possession of the humanity from which it was derived. His ideas encompassed a fully developed system of education (Steiner schools still thrive around the world), art and performance, sociology, therapeutic treatment for disturbed children (1924), a spiritual church called The Christian Community (founded 1921–22), medicine, and agriculture.

He wished people to test his ideas for themselves and desired that his tree be judged by its fruits. He was approached by doctors, therapists, businesspeople, academics, scientists, teachers, theologians, pastors, and farmers.

In 1989 the author was invited to explore the Warmonderhof Anthroposophical Farm in Holland and spoke to its director, Art Schiemann: "The application of Anthroposophy to agriculture is very diverse," he told me. "I think it boils down to taking care of the natural process. When you farm, you are bringing a piece of wild nature into culture. In essence that's what it's about. We try to do that in a most respectful way.

"We preserve and conserve as much as possible of the value that the landscape gives to us: all the living things in the earth. Anthroposophy teaches us the way to see these processes and their connection with the earth and the movements that exist in the cosmos.

"I learn daily to observe the life cycles in plants and animals along with the influences of astronomical conjunctions during the year. Everyone takes it for granted that the moon has an influence on the tidal movements of the sea, but Anthroposophy teaches me with every passing day that the influence of the cosmos reaches out far further than just the things we see with our eyes."

The Warmonderhof farm represents a very beautiful and orderly expression of Steiner's philosophy. Apart from the down-to-earth experience of finding the many plants and root crops to be very healthy (and tasty), Steiner's "biodynamic" farming methods, incorporating a host of occult lore, give the farm an extraordinary atmosphere. It is a strange experience to feel the presence of the stars and the great patterns of cosmic movement (so little of which we really understand) in the bright blue daytime. It is also fascinating to witness how well nature responds to techniques practiced in a state of spiritual mindfulness. I asked the director if he considered himself to be a gnostic: "In a meditative sense, yes, I would," he answered, "but a very modern one, pretty skeptical, very shortsighted, very short of all the sense instruments I presumably had about three or four centuries ago. I can just about observe something of the movement of the stars, but I can't observe Venus in daylight as they did four hundred or five hundred years ago when they had to navigate on the sea. I know the tidal movement is there, and when I meditate early in the morning if I'm not too tired, I get a real feeling that I relate to spiritual levels that help and stimulate me to do the daily tasks I have to do."

Warmonderhof is not only a government-approved agricultural training center, but it is also able to support itself by selling fresh bio-dynamic food, for which there is a growing market.

Anthroposophical farming has also pioneered the use of "flow-form" sculptures through which water passes downward in a step system, purifying itself through rythmical impulses.[2] Within each step is a sculpted imprint that encourages the water to cascade in figure eights. Advanced ecologists on the Continent and in England (such as the hydrosopher Julian Jones, based in Stroud) are now using flow-forms in conjunction with reed beds to effect a cheaper and far more effective sewage purification system than those available through chemical treatment methods.

It has been said that if we get our understanding of water flow right, as a worldwide phenomenon, innumerable ecological benefits will follow.[3] Steiner and his followers have pioneered a new and eminently practical understanding of the occult (hidden) properties of water. I asked Art Schiemann if he considered Steiner to be a prophet: "I think that Rudolf Steiner foresaw, years before it happened, that humankind—and not only Western humankind, but humankind all over the world—has to be helped through a narrow passage into another time.

"There is a fast movement going on. I have the feeling I'm part of it, a very small particle, but it's a fast movement from a very mystical kind of knowledge hundreds of years ago, through a very difficult time now where everything has become mechanical, into a time in which I expect and trust humankind will again have contacts with the spiritual levels and with spiritual beings, and will recover a natural relation to its origin and its destiny."

GNOSIS AND ECOLOGY

I once met a representative of England's Green Party at a local by-election. He showed me a list of things about which the Green candidate was discouraged from speaking. On the list of contentious issues was the word *spirituality*. It was presumably considered that a spiritual interpretation of phenomena might bring disgrace and embarrassment to the Green cause.

From the point of view of spiritual philosophy, we might also think it strange to posit a positive relationship between gnosis and the general ecological crisis. We might assume that the world of nature is inimical to gnostic concerns, insofar as gnosis has too often been considered to be a totally dualist philosophy, regarding nature as something at worst to be fled from and at best something to be suspicious of. We ought also to remember that humankind's mastery over some natural forces has been hard won, and is a recent development.

In fact the Hermetic gnostic experience is of great significance to the ecological debate. The Smaragdine Table of Hermes Trismegistus declares, "That which is above is like that which is below; and that which is below is like that which is above: to work the miracle of the one thing."[4]

The realization of the "one thing," the whole movement of spirit and matter, is a bona fide gnostic experience. It is a question of state of mind. A holy mind will manifest in an ordered environment; an unbalanced mind will manifest in a chaotic environment. A mind dominated by materialist consciousness has no sound relationship with the world of nature, for in the Hermetic gnosis, mind and nature form a single spiritual system.

As quantum physics demonstrates, nature is not essentially material. From the gnostic point of view, nature is involved in a graded system of being that encompasses a range of visible and invisible worlds. The appearance of materiality is a passing and transient vision suitable to the discernment of the physical senses. There are countless records of visionary experiences where these principles have become apparent to consciousness. Such consciousness has been the prized possession of holy men and women throughout the ages. From the gnostic point of view, the materialist vision is a fixation of the person who is afraid to let go.

William Blake, for example, in his opposition to Deism, wrote that "God is in the lowest effects as well as in the highest causes."[5] The magus John Dee inscribed in the margin of his copy of the Hermetic *Pymander*, "Mundus imago dei"—the world is the image of God; nature is a divine projection.

Neoplatonists and Hermetic gnostics have spoken with awe of the soul of the world, clearly realizing that the planet is a living being of which, insofar as we are in the natural body, we are part (see the Gaia hypothesis that the planet is a living being—with consciousness). True mastery of nature belongs only to those who realize the full and total correspondence between spirit and matter.

In their quest for a reformed science, the first Rosicrucians sought knowledge of the full range of possible correspondences between the natural and the spiritual. In ignoring the spiritual dimension to life (that is, until recently) our scientific technology has become a suicidal force. The author asked Dr. Christopher McIntosh for his opinion on the relevance of the Rosicrucian vision today, and he responded: "The Rosicrucian mythology is important to us today because the needs of the age are the same as they were then. There is the same need for holistic vision, bringing together science, religion, art, and philosophy; there's the same need to heal religious divisions; there's the same need to read the 'Book of Nature' (as the Rosicrucians put it) if we are to save the environment. And we are still very much in need of the transformative vision, and the Rosicrucian vision still has the capacity to inspire us."[6]

According to some alchemists, the philosopher's stone is hidden in the earth. A deep vision of planetary life has in itself led many to a spiritual awareness. Nature, in general, can be regarded as the alchemist's prima materia, the "first matter" of the alchemical work. The natural world enfolds and is enfolded within the spiritual world. Most of the time (and for many all the time) our consciousness is cut off from IT— it is still there, it is real, and indeed may be described as reality itself, but we are rarely conscious of IT. Gnosis aims to wake humankind from this sleep, so that, putting the matter bluntly, we can "Get on with IT!"

The Hermetic philosophy begins with the conception that there was once a unity between humanity and God. This unity has been lost, and the Great Work of the Hermetic student is to restore it. Insofar as ecologists are encouraged to see the problem in terms of symptoms, such as pollution, emissions, and so forth, the great challenge remains unmet. As Crowley put it, "We need revolution at the root of life." The chief problem is that our conception of the cosmos is not yet equal to the challenge of humanity's life crisis.

In the language of a spiritual freemasonry, gnosis is the rejected stone necessary for the completion of the structure of a new cosmic understanding, a new Temple. Gnosis demands that we work to a new conception of the cosmos and of our place within it, integrating the best of past discoveries in science, art, and religion with a new consciousness of humankind's true identity—our centrality to a universe that is coterminous with our imagination. If we think hell, we shall get hell. If we open our eyes, we shall see infinity.

The crisis is not terminal; it is, in fact, our greatest opportunity. This vision represents the contribution of gnosis to both ecological and general scientific thought and practice.

NEO-GNOSTICS

One man who attended Steiner's Theosophical lectures in Berlin in the 1900s was Max Heindel. Heindel, born Max Grashof in Denmark in 1865, emigrated to the United States, where he founded the Rosicrucian Fellowship, members of which received his "Rosicrucian letters of instruction," taken largely from Rudolf Steiner's lectures.

The founding of the fellowship followed a somewhat unusual—although in the annals of neo-Rosicrucian initiation not exceptional—event. Heindel claimed that while in Europe in 1907, he met a "marvelous being," whom he later came to know as a senior adept of a secret Rosicrucian order. This adept allegedly took Max Heindel to a temple of the Rose-Cross near the German–Bohemian border. There he spent a month receiving personal instruction from a number of "elder brethren." This teaching was, Heindel claimed, incorporated into his eccentric work *The Rosicrucian Cosmo-Conception,* first published in 1909, which strongly reflected his own interest in astrology and discarnate entities endowed with the power to travel from planet to planet. It reads strangely.

Although Heindel's Rosicrucian Fellowship still exists in the United States, a schismatic Dutch body, since 1946 called the Lectorium Rosicrucianum and based in Haarlem, now claims to be the European gateway to authentic Rosicrucianism and the authentic gnosis.

The Lectorium Rosicrucianum, founded by Jan and Wim Leene

together with Henny Stock-Huyser from the Dutch branch of Heindel's Rosicrucian Fellowship, sees itself as the "young Gnostic Brotherhood" and claims to reveal "to all who seek a way out, the ancient message of the only path to deliverance." This organization is self-confessedly gnostic and now has branches in countries all over the world, including the United Kingdom, France, Germany, Italy, Spain, Sweden, New Zealand, the United States, Brazil, Bolivia, Ghana, and Nigeria, to name just a few.

The Lectorium has combined and to an extent synthesized concepts deriving from the ancient Gnostics, the Hermetic writings, an idealized Catharism, the symbology surrounding the Holy Grail, alchemy, Freemasonry, Theosophy, Rosicrucianism, and Johannine Christianity into a system of initiation that leads students from an outer school to an inner school. The inner school promises freedom from further incarnations and a life of Christo-Hermetic liberation.

The author asked a leading member of the Lectorium, Joost Ritman, founder of the highly significant Bibliotheca Philosophica Hermetica in Amsterdam, why he saw a necessity for having organized gnostic groups. He replied: "I think it is what enspirits the group that is important. I should compare it to the discovery of the Nag Hammadi library. The manuscripts were found in a jar, a container, but what was hidden in the jar was the reality of the inner message. The gnostic groups of today are not building their kingdom on earth; they are not building a power—as the Church did very successfully for a thousand years. The value is in the inner spark of light. So if you look to these groups, these organizations, they are the earthly vessels that can contain the truth.

"It is not the organization or the vessel that is the truth. You have the symbol of the Grail: a symbol for the coming together of the twelve disciples—eleven when Judas left—with Christ at the center. After that, the blood and water that came from the body of Christ fell into the vessel afterward called the Grail. So if you look to these groups, look how that energy, that blood of the Christ, that inner reality that you find in the codices of Nag Hammadi, is treated, as the first important question for the group: to turn away from life; to go to an inner center, an inner reality in life. And then you will find, like the butterfly, that at a certain moment, you leave the organization, you leave the form, and you fly to the sun, who is the 'visible God.' "

Founders of the Lectorium Henny Stock-Huyser and Jan Leene, changed their names to Catharose de Petri and Jan van Rijckenbourg for reasons best known to themselves. (Henny, by so doing, became "Cathar rose of the Stone" and Jan became a "rich castle.") These names were nonetheless recognized by one Antonin Gadal.

Gadal was the head of the Syndicat d'Initiative for the region of Ussat-Tarascon in the Pyrenean Languedoc between the wars.[7] Before World War II, he claimed that he had been initiated as patriarch of the "ancient Cathar Brotherhood" and was therefore the chief inheritor of the Cathar tradition. However, his conception of the Cathars does not tally with the picture of the Cathars provided by careful histori-cal scholarship based on the extant evidence. Gadal was nevertheless sincere in his wish to see the tradition of the Cathars persist into a new age.

The Cathars are now a Languedoc tourist attraction, for better or for worse. The appearance of Dutch Rosicrucians answered Gadal's need to find proper successors. Before the war, Gadal had begun an exploration of the caves of the Sabarthès, around Ussat and Tarascon, and declared that he had discovered a system deriving from mystical Hermetic schools in ancient Egypt. He claimed the system was that whereby medieval Cathars had been progressively initiated into a state of spiritual perfec-tion, the process running from one cave to another—a fascinating idea, but held independently of any substantial historical evidence.

Gadal's peculiar vision of esoteric Catharism was of enormous interest to Jan van Rijckenbourg and Catharose de Petri, and they encouraged members of the Young Gnostic Brotherhood, among whom in the 1950s was the young Joost Ritman, to seek their spiritual roots within Gadal's vision of Catharism.

To this day, at five-year intervals, members of the Lectorium visit the cave of Lombrives at Ussat-les-Bains—a section of whose vaulted caverns has earned it the name The Cathedral—to sing and hear hymns based on twelfth- and thirteenth-century Cathar and trouba-dour writings. The emphasis is on a shared activity, a group con-sciousness, which, they say and believe, vibrates as a magnetic field of spiritual power. The effort is made to benefit humankind at large, as humans are still, they assert, lost in a materialist dialectical game or play, a show of power and egoism. The mass of humankind is blind to the spiritual life, heedless of what the Lectorium calls the Rose-Heart, or divine core of the awakened gnostic.

Should readers find this format of neo-Gnosticism attractive, the Lectorium Rosicrucianum is open to inquiry. For those who are not seeking group affiliation, there are many other ways that gnosis can be experienced today.

CINEMA

It is significant that the first major British film to emerge from the end of World War II, *A Matter of Life and Death* (made by the mystically minded team of Michael Powell and Emeric Pressburger in 1946), used the allegory of a love story between two young people. One was a poet (played by David Niven), mentally disturbed by war experience; the other was a romantic American girl (played by Kim Hunter).

The film represents not only a quest for genuine spiritual values, but also a vision of a better future. The U.S. title was *Stairway to Heaven,* a reference to the brilliantly constructed escalator that joins the two worlds of earth and the poet's mind within a single universe. Designed by Alfred Junge, the scene closely resembles nothing so much as the first-degree tracing board of Craft Freemasonry, including vast statues of inspired figures of history, such as, tellingly, Plato and Solomon.

In the film, the girl, June, must prove the depth of her love for poet Peter Carter, whose case for survival is being judged by a court held in "another world."

Peter's redemption is effected by a French romantic aristocrat who lost his head in the Revolution and is now a heavenly conductor guiding the newly dead to their new world—a surprisingly egalitarian, monochrome bureaucracy (a great joke on postwar Labor Party plans; no wonder Carter wants to keep his feet on terra firma!).

To prove June's love for Peter (who spends the last part of the film simultaneously on an operating table and in the heavenly court), the French conductor collects a tear from the anxious June's eye within a red rose.

This intuitive image is quite astounding. The tear in the rose: It would be hard to find a purer image for the suffering Sophia than this beautifully simple and deeply evocative image. The rose becomes the living link between the two worlds, and it is presented as evidence in justification for Peter Carter's right to life. Meanwhile, Carter's friend, the neurologist-philosopher-mystic Dr. Reeves, makes a most eloquent speech to the assembled court: "In this tear are love and truth and friendship. Those qualities, and those qualities alone can build a new world today, and must build a better one tomorrow! That is my case, and upon it I demand a verdict that Peter Carter shall live!"

The wisdom of the court is to allow the young couple a long life on earth after June shows her readiness to sacrifice her life in this world and die for Peter, should such self-sacrifice save his life. The couple are rejoined on earth and become a kind of living talisman of postwar hope. Three hundred and thirty-four years after the physician Michael Maier invited King James I to rally behind the Rose, that flower becomes once more a symbol for a new age at yet another alchemical wedding. The film ends and a new world begins.

We do not know what happened to Peter and June's children, but this author has the feeling that they would live to fulfill, against the odds, the expectation of the last great Anglican, William Ralph Inge. In a book published at the time of the film's release, he wrote that the prophets of the vital new spirituality would come not from within the Church but from young people outside of it, people who would understand that "where the spirit of the Lord is, there is liberty." In the book *Mysticism in Religion,* Dean Inge wrote, "Theirs also is faith; but it is the faith of insight and of knowledge, the faith which is gnosis."[8]

It was in part the horror of war—the duality that combatants refuse to transcend—that generated from within the depths of the collective psyche the need and desire for the principle of unity that created the movement of youthful consciousness and the original impulse for the remarkable Love Generation. Among its authentic progenitors, this was possibly the best, as well as the most reviled and misrepresented, aspect of the 1960s. That all too easily banalized and commercialized imperative to "make love, not war" is a micro- and macrocosmic necessity. War divides; love brings together—and sure enough, the young prophets prophesied by Inge emerged. People wondered where they had come from. (When they had gone, they were missed; only the image remains.)

HIPGNOSTICS: POPULAR MUSIC

The 1960s saw the rise to prominence of two popular musicians, both of whom can be identified as being part of the gnostic stream—among many others, of course—whether as neo-troubadours or as gnostic visionaries. In searching to the heart of the poetic life, these men (though not by any means alone) uncovered and expressed classical gnostic archetypes. Insofar as their vision coincided with the yearnings of a new generation, they became leaders and, in the sense of the Hebrew term *nabu* (one who overflows), prophets. This was often to their individual dislike—no true prophet desires this appalling mantle. Their ecstasies and despairs became a light for a lost generation, a generation drowning amid the welter of new money and materialistic grasping that they intuitively sensed aimed to overwhelm them with false promises of a better life.

These men were young. Their names: John Lennon and Jimi Hendrix. Their lyrics and music continue to exercise a great fascination on the minds of musicians and listeners across Europe and America. I could fill the following paragraphs with quotations from the works and interviews of these men to justify their place in this story. But I am convinced that those who know will know and those who do not may seek for themselves. Regarding John Lennon, I should like to offer a small anecdote from my own life.

In October 1985 I was staying with some German *Alternativen,* friends of mine near Korbach in northern Germany, good people I had met while investigating the origins of the great German Green movement of the late 1970s and early 1980s. I had been seeking an objective correlative for my own ideals. The spirit in West Germany among some young and not-so-young people in the early 1980s had perhaps something in common with the spirit of the early German Reformation.

The German media establishment was not favorable, suggesting to this author that the international media now occupy the position once held by the medieval Roman Church: the controllers of images, with all that that implies.

My friend Heinz and I had gone for a long walk through the countryside with his wife, Eva, who had escaped the communist state of Poland to live in Berlin, and whom Heinz had married so that she could stay in the free West. At the end of the walk we found ourselves in a dim village bar, full of rather red-necked German farmers in the ubiquitous dress of checked shirts and jeans.

Eva was talking of a spate of sightings of the Virgin Mary across Poland, in which many people traveled great distances to share. Something was afoot in the Eastern Bloc. (Nobody at the time could have guessed how close the Soviet Union and its economic satellites were to political meltdown.)

The conversation turned to spirituality. Eva said that in her school, after the murder of John Lennon in December 1980, somebody had put up a poster of the musical star, and to everyone's surprise no one had taken it down. I asked her what it meant to her and her friends. She said: "Freedom, love, and the truth of the spirit. John Lennon had an inner life. He gave us hope."

John Lennon's interest in spirituality and, in later life, in the Gnostics, whom he regarded as the true Christians, is now well known, if rarely reported. Before we left the bar, I burned a ten-Deutschmark note before the eyes of the farmers. They were shocked; I had profaned the sanctuary of the Free West.

David Henderson's droll book about Jimi Hendrix (1942–70), *'Scuse Me While I Kiss the Sky* (1978), revealed the depth of Hendrix's spirituality. It is the signal quality that prevents so many other guitar virtuosos from equaling or surpassing his musical achievements. His intuitive gnosis, reinforced by a number of spiritually minded friends and contacts, led him to a sense of his own visionary role:

> We're in our little cement beehives in this society. People let a lot of old-time laws rule them. The establishment has set up the Ten Commandments for us saying don't, don't, don't. Once you say "don't" you've made two points against yourself.
>
> Then all of a sudden kids come along with a different set of brain

cells and the establishment doesn't know what to do. The walls are crumbling and the establishment doesn't want to let go. We're trying to save the kids, to create a buffer between young and old. Our music is shock therapy to help them realize a little more of what their goals should be.[9]

The soul must rule, not money or drugs. If you can do your own thing, just do it properly. A guy can dig ditches and enjoy it. You should rule yourself and give God a chance. . . . Definitely I'm trying to change the world. I'd love to! . . . My goal is to erase all boundaries from the world.[10]

We're making our music into electric church music—a new kind of Bible, not like in a hotel, but a Bible you carry in your hearts, one that will give you a physical feeling. We try to make our music so loose and hard-hitting so that it hits your soul hard enough to make it open. Rock is like a young dragon until the establishment gets hold of it and turns it into a cabaret act with the big voice and the patent-leather shoes and the patent-leather hair.[11]

Jimi Hendrix's "establishment" clearly fulfills the exact psychological role of the Gnostic archons, the grim rulers who are afraid of the bright-light spirit of free humans. Hendrix, above all the rock giants, was an intuitive, relying very little on learned or book culture. His rebellion has something almost angelic about it:

There's no telling how many lives your spirit will go through—die and be reborn. Like my mind will be back in the days when I was a flying horse. Before I can remember anything, I can remember music and stars and planets. I could go to sleep and write fifteen symphonies. I had a very strange feeling that I was here for something and I was going to get a chance to be heard. I got the guitar together 'cause that was all I had. I used to be really lonely.

A musician, if he's a messenger, is like a child who hasn't been handled too many times by man, hasn't had too many fingerprints across his brain. That's why music is so much heavier than anything you ever felt.[12]

Hendrix, like his predecessor the poet Blake, felt that everyone ought to be able to hear the spiritual voice, but the little flashes were constantly switched off by negativity—a negativity encouraged by the fraudulent and dominating materialism he discerned all about him. He looked to the cosmos for fraternity. At moments like that, he would become almost prophetic, as during an interview with the poet Jim Brodey for the *Los Angeles Free Press,* wherein he declared he was trying to move "toward a spiritual level through music":

There really are other people in the solar system you know, and they have the same feelings too, not necessarily bad feelings, but, see, it upsets their way of living for instance, and they are a whole lot heavier than we are. And it's no war game because they all keep the same place. But like the solar system is going through a change soon and it's going to affect the Earth in about thirty years, you know.

There's no whole lot of religions. Just one link because there's only a few chosen people that supposedly are to get this across; these chosen people, in the process, are now being distracted and they are drowning themselves. . . . In order to properly save them, they've got to take a break from people.[13]

Hendrix was talking about himself. He did not favor violence:

Like someone is going to have to go back to his childhood and think about what they really felt, really wanted before the fingerprints of their fathers and mothers got ahold of them or before the smudges of school or progress. . . . Most of them are sheep. Which isn't a bad idea. This is the truth, isn't it? That's why we have the form of Black Panthers and some sheep under the Ku Klux Klan. They are all sheep and in the beginning they were all following a certain path.[14]

Hendrix believed that the solution to our problems lay in getting back to a consciousness of our spiritual origins.

Thus spoke the "wild man of pop" who lived so long ago.

THE ARTS

The roll call of artists influenced by gnosis is practically endless. Gnosis has been called the religion of the artist. Valentinus was a poet. Images, dreams, reflections, ideas, abstractions, visions, ideals, archetypes, the limitless, the inexpressible: These are the stuff of art.

Michael Powell was fond of quoting Kipling's "All Art is one, man, one." The filmmaker Jean-Luc Godard, in spite of attempts at creating a materialist cinema (when he was not trying to be a sincere and, mercifully, questioning Maoist-socialist), has shown graphically the terrible materialism of our time. See *Je vous salue Marie* and the apocalyptic *Weekend*. Godard has found himself in the gnostic consciousness on more than one occasion. He almost despairs of the filmmaker's attempt to "create the imperishable with perishable means."[15]

> I escaped from the cutting room of a film I was struggling with called *The New Age and the New Man* (before the phrase "New Age" had been loaded with questionable connotations) in Wardour Street in the summer of 1989, and strolled into Mayfair for an exhibition of paintings. I met the abstract-expressionist Vanilla Beer. I heard her mention John Dee, and we fell into conversation. She was using his *Monas Hieroglyphica* as a visual theme.[16]

Another exhibition, this time by Yvonne Hawker, revealed a very fine figurative painter with a sense of the Symbolist about her. She told me how she had stayed in the Languedoc exploring the spirituality of the Cathars. It shows in her paintings: "Gnosis to me means a light that lights up in myself, in those quietest of moments, and binds me, and frees me with humankind. And it's something that happens on your own, and yet links you with so many others."

And Laurie Lipton, an enthusiast of the works of the gnostic master Gurdjieff, is a disturbing surrealist—and gnostic: "My work is searching, my work is questioning, and I think that's the basis of gnosis: to question. A lot of the religions, I think, tend to say 'Sleep, sleep, it's going to be all right'; whereas gnosis says: 'Awaken! Look! Question! Where are you? Who are you? And why?' And that is in my work and in me."[17]

There's Columba Powell, with a host of richly colored paintings inspired by Montségur and the landscape of the Languedoc. He has been a Sufi enthusiast and knows more about the spirituality of great cinema than anyone else I know.

Another phone call: "Do you want to go to the 'Spiritual in Art 1890–1985 Exhibition' at The Hague?" "I do."

Who would have thought that abstract artists and Abstract Expressionist painters owed so much to the gnostic stream? The exhibit was overwhelming. The catalogue included treatises on Hermetism, Theosophy, Éliphas Lévi, Gnosticism, Symbolism, Kabbalah, Paracelsus, alchemy, and Native American art: debts of influence suddenly revealed.

Judging by this selective exhibition, the visual canon of the twentieth century represents a kind of controlled explosion of gnostic dreams and ideas: Jean Arp, follower of Steiner and Böhme; Wassily Kandinski, influenced by Steiner and Theosophy; Paul Klee, influenced by Kandinsky and Steiner; Yves Klein, member of Heindel's Rosicrucian Fellowship; Hilma af Klint, influenced by Steiner and occult teachings; Kazimir Malevich, who said, "Science and art have no boundaries because what is comprehended infinitely is innumerable and infinity and innumerability are equal to nothing"[18] (cf. Crowley's 0 = 2 formula); Piet Mondrian, influenced by Madame Blavatsky; Jackson Pollock, influenced by Theosophy and Native American art; Mark Rothko, influenced by Jung; Jan Toorop, influenced heavily by neo-Rosicrucian and Symbolist ideas—and many more doubtless waiting to be discovered.

Should we be surprised at the heady confluence of gnosis and the visual arts? Of course not. Artists are trying to make us see. What is it that heals the blind?

In the fields of poetry, visual arts, and genuinely imaginative writing there now exists the Temenos Academy, founded by the world's expert on William Blake, the irreplaceable poet Kathleen Raine.

The academy's patron is H.R.H. Prince Charles. The academy is a foundation extending from Raine's influential review "devoted to the Arts of the Imagination," *Temenos*. The *Temenos* project was, according to Raine, "from the outset designed to carry a challenge to the values of current materialist culture in the field of the arts, and to re-affirm the spiritual ground from which all imaginative art must grow."[19]

Kathleen Raine's tireless work over many decades has borne fruit through conferences, articles, lectures, interviews, and a great body of poetry and prose in a new awareness of the centrality of the spiritual and of the experience of gnosis in the arts. For a long time, she felt like a lonely beacon in a dark alley; now there are a growing number of intelligent and enthusiastic supporters, aiming at the same goal: to assert by all means possible the primacy of the spiritual in human experience. *Temenos* is only one among many analogous initiatives throughout the world.

Who could say how much work is today accomplished under the aegis of the Thrice Greatest? Not all is done openly and in public; in fact, perhaps very little is truly achieved in this way: Silence is golden. "Therefore let Mind meditate on Spirit. Spirit is the Good in all."

And so we come back to front, to the timeless wisdom of the Upanishads, where we began. Could those who first uttered the words of spiritual liberation and insight have possibly known for how long men and women would read and gain inspiration from their words? Who can say? But the words shall be read, so long as humankind can still respond to this speech of Hermes Trismegistus, a greeting from the first book of the *Pymander*, addressed, upon his having been vouchsafed "the supreme vision," to all the people of earth:

> "O People! Earth born men, who have given yourselves up to drunkenness and sleep in your ignorance of God; wake up to sobriety, cease to be sodden with strong drink and lulled into mindless sleep.
>
> "O men of earth, why have you surrendered to death, when you have been given power to partake of immortality? Turn your minds round, you who have travelled with Error, and taken Ignorance for company; rid yourselves of darkness, and seize the Light; forsake corruption and share in immortality."

And some of them mocked at my words, and stood aloof; for they had given themselves up to the way of death. But others besought me that they might be taught, and cast themselves down at my feet. And I bade them stand up; and I made myself a guide to mankind, teaching them the doctrine, how and in what wise they might be saved. And I sowed in them the teachings of wisdom; and that which I sowed was watered with the water of divine life.

And when evening was come, and the light of the sun was beginning to go down, I bade them all with one accord give thanks to God. And when they had accomplished their thanksgiving, they betook them every man to his own bed.[20]

The Gnosis has returned? Indeed not. It is we who return.

Notes

Introduction

1. Rudyard Kipling—fondly and frequently quoted by British film director Michael Powell.
2. Adolf von Harnack, *The Mission and Expansion of Christianity in the First Three Centuries,* 2 vols. New York, 1908, quoted in Hans Jonas, *The Gnostic Religion* (New York: Beacon Press, 1958), 36.
3. A phrase characteristic of the mature thought of Samuel Taylor Coleridge and poetically expressed in his "Rime of the Ancient Mariner."
4. Aleister Crowley, "Chinese Music," in *Book of Lies* (York Beach, Maine: Samuel Weiser, 1990), para. 9.

Chapter 1 Before the Gnostics

1. Chandogya Upanishad 3:3–4, in *Ten Principal Upanishads.*
2. Dialogue of the Saviour, in *The Nag Hammadi Library,* 236.
3. Katha Upanishad 2:19, in *Ten Principal Upanishads.*
4. See S. G. F. Brandon, "Time as God and Devil" and "Zarathustra and the Dualism of Iran," in his wide-ranging collection of essays *Religion in Ancient History* (London: George Allen and Unwin, 1972), 49, 193.
5. Eudemus of Rhodes, in J. Bidez and Fr. Cumont, *Les Mages hellénisés* (Paris, 1938), ii. 69 (15) 70.
6. Plato, *Timaeus.* Cambridge, Mass.,: Harvard University Press, 1960.
7. Many centuries later, alchemists called this spirit *mercurius;* it was often symbolized as a serpent.
8. *Zurvan, a Zoroastrian Dilemma* (Oxford: Oxford University Press, 1955), 240–41, 398–99. See also *Bulletin of the School of Oriental and African Studies* 17, no. 2 (1955): 233.
9. Gerhard von Rad, *Wisdom in Israel* (London: SCM Press, 1978), 138.
10. The Gospel of Thomas, Codex 2, page 51, line 17, in *The Nag Hammadi Library.*

11. In the ancient Babylonian creation narrative, the *Enuma Elish,* Marduk, as leader of the young gods, slays Ti-amat and out of her body creates our world and the human beings who will serve him.

12. The Ogdoad generally refers to the eighth and ninth spheres, beyond the seven planetary spheres. The Ogdoad, the abode of the emanations of the highest divinity, is out of the control of the manifest world's zodiacal governors. Planet Earth, it should be noted, was seen as the center of a vast cosmic union, held in from all sides by superior forces.

13. Irenaeus, *Adversus Haereses* [Against the Heretics], Book 1, 17.2, in *The Ante-Nicene Fathers.*

14. For those who consider the trinity of Ohrmazd-Mithra-Ahriman to be of little consequence, it is instructive, as a codicil, to consider the persistence of the Mithraic image to as far as the eve of the European Reformation. In St. Thomas More's world-famous *Utopia* (Book 2), public worship is addressed only to the *hidden* deity: "They call on no peculiar name of God, but only Mithra, in the which word they all agree together in one nature of the divine majesty whatsoever it may be." The Renaissance Platonist Marsilio Ficino, on whose work More was leaning, had identified the "Chaldean" triad of Ohrmazd-Mithra-Ahriman as a vestige of the Christian Trinity.

Chapter 2 From the Magi to St. Paul

1. From Pico's 1486 *Oratio de dignitatis homini* [Oration on the Dignity of Man], called by Ernesto Garin "the manifesto of the Renaissance."

2. While later Christian apologists tried to interpret the coming of the Magi as an act of symbolic surrender to the new nonmagical Christian religion (see Justin's *Dialogue with Trypho* and Ignatius's *Epistle to the Ephesians* 19), reflecting a conflict between the Church and magic, the *magoi* of Matthew 2 are, according to the theologian Raymond E. Brown (*The Birth of the Messiah*, Garden City, N.J.: Doubleday, 1978), "wholly admirable. They represent the best of pagan lore and religious perceptivity which has come to see Jesus through revelation in nature ['his star']."

3. *Herodotus,* Book 1.101.

4. Ibid., Book 1.140. Herodotus is probably exaggerating laconically the Zarathushtrian practice of killing animals such as frogs, toads, snakes, mice, lizards, flies, and so on, supposed to have been created by the evil principle Ahriman. The reason dogs were spared is most likely because in the *Zendavesta,* the dog is represented as the special animal of Ohrmazd, the Good principle.

5. Ibid., Book 1.120. This somewhat lighthearted account bears uncanny parallels to the story of the Magi visiting King Herod in Matthew 2. In both there is a dream warning concerning a boy out in the country who is destined to be king. Far-fetched as it probably is, we might conjecture

that a tradition had grown up among the Magi following the unhappy events surrounding Cyrus that they had better make peace with future kings in advance!

6. Howard Clark Kee, *Medicine, Miracle, and Magic,* 107 ff.

7. A horoscope concerning the Roman king Antiochus I was found at an archaeological dig at Nemrud Dugh (Commagene). Astrological knowledge was frequently applied in composing horoscopes for royal births.

8. Current scholarly opinion dates Matthew between A.D. 85 and 105, especially since the Gospel appears to show knowledge of the destruction of the Jerusalem Temple in A.D. 70 (see Matt. 21:41, 22:7, 27:25). The problem, as ever, with the dating of the Gospels is that they exhibit all the features of being essentially composite works, and we do not have evidence of original texts. In any case, for our purposes, even if the Gospel is no older than A.D. 105, that is well within the limits of memory where the A.D. 66 Procession of Tiridates is concerned.

9. Their reputation for universality of thought was proverbial in the Florentine Renaissance. Little wonder that Lorenzo the Magnificent, patron of Pico della Mirandola and devotee of Hermetic philosophy, ensured that when he commissioned for his apartments a painting of the procession of the Magi to Christ's birthplace, he had himself included among the processional throng.

10. Of course, the whole account in Matthew could be fictitious. But this seems unlikely chiefly for two reasons. First, the account is straightforward and perfectly consistent with historically attestable Magian behavior. Second, the author of Matthew is usually keen to state that such and such happened "in accordance with the Scriptures," adding a quote from the Septuagint for good measure. For the visit of the Magi, there were a number of quotations he could have employed to beef up his message (e.g., Ps. 68:29, 31, 72:10; Isa. 49:7, 60:3, 60:10). He did not do so. The account is sober and reasonable. Even the references to "his star" make perfect astronomical sense. Later writers were responsible for embellishing the story with elements such as "three kings," the names Balthasar, Melchior, and Caspar, and the "miraculous" star that glided over the Fertile Crescent to hover directly above the Christmas crib.

11. The Gospel of the Infancy, in A. Walker, ed., *Apocryphal Gospels, Acts and Revelations* (Edinburgh: T. T. Clark, 1890).

12. Justin Martyr, *Dialogue with Trypho,* in *The Ante-Nicene Fathers,* 237.

13. David Hughes, *Star of Bethlehem Mystery,* 200. Based on Hughes's original article "The Star of Bethlehem," in *Nature* 264 (1976): 513–17, which received global attention.

14. Gilles Quispel, *GNOSIS,* undated typescript given to the author by Professor Quispel, January 1986, at Bilthoven, Netherlands, for the use of students.

15. Preserved in fragmentary form in the *Evangelical Preparation* (9.29) of the Christian bishop Eusebius of Caesarea, in Edwin Gifford, ed. and trans., *Eusebii Pamphili Evangelicae praeparationis libri XV,* 4 vols. (Oxford: Oxford University Press, 1903).

16. In the Greek translation of Ezekiel in the Septuagint, the figure of the divine Man (Hebrew: *demuth kemareh adam*) is translated in terms of a Greek Middle Platonist *idea* of Man: *homoioma hos eidos anthropou.*

17. Works attributed to this legendary figure appeared between the first century B.C. and, principally, the second century A.D., but they were pseudonymously backdated to a remote Egyptian antiquity. See my book *The Golden Builders.*

18. *Corpus Hermeticum,* Libellus 1.12–15 *(Poimandres),* Walter Scott, trans. (Boston: Shambhala, 1986). The title *Poimandres* usually refers to Marsilio Ficino's translation of the first fourteen books of the philosophical Hermetica, first printed in Treviso in 1471 and many times subsequently. The meaning of the title is disputed. The latest theory—noted in Peter Kingsley, "Poimandres: The Etymology of the Name and the Origins of the Hermetica," in *From Poimandres to Jacob Böhme: Gnosis, Hermetism and the Christian Tradition,* edited by Roelof van den Broek and Cis van Heertum—is that Poimandres is a corruption of the Egyptian P-eime nte rē, "the knowledge of Re" or "the understanding of Re." Poimandres is also thought to be related (perhaps as a pun) to the Greek for "shepherd of men." In the work itself, the name of the revealer to Hermes Trismegistus is given as the "authentic nous [mind]" or the "intelligence of the supreme power." Because the revelation of Poimandres appears in the first libellus of the *Corpus Hermeticum,* Ficino and subsequent compilers and translators took it for the title of the philosophical dialogues of Hermes.

19. See Luke's "Magnificat" hymn (Luke 1:46–55).

20. *The Thunder, Perfect Mind,* Codex 6, page 13, lines 1–5, 16–23, in *The Nag Hammadi Library.*

21. *Eugnostos the Blessed,* Codex 3, page 88, lines 3–11, in *The Nag Hammadi Library.*

22. The Gospel of Philip, Codex 3, page 63, lines 30–37; page 64, lines 1–5, in *The Nag Hammadi Library.*

23. This is strongly reminiscent of the more harmonious account of the heavenly Man in the Hermetic *Poimandres.*

24. The Apocryphon of John, Codex 2, page 15, lines 1–4, in *The Nag Hammadi Library.* Genesis 1:26 reads: "And God said, Let us make man in our image, after our likeness." Some Gnostics were convinced that the use of the plural pronoun and the possessive case was a direct giveaway that man (Adam) did not owe his origin to the work of a single creator alone.

25. The Apocryphon of John, Codex 2, page 19, line 34; page 20, lines 1–9, in *The Nag Hammadi Library.*

26. "Gnosis," undated typescript, given by Quispel to the author in January 1986 for students' use.

27. There must be something in the fact that both the orthodox Christian Irenaeus and the third-century pagan philosopher Plotinus (who regarded Christianity as a threatening fiction) complained about the arrogance of those who called themselves Gnostics. Moreover, the arrogance of the Gnostics seems most closely to resemble the arrogance of their own bête noire, Ialdabaoth, the devilish demiurge—a sign, perhaps, that something had gone spiritually adrift among the groups that Irenaeus and Plotinus encountered. Some who called themselves Gnostics may have come to regard themselves, in the most literal sense, as greater than their creator(s)— and the discovery went to their heads. Paul, of course, when addressing the Corinthians, had warned against the dangers of spiritual pride.

28. Henry Chadwick, "Philo of Alexandria," in *The Cambridge History of Later Greek and Early Medieval Philosophy,* A. H. Armstrong, ed. (Cambridge: Cambridge University Press, 1967).

29. Philo, *Philo,* "De plantatione," "Quod deterius potiori insidiare soleat," and "Quis rerum divinarum heres sit," Loeb Classical Library, 10 vols., trans. F. H. Colson and Rev. G. H. Whitaker (London: Heinemann, 1973), 6, 154, 156.

30. Ibid., "De opificio mundi," 141 ff.

31. Ibid., "De confusione linguarum," 41, 62, 146.

32. Ibid., "De agricultura," 51.

33. Ibid., "Quis rerum divinarum heres sit," 205 ff.; "De somniis," 2.188; "Quaestiones in exodum," 2.68.

34. Ibid., "De sacrificiis Abelis et Caini," 60, 131–32; "De Abrahamo," 122; "De fuga et inventione," 95–95; "De cherubim," 48.

35. Ibid., "Legum allegoriae," 2.85.

36. Ibid., "De ebrietate," 147.

37. Ibid., "De ebrietate," 146. Compare, of course, with the Pentecost account in Acts 2:13.

38. Ibid., "Legum allegoriae," 3.71.

39. Ibid., "De somniis," 2.226; cf. 1 Corinthians 8:3.

40. Ibid., "De posteritate Caini," 12; "De cherubim," 42–53. Philo even uses "mystery" terms reminiscent of both Plato's *Symposium* and Ephesians 5.

41. Ibid., "Legum allegoriae," 149; "De cherubim," 58–64.

42. It is surely significant that the great explosion of Gnosticism occurred after the total and suicidal collapse of Jewish resistance in Palestine in A.D. 138.

43. Reitzenstein, Nock, and Festugière translated the *Hermetica* and wrote authoritative commentaries on the Hermetic gnosis.

44. Rudolf Bultmann alerted scholars to the significance of the Mandaean (gnostic) community of Iraq and demonstrated gnostic influence in the New Testament, particularly in the Gospel of John. His idea that gnosis was of primarily Persian provenance is no longer accorded respect.

45. Hans Jonas's remarkable study *Gnosis und spätantiker Geist* [Gnosis and the Spirit of Antiquity;—1934, 1954], encapsulated in his great book *The Gnostic Religion,* demonstrated that we can speak of a gnostic religion irrespective of its ties to early Christianity and that its doctrines bear conceptual resemblances to contemporary existentialism. He saw the Gnostic phenomenon as a "world-historical event."

46. For example, Walter Birks' and R. A. Gilbert's *The Treasure of Montségur* (Wellingborough, Northamptonshire, U.K.: Crucible, 1987), 137–39.

47. Eisenman and Wise, *Dead Sea Scrolls Uncovered,* 83.

48. *Life of Josephus 2,* in *The Works of Flavius Josephus.*

49. Geza Vermes, *The Complete Dead Sea Scrolls in English.*

50. *Antiquities of the Jews,* Book 18, section 5.51, fragment 115, in *The Works of Flavius Josephus* translated by William Whiston (Edinburgh: William P. Nimmo 1865).

51. See John Burnet, *Early Greek Philosophy,* 4th ed. (London: A. and C. Black, 1930), 222.

52. This daemon corresponds to what the fifteenth-century magical document *The Sacred Magic of Abra-melin the Mage* calls the Holy Guardian Angel of the magus. This angel exists in a transcendent sphere independent of the human being and has been inadequately called the Higher or True Self—inadequate because this conception is too easily confused with contact with the soul. Gnosis in the context of this form of magic consists in becoming conscious of the transcendent nous, or as the nous becoming conscious of itself in the human being. The endeavor to make contact with the Holy Guardian Angel has also been called the Great Work of the Alchemist. The practice is fraught with psychic difficulties.

53. Although if the Essenes were in possession of the Book of Enoch, which seems not unlikely, they were familiar with the Son of Man figure, identified earlier with the Anthropos, who comes from the Throne of the Lord of Spirits to punish the fallen angels who have perverted humankind: "For from the beginning the Son of Man was hidden, and the Most High preserved him in the presence of His might, and revealed him to the elect" (*Book of Enoch,* 62.7).

54. Josephus, *Antiquities of the Jews,* Book 15, chapter 10, section 5, in *The Works of Flavius Josephus.*

55. Ibid., *War of the Jews,* Book 2, chapter 8, 2–14 in *The Works of Flavius Josephus.*

56. Ibid., *Antiquities of the Jews,* Book 18, chapter 5, section 2, in *The Works of Flavius Josephus.*

57. Compare the Essenes to the Mandaeans of Iraq. The Mandaeans hold John the Baptist in special reverence, and in many respects seem reminiscent of the Essenes by virtue of dress and ritual washing. The Mandaean theology is thoroughly Gnostic, but how far this might be true of Josephus's Essenes, with their "knowledge of divine revelations," cannot be asserted with certainty.

58. Josephus, *War of the Jews,* Book 2, chapter 8, section 7, in *The Works of Flavius Josephus.*

59. The significance of Enoch as one privy to divine secrets persisted in Hermetic, kabbalistic, and occult circles at least as late as the Renaissance. Medieval Arabic works equating the Hebrew patriarch with Hermes were passed underground throughout the Middle Ages. The English magus John Dee used the works of Enoch in defining the visionary scope of his gnostic angel magic. His chief sources were Friar Roger Bacon's notes on the *Secretum secretorum* and Guillaume Postel's (1510–81) *De originibus.* Postel, the French kabbalist, had met an Ethiopian priest who acquainted him with knowledge of the Ethiopian *Book of Enoch,* the work we are here describing.

60.
> *Marcus, thou former of idols, inspector of portents,*
> *Skilled in consulting the stars, and deep in the black arts of magic,*
> *Ever by tricks such as these confirming the doctrines of error,*
> *Furnishing signs unto those involved by thee in deception,*
> *Wonders of power that is utterly severed from God and apostate,*
> *Which Satan, thy true father, enables thee still to accomplish,*
> *By means of Azazel, that fallen and yet mighty angel,—Thus making thee*
> *the precursor of his own impious actions."*
>
> IRENAEUS, *AGAINST THE HERETICS* 1, 15.6

The poem may be by Irenaeus's teacher Pothinos, who, according to Irenaeus, was taught by Polycarp, who knew John the Apostle.

61. It cannot be stated strongly enough that when we read of "fire" in visionary and apocalyptic works, it must be understood that spiritual fire is intended: the fire *within* the visible fire. The material eye can see ordinary fire; the spiritual eye sees spiritual fire. This fire can also be called alchemical fire insofar as it is engaged in the purification of the soul and the release of the spirit. Fire in the above context means the divine agent of purification, akin to the alchemical stone, or firestone, from which sparks are struck. Visible fire is the projection in matter of that for which spiritual fire is the *idea.* Thus, in this context, the "house of fire" can refer to a temple or more particularly to a living spiritual body. In the gnostic symbology, human beings can become houses of fire. Even in common speech we have expressions such as "He was on

fire with what he had to say." Enormous grief has followed from this fundamental misunderstanding of spiritual and poetic language by materialists. Hence, it is not unknown to await the Second Coming in the wake of nuclear war and the like.

62. γνωσιν σωτηριας, *gnosin soterias.*

63. Around seventeen hundred years later, eighteenth-century Rosicrucian enthusiasts collected dew, thinking it to be the alchemical prima materia and "sugar of the stars," another classic case of what happens when a symbol is regarded from the perspective of material vision.

64. Josephus, *Antiquities of the Jews,* Book 1, chapter 3, in *The Works of Flavius Josephus.*

65. See the "The Three Steles of Seth and the Second Treatise of the Great Seth" in *The Nag Hammadi Library.* In the latter work, Seth, progenitor of the "immovable race," the "perfect," is identified with Jesus, founder of a new spiritual generation.

66. Josephus, *Antiquities of the Jews* 1, 3.1, in *The Works of Flavius Josephus.*

67. Norman Golb, *Who Wrote the Dead Sea Scrolls? The Search for the Secret of Qumran* (Toronto; Scribner, 1995).

68. Michael Baigent and Richard Leigh, *The Dead Sea Scrolls Deception* (New York: Simon and Schuster, 1993).

69. A strong theme in Robert Eisenman's seminal work *Maccabees, Zadokites, Christians and Qumran: A New Hypothesis of Qumran Origins.*

70. S. G. F. Brandon, *The Trial of Jesus of Nazareth* (London: Batsford, 1968); and *Jesus and the Zealots* (New York: Scribners, 1967).

71. Similar comments might properly be aimed at the churches that claim his name. An Egyptian Gnostic (Apocalypse of Peter 74.10–20) spoke of the orthodox Christian establishment as "cleaving to the name of a dead man." Is Jesus' conception of God too big for the churches to handle?

72. "But though I be idiot in speech, yet not in knowledge [*gnosei*]" (2 Cor. 11:6). In the same epistle, Paul records an ascent to the "third heaven," unsure in what dimension the vision took place ("God knoweth"). This kind of spiritual ascent was dear to those who brought the *Book of Enoch* to the Qumran area.

73. See the section "Kabbalistic Magic" in chapter 4.

74. Jesus' father, Joseph, was called a *tekton* (mason, craftsman, or master).

75. Nigel Pennick, *Sacred Geometry* (Wellingborough, Northamptonshire, U.K.: Turnstone Press, 1980).

76. Gordon Strachan, "The Temple of Solomon and the Cosmic Music," in *Occult Observer* 2, no. 3 (1992).

77. This (undated) psalm seems to refer to the building of Solomon's Temple in Jerusalem, a task apparently undertaken between 961 and 922 B.C.

This legendary account, however, makes no reference to a special cornerstone or head stone. For that we must look to the collection of prophecies gathered under the name of the prophet Isaiah, a man thought to have lived in and around Jerusalem between circa 745 and 686 B.C. (although some of the prophecies bearing his name have been dated at least a century after the prophet's death). In one singular prophecy (28:16) we have a reference to God laying a "precious corner stone" in Zion—a strange thing, perhaps, given that the Temple was apparently still standing. (The Temple did undergo repairs under the reign of King Josiah around the year 622 B.C.) Nevertheless, the kind of stone suggested in the Isaiah prophecy seems to have been more of the nature of a visionary hope and supernatural symbol than a visible object: "Therefore thus saith the Lord GOD, Behold, I lay in Zion for a foundation stone, a tried stone, a precious corner stone, a sure foundation: he that believeth shall not make haste. Judgement also will I lay to the line, and righteousness to the plummet and the hail shall sweep away the refuge of lies, and the waters shall overflow the hiding place." The idea behind the prophecy suggests a restoration of an ideal, combined with an ethical judgment (already prefigured in the divine mind), and so the prophecy may have been made after the destruction of the Solomonic Temple by the Babylonian king Nebuchadnezzar in 587 B.C., perhaps to encourage a (spiritual?) reconstruction after the exile of Jews in Babylon. (An attempt to rebuild the Temple was undertaken in an intermittently desultory fashion between 520 and 515 B.C.).

The important thing to bear in mind is that after the exile of the Jews in Babylon, the idea of the Temple became embroiled with prophetic visions of a spiritually or supernaturally redeemed Jewry (or even a visionary redemption of the world as a whole), while aspects of the Temple structure attained symbolic significance—in particular, the Temple cornerstone. The point is that the *true* head stone is laid "by the hand of God" and almost certainly represents not so much a physical and historical stone-laying but rather the *controlling principle* of any structure—physical or spiritual—built through its agency.

78. See Daniel 2:34–35, where the impact of a supernatural stone destroys the Babylonian Empire, which becomes "like the chaff of the summer threshing-floors; *and the wind carried them away,* that no place was found for them: and the stone which smote the image became a great mountain, and filled the whole earth" (my emphasis).

79. Thus in alchemy, the messenger god Hermes (also identified with John the Baptist in initiated circles) presides over the alchemical operation because Hermes' element is air and his movement is like the invisible but nonetheless penetrating wind. The name Mercurius (the Latin form of Hermes) is given to the penetrating *spiritus* in the alchemical operation—often symbolized as a regenerating and penetrating serpent who

enters into all substances and is the agent of division, transformation, and purification. (There is even a Jewish legend that Solomon used a supernatural *worm* to separate the building stones required for the Temple.)

80. For example, see Zechariah 11:10 ff. for a reference to thirty pieces of silver as the price of a prophet; Zechariah 12:10 and 11:6 on the wounding of God's chosen: "And I will pour upon the House of David, and upon the inhabitants of Jerusalem, the spirit of grace and of supplication: and they shall look upon me whom they have pierced, and they shall mourn for him, as one mourneth for his only son" (Zech. 12:10); "And one shall say unto him, What are these wounds in thine hands? Then he shall answer, Those with which I was wounded in the house of my friends" (Zech. 11:16).

81. *Stone* was also the word for a healing agent in the first century; according to Josephus, the Essenes were familiar with them.

82. C. G. Jung, "Psychology and Alchemy," in *The Collected Works of C. G. Jung*, 297, commenting on Berthelot's translation of *Collection des anciens alchimistes grecs* 4, 22.8.

83. Jung, "Psychology and Alchemy," 301 ff.

84. The Gospel of Truth, 18:20–35, in *The Nag Hammadi Library*.

85. Jung, "Psychology and Alchemy," 303–304.

86. "Undeniably, borrowings were made over and over again [by alchemists] from the Church, but when we come to the original basic ideas of alchemy we find elements that derive from pagan, and more particularly, Gnostic, sources. The roots of Gnosticism do not lie in Christianity at all—it is far truer to say that Christianity was assimilated through Gnosticism" (Jung, "Psychology and Alchemy," 357).

87. The Second Treatise of the Great Seth, Codex 7, page 49, line 35; page 50, line 1, in *The Nag Hammadi Library*.

88. The Book of Thomas the Contender, Codex 2, page 138, lines 7–10, in *The Nag Hammadi Library*.

89. The Gospel of Thomas, Codex 2, page 32, lines 10–14, in *The Nag Hammadi Library*.

90. Ibid.

91. Ibid., page 36, lines 5–9.

92. The Apocryphon of John, Codex 2, page 30, line 34; page 31, line 1, in *The Nag Hammadi Library*.

93. The First Apocalypse of James, Codex 5, page 28, lines 16–20, in *The Nag Hammadi Library*.

94. Eisenman and Wise, *The Dead Sea Scrolls Uncovered*.

Chapter 3 The First Gnostics

1. For example, in James M. Robinson's introduction to *The Nag Hammadi Library in English*: "The focus of this [Gnostic] library has much in common with primitive Christianity, with eastern religions, and with holy men of all times, as well as with the more secular equivalents of today, such as the counter-culture movements coming from the 1960s."

2. The use of the major seventh (itself of Eastern origin) accounts for the distinctively arch-romantic, yearning, and sometimes spiritually otherworldly flavor discernible in the music of Ravel, Debussy, Erik Satie (all touched by the gnostic-influenced Symbolist movement), Richard Strauss, Joseph Marie Canteloube's *Songs of the Auvergne* (with their hints of the medieval troubadours), and on to Burt Bacharach, Rodgers and Hammerstein, and John Barry. The major seventh is the ubiquitous magic chord suggesting home, spiritual ascent, sensuality, and the bittersweet pain of nostalgia. Some ancient Gnostics called their message the *knowledge of the heart*. It is also worth adding that the major seventh was regarded as discordant and subversive of the Western musical tradition based on church or sacred music. The use of the major seventh breaks the grip of a musical and religious dogma that was opposed to ambiguity of expression. Popular taste has thus been open to dissent. One could add that true romance is true subversion: *contra mundum*.

3. The Second Treatise of the Great Seth, Codex 7, page 55, lines 30–35; page 56, lines 14–19, in *The Nag Hammadi Library*.

4. See Pliny the Elder, *Natural History*, 35.15 ff.

5. Irenaeus, "The Deceitful Arts and Nefarious Practices of Marcus," in *Against the Heretics* 1, 13.

6. Ibid.

7. Robinson, introduction, *The Nag Hammadi Library*, 10.

8. It is noteworthy that the Nag Hammadi library contains four works described as "apocalypses." They all share in the idea of an apocalypse as a mystical ascent itinerary, apparently available to the Gnostic spirit. The word *apocalypse* seems to have lost its "end of the world" meaning. For the Gnostic, the world ends in symbolic fire on the discovery of the divine spirit, which burns the world away from Gnostic vision. This development of apocalyptic—if that is what it is—allowed the Gnostics a completely fresh understanding of the conventionally apocalyptic sayings ascribed to Jesus. Thus the cleansing "fire" can be understood alchemically. It is perhaps significant that it is from around the period of the composition of much of the Nag Hammadi library (c. A.D. 200–300) that our earliest extended alchemical commentaries derive: those of Zosimos of Panopolis—not surprisingly an Egyptian dedicated to achieving gnosis.

9. The Gospel of Philip, Codex 2, page 67, lines 9–14, in *The Nag Hammadi Library*.

10. Ibid., page 61, lines 31–38.

11. Ibid., page 69, lines 8–12.

12. Jonas, *Gnostic Religion.*

13. Conversation with the author, New Rochelle, New York, January 1986.

14. Elaine Pagels, *The Gnostic Gospels.*

15. See my book *The Gnostics.*

16. Conversation with the author, New Rochelle, New York, January 1986.

17. The Mandaeans derive their name from the Aramaic verb *mandâ*, "to know." They are the oldest surviving Gnostics and were last seen dwelling in the marshlands of Iraq and in obscure parts of Iran. Mandaean literature dates back at least as far as the fourth century A.D.

18. "According to what thou, great Life, saidst unto me, would that a voice might come daily to me to awaken me, that I might not stumble. If thou callest unto me, the evil worlds will not entrap me and I shall not fall prey to the Aeons."(Mandean Ginza 485) The spirit in man is called by the *Alien Man:* "I am an alien man. . . . I beheld the Life and the Life beheld me. My provisions for the journey come from the Alien Man whom the Life willed and planted. I shall come amongst the good whom this Alien Man has loved." (Ginza 273)

19. See my book *The Golden Builders: Alchemists, Rosicrucians and the First Free Masons,* chapter 2.

20. See the Bridal Chamber imagery ubiquitous in Valentinian texts.

21. The Gospel of Truth, Codex 1, page 28, line 31; page 30, line 12, in *The Nag Hammadi Library.*

22. The Gospel of Philip, Codex 2, page 71, line 35; page 72, line 4, in *The Nag Hammadi Library.*

23. The Gospel of Thomas, Codex 2, page 46, lines 23–28; page 51, lines 16–18, in *The Nag Hammadi Library.*

24. Neoplatonism features frequently throughout this book because the tradition of Neoplatonism, a partly gnosticized form of Platonic tradition, bore within it the seed of gnosis.

25. Clement of Alexandria, *Stromateis*, Book 7.

26. Ibid., 7, 2.8–9.

27. The Gospel of Thomas, Codex 2, page 32, lines 15–19, in *The Nag Hammadi Library.*

28. *Corpus Hermeticum,* Libellus 1.26a–26b.

Chapter 4 Magic in the Middle Ages

1. According to the magus Aleister Crowley, magick (he spelled it with a *k*) is the science and art of causing changes in nature in conformity with

will. It might be added: *in conformity with nature* as well. (Dion Fortune defined the range of magic as having to do with causing changes in *consciousness* in conformity with will.)

2. Von Eschenbach, *Parzifal,* 329.

3. See part 1 of my book *The Golden Builders.*

4. Quoted by Garth Fowden in *The Egyptian Hermes* (Cambridge: Cambridge University Press, 1986), 130, n. 55.

5. Porphyry, *De regressu animae* 4, quoted by Augustine in *Civitas dei,* 10.27, cited by Fowden, *The Egyptian Hermes,* 133–34.

6. Porphyry, *De regressu animae,* quoted in Fowden, 131.

7. Iamblichus, *De mysteriis,* I.1.1–2, quoted in Fowden, 136.

8. See part 3 of my book *The Gnostics.*

9. Iamblichus, *De mysteriis,* VIII.4.266–6.268, quoted in Fowden, 140.

10. Pleroma is the Greek word used in the Valentinian Gnostic itinerary of the second century A.D. to denote the "fullness" or plenitude of God in God's pure state. Within the Pleroma, all archetypes (divine ideas) exist in harmony until a catastrophic breach occurs within it. The healing of the Pleroma concerned the Egyptian Gnostic poet Valentinus (c. 160 B.C.). Consideration of the breach enabled him to understand the fallen nature of our world and our wills. The Pleroma, while unitary, is, however, in Gnostic understanding, still a coterie of divine powers. The breach in the Pleroma in the Valentinian system is caused when an aspect of "it" (the Aeon Sophia, or Wisdom) seeks knowledge of its nature—attempting to know its depth or source: the "unknowable Father." This myth precisely mirrors the process of coming to consciousness that typifies the pneumatic Gnostic who, in seeking his source, comes to a breach with the extended material world and experiences alienation: The seeking to know sets off the breach, and achieving gnosis heals the breach in the individual. This mystery of divine self-estrangement and autoconsciousness explains the perennial fascination of the gnosis, for the system so effectively turns both in and out on itself while vouchsafing a perpetual mystery of being: Being is fascinated by itself.

11. The influence of the pseudo-Dionysian *Celestial Hierarchies* on the leading figures of medieval mysticism can hardly be overestimated. Joannes Tauler (c. 1300–1366) in his *Sermon* (Leipzig: Cunradus Kacheloven, 1498) speaks of God in terms of Dionysius Areopagita's *theologia negativa* as the "unspeakable mystery," "the divine abyss," and calls God incomprehensible and anonymous; God is Nothing. This theme is almost certainly of Valentinian Gnostic provenance (where God in God's essential being is called Bythos, "the Depth"). The mystic Tauler also quotes from the Hermetic *Liber 24 philosophorum:* "God is darkness in the soul after all the light." In mystical union the unknown God can be experienced.

The theme of the deepest root of the human soul being God himself spelled trouble with ecclesiastical authorities for the great mystic Meister Eckhart (c. 1260–1328). Heinrich Seuse (c. 1295–1366) defended his teacher Eckhart against accusations of heresy. He himself composed works that took up key ideas of the *Celestial Hierarchies* and developed a Sophia (Wisdom) Christology in conjunction with Jewish Alexandrian Wisdom works (Wisdom of Solomon, or Ecclesiasticus) roughly contemporaneous with the (arguably) semi-gnostic works of Philo of Alexandria, in which the feminine Sophia and the Stoic Logos are identified in a manner that would have a marked effect on the development of Alexandrian gnosis.

In the late collection of Heinrich Seuse's works *Hier seind geschriben die capital des buchs dz do der Seusse heisset* (Augsburg: Antonius Sorg, 1482), Seuse identifies Wisdom with Christ: "When in fear and death agony, I was hanging, crucified, everybody mocked me. I had decided that I must empty the beaker of my bitter suffering alone and for all people." In the manuscript version of the work from which these lines are taken—*Die ewige Weisheit* [The Eternal Wisdom]), Nuremberg (?): 1435, *Bibliotheca Philosophica Hermetica*, Amsterdam—the Wisdom-Christ is depicted crucified on a floriate tree that bears ripe fruit, an image consistent with alchemical conceptions of the crucified yet spiritually penetrating *mercurius*, whose fruit is the *filius philosophorum*.

12. F. C. Copleston, *A History of Medieval Philosophy* (London: Methuen, 1972).

13. The Gospel of Thomas, Codex 2, page 47, lines 20–24, in *The Nag Hammadi Library*.

14. Garth Fowden, *The Egyptian Hermes*, 127.

15. "Hymn of Praise and Thanksgiving for the Paradoxical Opening of the (Inner) Eyes," Codex 6, pages 63–65, in *The Nag Hammadi Library*.

16. Announced by the so-called *Rosicrucian Manifestos* (1610–16).

17. See Brian Stock, *Myth and Science in the Twelfth Century* (Princeton, N.J.: Princeton University Press, 1972). For Neoplatonism in the school of Chartres, consult Helen Waddell's *The Wandering Scholars* (Ann Arbor: University of Michigan Press, 1989).

18. Moses Taku, quoted in Gershom Scholem, *Major Trends in Jewish Mysticism* (New York: Schocken, 1961), 102.

19. G. Scholem, *Major Trends in Jewish Mysticism* (New York: Schocken, 1961.

20. Hai ben Sherira, quoted in Scholem, *Major Trends in Jewish Mysticism*, 49. See the extensive heavenly itinerary of the *Book of Enoch*.

21. Nicholas Clulee, *John Dee's Natural Philosophy* (London: Routledge, 1988).

22. Walter Scott, trans., introduction to the *Hermetica*.

Chapter 5 The Sufis

1. Quoted in Laleh Bakhtiar's essay "Traditional Philosophy," in *Iran: Elements of Destiny* (London: Collins, 1978), 227.

2. "Mysticism" by R. A. Nicholson, in *The Legacy of Islam*, ed. Sir Thomas Arnold (Oxford: Oxford University Press, 1931), 212–13.

3. Titus Burckhardt, *An Introduction to Sufism* (Shaftesbury, Dorset, U.K.: Element Books, 1976).

4. Last words of al-Hallaj, in R. A. Nicholson, *The Legacy of Islam* (Oxford: Oxford University Press, 1931), 217.

5. Nicholson, *The Legacy of Islam*, 218.

6. "Al-Hallaj"(poem), in Nicholson, *The Legacy of Islam*, 218.

7. Dhu'l-Nun (quotes), in Nicholson, *The Legacy of Islam*, 215.

8. Anonymous, "Tractatus Aureus," in *Ars chemica* (Strasbourg, 1566), 21 ff., quoted in Jung *Psychology and Alchemy*, 358–59.

9. Abu Yazid of Bistam, in Nicholson, *The Legacy of Islam*, 215.

10. R. A. Nicholson on the mysticism of Muhyi-d-Din ibn 'Arabi, in Nicholson, *The Legacy of Islam*, 226.

11. It is thought that Ibn 'Arabi may have influenced Dante's Beatific Vision of Beatrice in *The Divine Comedy*, especially considering the many linguistic and visionary parallels between Dante's *Inferno* and *Paradiso* and the labyrinthine miseries of Ibn 'Arabi's passing hells. Blake's *Dante* (being gnostic) is closer to Ibn 'Arabi's redemptive vision than Dante's is.

12. Ibn 'Arabi, in Nicholson, *The Legacy of Islam*, 226.

13. Abu Hamid al-Ghazali, in Nicholson, *The The Legacy of Islam*, 221.

14. Averroës, *Tahafut al-tahafut* [The Incoherence of the Incoherence], in *A History of Medieval Philosophy* (London: F. C. Copleston/Methuen, 1972), 120.

15. Rumi, "House of Love," in Nicholson, *The Legacy of Islam*, 231.

16. St. Paul had preached in Iconium some twelve hundred years before.

17. Afzal Iqbal, *The Life and Work of Jalaluddin Rumi* (Oxford: Oxford University Press, 2000).

18. Ibid.

19. Rumi, *Mathnawi*, in Afzal Iqbal, *The Life and Work of Jalaluddin Rumi*.

20. Ibid.

21. Ibid., 1.133.

22. Ibid., 1.527–29.

23. Ibid., 4.2034.

24. Ibid., 4.3000–29.

25. Faridu'ddin 'Attar, in Nicholson, *The Legacy of Islam*, 232.

Chapter 6 The Troubadours

1. Such as Epiphanius (d. A.D. 403), author of the *Panarion,* an extravagant and thoroughly biased description of some sixty heresies current in his time, including a number of Gnostic cults.

2. The position of the Gnostic ascetic is asserted with great force and eloquence in the Book of Thomas the Contender (in *The Nag Hammadi Library*), a work characterized by its author's feeling of intense disgust at the capacity of sexual lust to overwhelm the mind and lead the soul into further imprisonment in the material realm.

3. A nickname from the Greek *katharos,* meaning "pure." The Cathars were the Pure Ones, known among their friends as the Good Men or Good Women. Their beliefs have much in common with the point of view of the Book of Thomas the Contender, and their peripatetic nature and concept of the soul resonate with what little we know of the first-century Essenes. Their liturgical works were already of great antiquity, and their claim to be the true church—or that their doctrines were older than those of orthodox Catholicism—is not without foundation.

4. See R. I. Moore, *The Origins of European Dissent* (Basil Blackwell, Oxford, U.K.,1985), 174 ff.

   > The suddenness with which dualism spilled from Constantinople, reaching northern Europe and Bosnia, so far as we can tell, almost at the same moment, suggests that it was precipitated by events rather than processes. In 1140 a monk named Constantine Chrysomalos, whose work was influential in monastic circles, was condemned as heretical on the charge that he taught Messalian and Bogomil doctrines on a number of points, including baptism, confession and the study of the Gospels. [Bogomil means "beloved of God" in Bulgar. The Bogomil was the supposed initiator of the fresh movement of Catharism.] The accession of Manual I to the imperial throne in 1143 was followed by renewed persecution of suspected Bogomils; it was through his friendship with one of those accused, the monk Niphon, that the patriarch Cosmas II was deposed as a heretic early in 1147. These episodes suggest that the atmosphere of the capital in those years was congenial to persecution, both in and outside Constantinople.

   > Moore deduces that these and related events led to a greater penetration of heresy in western Europe, Languedoc having been found to be particularly conducive to the transmission of Catharist doctrines, especially among the nobility.

5. Raimon de Miraval, "D'Amor es totz mos cossiriers" [Love Is All My Thought; Love Is My Only Concern] (song), in René Nelli, trans., *Le Roman de Raimon de Miraval* (Paris: Albin Michel, 1986). All English translations of songs by Raimon de Miraval quoted in this book are by the author.

6. Guillaume IX (song), in *Troubadour Lyric Poetry*, ed. A. R. Press (Edinburgh: Edinburgh University Press, 1971), 17.

7. Raimbaut d'Aurenja, "La Flors enversa" [The Inverted Flower], in *Troubadour Lyric Poetry*, 107.

8. In *Troubadour Lyric Poetry*, 107, v. 7.

9. Description by papal legate of the Languedoc, quoted by the historian R. I. Moore in an interview with the author in *Gnostics*, episode 2, Border TV for U.K. Channel 4, 1987.

10. Records attest to the existence of 460 troubadours from the Languedoc, Italy, Spain, and Portugal; 2,600 texts of original poetry have survived, along with 342 original melodies, signed by forty-four authors, as well as twenty-six anonymous melodies. There are 225 Provençal texts extant concerning the lives of 101 troubadours. (Source: The troubadour historian and interpreter Gérard Zuchetto, *Catalogue de l'Exposition Troubadours et Jongleurs*, 4. These date from the thirteenth and fourteenth centuries and are divided into the *vidas* ("lives," or notes on the poets themselves) and the *razos* (commentaries on their works). The vidas were romanticized, filled with summaries and stereotypes that present a curious mélange of truth and fiction. In spite of lacunae, errors, and legends, their value lies in the fact that they are the only near-contemporary writings available attesting to the existence of the troubadours and their distinctive personalities. Their authorship is usually attributed to non-scholarly *jongleurs* (Occitan: *jocglars*), musicians inaccurately described as minstrels and all too frequently confused with the troubadours themselves.

11. Loba was not the sentimental type. On one occasion, she asked Vidal to approach her castle disguised as a wolf. Refusal was out of the question, and he did as he was told. She then had the castle dogs set on him! This is the kind of story that the vidas revel in. The troubadours were living legends—the first celebrities.

12. Dante Alighieri, *De vulgari eloquentia*, ed. Steven Botterill (New York: Cambridge University Press, 1996).

13. Nelli, *Le Roman de Raimon de Miraval*, 15.

14. Miraval, "Entre Deux Désirs je reste songeur" [Between Two Desires I Remain Thoughtful] (song addressed to lady Azalaïs de Boissézon), in Nelli, *Le Roman de Raimon de Miraval*, 137, v. 9. "Bien que ma dame me soit cruelle" [Although My Lady Is Cruel to Me], in Nelli, *Le Roman de Raimon de Miraval*, 111, v. 2.

15. See my book *The Gnostics*, Barnes and Noble, 1997, part 2: *The Good Men*.

16. L. T. Topsfield, *Les Poésies du troubadour Raimon de Miraval* (Paris, 1971).

17. It is possible that Loba de Pennautier lived at Cabaretz, an important center of Cathar preaching, close to Miraval. Peire Vidal mentions a Loba, lady of the Carcassès, who has left him for a red-haired count, thought to have been the count of Foix, by whom she seems to have had an illegitimate and much loved child. Loba has been identified with Auda, wife of Arnaud d'Aragon. The Aragon family was one of the most considerable in the viscounty of Carcassonne, and the name resides in many documents next to those of the seigneurs of Cabaretz. Depositions made by the forfeit Arnaud de Laure in 1262 designate a certain Auda as daughter of Loubat de Pennautier. According to the razo, Loba was the daughter of Raymond de Pennautier. These men are known to history. Raymond plays a role as witness along with Peire Roger de Cabaretz in the marriage contract of 1211 made between Orbria de Durban and the knight Jordan of Cabaretz. Auda may have transmitted her father's name, Loubat, into a feminine form, Lobata, Louba, or Loba. The two men of Pennautier may have been the same. While there are only slight indications linking Miraval to the Loba celebrated by Peire Vidal, we may yet conclude that *Mais d'Amic* was probably Loba.

18. Miraval, "Rien ne garantit de l'Amour" [Nothing Guarantees Love] (song to Mais d'Amic), in Nelli, *Le Roman de Raimon de Miraval*, 77–80.

19. The *Ars amatoria* by Ovid was an ironic satire on the folly and pursuit of love for women, but it was taken as a serious code of conduct in twelfth-century court.

20. Minerve is an astonishing fortified town twenty miles east of Miraval, and was a great center of Catharism.

21. The author of *Razo* C [the title of an original manuscript commentary on the song; see W. T. Pattison, *The Life and Works of the Troubadours* (Minneapolis: University of Minnesota, 1952)] designates her as Gent Esquia of Minerba, a name already assumed by Miraval for his patron called `N Gent Esquieu. It is possible that they were married. It is possible that `N [Sir] Gent Esquieu was the *seigneur* of Minerve who figures under the designation of Esquivus de Menerba, among the guarantors of the act by which the young viscount of Béziers donated goods to the count of Foix in 1202. Under the name Schius de Menerba, he figures as a witness in the aforementioned marriage contract between Jordan of Cabaretz, son of Bernard, and Orbrisse, daughter of Guillaume de Durban (January 1211). The seigneur of Minerve had fairly good relations with the family of Cabaretz. It is clear that the marqueza was not the wife of Guilhem de Minerve, who by 1191 had for his wife Rixovende de Termes. We can thus date the period of Miraval's interest in Mais d'Amic and in the marqueza as being between about 1196 and 1204.

22. Miraval, "Rien ne garantit de l'Amour" [Nothing Guarantees Love] (song), in Nelli, *Le Roman de Raimon de Miraval*, 77–80. v. 6.

23. Ibid.

24. Ibid., "Entre Deux Désirs je reste songeur" [Between Two Desires I Remain Thoughtful] (song to Azalaïs de Boissézon), in Nelli, *Le Roman de Raimon de Miraval,* 137.

25. Ibid.

26. Ibid., "Maintenant que le Froid est dans toute sa force" [Now That the Cold Is in All Its Force] (comments to Pedro II about Azalaïs), in Nelli, *Le roman de Raimon de Miraval,* 145, v. 6.

27. Ibid., "Celui a qui convient la Joie" [The One to Whom Joy Is Suited] (song to Azalaïs de Boissézon), in Nelli, *Le Roman de Raimon de Miraval,* 147, v. 8.

28. The name of Miraval's wife is known to us by the sirventès of Uc de Mataplana, the Catalan lord with whom Miraval exchanged several works, as well as from razo D. It seems he had a falling out with Uc over differing views of duty toward his wife. The custom among the nobility—especially the Cathar nobility—was that once the honor of marriage had been accepted by the lady, she became linked to her future spouse as a vassal by "a sure *hommage,*" while he was at liberty to abandon her should she displease him. Among other examples is the aforementioned Jordan of Cabaretz, who brought upon himself the anger of the Catholic Church when he repudiated his wife, Orbria, under the cover of the Cathar doctrine that discouraged sex and marriage altogether (since they were believed to lead to the enslavement of more divine soul in the demonic world—that is, this one), and then lived in contented conjugality with Lady Mabilia. According to Uc de Mataplana, Gaudairenca was herself a poet and composer of dances, and Miraval was alleged to have said: "Two poets in one house is too many." Nevertheless, the razo appears to have greatly exaggerated the dispute between Raimon and his wife because, in a sirventès to Uc, he says that he is ready to be reconciled with Gaudairenca.

29. Miraval, "Je vais tout triste et plein de Hargne" [I'm Becoming All Sad and Bad-Tempered] (song to Brunissens or Brunessen de Cabaretz), in Nelli, *Le Roman de Raimon de Miraval,* 175, v. 5

30. Ibid., "Entre Deux Désirs je reste songeur" [Between Two Desires I Remain Thoughtful] (song to Azalaïs de Boissézon), in Nelli, *Le Roman de Raimon de Miraval,* 137, v. 6.

31. Ibid., "Longtemps j'ai eu des soucis" [For a Long Time I Have Had Cares] (song to Azalaïs de Boissézon), in Nelli, *Le Roman de Raimon de Miraval,* 131, v. 3.

32. Anne Brenon, *Le Vrai Visage du Catharisme,* 178.

33. Nelli, *Le Roman de Raimon de Miraval,* 121.

34. Miraval, "Maintenant que le Froid est dans toute sa force"[Now That

the Cold Is in All Its Force] (song), in Nelli, *Le Roman de Raimon de Miraval*, 145, v. 7.

35. In other words, an anima archetype, the soul conceived in gnostic psychology as feminine and exalted as the heavenly Sophia, or Wisdom, who falls to earth and whose resurrection is celebrated in the psychic life of the gnostic within the mystery of the alchemical wedding, the *mysterium coniunctionis*.

36. Miraval, "Celui qui ne veut pas écouter de chansons" [The One Who Doesn't Want to Hear Songs], in Nelli, *Le Roman de Raimon de Miraval*, 153, v.5.

37. Nelli, *Le Roman de Raimon de Miraval, troubadour*, 156

38. Miraval, "Celui a Qui Convient la Joie" [The One to Whom Joy Is Suited], in Nelli, *Le Roman de Raimon de Miraval*, 147.

39. Winters are quite miserable in the Languedoc. By the end of November, glorious summers are quickly cut off with the sudden appearance of winter—quite different conditions from those evoking the autumnal feelings found in English and German traditional minstrelsy. The courtly season is always associated with springtime, youth, valor, birdsong, flowers. This gives the works archetypal resonance and the power of rebirth in every age. There is more to the nostalgia theme, however. The golden age is simply a psychological archetype, and it is in everyone: *There was a time when . . .* This archetype is one of the most creative of all. The wish for the Arthurian legendary court that became popular in Miraval's day makes chivalry come alive and gives it a spiritual depth that military function does not permit. Time and time again these golden ages initiate periods that in retrospect appear themselves to have been golden ages, such as the High Middle Ages, the Renaissance (with its Hermetic golden age and Atlantean mythologies), the period of the Albion of Blake, and the Romantic era, with its spiritual radicals. There seems little doubt, however, that the archetype functions better when it is activated unconsciously and in innocence, as in the case of the troubadours. Of course, Miraval did not need the legend of Arthur and his knights. The history of the region of Occitania itself was inspiring enough, and the classical world and Rome of late antiquity must have seemed in the twelfth century to be psychologically close, especially since the language and even costume had barely changed since the time of Joseph of Arimathaea, regardless of Visigothic settlement and occasional Frankish incursions.

40. Miraval, "Blessed be the Message," in Nelli, *Le Roman de Raimon de Miraval*, 159.

41. Ibid., "Celui qui ne veut pas écouter de chansons" [The One Who Doesn't Want to Hear Songs], in Nelli, *Le Roman de Raimon de Miraval*, 153.

42. To clarify this much misunderstood dimension of troubadour life: After *le jazer,* real love begins. Carnal and cordial love cannot be separated

unless spiritual love is at risk, in which case carnal love must be rejected as not being real love. (This would hardly be possible or conceivable in a marriage situation.)

43. In alchemical language, the *mercurius* crucified upon the four elements of nature.

44. Miraval, "Rien ne garantit de l'Amour" [Nothing Guarantees Love], in Nelli, *Le Roman de Raimon de Miraval,* 77, v. 2.

45. Quoted in Lewis, *Allegory of Love,* 18–19.

46. Andreas Cappelanus, "De arte honeste amandi" [The Virtuous Art of Loving], in Lewis, *Allegory of Love,* 40.

47. Our word *bugger* comes from Bulgar or Bougre—that is, Bulgarian, for the Cathars came originally to the Languedoc via Bulgaria.

48. Capellanus, "De arte honeste amandi" [The Virtuous Art of Loving], quoted in Lewis, *Allegory of Love,* 41.

49. The Cathar Church was divided into the *perfecti* (French: *parfaits*) and the *auditores.* The perfecti, the leaders of the church, renounced marriage, sex, meat, all food connected with procreation (such as milk, eggs, and cheese), money, and property. Most followers waited until they were older before entering upon the definitive rite of the Consolamentum, after which the practice of charitable love, laying-on of hands, teaching, and, above all, the meditative commitment to divine knowledge became their sole business on earth. Jordan de Cabaretz could thus find Catharist justification for renouncing his marriage to Orbria. There is no indication as to whether this motive was applied cynically or not; lords generally did as they pleased.

50. Anne Brenon, *Le Vrai Visage du Catharisme,* 176.

51. Perfected Cathar; one who had received the sacrament of the Consolamentum, a rite that severed the spirit from bondage to the material world and its passions.

52. Peire Vidal, "A per pauc de chantar nom lais" [For a Little I'd Give Up Singing], *Troubadour Lyric Poetry,* ed. A. R. Press (Edinburgh: University Press), 205, v. 2.

53. Brenon, *Le Vrai Visage du Catharisme,* 180.

54. Ibid., 181.

55. Jung, introduction to *Psychology and Alchemy.*

56. Miraval, "Il me plait de chanter et de me montrer aimable" [It Pleases Me to Sing and Appear Lovable], in Nelli, *Le roman de Raimon de Miraval,* 179.]

57. Nelli, *Le Roman de Raimon de Miraval,* 181.

58. The Gospel of Truth, in *The Nag Hammadi Library,* Codex 1, page 16, line 32; page 17, line 4.

59. The Gospel of Philip, in *The Nag Hammadi Library,* Codex 2, page 77, line 35; page 82, lines 1–11 (précis).

60. Ezra Pound, "The Psychology of the Troubadours," in *The Spirit of Romance* (New York: New Directions, 2000).

61. Omar Garrison, *Tantra: The Yoga of Sex* (London: Academy Editions, 1972).

62. John Kimsey, *Gnosis* (Winter 1988).

63. Such as the Rolling Stones' "Sympathy for the Devil" (1968), which refers to "troubadours who get killed before they reach Bombay." In 1980 a journalist compared John Lennon's song "Woman" to that of a medieval troubadour in an interview with the songwriter. Lennon did not demur.

Chapter 7 The Knights Templar

1. The Vatican was at times deeply interested in the new knowledge coming from the East. Before 1090, Pope Sylvester II went to Toledo in person to investigate new literary arrivals; it would be interesting to know what this savant was looking for (source: Matthew Scanlan, from a conversation with the author, London, 1997). The papacy's attitude to new learning depended on the particular pope.

2. Quoted in Howarth, *Knights Templar* (London: Macmillan, 1982), 118.

3. The wearing of the cross began in 1147 by order of Pope Eugenius III, the first Cistercian pope and a pupil of St. Bernard of Clairvaux.

4. For example, Abbé Barruel, *Mémoires pour servir à l'histoire du Jacobinisme* [Memoirs to Contribute to the History of Jacobinism], 3 vols. (London, 1797–98); Joseph von Hammer-Purgstall, "Mysterium Baphometis revelatum" (The Mystery of Baphomet Revealed), *Fundgruben des Orients* 6 (1818): 1–120, 445–99. These works linked the Templars to a pattern of secret transmission of Gnostic practice stemming from the time of the persecution of the Manichees (third and fourth centuries A.D.) and set off a stream of extravagant speculation that persists to the present day.

5. One of the chief problems is that the great bulk of Templar records disappeared at the time of the trials. A significant cache of Templar documents is thought to have been in the hands of the Knights of Malta at the time of the siege of Cyprus by the Ottoman Turks in 1525. Allegedly, the documents were left to the Turks when the Knights of Malta left the island. According to the Masonic historian Matthew Scanlan, there are reasons for not accepting this story at face value.

6. Recently translated into English by Judi Upton-Ward as *Rule of the Templars.*

7. Baigent, Lincoln, and Leigh, *Holy Blood, Holy Grail,* 63.

8. Wolfram von Eschenbach (*flor.* c. 1195–1225), an admirer of the Languedoc troubadours, was the greatest of the German narrative poets.

Little is known of his life. He belonged to a Bavarian family of the lower nobility. He may have served a Franconian lord and was patronized in his writing by Hermann, Landgrave of Thuringia.

9. According to A. T. Hatto, translator of the Penguin *Parzifal,* in Wolfram's original work the "Templars are *templeis.* Since he gives us a Gral Temple, it seemed legitimate to render *templeis* as 'Templar': yet it would be wrong to read into this term, by association, any more than is told of these knights in *Parzifal.*" It is obvious from Wolfram's text that the Gral knights were not Templars as one would see in his lifetime. They wear "a surcoat either of brocade or samite," not the plain wool of the historical Templars. Of course, Wolfram might be playing with concepts, and his Gral knights could represent idealized Knights Templar translated to a higher existence of special service. The real issue here is how Wolfram's contemporaries would have read the word *templeis.* The battered appearance of Templars from *Parzifal* that opened this chapter would, I think, have suggested something very much like the Knights Templar to people in the early thirteenth century.

10. The relevant lists of defenders have been exhaustively studied in Michel Roquebert's seminal study *L'epopée Cathare* [The Cathar Epoch], vol. 1: "L'Invasion" (1979); vol. 2: "La Dépossession" (1977); vol. 3: "Les Lys at la croix" (1986) (Toulouse: Privat).

11. Reznikov, *Cathares et Templiers,* 3.

12. Ibid., 154–55.

13. Ibid. 155.

14. Words of pardon and valedictory blessing offered to confessing sinners at the end of Temple services, original version versus DeMolay's, quoted in Howarth, *Knights Templar,* 81 ff.

15. G. C. Addison, *History of the Knights Templars* (London, 1842), 263.

16. *Docetic* is from the Greek *dokein,* "to seem." Thus, Jesus only seemed to be what people ordinarily understand as a human being; the physical constraints on him were apparent and not absolute.

17. This area requires further investigation. The Templar Rule required that temples in the East have either a master who spoke Arabic or, at the least, a translator. Complaints were made against masters of temples in Palestine that they had free intercourse with "heathens" (Muslims), even allowing them to celebrate religious rites in their homes (see Forey, *Military Orders*). Clearly, there must have been an exchange of ideas and philosophy. It can hardly be stated too strongly that the task of the Templars was to protect pilgrims and ensure easy passage to the holy places, not to generate conflict with Muslims at every opportunity. Having diplomatic contact with Muslim authorities was essential for their task. Gnostic influences were entering the West through (Sabian) translations (from Greek and Syriac to Arabic) of Neoplatonic, Hermetic,

alchemical, and magical works. Tolerance of Islam must have increased over a long period of familiarity. We know that two masters of English temples ordered the translation of certain books of the Bible (including the books of Maccabees) into French, along with Hebrew and Arabic supplementary commentaries. (The Church forbade reading the Bible in the vernacular at this time.) To some Westerners with no experience of the East, such interests may well have appeared suspect. Catholics were taught to regard Muhammad ("Mahomet") as a devil.

The problem in comprehending Templar culture has been exacerbated by attempts to find specifically heretical ideas among them (such as Catharism). Hermes, for example, was regarded as an authority in Western universities, and as long ago as c. A.D. 400 (by Lactantius) as a prophet who foretold Christ. Hermes was also a name with authority in matters of architecture and practical masonry—as well as alchemy.

18. The Shroud appeared in France after the dissolution of the temple in the family of de Charney. Disputed, however, is whether this was the same de Charney family as that which produced Geoffrey de Charney, the Templar Preceptor of Normandy who was burned alongside Jacques de Molay. (For those who would assert a Templar continuity in Scotland after its official suppression there in 1360, when its lands were given to the Knights of St. John, it is noteworthy that *a* Geoffrey de Charney fought against the English alongside King Robert II of Scotland (of the family of Stewarts who came to the Scottish throne on March 26, 1371). Regarding the Shroud of Turin itself, it has recently been proved to be a late medieval forgery. An investigation in South Africa into how the forgery was achieved revealed the possibility that the Shroud could have been produced by a photographic process of great ingenuity—making it the world's first photograph, or rather photographic negative. The technology required was available at the time. The Templars themselves, of course, had access to the sciences of the East, including alchemy, knowledge of which could have furnished an artist-forger with the requisite capability. The important thing for us is that knowledge was available in the East that astonished Westerners, and the Templar leadership, by the thirteenth century at least, was certainly interested in acquiring it. The Order of the Temple was, after all, a monastic-type order with many links both to other monastic orders and to tradesmen, artisans, and trade guilds.

19. Wolfram von Eschenbach, *Parzifal,* 232.

20. Spurious connections between the Gral and Catharism are explored in a scholarly and thorough fashion in Michel Roquebert's exhaustive work *Les Cathares et le Graal.* Roquebert makes it plain that the major accounts of the Holy Grail in the period of flourishing Catharism (c. 1160–1256) owe their Christological background to Catholic eucharistic doctrines (the holy cup of sacramental wine/blood), whatever the sources

of the Grail or Gral image might be. Visionary mysticism was not the prerogative of heretical movements, whether gnostic or any other kind. Anyone can use a symbol for his or her own purposes. There is no evidence that the Cathars had any interest in the Gral symbology—and even if they did, and the evidence has yet to come to light—they would certainly not have linked it to the eucharistic cup in the way that Chrétien de Troyes does, since Cathars found the transubstantiation concept of the Eucharist abhorrent in any form. Chrétien de Troyes's patron, Philippe d'Alsace, count of Flanders—who commissioned *Perceval the Gaul or the Story of the Graal* when he came to Troyes in 1182, hoping to marry Marie of Champagne, daughter of King Louis VII of France—was a determined persecutor of all heretics, including the Cathars.

21. According to Hatto (*Parzifal*, 431 ff.), Wolfram has apparently taken the word from a work (which he knew and used in *Parzifal*) called *Alexander*, written in early German, wherein we hear of a miraculous stone that a Latin translator calls the *lapis exilis*, the "small" or "slight stone." Subsequent versions of Wolfram's work have apparently repeated a mistake by an early copyist, unless Wolfram was indulging in an obscure pun. The small or uncomely stone is of course completely consistent with traditional alchemy's assessment of the stone as being something unnoticed or invisible to the eyes of the world, deriving from what Jung calls the "psychic non-ego" or "unconscious": a direct link to the spiritual world.

22. The Phoenix that emerges from alchemical fire is a staple symbol for resurrection in medieval alchemy and beyond. In the polyvalent world that is alchemy, it is related to the peacock and to Christ, who, from a Christian reading of the medieval Arabic *Tractatus aureus,* can be identified with the stone. It is from the stone that the knights ride out in quest of adventure. The mountain itself is also a polyvalent alchemical symbol. The stone is generally both the start and the goal of the alchemical opus of transformation.

23. It is significant that access to the stone can be achieved in this world.

24. We have already learned from Flegetanis that a troop of angels left the stone on earth in the first place. The mythology behind this story is strongly reminiscent of the account in the *Book of Enoch* (c. first century B.C.), wherein Enoch is told that the secrets of heaven were brought illegitimately to humans by the Watchers, stellar angels who rebelled against the Lord of Spirits. Rebel angels having brought the stone, neutral angels had to descend to earth, in what was apparently a punishment, to make contact with the stone. From the psychological point of view, this myth is highly suggestive.

25. Wolfram von Eschenbach, *Parzifal,* chapter 9.

26. *Corpus Hermeticum,* Libellus 4.25.

27. The Egyptian alchemist Zosimos of Panopolis had, nine hundred years before, recognized the Hermetic *krater* as being directly linked to the spiritual alchemical opus.

28. In 1192, Richard left the Holy Land dressed in the guise of a Templar, after having lived with the Templars in Acre [G. C. Addison, *The History of the Knights Templars* (London, 1842), 148].

29. Carefully tutored by William Marshall, Henry III was responsible for the building of Westminster Abbey.

30. Malcolm Barber, *Trial of the Templars* (Cambridge: Cambridge University Press, 1978), 249 (the list is abridged).

31. According to Matthew Scanlan, the Valetta Palace of the Knights of Malta featured a chamber of reflection in which was placed a skull upon which to meditate. The room was surrounded by images of skulls and bones. This suggests a monastic-type meditation on death, its meaning and denouement: resurrection, rebirth—even germination, by extension to the natural world. Perhaps the practice was derived from or shared with Templars. We cannot stress enough the spiritual intensity of the discipline of conscientious Templars—and, because most were illiterate, their dependence on symbols.

32. It may be that some of these masons were Saracens. At Biddulph Moor in northern Staffordshire live the so-called Biddulph Moors, who are dark-skinned and smaller than the average English person, with full eyes having large, arresting black pupils. Their origins have caused much speculation. Some say they are Egyptians or even Phoenicians. From Doug Pickford's fascinating book, *Staffordshire: Its Magic and Mystery* (Wilmslow, Cheshire: Sigma, 1994):

    > One person credited with bringing these dark-skinned people to the Moor was the Overlord of Biddulph, Bertram de Verdon, who took part in the third Crusade and died at Joppa in 1192 and was buried at Acre. However, according to a *History of Leek* by John Sleigh, these servants or whatever, went by the name of "Paynim" and were brought here by another Lord who wrote: "A Knight Crusader is reputed to have brought over in his train from the Holy Land, Paynim, whom he made bailiff of his estate and from whose marriage with an Englishwoman the present race of 'Biddulph Moor Men' are traditionally said to have sprung." This Knight Crusader, who is thought to have been a Knight Templar named Ormus le Guidon, was the supposed son of Richard Forestarius, Lord of Darlaston, Buckinhall, Biddulph &c. According to the *Shell Guide to Staffordshire*, the Biddulph family used these Saracens, who were stonemasons, to produce the intricate carvings at St. Chad's Church in Stafford and settled them as bailiffs on the moor. These carvings have a "strangely oriental look" and there is an inscription in the

church that reads "Orm Built me," referring to Ormus le Guidon. There is no hard-and-fast evidence that the crusading knights of Biddulph were Knights Templar, although at St. Lawrence's church, Biddulph, there are a number of grave headstones of obvious antiquity. On these stone slabs are carvings of crusader's crosses and several of them are very similar to Templar crosses.

Having investigated these carvings with Matthew Scanlan, I have found them to be consistent in detail with known Templar gravestones elsewhere. The whole area, it should be noted, is bounded by Cistercian monasteries: Croxden (where King John's heart was buried), Dieulacres, and Hulton. The nearest known center for these Knights Templar was at Keele, while nearby Hulton Abbey, a Cistercian monastery, owned the pasture rights for sheep on the moor and at Biddulph; these white-robed monks had strong connections with the Templars. This is all suggestive of how much serious research remains to be done in the field of Templar beliefs.

33. Peter Partner, *The Murdered Magicians: The Templars and Their Myth* (Oxford: Oxford University Press, 1982). As the title suggests, the book is most effective in debunking the myth of esoteric Templarism that developed within Continental Freemasonry in the eighteenth century. There is also a tendency to debunk the Templars themselves by stressing so much of the criticism aimed at them by their contemporary opponents. The book is valuable, however, as a balance to the excesses of romantics.

34. Marsilio Ficino, publisher of the first printed edition of the *Pymander* of Hermes Trismegistus (Treviso, 1471), while seeking pagan vestiges of the Christian Trinity found the Chaldean trinity of Ohrmazd-Mithra-Ahriman in Plutarch's (c. A.D. 46–120) *De Iside et Osiride,* 46, and *Moralia,* 369E; while the biographer of Ficino's friend Pico della Mirandola, Thomas More, wrote in Book 2 of his world-famous *Utopia* that the Utopians "call on no peculiar name of God, but only Mithra, in which word they all agree together in one nature of the divine majesty whatsoever it may be." More understood Mithra to be a universal name for the universal giver of life.

35. The three-faced head is highly suggestive of a cyclic process enacted in the life of human beings. While this is not the only use of the image in postmedieval iconography, the following incidence of the image does demonstrate how an author adept in traditional (and particularly alchemical) symbolism uses it to denote a cyclic process: On the title page of Book 3 of Johann Valentin Andreae's *Mythologiae Christianae sive virtutem & vitiorum vitae humanae imaginum* (Strasbourg: Lazarus Zetzner, 1619) is engraved a head on a plinth with three faces: youth, maturity, and old age. On the front of the plinth is a pyramid (the triadic theme again), below which is a Latin imperative for each of the faces of life: For youth, *discuss* it; for maturity, *pursue* it; for old age, *be wise.*

36. This was Monsieur Hersent, priest to Baron de Poly (buried in Banbury), who, though a German baron, had fought for Louis XVI and had escaped to England from the Reign of Terror, bringing with him his Catholic priest. (I am indebted to my father, Victor Churton, for this information and for access to the Churton Papers, which he discovered and catalogued.)

37. Churton Papers (Ralph Churton–J. B. Blakeway correspondence, 1821–1825), letter dated Friday, February 21, 1823, from Middleton Cheney rectory to the Council House, Shrewsbury.

38. If the purpose of the supposed Templar excavation around the Stables of Solomon was more than merely the practical one of providing stabling for their horses—and it should be recalled that a good warhorse had the value in medieval warfare of a tank in modern warfare—then any supposed discoveries beneath the Temple site might have been more mundane than the symbolically powerful stones of the ancient altar. The "Copper Scroll" from the Qumran corpus (Dead Sea Scrolls, c. second century B.C.–first century A.D.) gives an account of at least twenty-four hoards of treasure alleged by the author or authors of the "Copper Scroll" to have been hidden beneath the Temple. Even if such had existed at that place, however, more than a thousand years had passed between the time the Qumran community flourished and the coming of the Templars; practically anything could have happened in the meantime—not to mention the fact that at the destruction of the Temple by Titus in A.D. 70, a great treasure was translated to Rome.

39. Matthew Scanlan, "A Town called Kilwinning," in *Freemasonry Today*, no. 13 (October 2000): 20–22.

40. Andrew Michael Ramsay, "Oration."

41. A. C . F. Jackson, *Rose Croix* (London: Lewis Masonic, 1980).

42. D. Murray Lyon, *History of the Lodge of Edinburgh*, 9–11.

Chapter 8 Jacob Böhme's Theosophick Cosmos

1. Paul Tillich, preface to John Joseph Stoudt, *Sunrise to Eternity: A Study of Jacob Boehme's Life and Thought* (Philadelphia: University of Pennsylvania Press, 1957).

2. Scholem, *Major Trends in Jewish Mysticism*, 206.

3. For a study on Schwenckfeld, Franck, Weigel, and Paracelsianism, see my book *The Golden Builders*.

4. Quoted in Rufus M. Jones, *Spiritual Reformers in the 16th and 17th Centuries* (Boston: Beacon Press, 1959), 159.

5. *De Vita et Scriptis Jacobi Bohmii* (with Böhme's Works), ed. J. G. Gichtel (Amsterdam, 1682), para. 12, quoted in Hirst, *Hidden Riches*, 85.

6. Ibid., para. 11, 85.

7. Jacob Böhme, *Von 117 theosophischen Fragen* (Amsterdam, 1693), 3.34, 7.11.

8. Account of Dr. Tobias Kober, quoted in Stoudt, *Sunrise to Eternity*, 191.

9. Jacob Böhme, closing paragraph from "Of Heaven and Hell: A Dialogue Between Junius, a Scholar, and Theophorus, His Master," in G. Ward and T. Langcake, eds., *The Works of Jacob Behmen*, trans. William Law, 4 vols. (London, 1764–81).

10. There is a conceptual correspondence between Böhme's Ungrund and the Valentinian Gnostic Bythos, or "depth," at the heart of the divine Pleroma or Fullness.

11. Hirst, *Hidden Riches*, 89.

12. Jacob Böhme, *An Apology and Reply upon Esaiah Stiefel*, trans. John Sparrow (London, 1651), no. 16, 90.

13. Ibid., *40 Questions of the Soul* (London, 1655), no. 11, 12.

14. Ibid., *Sämtliche Schriften* (Collected Writings), ed. W. E. Peuckert, vol. 16 (Stuttgart, Germany: Frommann, 1957), 233.

15. Edward Taylor, *Jacob Behmen's Theosophick Philosophy Unfolded*, 2 (preceding the preface).

16. Jacob Böhme, *Mysterium magnum* (London, 1654), chapter 18, no. 2.

17. Quoted in Evelyn Underhill, *Mysticism: A Study in the Nature and Development of Man's Spiritual Consciousness*, 2nd ed. (London, 1912), 142.

18. Ibid., "The Supersensual Life," in G. Ward and T. Langcake, eds., *Works of Jacob Behmen*, 1764–81.

19. Ibid., *Of the Election of Grace*, trans. John Sparrow (London, 1655), 6, no. 29.

20. Ibid., *Mysterium magnum*, quoted in Stoudt, *Sunrise to Eternity*, 264–66.

21. Ibid., *The Three Principles*, 13, 41.

22. C. H. Josten, ed., *Elias Ashmole, 1617–1692*, vol. 2 (Oxford: Oxford University Press, 1966), 554, note 1.

23. Anthony Wood, *Athenae Oxoniensis*, ed. Bliss and J. Ferguson, *Bibliotheca Chemica*, vol. 2 (Glasgow, 1906), 214–15.

24. MS. Ashm. 374, f. 74, Bodleian Library, Oxford, U.K.

25. "On the Rise and Progress of the Philadelphian Society," Bodleian MS. Rawlinson, D. 833. fol. 65 recto, Bodleian Library, Oxford, U.K.

26. Quoted in Gordon L. Miller, *The Way of the English Mystics: An Anthology and Guide for Pilgrims*.

27. William Law, *The Spirit of Prayer*, vol. 7 in *The Works of the Rev. William Law* (Brockenhurst, U.K.: G. B. Morgan, 1892–93), 28.

28. Ibid.

29. Quoted in Hirst, *Hidden Riches.*

30. Ibid.

31. William Law, *An Appeal to All That Doubt or Disbelieve the Truths of the Gospel* (1742).

32. Ibid., *The Spirit of Prayer, or the Soul Rising Out of the Vanity of Time, into the Riches of Eternity* (London, 1750), 8–10.

33. Hirst, *Hidden Riches,* 181.

34. William Law, *The Spirit of Love.*

35. William Ralph Inge, "Studies of English Mystics." *St. Margaret's Lectures, 1905* (London: John Murray, 1906).

36. Quoted in Inge, *Studies of English Mystics, St. Margaret's Lectures, 1905* (London: John Murray, 1906).

37. Harriett Watts, "Arp, Kandinsky, and the Legacy of Jacob Böhme," in Nancy Grubb, ed., *The Spiritual in Art: Abstract Painting 1895–1985* (New York: Abbeville, 1987), 239 ff.

38. Alexandre Koyré, *La Philosophie de Jacob Böhme* (Paris: J. Vrin, Librairie Philosophique, 1929).

39. Harriett Watts, *Spiritual in Art,* 239.

40. Ibid., 241.

41. Friedrich von Schelling, *The Ages of the World,* trans. Friedrich Bohmann (New York: Columbia University Press, 1942), 215.

42. Kathleen Raine, *Blake and Antiquity,* 74.

43. Compare this with the journey of young Christian Rosenkreuz in Johann Valentin Andreae's *Chymische Hochzeit* (Strasbourg: Lazarus Zetzner, 1616).

44. For a thorough treatment of the outlook of the original Rosicrucians, see my book *The Golden Builders,* part 2, "The True Story of the Rosicrucians," 79 ff.

45. Kathleen Raine, *Blake and Tradition.*

46. Quoted in Raine, *Blake and Antiquity,* 70.

47. Hirst, *Hidden Riches,* 94.

48. Jacob Böhme, quoted in Raine, *Blake and Antiquity,* 74.

49. William Blake quoted in Raine, *Blake and Antiquity,* 74.

50. William Blake, "A Memorable Fancy," in *Marriage of Heaven and Hell* (1790).

51. William Blake, quoted in Raine, *Blake and Antiquity,* 74.

52. Jacob Böhme, *Aurora* (1612), in *The Works of Jacob Behmen,* ed. George Ward and Thomas Langcake, 4 vols. (London, 1764–81).

53. William Blake, "The Tyger," in *Songs of Experience* (1794).

54. Jacob Böhme, quoted in Raine, 81, from *The Works of Jacob Behmen*, ed. George Ward and Thomas Langcake, 4 vols. (London: 1764–81). This edition is commonly known under the name of William Law; each work in each volume is separately paginated.

55. Kathleen Raine, *Blake and Antiquity*, 75.

56. William Blake, "Proverbs of Hell," in *The Marriage of Heaven and Hell*.

57. William Blake, "Auguries of Innocence," in *Blake: Complete Writings*, ed. Geoffrey Keynes, Oxford Standard Authors (London, 1966), 431.

58. Quoted in Underhill, *Mysticism*.

59. Jacob Böhme, quoted in Raine, 81.

60. Kathleen Raine, *Blake and Antiquity*, 81.

61. Jacob Böhme quoted in Raine, 87.

62. Kathleen Raine, *Blake and Antiquity*, 87.

Chapter 9 Germany 1710–1800: The Return of the Rosy Cross

1. McIntosh, *Rose Cross*, 10.

2. Max Weber, *Geschichtliche Grundbegriffe*, vol. 1, eds. Otto Brunner, Werner Conze, and Reinhart Koselleck (Stuttgart, Germany: Ernst Klett/JG Cotta, 1972–82), 245.

3. See Vico's *The New Science*, excerpted by Franklin Le Van Baumer, *Main Currents of Western Thought* (New Haven, Conn.: Yale University Press, 1978), 448–50.

4. See part 2 of my book *The Golden Builders* for a full account of the historical origins of the Rosicrucian manifestos.

5. McIntosh, *Rose Cross*, 21.

6. Ibid., 30.

7. Sincerus Renatus, *Die wahrhaffte und volkommene Bereitung des philosophischen Steins der Brüderschaft aus dem Orden des Gulden und Rosen Kreutzes*, quoted in McIntosh, *Rose Cross*, 32.

8. Frankfurt/Leipzig/Erfurt, Jungnicol (1737); two copies in the Wellcome Institute Library (1737); and a cruder copy of 1750 (MSS. 4808 and 4809).

9. Archarion, *Von Wahrer Alchemie*, Freiburg-im-Breisgau, Hermann Bauer, 1967, 153–56, quoted in McIntosh, *Rose Cross*, 35.

10. Statistics from Michael Voges, *Aufklärung und Geheimnis* (Tübingen, Germany: Max Niemeyer, 1987), 64 ff.

11. Arnold Marx, *Die Gold und Rosenkreuzer* (Zeulenroda/Leipzig, Germany: Freimaurer-Museum, 1930).

12. Ludwig Abafi-Aigner, "Die Entstehung der neuen Rosenkreuzer" [The Rise of the New Rosicrucians], in *Die Bauhütte* 36, no. 11 (March 18, 1893): 81–85.

13. Ibid., 82.

14. Arnold Marx, *Die Gold und Rosenkreuzer,* 19.

15. McIntosh, *Rose Cross,* 52.

16. Johannes Schultze, "Die Rosenkreuzer und Friedrich Wilhelm II," in *Forschungen zur brandenburgischen und preussischen Geschichte* [Investigations into the Brandenburg and Prussian Affair] (Berlin: de Gruyter, 1964), 241–42.

17. As is well known, Freemasonry was to play a highly significant and instrumental role in the forming of the ideals on which George Washington (Alexandria Lodge No. 22) and his associates based the United States Constitution.

18. Gerhard Steiner, *Freimaurer und Rosenkreuzer: Georg Forsters Weg durch die Geheimbünde* [Freemasons and Rosicrucians: Georg Forster's Path through the Secret League] (Berlin: Akademie-Verlag 1985), 65 ff.

19. From *Geistliches Blumen-Gärtlein inniger Seelen* [The Spiritual Flower Garden of Profound Souls] (Lancaster, Pa., 1823), quoted in *Pietists: Selected Writings,* trans. and ed. Peter C. Erb (London: SPCK, 1983), 249.

20. Library of the Grand Lodge of the Netherlands (Den Haag, Kloß Collection), 1198 17, 193.A.9, unnumbered folios of letters.

21. Indeed, we find Weishaupt's name among the saints of Aleister Crowley's *Gnostic Mass,* although exactly how much Crowley knew about the Illuminati is debatable. Of course, to the convinced conspiracy theorist, the mere mention of Crowley's name is enough to damn Weishaupt and his aims: Was not Crowley the arch-Satanist dedicated to subversion of prevailing religious authority?

22. McIntosh, *Rose Cross,* 102.

23. J. M. Roberts, *The Mythology of the Secret Societies* (London: Secker and Warburg, 1972), 119–21.

24. *Einige Originalschriften des Illuminatenordens welche bey dem gewesenen Regierungsrath Zwack durch vorgenommene Hausvisitation zu Landshut den 11 und 12 Oktober 1786 vorgefunden wurden* (Munich: Anton Franz, 1787); sequel: *Nachtrag von weiteren Originalschriften welche die Illuminatensekte überhaupt, sonderbar aber den Stiften derselben Adam Weishaupt, gewesenen Professor zu Ingolstadt betreffen* (Munich: 1878), 53 ff.

25. For information on the order's structure and history, consult J. M. Roberts, "The Mythology of the Secret Societies"; Richard van Dülmen, "Der Geheimbund der Illuminaten"; and Ludwig Hammermayer, "Höhepunkt und Wandel: Die Illuminaten," in Max Spindler, ed., *Handbuch der bayerischen Geschichte,* vol. 4 (Munich, 1988), 1269–70; and Hans Graßl, *Aufbruch zur Romantick* (Munich: Beck, 1968).

26. Weishaupt, *Originalschriften,* 148–49.

27. Decree sent to Maltzahn, March 17, 1783, from the Vice Generalats Secretariat, Library of the Grand Lodge of the Netherlands (Den Haag: Kloß Collection).

28. McIntosh, *Rose Cross*, 109.

29. Schultze, "Die Rosenkreuzer," 245.

30. For a summary and quotations from Wöllner's *Abhandlung*, see Paul Schwartz, *Der erste Kulturkampf in Preußen um Kirche und Schule (1788–98)*, in Monumenta Germaniae Pedagogica, vol. 58 (Berlin: Weidmann, 1925), 73–91.

31. The text of the "Edict Concerning Religion" is printed, *inter alia*, in C. L. H. Rabe, *Sammlung Preußischer Gesetze* (1893), 11–12.

32. Eckartshausen's work *The Cloud upon the Sanctuary* would convince a young Aleister Crowley a century later (1898) of the usefulness of joining another Hermetic society, the Golden Dawn, based in Paris and London.

33. McIntosh, *Rose Cross*, 148.

34. Eugen Lennhoff and Oskar Posner, *Internationales Freimaurer-Lexicon* (Vienna/Munich, Amalthea Verlag, 1980), 207 ff.

35. Bon Pasteur "Instruction to Candidates"; M. Thalmann, "Das System der Loge 'du Bon Pasteur,' " in *Das Freimaurer-Museum*, vol. 2 (Leipzig: Bruno Zechel, 1926).

36. Antoine Faivre, *Eckartshausen et la théosophie chrétienne* [Eckartshausen and Christian Theosophy] (Paris: Lincksieck, 1969), 620, note 329.

37. Georg von Rauch, "Johann Georg Schwarz und die Freimaurer in Moskau," in *Beförder Aufklärung in Mittel-und Osteuropa* [Promoting the Enlightenment in Central and Eastern Europe], eds. Eva H. Balázs, Ludwig Hammermayer, Hans Wagner, and Jerzy Wojtowiccz (Berlin: Ulrich Camen, 1979), 213, 216–17.

38. Faivre, *Eckartshausen et la théosophie chrétienne*, 623–24.

39. It was said of Blake that had he lived in Germany, his works would have come under the survey of the finest minds and earned him widespread appreciation. I hope this chapter demonstrates how accurate that view is. Alas, Blake was a prophet both for and in his own country.

40. McIntosh, *Rose Cross*, 161 ff.

41. Jacob Katz, *Jews and Freemasons in Europe, 1723–1939* (Cambridge, Mass.: Harvard University Press, 1970), 84.

42. McIntosh, *Rose Cross*, 164.

43. Katz, *Jews and Freemasons*, 41.

Chapter 10 Freemasonry in France

1. John Henry Newman's phrase for the effect of liberalism in theology.

2. Auguste Viatte, *Les Sources occultes du romantisme* [The Occult Sources of Romanticism], vol. 1 (Paris: Champion, 1928), chapter 2.

3. René le Forestier, *La Franc-maçonnerie occultiste au XVIIIe siècle et l'ordre des Elus Coëns* [Eighteenth-century Occult Freemasonry and the Order of Elect Cohens] (Paris: Dorbon, 1928).

4. See A. E. Waite, *The Unknown Philosopher: The Life of Louis Claude de Saint-Martin and the Substance of His Transcendental Doctrine* (New York: Rudolph Steiner Publications Blauvelt, 1970).

5. Martines de Pasqually, *Des Érreures et de la Verité* (Edinbourg [Lyon], 1782), quoted in McIntosh, *Rose Cross*, 41.

6. Ibid., 44.

7. Ibid., 287.

8. Éliphas Lévi, *L'Assomption de la Femme,* quoted in McIntosh, *Éliphas Lévi,* 77.

9. Quoted in ibid., 83.

10. Quoted in ibid., 94.

11. Quoted in ibid., 97–98.

12. Quoted in ibid., 99–100.

13. Ibid., 117.

14. Quoted in ibid., 136.

15. Five months later, Edward Alexander Crowley was born in Leamington Spa, Warwickshire. Crowley thought there was a good chance that he was the reincarnation of Éliphas Lévi, but he didn't belabor the point.

16. Lévi, *Les Portes de l'avenir: Dernières Paroles d'un voyant* [The Gates of the Future: Last words of a Seer] (1870). This unpublished manuscript formerly belonged to Wynn Westcott (founder-member of the Hermetic Order of the Golden Dawn, and in 1972 was in the possession of Geoffrey Watkins. See McIntosh, *Éliphas Lévi,* 136.

17. McIntosh, *Éliphas Lévi,* 146.

18. Quoted in ibid., 149.

19. Quoted in ibid., 149–50.

20. Quoted in ibid., 151–52.

21. Éliphas Lévi (last words), *Clés Majeures et clavicules de Salomon* (Major Keys and Minor Keys of Solomon) (Paris: Chaumel, 1895), quoted in McIntosh, *Éliphas Lévi,* 151–52.

22. Joséphin Péladan, *L'Art idéaliste et mystique: Doctrine de l'ordre et du salon des Rose Croix* [Idealist and Mystical Art: Order Doctrine of the Rosicrucian Salon] (Paris: Chamuel, 1894).

23. Quoted in McIntosh, *Éliphas Lévi,* 174–75.

24. Oswald Wirth, *Stanislas de Guaita: Souvenirs de son secrétaire* (Paris: Éditions du Symbolisme, 1935).

25. Quoted in McIntosh, *Éliphas Lévi*, 176.

26. *The Confessions of Aleister Crowley,* eds. John Symonds and Kenneth Grant (London: Routledge and Kegan Paul, 1979), 196.

Chapter 11 A New Aeon: Aleister Crowley

1. Yorke Collection, Warburg Institute, AC Holograph Letters, folder D.9.A4.1.

2. Yorke Collection, folder 117c.

3. Yorke Collection, Royal Court Diaries, 1929–34, folder 20b. On March 25, 1931, nine black youths aged thirteen to twenty were found guilty in Alabama of raping two white prostitutes. Eight of them were sentenced to the electric chair.

4. Yorke Collection, Royal Court Diaries, 1929–34, Folder 20b. On March 10, 1933, Crowley noted in his diary: "Great public meeting to protest against Scottsborough Outrage turned to African Rally 8PM. It would have been a perfect party if the lads had brought their razors! I danced with many whores—all colours."

5. Yorke Collection, folder 117c.

6. In the south of France in the 1920s, Crowley enjoyed the joke of asking women if they wanted the "serpent's kiss." Those who agreed offered their hand and received a bite—an anarchic *frisson* from a bygone age.

7. Yorke Collection, folder 117c.

8. Aleister Crowley, *The Magical Record of the Beast 666,* eds. John Symonds and Kenneth Grant (London: Duckworth, 1972), 108.

9. Yorke Collection, AC Holograph Letters 1899–1906, folder D6.A.1a.

10. Crowley, *Confessions*, 73.

11. Crowley achieved the world's record for height reached on K2 (Chogo Ri) in 1902 and made a heroic assault on Kangchenjunga in 1905, reaching 21,000 feet and establishing another world's record for time spent at the highest altitude. His climbs on Beachy Head and solo ascents of the Matterhorn and Eiger have become legendary. His animosity toward the Alpine Club of Great Britain ensured that his achievements were largely known only to fellow climbers.

12. The first part of Crowley's famous watchword—"Do what thou wilt shall be the whole of the law"—comes from the rule of the Abbey of Thelema (Greek for "will") in François Rabelais's *Heroic Deeds of Gargantua and Pantagruel* (c. 1532). Rabelais was included as a saint of the Gnostic Church in Crowley's *Gnostic Mass*. Taking the following extract into account, it is not difficult to see why:

All their life was spent not in laws, statutes, or rules, but according to their own free will and pleasure. They rose out of their beds when they thought good: they did eat, drink, labour, sleep, when they had a mind to it, and were disposed for it. None did awake them, none did offer to constrain them to eat, drink, nor to do any other thing; for so had Gargantua established it. In all of their rule, and strictest tie of their order, there was but one clause to be observed, DO WHAT THOU WILT. Because men that are free, well-born, well-bred, and conversant in honest companies, have naturally an instinct and spur that prompteth them unto virtuous actions, and withdraws them from vice, which is called honour. Those same men, when by base subjection and constraint they are brought under and kept down, turn aside from that noble disposition, by which they formerly were inclined to virtue, to shake off and break that bond of servitude, wherein they are so tyrannously enslaved; for it is agreeable with the nature of man to long after things forbidden, and to desire what is denied us. . . . So nobly were they taught, that there was neither he nor she amongst them, but could read, write, sing, play upon several musical instruments, speak five or six languages, and compose in them all very quaintly, both in verse and prose. . . . Never were seen so valiant knights, so noble and worthy, so dexterous and skilful both on foot and a horseback, more brisk and lively, more nimble and quick, or better handling all manner of weapons than were there.

13. Yorke Collection, AC Holograph Letters 1899–1906, folder D6.A.1.a.

14. Yorke Collection, AC Holograph Mss., folder 22.4. Rough working notes of rituals for the Temple of L.I.L. in Mexico City, 1901.

15. This is curious for many reasons pertaining to the history of Freemasonry. According to the Masonic historian John Hamill, Crowley was at some time made inspector general of John Yarker, the "Manchester Mason's" Ancient and Accepted Right of Memphis and Mizraim, being commissioned by Yarker to reduce the cumbersome ninety-seven degrees thereof to thirty-three. Crowley received his charter for the thirty-third degree in 1910. He made the rituals work, but it was too late. John Yarker had overextended his ideas, and these degrees no longer worked. Contrary to contemporary Masonic lore, Yarker was not expelled from United Grand Lodge, but rather chose to leave. Crowley's charter to work the degrees was therefore valid. As it happened, he did not do so, but incorporated them into his revised ten-degree OTO system.

16. Crowley, *Confessions*, 203.

17. Yorke Collection, AC Holograph Mss., folder 22.4. Rough working notes of rituals for the Temple of L.I.L. in Mexico City, 1901. It is interesting to see the figures of Horus and Hoor Paar Kraat (Harpocrates— the power of silence, an aspect of Horus) given such prominence,

considering their centrality to Crowley's "Great Revelation," still three years away.

18. Yorke Collection, Holograph Mss., folder 22.7.

19. Ibid.

20. Yorke Collection, AC Holograph Letters 1899–1906, folder D6.A.1. a.

21. P. R. Stephenson and Israel Regardie, *The Legend of Aleister Crowley*, 2nd ed. (St. Paul, Minn.: Llewellyn, 1970), 48.

22. Crowley, *Magical Record*, 222.

23. Quoted in *Legend of Aleister Crowley*, 48.

24. Yorke Collection, folder D.6.A1.a. Letter from Colombo, Ceylon.

25. Yorke Collection, AC Holograph Mss., Japanese vellum diary, folder 20.1.

26. Crowley, *Magical Record*, 110.

27. Ibid., 121.

28. Yorke Collection, AC Holograph Letters 1899–1906, folder D6.A.1.a.

29. Inge, *Mysticism in Religion*, 150.

30. Yorke Collection, AC Holograph Letters 1899–1906, folder D6.A.1.a.

31. Foyers Boleskine, August 12, 1903, Yorke Collection, AC Holograph Letters 1899–1906, folder D6.A.1.a.

32. Yorke Collection, small Japanese vellum notebook, "Book of Results," folder 27.5, Cairo, 1904.

33. Yorke Collection, small Japanese vellum notebook, "Invocation of Horus according to the Divine Vision of Ouarda [Rose Kelly] the Seer," folder 27.1, 1904.

34. Yorke Collection, "Book of Results," folder 27.5.

35. Ibid.

36. The stele is a funerary monument of Ankh-f-n-Khonsu, a Theban priest of Mentu who flourished circa 725 B.C. in Egypt's twenty-fifth dynasty. According to the Egyptologist Abd el Hamid Zayed, who made a study of the stele in 1968, the second part of the inscription is part of the Book of the Dead, chapter 2, "and in the Theban Recension, it was entitled: 'The chapter of coming forth by day and living after death'. Its object was to allow the astral form of the deceased to revisit the earth at will." *Revue d'égyptologie* 20 (1968): 149–52 and plate 7. See *The Holy Books of Thelema*, ed. Hymenaeus Beta (New York: 93 Publishing, 1993).

37. Yorke Collection 27.5, "Book of Results."

38. Ibid.

39. Crowley, *Confessions*, 395.

40. Yorke Collection, AL, "The Commentary called D(jeridensis) provisionally by 666" (1923), folder 16.

41. Yorke Collection, letter to Clifford Bax from Hong Kong, S. China, diary entry for March 28, 1906, folder D6.A1.d.

42. Yorke Collection, "Commentary called D(jeridensis)."

43. Yorke Collection, Crowleyana, AC Diaries.

44. Yorke Collection, AC Holograph Mss., Letter to Tränker (Notebook 1925–26), folder 12.

45. Yorke Collection, AC Holograph Letters, Letters to Louis Wilkinson, folder D.9.A4.1.

46. Yorke Collection, Cephaloedium Working (1920–21), folder K.1.

47. Ibid.

48. Ibid.

49. Ibid.

50. Ibid.

51. Ibid.

52. Yorke Collection, Royal Court Diaries (1929–34), diary entry for Saturday, June 28, 1930, folder 20.b.

53. Yorke Collection, AC's letters (1913–14), folder 12.a, b, c.

54. Yorke Collection, Royal Court Diaries (1929–34), folder 20.b.

55. William Blake, "The Marriage of Heaven and Hell," in *The Poems of William Blake, Edited by W. B. Yeats* (London: Routledge and Kegan Paul, 1979), 176 ff.

56. Yorke Collection, Letters, folder D.9.A4.2.

57. Aleister Crowley, *Magick in Theory and Practice* (London: Routledge and Kegan Paul, 1973), 308.

58. Asclepius 21, in *The Nag Hammadi Library.*

59. Yorke Collection, Royal Court Diaries (1929–34), folder 20.b.

60. Yorke Collection, AC Holograph Mss., Letter to Tränker (Notebook 1925–26), folder 12. There is, I think, something quite disingenuous about this account. The first problem is the date when all this is supposed to have occurred. In the 1930 diary entry referred to earlier, Crowley writes that he was involved with ceremonial magic for fourteen years before attempting sexual magick. That brings us to 1912, two years after he says he met Reuss for the first time. The *Book of Lies* passage that Crowley's *Confessions* says is what brought Reuss to his door with the offer of the ninth-degree secret was not published until 1913. Something is amiss here. The connection both men had with John Yarker's Ancient and Accepted Scottish Rite of Freemasonry might hold a clue for further research. Crowley was made a Sovereign Grand Inspector General of this rite in 1910, the year in which he says he met Reuss for the first time, and had the task of reducing the system to workable proportions—a task

finally consummated within the OTO. It is noteworthy that Crowley says that Reuss tried to "bully him" into something. Crowley must have known about the OTO, and it is hard to believe its supreme secret came as much of a surprise to him. It would also be interesting to know why Crowley initially reacted against the ninth degree.

61. Yorke Collection, AC's letters (1913–14), folder 12.a, b, c.

62. Ibid.

63. Yorke Collection, Letters, folder 117.C.

64. Ibid.

65. Incidentally, Crowley undoubtedly did hold to a master race idea—as does, arguably, biological evolution. His master race was not racist in the nationalistic or tribal-blood sense. "The [Thelemic] Law is for All." A member of Crowley's master race is one who has mastered his or her self and who is doing his or her True Will, whoever he or she may appear to be.

66. Yorke Collection, letter to G. Cowie, AC's letters (1913–14), folder 12.a, b, c. See also the following from an unfinished article on Prohibition, written when Crowley was in the United States, entitled "The Verbotenist" (1919): "The old antithesis between matter and spirit is disappearing. The materialists went so far as to say 'Thought is a secretion of the brain' while their opponents retorted that the brain itself was but an idea in the mind. So we find mind reacts on body, and body on mind, until the question as to which first arose is as foolish as that old joke: 'which came first, the hen or the egg?'"

67. That is, the Newton of the sanitized, received history of science. The real Newton believed the universe was an expression of a spiritual mind. See Michael White, *The Last Sorcerer* (London: Fourth Estate, 1998).

68. The following letter, written by Crowley in his last year to his son Aleister Ataturk (Yorke Collection, folder 30.5.47), could hardly come, one would think, from a Satanist as commonly understood:

> My dear Son, This is the first letter that your father has ever written to you, so you can imagine that it will be very important; and you should keep it and lay it to your heart. [. . .] I want you to learn to behave as a Duke would behave. You must be high-minded, generous, noble, and above all, without fear. For that last reason you must never tell a lie; for to do so shows that you are afraid of the person to whom you tell it, and I want you to be afraid of nobody. [. . .] There is one more point that I want to impress upon you! The best models of English writing are Shakespeare and the Old Testament, especially the Book of Job, the Psalms, the Proverbs, Ecclesiastes, and the Song of Solomon. It will be a very good thing for you to commit as much as you can, both of these books and of

the best plays of Shakespeare to memory, so that they form the foundation of your style: and in writing English, the most important quality that you can acquire is style. [. . .] Your affectionate father, Aleister.

69. Yorke Collection 26.2. Small Japanese vellum notebook, "AGAPE AZOTH, Sal Philosophorum, The Book of the Unveiling of the Sangraal wherein it is spoken of the Vine of the Sabbath of the Adepts."

70. Ibid.

71. Ibid.

72. Ibid.

73. Ibid.

74. Shin is the Magic Fire or Elixir, and as such the first part of Shaitan, when followed by the letter *T*, the Hebrew Teth, which Crowley interprets as the Lion-Serpent, and subsequently the letter *N*, the Hebrew Nun, which for Crowley stands for his female partner, the Scarlet Woman. Thus did Crowley consider the word *Shaitan* to encompass the essence of sexual magick. The letter Shin was also identified with the coming of Christ into the Tetragrammaton, or the spirit made flesh, by Christian kabbalists since Reuchlin and Pico della Mirandola.

75. Yorke Collection, folder 26.2, AGAPE AZOTH.

76. Ibid.

77. Yorke Collection, "Commentary called D(jeridensis)," folder 16.AL.

78. Yorke Collection, Letter to John Symonds, June 25, 1946, folder 117.c.

79. Yorke Collection, Crowleyana in possession of G. J. Yorke (195).

80. Yorke Collection, Scrapbook of letters to John Symonds when writing "The Great Beast," folder No. 96.

81. Ibid.

82. Ibid.

83. Yorke Collection, Letters to Karl and Sascha Germer, folder D9.A4.6.

Chapter 12 Light in the Jar

1. Stephan A. Hoeller, *The Gnostic Jung and the Seven Sermons to the Dead* (Wheaton, Ill: Quest Books, 1982), 44.

2. Jung, "Psychology and Alchemy," 35.

3. The Gospel of Thomas, in *The Nag Hammadi Library*, Codex 2, page 45, lines 30–34.

4. The "chemical wedding" of the divided soul, animus (male) and anima (female), the archetypal symbol of individuation—that is, to become fully human, the Gnostic Anthropos archetype.

Chapter 13   Gnosis and the New Physics

1. Comenius, *Via lucis* (The Way of Light), 1668.

2. David Bohm, *Wholeness and the Implicate Order,* 69.

3. John Gribbin, *In Search of Schrödinger's Cat*, 161.

4. Albert Einstein, quoted in Abraham Pais, *Subtle is the Lord . . .* (Oxford: Oxford University Press, 1982). From a paper "Can quantum-mechanical description of physical reality be considered complete?" by A. Einstein, B. Podolsky, N. Rosen, reprinted in the volume *Physical Reality,* ed. S. Toulmin (San Francisco: Harper and Row, 1970), 456.

5. John Gribbin, *In Search of Schrödinger's Cat*, 4.

6. William Ralph Inge.

7. *Corpus Hermeticum,* Libellus 2.12a–13.

8. David Bohm, *Giordano Bruno: His Life and Thought* (New York: Schuman, 1950).

9. See Giordano Bruno, *On the Infinite Universe and Worlds,* in Singer, *Giordano Bruno.*

10. Renée Weber, *Dialogues with Scientists and Sages* (London: Routledge and Kegan Paul, 1986).

11. Larry Dossey, *Recovering the Soul: A Scientific and Spiritual Search* (London: Bantam New Age Books, 1989).

12. Bronowski, *A Sense of the Future* (Cambridge, Mass.: MIT Press, 1977).

13. Erwin Schrödinger, *Mind and Matter* (Cambridge: Cambridge University Press, 1958).

14. Paul Davies, quoted in Larry Dossey, *Recovering the Soul: A Scientific and Spiritual Search,* Bantam (London: New Age Books, 1989).

15. Bertolt Brecht, *Threepenny Opera.*

16. *Corpus Hermeticum,* Libellus 1.7–8: The Authentic Nous Speaks to Hermes Trismegistus.

Chapter 14   Gnosis Today: A Personal View

1. Rudolf Steiner, *Christian Rosenkreutz: From the Works of Rudolf Steiner,* compiled by Steven Roboz (Vancouver: Steiner Book Centre, 1982), 12.

2. Designed by John Wilkes, ARCA, at Emerson College, Sussex, U.K.

3. "Only now are we understanding the mysteries of water's global circulation." In John Wilkes, *Hoechst High-Chem* magazine (December 1991).

4. Tobias Churton, *The Hermetic Philosophy,* part 1 of *The Golden Builders: Alchemists, Rosicrucians and the First Free Masons* (York Beach, Maine: Weiser, 2005), 21.

5. William Blake, quoted in Tobias Churton, *The Gnostics* (London: Weidenfeld and Nicolson, 1987), 121.

6. Christopher McIntosh, from an interview with the author for the documentary *The New Age and the New Man* (Lichfield, U.K.: Spirit Level Productions, 1989).

7. See Walter Birks and R. A. Gilbert, *The Treasure of Montségur* (Wellingborough, Northamptonshire: Crucible, 1987), and the more hostile Christian Bernadac, *Le Mystère d'Otto Rahn: Du Catharisme au Nazisme* (Paris, 1978).

8. Inge, *Mysticism in Religion*, 9.

9. David Henderson, *'Scuse Me While I Kiss the Sky* (London: Bantam, 1981), 206.

10. Ibid.

11. Ibid., 205.

12. *Life* magazine, 1969, quoted in Henderson, 233.

13. Jim Brodey, *Los Angeles Free Press,* quoted in Henderson, 272.

14. Ibid., 272.

15. Jean-Luc Godard, quoted in the excellent study by David Sterritt *The Films of Jean-Luc Godard: Seeing the Invisible* (Cambridge: Cambridge University Press, 1999).

16. Ibid.

17. Laurie Lipton, from an interview with the author for *The New Age and the New Man* (Lichfield, U.K.: Spirit Level Productions, 1989).

18. Kazimir Malevich, cited in *The Spiritual in Art: Abstract Painting 1890–1985,* ed. Maurice Tuchman (New York: Abbeville, 1987), 408.

19. Kathleen Raine, from an interview with the author, London, May 1989.

20. Hermes Trismegistus, *Pymander,* Libellus I, final para., *Hermetica,* ed. W. Scott (Boston: Shambhala, 1985).

Bibliography

Agrippa, Heinrich Cornelius. *De occulta philosophia*. English translation: London: J. Freake, 1651. Facsimile: Agrippa, Heinrich Cornelius. *De occulta philosophia*. London: Chthonios Books, 1986.

Arnold, Thomas, ed. *The Legacy of Islam*. Oxford: Oxford University Press, 1931.

Baigent, Michael, Richard Leigh, and Henry Lincoln. *The Holy Blood, Holy Grail*. London: Jonathan Cape, 1982. Published in the United States as *Holy Blood, Holy Grail*. New York: Delacorte, 1982.

Barber, Malcolm, ed. *The Military Orders: Fighting for the Faith and Caring for the Sick*. Aldershot, U.K.: Ashgate Publishing, 1994.

Beamon, Sylvia P. *The Royston Cave: Used by Saints or Sinners? Local Historical Influences of the Templar and Hospitaller Movements*. Baldock, U.K.: Cortney, 1992.

Beny, Roloff. *Iran: Elements of Destiny*. London: Collins, 1977.

Bettenson, Henry, ed. *Documents of the Christian Church*. Oxford: Oxford University Press, 1977.

Blair, H. A. *The Kaleidoscope of Truth, Types and Archetypes in Clement of Alexandria*. Worthing, W. Sussex, U.K.: Churchman Publishing, 1986.

Blake, William. *Jerusalem*. London: Blake Trust/Tate Gallery, 1991.

Blake, William, "The Marriage of Heaven and Hell." In Yeats, W. B., ed. *The Poems of William Blake*. London: Routledge and Kegan Paul, 1979.

Bohm, David. *Wholeness and the Implicate Order*. London: Routledge and Kegan Paul, 1981.

Brandon, S. G. F. *Religion in Ancient History*. London: George Allen and Unwin, 1972).

Brenon, Anne. *Le Vrai Visage du Catharisme* [The True Face of Catharism]. Portet-sur-Garonne, France: Loubatières, 1987.

Brenon, Anne, Annie Cazenave, and Dieter Harmening. "Christianisme Mediéval: Mouvements Dissidents et Novateurs" [Medieval Christianity:

Dissident and Renewal Movements]. In *Heresis* 13, 14. Villegly, France: Centre René Nelli, 1990.

Buckley, Jorunn Jacobsen. "An Interpretation of Logion 114 in the Gospel of Thomas." In *Novum Testamentum* 27, no. 3 (July 1985).

Burckhardt, Titus. *An Introduction to Sufism*. Shaftesbury, Dorset, U.K.: Element Books, 1976.

Burkitt, F. C. *Church and Gnosis*. Cambridge, U.K.: University of Cambridge Press, 1931.

Casaubon, Meric, ed. *A Strange Relation of What Passed Between Dr John Dee and Some Spirits*. London: A.C. Daniel, 1977.

Chadwick, Henry. *The Early Church*. Harmondsworth, Middlesex, U.K.: Pelican, 1978.

Charles, R. H., trans. *The Book of Enoch*. London: SPCK, 1984.

Churton, Tobias. *The Golden Builders: Alchemists, Rosicrucians and the First Free Masons*. York Beach, Maine: Weiser, 2005.

———. *The Gnostics*. New York: Barnes and Noble, 1997.

Clulee, Nicholas. *John Dee's Natural Philosophy*. London: Routledge, 1988.

Copenhaver, Brian. P., trans. *Hermetica*. Cambridge: Cambridge University Press, 1997.

Copleston, F. C. *A History of Medieval Philosophy*. London: Methuen, 1972.

Crowley, Edward Alexander ("Aleister"). Ms. collection bequeathed by Gerald Yorke (the Yorke Collection). London: Warburg Institute, University of London.

———. "Chinese Music." In *Book of Lies*. York Beach, Maine: Samuel Weiser, 1990.

———. *The Holy Books of Thelema*. Edited by Hymenaeus Beta (W. Breeze). New York: 93 Publishing, 1989.

Dart, John. *The Laughing Saviour*. New York: Harper and Row, 1976.

Dee, John. *Monas hieroglyphica* [The Hieroglyphic Monad]. Antwerp, 1564.

De Jong, M., ed. *Les Symboles spirituels de l'alchimie*. Exhibition catalogue, Bibliotheca Philosophica Hermetica. Amsterdam: In de Pelikaan, 1988.

De Lugio, Jean. *Le Livre des deux principes*. Edited by Christine Thouzellier. Paris: Éditions du Cerf, 1973.

Domini, Donatino. *Chymica vannus* [The Alchemical Fan]. Ravenna: Longo Editore, 1986.

Doresse, Jean. *The Secret Books of the Egyptian Gnostics*. London: Hollis and Carter, 1960.

Edighoffer, Roland. *Rose Croix*. Paris: PUF, 1995.

Eisenman, Robert. *Maccabees, Zadokites, Christians and Qumran*. Leiden: E.J. Brill, 1983.

Eisenman, Robert, and Michael Wise, eds. and trans. *The Dead Sea Scrolls Uncovered.* Harmondsworth, Middlesex, U.K.: Penguin, 1992.

Forey, Alan J. *Military Orders and Crusaders.* Aldershot, U.K.: Ashgate Publishing, 1994.

———. *The Military Orders: From the 12th to the Early 14th Centuries.* Basingstoke: Macmillan Education, 1992.

Fowden, Garth. *The Egyptian Hermes.* Cambridge: Cambridge University Press, 1986.

Gentile, Sebastiano, and Carlos Gilly. *Marsilio Ficino and the Return of Hermes Trismegistus.* Exhibition catalog, Bibliotheca Philosophica Hermetica Publications. Amsterdam: In de Pelikaan, 1999.

Gilchrist, Alexander. *The Life of William Blake.* London: Dent, 1971.

Gilly, Carlos. "Iter Gnostico-Russicum." In *500 Years of Gnosis in Europe.* Exhibition catalog, Bibliotheca Philosophica Hermetica Publications. Amsterdam: In de Pelikaan, 2002.

———, ed. *Johann Valentin Andreae, 1586–1986: Die Manifeste der Rosenkreuzer-bruderschaft.* Exhibition catalog, Bibliotheca Philosophica Hermetica Publications. Amsterdam: In de Pelikaan, 1986.

Gimpel, Jean. *The Cathedral Builders.* Salisbury, Wiltshire, U.K.: Michael Russell, 1983.

———. *The Medieval Machine.* London: Victor Gollancz, 1976.

Grant, R. M., ed. *Gnosticism: An Anthology.* London: Collins, 1961.

Gribbin, John. *In Search of Schrödinger's Cat.* London: Black Swan, 1984.

Haeri, Shaykh Fadhlalla. *The Sufi Way to Self-Unfoldment.* Shaftesbury, Dorset, U.K.: Element, 1987.

Heindel, Max. *The Rosicrucian Cosmo-Conception.* Chicago: Independent, 1909.

Henderson, David. *'Scuse Me While I Kiss the Sky.* New York: Bantam, 1981.

The Hermetick Art by a Lover of Philalethes. London, 1714. Text available at www.levity.com/alchemy/shortenq.html.

Hirst, Désirée. *Hidden Riches: Traditional Symbolism from the Renaissance to Blake.* London: Eyre and Spottiswoode, 1964.

Herodotus. *The Histories.* Trans. by Walter Blanco. New York: Norton, 1992.

Hoeller, Stephan. *The Gnostic Jung and the Seven Sermons to the Dead.* Wheaton, Ill.: Quest Books, 1982.

Holmes, Richard. *Coleridge: Early Visions.* Harmondsworth, Middlesex, U.K.: Penguin, 1989.

Holroyd, Stuart. *Magic, Words, and Numbers.* London: Aldus, 1976.

Howarth, Stephen. *The Knights Templar.* London: Macmillan, 1982.

Hughes, David. *The Star of Bethlehem Mystery.* London: Dent, 1978.

Inge, William Ralph. *Mysticism in Religion*. London: Hutchinson University Library, 1947.

———. *Personal Idealism and Mysticism*. London: Longmans, London, 1907.

———. *Studies of English Mystics*. London: John Murray, 1906.

———. *The Philosophy of Plotinus*. 2 vols. London: Longmans, 1929.

———. *Truth and Falsehood in Religion*. London: John Murray, 1907.

Iqbal, Afzal, *The Life and Work of Jalaluddin Rumi*. Oxford: Oxford University Press, 2000.

Irenaeus. *Against the Heretics* [Adversus Haereses], in *The Ante-Nicene Fathers*. Translated by Alexander Roberts and James Donaldson. Grand Rapids, Mich.: William B. Eerdmans, 1981.

Jonas, Hans. *The Gnostic Religion*. Boston: Beacon Press, 1958.

———. *The Imperative of Responsibility*. Chicago: University of Chicago Press, 1986.

———. *Philosophical Essays*. Chicago: University of Chicago Press, 1974.

Josephus, Flavius. *The Works of Flavius Josephus*. Translated by William Whiston. Edinburgh: William P. Nimmo, 1865. www.ccel.org/j/josephus/JOSEPHUS.HTM or www.sacred-texts.com/jud/josephus).

Jullian, Philippe. *Dreamers of Decadence*. London: Pall Mall, 1971.

Jung, C. G. *The Collected Works of C. G. Jung*, vol. 12. London: Routledge and Kegan Paul, 1981.

Kee, Howard Clark. *Medicine, Miracle and Magic in New Testament Times*. Cambridge: Cambridge University Press, 1988.

Kelly, J. N. D. *Early Christian Doctrines*. London: A and C Black, 1977.

King, Francis. *Magic: The Western Tradition*. London: BCA, 1975.

Kristeller, P. O., and E. Cassirer, eds. *The Renaissance Philosophy of Man: Petrarca, Valla, Ficino, Pico, Pomponazzi, Vives*. Chicago: University of Chicago Press, 1948.

Lake, Kirsopp, trans. *Eusebius: Ecclesiastical History*. London: Loeb Classical Library, 1975.

Lewis, C. S. *The Allegory of Love*. Oxford: Oxford University Press, 1986.

Logan, A. H. B., and A. J. M. Wedderburn, eds. *New Testament and Gnosis*. Edinburgh: T and T Clark, 1983.

Mahé, Jean-Pierre. *Hermès en haute Egypte*. 2 vols. Quebec: University of Quebec Press, 1978.

McIntosh, Christopher. *Eliphas Lévi and the French Occult Revival*. London: Rider, 1972.

———. "Gold und Rosenkreuz and the German Counter-Enlightenment." Ph.D. thesis, Oxford University, 1989.

————. *The Rose Cross and the Age of Reason: Eighteenth-Century Rosicrucianism in Central Europe and Its Relation to the Enlightenment.* Leiden: E. J. Brill, 1992.

Mino, Gabriele. *Alchimia: La Tradizione in Occidente* [Alchemy: The Western Tradition]. Venice: Edizione La Biennale, 1986.

Moore, R. I. *The Origins of European Dissent.* Oxford: Basil Blackwell, 1985.

Nelli, René. *Le Roman de Raimon de Miraval, troubadour.* Paris: Albin Michel, 1986.

Nicholson, Helen. *Templars, Hospitalers and Teutonic Knights: Images of the Military Orders, 1128–1291.* Leicester, U.K.: Leicester University Press, 1993.

Nock, A. D., and A. J. Festugière, trans. *The Asclepius.* In *La Révélation d'Hermès Trismégiste.* 4 vols. Paris: Société d'édition "Les Belles lettres," 1960.

Pagels, Elaine. *The Gnostic Gospels.* London: Weidenfeld and Nicolson, 1979.

Philo. *Philo.* Translated by F. H. Colson and G. H. Whitaker. London: Heinemann, 1973.

Pickford, Douglas. *Staffordshire: Its Magic and Mystery.* Wilmslow, Cheshire, U.K.: Sigma, 1994.

Press, A. R., ed. *Troubadour Lyric Poetry.* Edinburgh: Edinburgh University Press, 1971.

Quispel, Gilles. *Gnostic Studies.* 2 vols. Leiden: E. J. Brill, 1974.

————. "Review of *Neues Testament und Gnosis* by Walter Schmithals." In *Vigiliae Christianae* 39 (1985).

Rabelais, François. *The Heroic Deeds of Gargantua and Pantagruel.* Translated by Thomas Urquhart. London: J. M. Dent, 1929.

Raine, Kathleen. *Blake and Antiquity.* London: Routledge and Kegan Paul, 1979.

————. *Blake and Tradition.* London: Routledge and Kegan Paul, 1979.

————, ed. *Temenos: Review Devoted to the Arts of the Imagination.* London: 47 Paultons Square, 1986.

————, ed. *Coleridge: Poems and Prose Selected.* Harmondsworth, Middlesex, U.K.: Penguin, 1986.

Rawlinson, Canon, trans. *Herodotus.* 2 vols. London: John Murray, 1897.

Regardie, Israel, ed. *The Golden Dawn.* St. Paul, Minn.: Llewellyn, 1992.

Reznikov, Raimonde. *Cathares et Templiers.* Portet-sur-Garonne: Loubatières, 1993.

Ritman, J., and F. Janssen, eds. *Hermes Trismegistus, Pater Philosophorum: A Textual History of the Corpus Hermeticum.* Exhibition catalog, Bibliotheca Philosophica Hermetica Publications. Amsterdam: In de Pelikaan, 1991.

Roberts, Alexander, and James Donaldson, trans. *The Ante-Nicene Fathers.* Grand Rapids, Mich.: William B. Eerdmans, 1981.

Robinson, James M., ed. *The Nag Hammadi Library in English.* Leiden: E. J. Brill, 1977.

Roquebert, Michel. *Les Cathares et le Graal.* Toulouse: Éditions Privat, 1994.

———. *L'Épopée Cathare.* [The Cathar Era]. 5 vols. Toulouse: Privat, 1985.

———. "En Face de Catharisme" [Opposite Catharism]. In *Cahiers de Fanjeaux.* Toulouse: Privat, 1985.

Ryan, R. F. "The Great Beast in Russia: Aleister Crowley's Theatrical Tour in 1913 and His Beastly Writings on Russia." In *Symbolism and After: Essays on Russian Poetry in Honour of Georgette Donchin.* Edited by Arnold McMillin. London: Duckworth, 1992.

Rudolph, Kurt. *Gnosis.* Translated by R. McL. Wilson. San Francisco: Harper and Row, 1985.

Schelling, Fredrich. *Of Human Freedom.* Chicago: Open Court, 1936.

Scholem, Gershom. *Major Trends in Jewish Mysticism.* New York: Schocken Books, 1961.

Scott, Walter, trans. *Hermetica.* Boston: Shambhala, 1986.

Secret, François. *Kabbale et philosophie hermétique.* Amsterdam: BPH, 1989.

Shah, Idries. *The Secret Lore of Magic.* London: Abacus, 1972.

Shepherd, A. P. *A Scientist of the Invisible: An Introduction to the Life and Work of Rudolf Steiner.* Edinburgh: Floris Classics, 1983.

Singer, Dorothea. *Giordano Bruno: His Life and Thought, with Annotated Translations of His Work "On the Infinite Universe and Worlds."* New York: Schuman, 1950.

Steiner, Rudolf. *Christian Rosenkreutz: Collected Extracts.* Vancouver: Steiner Book Centre, 1982.

Stoyanov, Yuri. *The Other God: Dualist Religions from Antiquity to the Cathar Heresy.* New Haven, Conn.: Yale University Press, 2000.

Swami, Shree Purohit, and W. B. Yeats, trans. *The Ten Principal Upanishads.* London: Faber and Faber, 1975.

Symonds, John, and Kenneth Grant, eds. *The Confessions of Aleister Crowley.* London: Routledge and Kegan Paul, 1977.

Taylor, Edward. *Jacob Behmen's Theosophick Philosophy Unfolded.* London, 1691.

Tuchman, Maurice, ed. *The Spiritual in Art: Abstract Painting 1890–1985.* New York: Abbeville, 1987.

Upton-Ward, J. M., trans. *The Rule of the Templars.* London: Boydell and Brewer, 1992.

Van den Broek, Roelof, and Cis van Heertum, eds. *From Poimandres to Jacob Böhme: Gnosis, Hermetism and the Christian Tradition*. Exhibition catalog, Bibliotheca Philosophica Hermetica Publications. Amsterdam: In de Pelikaan, 2000.

Van Lamoen, Frank. *The Hermetic Gnosis*. Exhibition catalog, Bibliotheca Philosophica Hermetica. Amsterdam: In de Pelikaan, 1988.

Van Rijckenbourg, Jan. *The Egyptian Arch-Gnosis*. Haarlem: Rozekruis Pers, 1982.

Vermes, Gezu. *The Complete Dead Sea Scrolls in English*. Harmondsworth, Middlesex, U. K.: Penguin, 1988.

Vickers, Brian, ed. *Occult and Scientific Mentalities in the Renaissance*. Cambridge: University of Cambridge Press, 1984.

Von Eschenbach, Wolfram. *Parzifal*. Edited by A. T. Hatto. Harmondsworth, Middlesex, U.K.: Penguin, 1980.

Wilson, R. McL. *The Gnostic Problem*. London: Mowbray, 1958.

———. *Gnosis and the New Testament*. Oxford: Blackwell, 1968.

Wind, Edgar. *Pagan Mysteries in the Renaissance*. Oxford: Oxford University Press, 1980.

Zaehner, R. C. *Our Savage God*. London: Collins, 1974.

Zuchetto, Gérard. *Catalogue de l'Exposition Troubadours et Jongleurs*. Carcassonne: Center de Recherche et d'Expression des Musiques Medievales, 1985.

Index

Abafi, Ludwig, 268
Abano, Peter, 123
Abhandlung der Religion, 279
Abulafia, Abraham ben Samuel,
　138
Abu Yazid of Bistam, 150
"Aceldama," 318
Adalbert, Johann, Prinz de Buchau,
　265
Adam Kadmon, 35, 238
Against the Heretics, 90, 104
Agrippa, Henry Cornelius, 248
Ahriman, 18, 19, 29
Ahura Mazdah, 12
Aiwass, 329 ff.
Albigensian Crusade, 195
Aleppo, 30
Alexander, 17, 19, 31
Alexander I, Tsar, 286
Alexander Jannaeus, 64
Alfonso II, of Castile, 165
al-Ghazali, 152, 220
al-Hallaj, 147
Ali (brother to Muhammad), 150
al-Jilani, Abd al-Qadir, 144
al-Junaid, Abu'l Qasim, 144
al-Kindi, Abu Yusuf Ya'qub ibn,
　131
Allegory of Love, The, 186 ff.
Allenbach, Adèle, 298
Amesha Spentas, 13
Anat Jahu, 38

Anaxilaus, 96
Andreae, Johann Valentin, 263, 276,
　292
Anthropos, 36 ff., 54, 81, 380
Antigonus, 64
Antiochus III, IV, 17, 64, 223
Antiquities, 54, 56
Apocalypse of Peter, 98
Apocalyptic, 57 ff.
Apocryphon of John, 23, 40, 41,
　98
Aquinas, Thomas, 130, 134,
　150
Arnold of Villanova, 123
Arp, Jean, 251
Asclepius, 141, 148, 345
Ashera, 38
Ashmole, Elias, 245, 248, 254,
　381
Aspect, Alain, 377
Assadai, 295
as-Suhrawardi, 144
Asthanes, 26
Astyages, 27, 28
Atalanta fugiens, 371
Attar, Faridu'ddin, 159
Attis, 21
Augustine, 125, 134
Aurora, 237, 257
Aureum vellus, 268
Averroes, 153
Avesta, 13

Avicenna, 156
Azazel, 58, 60, 61, 96

Babylon, 407, 414
Bacon, Friar Roger, 123, 131 ff., 371
Bahir, 136
Bailly, 296
Banus, 52, 53
Baphomet, 219 ff., 225, 340, 359
Bar Kokhba rebellion, 63
Barrett, Francis, 319
Bathurst, A, 246
Bax, Clifford, 335
Bayona, 165
Beamon, Sylvia, 222
Beatles, 341
Beckett, Samuel, 315
Beer, Vanilla, 402
Bennett, Allan, 321, 350
ben Sherira, Hai, 136
Bergson, 234
Bibliotheca Philosophica
    Hermetica, xv
Birks, Walter, 411
Bisol (or Bisot), Geoffrey, 202
Blake, William, 234, 255 ff., 289,
    357, 383, 391
  and Tradition, 255
Blakeway, John Brickdale, 225
Blavatsky, Madame Helena
    Petrovna, 305, 306, 403
Bogomil, 52, 162
Bohm, David, 376
Böhme, Jacob, 234 ff., 263, 284, 369
Bohr, Neils, 337, 373, 376
Boniface of Monferrat, 213
Book of Enoch, 57 ff., 66
"Book of Results," (Crowley), 330
Book of the Law, 332 ff.
Book of Lies, The, 348, 351
Book of Thomas the Contender, 421
Born, Max, 373
Boron, Robert de, 214
Bouillon, Baldwin de, 202
Bouillon, Godfroi de, 201

Brandon, S. G. F., 67
Braszynski, Alexander, 301–2
Brenon, Anne, 178, 189, 192, 193
Bruno, Giordano, 282, 380
Bultmann, Rudolf, 51
Bulwer-Lytton, Edward, 301
Burckhardt, Titus, 146

Cabalistic Order of the Rosy Cross,
    308
Cadiot, Noémi, 301
Cagliostro, 296
Cambyses, 28
Capellanus, Andreas, 187
Capra, Fritjof, 375
Cathars, 52, 162 ff.
Cathares et Templiers, 207
cave of the Lombrives, 395
caves of the Sabarthès, 395
Celestial Hierarchies, 129 ff.
Cephas, 74
Chadwick, Henry, 42, 45
Chaldeans, 30
Chaldean Oracles, 125
Chandogya Upanishad, 11
Christ and the Cosmos, 74
Chrysomander, 286
Churton, Ralph, 221
Churton Papers, 433
Cicero, 31
Clement of Alexandria, 115 ff.
Clinschor, 122 ff.
Cloud upon the Sanctuary, The,
    286, 318
Clulee, Nicholas, 142
Coleridge, Samuel Taylor, 234
Comenius, 371
Commagene, 30
Condorcet, 208, 270
Confucius, 6
consolamentum, 185
Constant, Alphonse Louis, 298 ff.
Copenhagen interpretation, 375
Coplestone, Father, 130
Corpus Hermeticum, 215

Cowie, George Macnie, 354
Crowley, Edward Alexander ("Aleister"), 8, 40, 310, 314–64, 382
Cunard, Nancy, 314, 315, 364
Cybele, 21
Cyrus, 27, 28

d'Alembert, 270
Daniel, Arnaut, 193
Dante, 165
Danton, 296
d'Aurenja, Raimbaut, 164
d'Auvergne, Peire, 164
Dead Sea Scrolls, 63 ff.
Dead Sea Scrolls Deception, The, 65
de Blanchefort, Bertrand, 206
de Blaye, Jaufré Rudel, 164
de Boissézon, Azalaïs, 173ff.
Debussy, Claude, 309
de Castres, Ermengarda, 176, 178
Deceitful Arts and Nefarious Practices of Marcus, The, 96
de Charney, Geoffrey, 429
de Clairvaux, Bernard, 210
De doctrina Christiana II, 134
Dee, John, 140–1, 383
de Gonneville, Godfroi, 211
de Guaïta, Marquis Stanislas, 307 ff.
de Guyon, Madame, 284
De imaginibus, 131
de Langes, Savalette, 296
de la Rochefoucauld, Comte Antoine, 309
del Villar, don Isidore Villerino, 349
Delville, Jean, 309
de Miraval, Raimon, 163ff.
Demiurge, 23, 24, 40, 81, 92, 105, 111, 146, 178, 383
de Molay, Jacques, 204, 210 ff., 292
de Montbard, André, 202
de Montdidier, Payen, 202
de Montfort, Simon, 209
De mysteriis, 126
de Pasqually, Martines, 293

de Pennautier, Loba, 165, 170
De radiis, 131–32
de Salverte, Toux, 282
Des erreurs et de la verité, 284
de Stapelbrugge, Stephen, 211
de St.-Germain, Comte, 288
de St.-Martin, Louis Claude, 284–85
de Stoke, John, 211
de St.-Omer, Godfroi, 202
de Troyes, Chrétien, 190, 214
de Ventadour, Bernard, 164
de Verdon, Bertram, 431
Dhu'l-Nun, 148
Dhu Nowas, 32
Dialogue of the Saviour, The, 11
Dialogue with Trypho, 32
Diderot, 279
Die Wolke über den Heligtum (The Cloud upon the Sanctuary), 438
Dio Cassius, 30
Dionysus the Areopagite, 129
Doctrine et rituel de la haute magie, 304
doge of Venice, 213
d'Olivet, Fabre, 300
Dossey, Larry, 384

Eckhart, Meister, 156
Edessa, 30
"Edict Concerning Religion," 280
"Edict of Censorship," 280
Eglinton, Eighth Earl, 229
Einstein, Albert, 373
Eisenman, Robert, 64, 73
Eleanor of Aquitaine, 163
Elect Cohens, 293 ff.
Elymas (Bar-Jesus), 29
Empedocles, 54
Encausse, Gérard, 305
Enochian Walks with God, 246
Enuma Elish, 407
Epistle to Rheginos, 104
Essenes, 51 ff.
Eudemus of Rhodes, 14

Eugnostos the Blessed, 38, 98
Exodus, 35
Ezekiel, 18, 34, 37, 92, 382
Ezekiel Tragicus, 35

Faucheux, Alfred, 308
Fénelon, François, 227
Festugière, 51
Feuerbach, Ludwig, 234
Fichte, 252
Ficino, Marsilio, 141
Fictuld, Hermann, 268
Flegetanis, 213, 215
Fludd, Robert, 254
Forniers, 165
Forster, Georg, 270, 271
Francis, St., 156
Francis, duke of Lorraine, 266
Francke, 265
Franklin, Benjamin, 271
Freher, Dionysius, 246
Friedrich August, duke of
    Braunschweig, 270
Friedrich Wilhelm, crown prince of
    Prussia, 270, 277, 279 ff.
Fulcher of Chartres, 202
Fuller, J. F. C., 350

Gadal, Antonin, 395
Galahad, 197
Garrison, Omar, 199
Germer, Karl and Sascha, 364
Gilbert, R. A., 411
Gnostic Gospels,The, 103
Gnostic Religion, The, 4
Gnostics, The, 1
Godard, Jean-Luc, 402
Gödel, Kurt, 383
Goethe, 388
Golb, Norman, 65
Golden Builders, The, 4
Gondemare, 202
Gospel of Mary, 39
Gospel of Philip, 39, 94, 98, 99,
    100, 113

Gospel of the Infancy, 32
Gospel of Thomas, 20, 117,
    136
Gospel of Truth, 367
Gotama, 13
Gotthelf, Karl, Baron Hund, 216
Grantwood, 349
Gribbin, John, 377
Grosseteste, Robert, 132, 141
Guillaume IX, count of Poitou,
    163

Halevi, Jacob, 137
Harran, 31, 322
Hasmonaean dynasty, 64
Hatto, A. T., 428
Haven, Marc, 308
Hawker, Yvonne, 402
Hawking, Stephen, 383
Hegel, 234
Heindel, Max, 393
Hekhaloth texts, 130
Heidegger, Martin, 101, 234
Heisenberg, Werner, 373
Helena, 40
Helvetius, 296
Henderson, David, 399
Hendrix, Jimi, 399–401
Henry II, 217
Hermes (Daniel Hermann), 280
Hermes Trismegistus, 36, 142, 144,
    215, 345, 379, 404
Herod the Great, 31, 33, 54,
    55, 65
Herodotus, 26, 27, 32
Hilton, James, 306
Hirschfeld, Joseph, 288, 289
History of Leek, 431
History of Medieval Philosophy, 138
Hitler, Adolf, 353
Hodler, 309
Holy Blood, Holy Grail, 206
Hoor-paar-Kraat, 340
Hughes, David, 33
"Hymn to King Jonathan," 65

Ialdabaoth, 24, 40, 41, 410
Iamblichus, 124-5
ibn 'Arabi, Muhyi-d-Din, 150
ibn Rushd, Abu'l Walid, 152
ibn Sina, 152
Illuminati, 252 ff.
Inge, William Ralph, 248, 250,
    327, 387
In Search of Schrödinger's Cat,
    377
Iqbal, Afzal, 155
Irenaeus, 24, 33, 39, 51, 58, 89ff.
Isis, cult of, 21

Jehudah the Hasid, 135
Jeremiah, 18, 27, 34
Jerome of Ascoli, 139
Jesus, 19, 20, 23, 29, 39, 42, 50,
    56, 60, 66, 67, 68, 69, 73 ff.
John of Salisbury, 223
Johnson, Samuel, 246
John the Baptist, 56, 67
Jonas, Hans, 41, 51, 101 ff.
Jones, George Cecil, 318, 350
Jordan, Pascual, 373
Joseph ou l'Estoire dou Graal, 214
Josephus, 30, 51, 52, 53, 58, 61,
    62, 63
Judas Maccabaeus, 18, 64
Jung, Carl Gustav, 82, 149, 193,
    366, 367 ff., 375
Justin Martyr, 32

Kant, Immanuel, 6
Kelly, Gerald, 316, 328, 350
Kempis, Thomas à, 263
Khan, Chingiz, 155
Khan, Hulagu, 156
Kilwinning, 227 ff.
Kilwinning Abbey chartulary,
    229
Kober, Tobias, 237
Kokabiel, 58
Krumm-Heller, Herr, 352
Kyot of Provence, 217

La Bible de la liberté, 299
Lactantius, 127
*La Décadence Latine, le vice
    supreme*, 307
Lamp of the Invisible Light, 322
Law, William, 246 ff., 284
Leadbeater, Charles, 305
Lead, Jane, 245, 246
Lectorium Rosicrucianum, 393
Leene, Jan and Wim, 393
Les Cathares et le Graal, 429
*Les Poésies du troubadour Raimon
    de Miraval*, 422
Les vers dorés de Pythagore, 298,
    306
Le Testament de la liberté, 300
Lewis, C. S., 186–89
L'Initiation, 308
Lipton, Laurie, 402
Lombard, Peter, 134
Lopuchin I. V., 284
Lost Horizon, 306
Luke, 160

Maaseh Berashith, 136
Maat, 38
Mackenzie, Kenneth, 301
Magi, 26 ff.
Maier, Count Michael, 371, 397
Major Trends in Jewish Mysticism,
    433
Malachi, 78
Manahem, 54, 55
Mandaeans, 58, 108
Mani, 107
"Mantiqu'l Tayr," 159
Marcabrun, 164
Marcosians, 24
Marcus, 24, 58, 96
Marduk, 22
Mariamme, 64
Mark Anthony, 64
Marriage of Heaven and Hell, The,
    255, 258

Marshall, William, 217
Martinism, 285
Mary Magdalene, 8, 39, 196
Marx, Eleanor, 351
Marx, Karl, 234
Masonic Templars, 208
Mather, Ralph, 249
Mathers, Samuel Liddell
    "MacGregor," 311, 319
Mathnawi, 156ff.
Matter of Life and Death, A, 396–97
McIntosh, Christopher, 260, 261
Medina, Don Jesus, 322
Melinge, Abbé, 308
Merkabah literature, 136, 137
Metatron, 137
Meynell, Wilfrid, 359
Minerve, 423
Mirandola, Pico della, 11, 27, 141
Mithra, 20-22, 41, 220
Mniszeck, Count Georges, 302
Monas Hieroglyphica, 142
Montségur, 206
Münter, Friedrich, 288
Murdered Magicians: The Templars
    and their Myth, The, 220
Mysterium Magnum, 237
Mysticism in Religion (Inge), 327,
    397

Nag Hammadi library, the, 11,
    51–52, 62, 63, 345, 367,
Nag Hammadi Library, The, 98
Natural History, 26
Negev, 38
Nelli, René, 179 ff.
Neoplatonism, 124 ff.
Nergal Sharezar, 27
Nero, 30
Newton, Isaac, 375
Nicholson, Helen, 223
Nicholson, R. A., 146
Nietzsche, 6
Nock, 51
Novikov, Nikolai Ivanovich, 283–86

Olcott, Colonel, 305
Ophism, 21
Ophites, 61
Order of Asiatic Brethren, 287–89
Order of Elect Cohens, 293–97
Order of the Golden Dawn, 318 ff.
Order of Oriental Templars, 338 ff.
Origen, 65, 150
Oxenbridge, Joanna, 246

Pagels, Elaine, 103, 104–9
Papus, 306
Paracelsus, 235, 255, 302
Partner, Peter, 220
Parzifal, 122, 206, 213
Path of the Names, 138
Paul, St., 20, 29, 44, 56, 70, 83ff.,
    384
Pauli, Wolfgang, 373
Peire II, king of Aragon, 175, 209
Péladan, Joséphin, 307 ff.
Pennick, Nigel, 74
Pernety, Antoine-Joseph, 294–96
Philadelphian Society, 245
Philippe le Bel, 204
Philo of Alexandria, 26, 29, 40, 42
    ff., 52
Pickford, Douglas, 431
Pietists, 235, 263 ff.
"Pilgrim's Thought," 271
Planck, Max, 373
Plato, 131
Pliny, 26, 30
Plotinus, 6, 106, 114, 124 ff., 139
Poimandres, 36, 82, 118, 120, 150,
    386
Poland, Rosicrucians in, 282
Ploycarp, 89
Polycratus, 223
Pordage, John, 245, 284
Porphyry, 124 ff., 139
Pothinos, 89
Pound, Ezra, 199
Powell, Columba, 403
Powell, Michael, 396–97, 402

'ressburger, Emeric, 396–97
Proclus, 124, 130
Psellus, 143
Pymander, 391
Pythagoras, 29, 51, 53, 54

Qedemites, 32
Queste del Saint Graal, 197
Quispel, Gilles, 35, 39, 41, 103
Qumran, 51, 63, 67

Raguel, 58
Raimonde VI, count of Toulouse,
    165, 168
Raine, Kathleen, 253, 255, 258,
    403
Ramsay, Andrew Michael
    ("Chevalier"), 208, 227
Raphael, 58
Raza Rabba (The Great Mystery),
    136
Reitzenstein, 51
*Religion within the Limits of Pure
    Reason,* 281
Republic, the, 131
Reuss, Theodor, 348, 349
Reznikov, Raimonde, 207, 208
Richard the Lionheart, 217
Richter, Gregory, 237
Richter, Samuel, 264, 265
Riquier, Guiraud, 196
Ritman, Joost, 394
Rodin, Auguste, 309
Roman de la Rose, 186
Roquebert, Michel, 429–30
Rosicrucian, The, 255
*Rosicrucian Cosmo-Conception,
    The,* 393
Rosicrucian and Red Cross, The,
    301
Rossal (or Roland), 202
Royal Society, 384
Royston Cave, 230
Rumi, Maulana Jalal-ud-din, 144 ff.
Rutherford, Ernest, 373

Sabians, 142, 151, 339
Sacred Geometry, 74
*Sacred Magic of Abramelin the
    Mage, The,* 411
Saint-Yves, Joseph-Alexandre, 306
Saklas, 40
Samael, 58
Satan, 19
Satie, Erik, 309
Scanlan, Matthew, 227
Schaw Statutes, 228
Schiemann, Art, 389
Scholem, Gershom, 137, 235
Schrödinger, Erwin, 373
Schultze, Johannes, 278
Schwartz, Georg, 284
Schwenckfeld, Caspar, 235–36
*Second Treatise of the Great Seth,
    The,* 94
Secretum secretorum, 140
Sefer Yetsirah, 136, 137
Semiazaz, 58
*Serious Call to a Devout and Holy
    Life, A,* 247
Seth, 62
Sheba (Yemen), 32
Shelley, Mary, 255
Shelley, Percy Bysshe, 255
Shiites, 150
Sicarii, 53
Silesius, Angelus, 260, 284
Simon Magus, 33, 39, 40
Simon Peter, 74
Sleigh, John, 431
*Smaragdine Table of Hermes
    Trismegistus,* 100
Smith, Adam, 275
Sophia, 37 ff., 96, 194, 243
Sophia of Jesus Christ, The, 98
Spencer-Lewis, H., 352–53
Spirit of Romance, The, 199
Starck, Johann, 266
Star of Bethlehem Mystery, The, 33
Statius, 21
Steiner, Rudolf, 353, 387 ff.

Stommeln, Kristina af, 156
Stock-Huyser, Henny, 394
Strachan, Gordon, 74
Stromateis, 117 ff.
Studies of English Mystics, 250
Suetonius, 30
Summers, Montague, 1
Swift, Jonathan, 229
Symonds, John, 363, 364

Taku, Moses, 135
Tantrics, 199, 355 ff.
Tao of Physics, The, 375
Taylor, Edward, 434
Teerstegen, Gerhard, 271
Temenos Academy, 403
Tertullian, 109, 116
Thabit ibn Qurra, 131
Thunder, Perfect Mind, The, 38
Timaeus, 48
Timotheus, 65
Tiridates, king of Armenia, 30
Toorop, Jan, 309, 403
Topsfield, L. T., 168
Tractatus aureus, 149, 430
Tränker, Heinrich, 338, 352
Treasure of Montségur, The, 411
Tripartate Tractate, 104
Tristan, Flora, 299
Turgenev, I. P., 284
Turin shroud, 429

Upanishads, 10, 11, 35, 404
Uriel, 58

Vaishnava sect, 355
Valentinians, 89 ff., 160, 378
Valentinus, 49, 89 ff., 198
Varuna, 21
Vaughan, Thomas, 248
Vico, Giambattista, 262
Vidal, Peire, 165, 188
Voltaire, 296
von Bischoffswerder, Johann Rudolf, 278 ff.

von Eckartshausen, Ka 318
von Ecker und Eckhoffen, Hans Friedrich, 288
von Ender, Carl, 237
von Eschenbach, Wolfram, 122 ff., 201, 206, 207, 213, 224, 292
von Frankenburg, Abraham, 236, 242
von Frisau, Imperator Johann Carl, 265
von Gugomos, Baron, 270
von Hammer-Purgstall, 222
von Harnack, Adolf, 5
von Knugge, Adolf Freiherr, 267, 275
von Krüdener, Baroness Julie, 286
von Maltzahn, 272
von Rad, Gerhard, 17
von Schelling, Friedrich, 252, 253
von Schlegel, Friedrich, 252

Warburg Institute, 321
Warmanderhof Anthroposophical Farm, xv, 389
Warren, Charles, 224
War Scroll, 52, 53
Watt, Alexander, 364
Watts, Harriett, 251
Wealth of Nations, The, 275
Weber, Max, 261
Weishaupt, Adam, 267, 271, 272, 273 ff., 296
Wesley, John, 246, 249
Who Wrote the Dead Sea Scrolls?, 65
Wholeness and the Implicate Order, 380
Wiener Zeitschrift, 281
Wilhelmsbad Masonic Conference, 284, 297
Wilkinson, Louis, 314, 339
Willermoz, Jean Baptiste, 294
William of Auvergne, 133
Wisdom of Illumination, The, 145

Wisdom of Solomon, 37, 39
Wise, Michael, 64, 73
Wittgenstein, Ludwig, 68
Wolff, Christian, 244
Wöllner, Johan Christof, 278 ff.
Wronski, Hoene, 300, 301

Yarker, John, 348, 350, 353
Yasna, 13
Yeats, W. B., 311
Yorke, Gerald, 315, 355

Xerxes, 26

Zaquiel, 58
Zanoni, 301
Zarathushtra, 12, 13, 15, 16, 19,
    21, 32, 98
Zealots, 52, 67, 85
Zeus Olympius, 18
Zuchetto, Gérard, 422
Zurvan, 13, 15
Zurvan-Ahriman, 22, 23, 24, 25

BOOKS OF RELATED INTEREST

Gnostic Secrets of the Naassenes
The Initiatory Teachings of the Last Supper
by Mark H. Gaffney

The Way of the Essenes
Christ's Hidden Life Remembered
by Anne and Daniel Meurois-Givaudan

The Discovery of the Nag Hammadi Texts
A Firsthand Account of the Expedition That Shook
the Foundations of Christianity
by Jean Doresse

The Mystery of the Copper Scroll of Qumran
The Essene Record of the Treasure of Akhenaten
by Robert Feather

The Gospel of Mary Magdalene
by Jean-Yves Leloup
Foreword by Jacob Needleman

The Gospel of Philip
Jesus, Mary Magdalene, and the Gnosis of Sacred Union
by Jean-Yves Leloup
Foreword by Jacob Needleman

The Gospel of John in the Light of Indian Mysticism
by Ravi Ravindra, Ph.D.

The Brother of Jesus and the Lost Teachings of Christianity
by Jeffrey J. Bütz

Inner Traditions • Bear & Company
P.O. Box 388
Rochester, VT 05767
1-800-246-8648
www.InnerTraditions.com

Or contact your local bookseller